S0-BOM-883

Treating the Disruptive Adolescent

Finding the Real Self Behind Oppositional Defiant Disorders

Eduardo M. Bustamante, Ph.D.

Jason Aronson Inc.
Northvale, New Jersey
London

This book was set in 11 pt. New Baskerville by Pageworks of Old Saybrook and Lyme, CT, and printed and bound by Book-mart Press, Inc. of North Bergen, NJ.

Copyright © 2000 by Eduardo M. Bustamante

10 9 8 7 6 5 4 3 2 1

All rights reserved. No part of this book may be used or reproduced in any manner whatsoever without written permission from Jason Aronson, Inc. except in the case of brief quotations in reviews for inclusion in a magazine, newspaper, or broadcast.

Library of Congress Cataloging-in-Publication Data

Bustamante, Eduardo M.
    Treating the disruptive adolescent : finding the real self behind
oppositional defiant disorders / by Eduardo M. Bustamante.
        p. cm.
    Includes bibliographical references and index.
    ISBN 0-7657-0235-5
    1. Oppositional defiant disorder in adolescence. 2. Attention-
deficit disorder in adolescence. I. Title.
RJ506.O66B87   1999
616.89'00835—dc21   99-37817

Printed in the United States of America on acid-free paper. For information and catalog write to Jason Aronson Inc., 230 Livingston Street, Northvale, NJ 07647-1726, or visit our website: www.aronson.com

Contents

PART III: TREATMENT

PART IV: SPECIAL PROBLEMS

11 Special Problem 4: Negative Peer Influences

Preface

This book characterizes oppositional defiant disorder (ODD) as a disguised and misunderstood version of a common psychiatric problem, namely alienation. Modern psychiatry has described a variety of syndromes that involve alienation from the true self. Some theoretical schools informally refer to these conditions as mind-body splits, manifestations of which range widely from the most common syndromes, such as anxiety and depression, to the most complex, such as disorders of the self, identity disorders, eating disorders, and narcissistic personality disorders.

The existential dilemmas that result from a split between an individual's ego and his true self have received extensive attention. Many treatments have been developed to address these conditions. Pioneers in the mental health field have developed primal scream therapy, gestalt therapy, Tavistock group therapies, and a host of others. Founders of these movements have produced landmark works dating back to the early 1960s that have addressed the problems of alienation, and the phenomenon of the mind-body split. Some of the most popular works are those of existentialists such as Fritz Perls and R. D. Laing, and humanists such as Carl Rogers

and Abraham Maslow. The psychoanalytic schools of object relations and self psychology have addressed the problem of false-self
disorders, and developed entire schools of thought around reintegration of the self.

It is my contention that ODD in adolescence involves the same
existential dilemma as the identity disorders. However, it has been
viewed differently, and therefore mishandled. Mainstream perceptions of ODD depict the condition as a misguided demand for
attention, a test of authority, and a call for firm behavioral limits.
ODD youths are seen as selfish, immature, and prone to deviant
behavior.

Established methods seek to curb the rebellion of the ODD
child, and use behavior modification to treat deviant behavior. If
ODD were indeed a simple call for attention and firm limits, our
treatments for ODD would yield positive results. However, they
have not. (See Appendix A for a review of the literature on disruptive disorders.) But if ODD represents an existential crisis and
a need for integration of the mind and body, then the attempt to
normalize the behavior of ODD youths seems absurd and destined
to fail.

The perspective of mind-body integration calls for fostering
increased expression and awareness in the individual and for acceptance of his true nature. But behavior modification extinguishes
the child's expression of his state of alienation without attending
to and responding to his cry for help.

Adolescents' energy is in a constant state of flux, and they fall
into states of imbalance as they try out their different abilities. Many
of the irresponsible acts of teenagers represent nothing more than
efforts to taste different experiences. Doing things wrong will feel
wrong, and will lead to the urge to do things right. But if teenagers are prevented from pursuing interests and experiences of which
parents and others may not approve, and making the mistakes from
which they can learn, then their development may be thwarted.

Teenagers often ignore certain essential aspects of their lives,
such as book learning, while devoting themselves to other aspects
of development, such as social and emotional growth. If the parents force the teenager to study, and if they curb his social free-

dom, he might be better behaved. But the parents may cause him a series of problems in the long run.

The teenager will sooner or later try everything he wasn't allowed to experience because he needs that experience to complete his development. Some people will pursue these experiences into their forties and fifties as part of a mid-life crisis. In the case of the teenager, much of his energies will remain on hold and the other aspects of personality development that would have followed social growth will be deferred. The end result will be an incomplete human being.

However, if the parents recognize that the teenager is now developing socially and emotionally and allow that to continue, the teenager may mature sufficiently in those areas to demonstrate a taste for education.

Teenagers become deceptive and distrustful when they sense lack of wisdom in teachers, parents, and other adult authority figures. They learn to distrust authority, lie, and indulge in clandestine activities. This developmental process takes some deviant turns as the teenager seeks the precious experiences he needs to mature and realize his full potential. This book suggests interventions that can be used in working with teenagers who have these problems.

To develop effective therapy for ODD it is first necessary for the clinician to recognize and understand attention deficit/hyperactivity disorder (AD/HD). The rate of comorbidity is high, and ODD is often the emotional expression of AD/HD. AD/HD is, as a result, cited frequently in this book.

My personal experience with attention deficit/hyperactivity disorder has given me a unique perspective on its diagnosis and treatment. My 17-year-old son suffers from AD/HD and I suffer from that condition myself. My son and I both have tremendous self-discipline, resilience, ethical convictions, and determination. We still have traces of AD/HD, including high energy levels, impetuousness, and difficulty in being on time.

My AD/HD has lured me into all kinds of traps in life and has forced me to develop the adaptive skills necessary to work my way out of them. Thanks to my training in psychology, I was able to study my own attempts at coping with AD/HD from a scientific perspective. I became my own guinea pig.

This book emphasizes two constructs that form the heart of the treatment method I have developed. One is forming an alliance with that part of the youth referred to in the literature in a variety of ways, including emotional mind, attachment brain, midbrain, and limbic system. This alliance addresses the body component of the mind-body split, since the emotional mind drives the behavior of the body. The second involves turning failure into growth, which is a key adaptive strength in dealing with AD/HD or ODD. This adaptive function addresses the rational mind part of the split.

I learned how to bond with ODD teenagers by living for two or three years among a group of miscreants after I finished high school. I roamed the inner-city streets with them and learned about youth culture directly from tough, streetwise teenagers and young adults. I came to love some of these youths who were my companions, and they became my family. I saw some of them die young.

I was motivated to work with this population by my own experience with AD/HD combined with what I observed on the streets. I became a pioneer in the field of brief therapy with AD/HD and other disruptive disorders. I trained and worked in a brief therapy clinic. I was trained as a child psychologist and was at one time coordinator of children's services at the University of Massachusetts, Amherst. I have since taught doctoral students in seminars and have lectured extensively on the subject of raising and treating difficult children.

My work and studies in psychology taught me the second key construct presented in this book. I learned to accept failure and to turn it into growth. I learned to laugh at the errors I committed, and through my professional training and years of psychoanalysis, I learned to turn them into growth opportunities.

In my work in brief therapy and AD/HD I developed the tools of my trade through trial and error. I participated in experimental protocols for the treatment of AD/HD. One was an experimental neurofeedback project that studied electroencephalogram training to improve attention. The protocol failed, and my response was to turn failure into growth. My practice gained strength, in part because of what I had learned about the brain and about AD/HD in the training and pilot study on neurofeedback. This knowledge gave me a new perspective on the needs of ODD and AD/HD teenagers, a perspective that is the subject of this book.

Acknowledgments

I dedicate this book to my dear wife, Hilda, from the bottom of my heart, and to our three children, who are the greatest gift a man could wish for. I also thank Carroll Robbins for his editing and advice. This work would not have been possible without the teachings of my mentor in brief therapy, Dr. Robert Mendelsohn, my many teachers throughout the years, and my brother, Andrew, who has worked hard to support and scientifically validate my work. Last, I thank the many spirited teenagers and the dedicated families who have challenged and taught me throughout the years.

Introduction

This book offers clinicians an effective method of dealing with oppositional, resistant, and disruptive older children and teenagers. It introduces a comprehensive program that clinicians can use to evaluate and treat the most common and troubling behavior disorders, and guides clinicians through the process of diagnosing and treating these youths. The book presents special intervention strategies for such problems as school failure, neurotic parents, excessive aggression, negative peer influences, and drug involvement.

For years there has been a need for a cost-effective method of treating the symptoms of disruptive disorders including attention deficit/hyperactivity disorder (AD/HD), oppositional defiant disorder (ODD), and conduct disorder (CD). Numerous strategies have been attempted, but the results have been largely disappointing, especially with teenagers and those suffering from AD/HD. This book discusses the most common reasons for these treatment failures, and offers clinicians effective solutions to these problems.

The program presented here was derived from years of testing interventions, collecting data on their impact, and studying treatment failures to discover the obstacles that undermined successful implementation. The interventions were tested on children of all ages and delivered in the form of a parenting program in a group format. Clinically significant changes were eventually achieved in standard measures of oppositional defiance and family functioning, including Barkley's Home Situations Questionnaire (HSQ), Olson's Family Satisfaction Questionnaire (FSQ), and a modified version of the Consumer Satisfaction Questionnaire (CSQ), a rating scale developed for evaluating behavioral parent training programs. These improvements were documented upon completion of a twelve-week training and support program in four different sites and most recently with a waiting-list control group.

The research continues. My observations suggest that a significant portion of ODD youths respond naturally to the parenting program developed for this difficult population.

The program presented here assists mental health practitioners in establishing an effective treatment focus, in introducing a new and useful understanding of the problem behaviors (a reframe), and in using interventions derived from this new understanding. The interventions target a comprehensive set of problems, from the most common to the most difficult that clinicians are likely to encounter. These three elements—an effective focus, a reframe, and a set of interventions—conform to guidelines set forth by authors of programs designed to address specific syndromes, including various forms of brief therapy, cognitive behavior modification, and family psychology. Such programs offer a sound scientific basis for intervention and the instrumentation necessary to determine the effectiveness of the treatment delivered. They have been applied to depression, anxiety disorders, eating disorders, personality disorders, and posttraumatic stress disorder, to name a few.

This book establishes the fundamental importance of "thinking developmentally." Chapter 1 begins by clarifying the impact of expectations on development. This chapter is based on the work of Chess and Thomas on temperament and goodness of fit, which explains how reasonable expectations (a good fit) yield healthy development, and how unreasonable expectations (a poor fit) arrest development or foster deviant behavior. This chapter supports the tenets of the goodness-of-fit hypothesis with the work of cognitive behavior-modification theorists. It also discusses a series of popular assumptions about child rearing that predate the notion of psychological development. These beliefs stem from an old child-rearing paradigm that treats the young as though they were simple creatures of habit waiting for their elders to mold and shape them into perfect little adults. These assumptions invite a form of parenting that causes a poor fit with challenging youths, and produces problems.

Chapter 1 also introduces a new paradigm of natural growth that can reverse the problems inherent in the old creatures-of-habit system of beliefs. It details the central assumptions that stem from the new paradigm, and contrasts it clearly with the old. The child-rearing assumptions that stem from this new belief system encourage a form of parenting that can bring out the best in difficult children. I call it *natural-consequences parenting*.

Chapter 1 also familiarizes the reader with the dynamics that take place during natural development. It describes a cycle of three distinct phases that children go through when they encounter a developmental milestone (a need that is difficult to gratify or a challenge that feels formidable). The child first regresses to a state of dependency. The dependent child seeks to escape obligations by having others handle them. The child gradually outgrows the dependent phase and enters an oppositional phase. The oppositional phase prepares the child to separate from those he has depended upon and to take matters into his own hands. This stage is fraught with problem behaviors. Any attempt to control an oppositional child will heighten the opposition and possibly cause a developmental fixation. Given the right conditions, the child outgrows the oppositional phase and moves into the mastery phase of the cycle, in which he engages in constructive attempts to overcome the developmental challenge on his own.

By meeting key development needs, parents can help children outgrow deviant behaviors that would otherwise prove impossible to change. Each developmental phase presents a unique set of needs. Each manifests a series of predictable behaviors that can be identified and used to determine the developmental state of that child. Adults dealing with disruptive children can resolve the problem behaviors that stem from each developmental phase by properly addressing the attendant needs of that state. Chapter 1 specifies the needs of each developmental phase and explains how to respond productively to these needs. The chapter ends with the central goal of this program: to evoke the mastery phase of the developmental cycle and encourage children to remain in this state.

Chapter 2 presents the reframe of ODD that lies at the heart of this treatment method—a developmentally fixated youth trapped in a state of inner conflict that the chapter describes as "two minds at odds." The chapter describes the ODD youth as hiding his true essence because of the shame he has developed from enduring prolonged situations that enforced unreasonable expectations, and left vital emotional needs unmet. The ODD youth has also learned to exercise his inherent drive for success and mastery in a negative manner, that is, by bringing others down with him. The chapter reviews the literature on mind-body splits, describes the nature of the two minds that are at odds, and introduces the reader to the wisdom and characteristics of the emotional mind, the centers of the brain that drive the dysfunctional behavior of the teenager. The chapter addresses the role of trauma in the formation of the ODD syndrome and the treatment steps necessary to achieve the central goal of treatment with these youths—the integration of the two minds.

Chapters 3 and 4 guide clinicians through the complex assessment process necessary to treat these cases effectively. An accurate and comprehensive diagnosis is critical to the determination of the proper treatment focus and intervention. There is a high frequency of comorbid conditions in this population. Hence, several conditions must be systematically ruled out in the disruptive child. The parents and the family system must also be evaluated.

The disruptive teenager needs to be evaluated for attentional, learning, and emotional functioning. If the child is diagnosed with AD/HD, the parents should be screened for this condition as well, as it is considered an inherited disorder. Parents with untreated AD/HD will weaken the treatment team. Clinicians depend upon parents to play a key role in the intervention process, but those with untreated AD/HD will often fail to follow through. Parents should also be screened for marital problems, and for other psychiatric conditions, such as anxiety or depression. These complications are common in families of disruptive and disordered children and they interfere with successful intervention.

In this book, specific assessment instruments are recommended and discussed for each component of this elaborate evaluation process. Guidelines are provided for when to go beyond the clinical interview and employ specific rating scales and performance tasks, and when to refer to a specialized diagnostician, such as a neurologist, neuropsychologist, or learning specialist.

Chapter 4 serves as a reference source that clinicians can use to prepare individualized treatment plans. Each diagnostic category is discussed along with appropriate interventions for the problems involved. This helps clinicians handle insurance and managed care planning and reporting.

Chapters 5 to 12 provide a new understanding of the disruptive adolescent that prepares clinicians to implement the standard parenting program that is the backbone of this model.

The program presented here integrates elements from attachment, self-esteem, family satisfaction, self-mastery, play, behavior modification, goodness of fit, and cognitive learning theories. It borrows interventions from the behavioral, cognitive behavioral, systemic, and strategic schools of therapy. Families that have struggled with the standard implementation of this program have responded particularly well to specific strategies derived from these various schools of therapy. The book combines these different interventions into a systematic model.

The eclectic nature of the approach presented here calls for easy-to-understand summaries of key theories from which its interventions were derived. These summaries are provided for readers who are unacquainted with them and for clinicians who wish to implement these protocols with reasonable comfort and ease.

Chapters 5 to 7 introduce the three fundamental steps for treating ODD—taking failure to the limit, turning failure into growth, and addressing the mind-body split. The oppositional child

uses failure as his main manipulation tool. Adults have tradition-
ally countered this maneuver by implementing structures that force
the child to succeed. This sets the stage for the development of
ODD.

Indeed, as a result of societal pressures, many parents end up
micromanaging their children's lives. They take what they believe
to be perfectly reasonable behavioral prescriptions and turn them
into excessive control struggles. They shepherd their children
through daily routines with seemingly successful results. But, despite appearances, they are committing the grave error of inhibit-
ing the development of their children's own critical adaptive brain
functions. They interfere with the maturation process, induce
oppositional behavior in even normal children, and encourage
rebellion.

Chapter 5 deals extensively with formal treatment. It shows
clinicians how to use the teenager's failure as a catalyst for growth.
This is a strategic move that instantly reverses the ODD. It throws
the ODD teenager into a state of imbalance. The chapter shows
the clinician how to prescribe failure in a way that helps the child
become invested in succeeding. However, the objective of this stage
of the intervention is not to avoid failure. On the contrary, the
process described in Chapter 5 seeks to help the child face his
limitations. This encourages him to invest in self-improvement.

The parents learn to develop an attitude of welcoming the
failure once they realize that exposing weaknesses is a prerequi-
site to correcting them. The clinician teaches the parents to help
their children develop strong adaptive brain functions of their own.
The book relies on the tenets of attachment and play theory for
their effectiveness in this regard. It introduces a parental attitude
that is playful, but not helpful. The lightheartedness buffers the
child's emotional and attachment system against trauma, while the
nonhelpfulness challenges the child to exercise vital mental functions for himself. This chapter emphasizes the importance of inducing the right kind of anxiety in the child to encourage the
exercise of vital adaptive functions and to facilitate brain maturation.

Chapter 6 shows clinicians how to confront difficult teenagers and older children with consequences that teach and strengthen them, using a combination of behavior modification and cognitive learning theories. Clinicians learn to apply the same effective psychology behind the time-out to older children and teenagers, and in special situations when it becomes necessary to remove them from their regular activities. This section has much in common with behavioral programs, except that the emphasis here is on strengthening rather than supplementing, that is, persuading the child to exercise the mental abilities involved, rather than performing them for him. Established programs developed in the past share the conviction that exposing disruptive children to natural and reasonable consequence—ways of experiencing the difference between good and bad behavior—is a critical component of effective treatment. This book adds a cognitive element to facilitate the development of important abilities, namely, to learn from experience, feel concern, and develop a conscience.

This book shows clinicians how to expose unruly children to reasonable consequences without hurting them. Chapter 6 turns to a combination of self-esteem and self-mastery theories to achieve this end. It emphasizes the value of putting children in charge of themselves and teaching them how to see failures as learning opportunities.

Chapter 7 discusses how to handle the ODD teenager's tendency to deceive. Brief therapy tactics are used to deal with resistance. The chapter discusses how to detect and expose deception at a point when the teenagers have nothing to lose because their parents have already doled out the consequences for their infractions, and they have performed reparative acts to demonstrate respect for the privileges they have violated. This chapter shows how to help ODD teenagers discover the value of trust, the importance of becoming trustworthy, and the importance of testing their peers for trustworthiness. Teenagers can discover the peace of mind to be derived from a life they like. They learn that it is possible to gratify their social needs while maintaining a good relationship with their parents in which they have nothing to hide. The chapter shows how to accomplish this with individual, parent, and family sessions.

The book combines all of the above elements in a working treatment model that addresses the consequences of actions. The program shows how to prepare consequences. It shows clinicians how to put children in charge, how to help families escape conflict-laden situations, and how to help parents decide if the consequences should be meted out or dispensed with. Finally, it shows clinicians how to use the family unit to encourage honesty and mind-body integration in the teenager. Proper implementation of this working model yields rapid results in families whose members are relatively intact and healthy. This level of intervention suffices for a significant portion of the population. However, many struggling families require further work, and Chapters 8 to 12 help clinicians resolve the most common obstacles to implementation of this program. Some of these obstacles are presented by the teenagers: scholastic resistance, excessive aggression, negative peer influences, and drug dependency. Others are presented by the parents: excessive dependency, neuroticism, and a history of trauma that renders them helpless when facing persistent badgering and disrespect.

Chapters 8 to 12 offer ways to assess and intervene in each of the obstacles presented, including school failure, parental neurosis, excessive aggression, negative peer influences, and addictions. Interventions for these specific problems share the strategy of the basic program, and hence will be familiar to the trained practitioner. These chapters also provide important information pertinent to each problem and draw from established treatments to provide a comprehensive approach to each area of focus.

Chapter 12 addresses other special problems and contraindications to the use of this model for treating ODD. This chapter discusses lack of parental support, increased acting out at the start of treatment, the distorting of session material to manipulate others, incompetent custodial parents, medical complications, and serious trauma. Guidelines are offered on how to modify this program to prevent or address these special problems, or when to refer to the appropriate specialists. Case studies are presented to illustrate the diagnostic and treatment process for each type of obstacle the clinician is likely to encounter.

Families that undergo the treatment method outlined here find unexpected benefits and growth for everyone involved. They are pleased with the welcoming response it elicits from the oppositional and disruptive older child or teenager who has resisted traditional counseling for years. The intervention program is sensible and easy to implement by parents after an initial adjustment period. The parents discover new health and happiness in their own personal lives, a welcome change for those who, without the benefits of the program, have all but given up any semblance of a satisfying personal life.

This book takes the mystery out of the treatment failures commonly seen in adolescent disruptive disorders. Clinicians learn a complex evaluation process and a cost-effective treatment process capable of meeting the needs of ODD teenagers. The book offers clinicians effective ways to manage school failure, parental neurosis, excessive aggression, negative peer influences, drug involvement, and a host of other problems that have plagued families and schools and baffled the mental health industry for years.

Part I

Understanding Oppositional Defiant Disorder (ODD)

Thinking Developmentally

My heart sank when I first met Carl. He was so closed off that the mere thought of seeing him on a regular basis left me drained. Trying to connect with him, I thought, will be a monumental task. His life had been painfully boring for prolonged periods, interrupted by dramatic bursts of acting out that caused him and his family significant trouble. He was 13 and very thin. His blond hair was uncombed. He presented a disheveled appearance. He wore thick-rimmed black glasses on a long, stone-cold face. He avoided eye contact. His face was a blank and frequently I could not tell whether he was listening to me. I knew that at some level, Carl was developmentally stuck, and that to do him any good I would have to uncover and understand the factors that fueled his oppositional behavior.

At this point, only through intense or perverse behavior could Carl obtain any release from his closed-off state. He seemed to live for those times. The remainder of his time was spent watching television in what seemed to be an electronic fix.

His mother was worried about her son's inappropriate behavior, which fluctuated from extremely withdrawn and passive to deceptive or aggressive. She wondered, especially, how much sex fantasy was normal for a boy his age. He watched pornographic videos and played the sound tracks to his mother over the phone. He hung pinups on all the walls of his room. At one point, he spent over $900 on toll calls to 1–900 sex phone lines. He was in the bathroom for long periods. In behavior that his mother considered the last straw, he sat in front of the television, unembarrassed, playing with his erect penis.

His ability to cause trouble did not end there, however. On one occasion he stole his grandmother's Social Security check, took $400 to school, and handed out $10 bills randomly to passersby in the hallway. Carl longed for toys that his mother, with her meager resources, couldn't afford.

In school Carl was flunking all his subjects. He did not respond to offers of support. He refused medication. He tormented his younger brother, one night kicking off the doorknob to his brother's room when the brother refused to open the door. He teased and bullied others outside the family and appeared to be enjoying their discomfort. He seemed to thrive on the pain he caused others but could not stand teasing directed at him.

I did not fully understand Carl's condition at this time. His refusal to do schoolwork, and his apathy, low energy, explosive behavior, and deviant tendencies were plain to be seen, but I could not establish a common thread in the various aspects of his behavior, or find the root cause. I knew that individual and family therapy, medication, behavioral programs, tutoring, and other academic supports had all been tried, but none had worked. I believed that allowing him to fail, without deriving gratification from his mother's worry, would help free him of the oppositional phase of development in which he was lodged, and that until then Carl would not respond to any intervention.

Carl was receiving special educational services, but to no avail. He was performing significantly below grade level. He was inattentive and had verbal retrieval problems and graphomotor deficits. He was becoming increasingly demanding and impulsive.

His mother reported that Carl had been an easy-to-care-for baby. Problems first surfaced when he entered school. He was seldom engaged with other children and their activities. Carl's parents divorced and he and his mother moved. By this time, he already had a history of problems in school. He barely engaged with peers for months after the move and was traumatized by the isolation and loss he was bringing upon himself. His depression and other symptoms worsened dramatically.

According to a social worker who had worked with him in school, Carl "exhibited a pattern of negative attention-seeking behavior, and was unresponsive to varied management strategies over a two-year period." The social worker noted that Carl was a disruptive influence, even in her counseling group.

Carl, however, was not without strengths. He was intellectually gifted. He had a verbal IQ of over 140, which placed him in the very superior range. His performance score, on the other hand, was simply average—around 100. He was considered gifted in school, but school was a negative experience for him from the start.

My assessment of Carl revealed attention deficit/hyperactivity disorder (AD/HD) in the severe range, oppositional defiant disorder (ODD), learning disability (LD), anxiety, and depression. His profile on the Achenbach Child Behavior Checklist, which is a test of emotional problems, placed him in the severe range for conduct and learning problems and hyperactivity. He was described as sassy, quarrelsome, disobedient, and aggressive, but extremely vulnerable. Carl would feel humiliated if he were to be punished for his blatantly disruptive behavior. Teachers rated him as being on-task 20 percent of the time. He tested extremely high on anxiety and depression. He had a history of excessive worrying, beginning in early elementary school.

Carl's condition worsened markedly after visits to his father. The father had a history of mental disorder, alcoholism, and spousal abuse, and had been convicted of driving while intoxicated. He resented his wife's leaving him and vented his anger by making her life miserable in any way he could. He often skipped child-support payments and had periods of unemployment. He tried to turn his son against the mother and described her as a traitor.

Carl would return from visits to his father obsessed with a desire to punish his mother for the pain he felt she had inflicted on his father. He attempted to spoil any relationship with other men that his mother tried to develop. It would take days after a visit for Carl to recover from the hateful influence of his father.

I eventually learned to connect with Carl by talking with him as though I were a fellow conspirator. At one point, however, he told me he considered me untrustworthy. "I don't want to feel like a rat," he said, to explain his earlier reticence to talk about himself and his family. We exchanged "crime" stories and I told him about some things I had done during my own adolescent years that I wished I hadn't. He responded by telling me some of his uglier secrets.

Once we connected at this level, Carl came temporarily to life. He talked incessantly about his plans to follow a life of crime as a way of obtaining some of the better things in life. He wouldn't do drugs but he would sell them to the poor suckers who would. He would use drugs to make girls do things they otherwise wouldn't do. He would hire "muscle" and have people rubbed out.

Talking like partners in crime helped us bond but I saw no real benefit coming from this kind of connection, nothing that would justify charging his mother a fee for therapy. I decided to let the case proceed by means of parenting intervention alone. It took two years for this plan to yield the desired result.

During this period, Carl's mother was following several recommendations I made for improving her parenting approach to him. She was able to separate her conduct from her desire to see her son do well—an important tactic in coping with oppositional behavior. Without intervening, she allowed him to experience failure in various ways. When it became necessary to impose consequences for misdeeds affecting the family, however, she cut off his access to money and electronics. She let him know what it was like to lose family support by going "off duty," that is, by ignoring him and his needs. Some improvements were noticeable right way. For example, his sex fantasies seemed to diminish.

The breakthrough in Carl's life came when, encouraged by his mother and his brother, he tried out for his high school basketball team, showed considerable promise during practice sessions, and was invited by the coach to join the squad, only to learn that he did not qualify academically. Uncharacteristically, he cried when he heard the news that he could not play. This was a major blow to his hopes because his interest in the game had now become passionate. He decided not to give up, however. He worked hard on his studies, and, to the surprise and delight of his mother and teachers, turned in excellent performances in the classroom and in his homework. He made the honor roll and was allowed to join the team. There was now a temporary resolution of the opposition stage of development. Gone was the surliness he had previously exhibited in school. At home, he was gracious and respectful toward, and appreciative of, his mother.

UNDERSTANDING OPPOSITIONAL STATES

The oppositional child may not be able to say why he resists the best efforts of his parents and teachers to modify his conduct. The reason may be elusive, even to him. Yet, conscious of it or not, he is engaged in a quest. He is seeking the opportunity to develop his abilities naturally through following his instincts and not necessarily according to the standards for correct behavior and success established by others. The intensity and duration of his revolt against efforts to control him, however, will depend on how well his needs are understood, and the amount of parental intervention involved, if any, when behavior becomes a problem.

Oppositional states are normal, especially during early childhood and adolescence. All children experience them at one time or another. The three common explanations for their occurrence are natural growth, unreasonable expectations, and trauma. Children enter oppositional states once they mature to the point where they are capable of performing certain functions for themselves but have not yet realized this potential. At this stage in their development, children signal their readiness to take over by resisting assistance, but at the same time demanding that their parents continue in a helping role. Children convey the message, "I need you but I can't stand you." The oppositional phase encourages those on whom they depend to give up their helping, rescuing roles. This withdrawal offers proof to children that the parents are willing to grant autonomy. Once children do things that result in negative effects and the parents do not interfere, the children know they are on their own.

The second cause of oppositional behavior is unreasonable expectations. When children face unreasonable expectations that threaten to undermine their confidence, they naturally seek to escape the demands placed upon them. If their parents or teachers attempt to force them to deal with the dreaded expectations, they adopt an oppositional stance.

The third cause of oppositional behavior involves the threat of trauma. When children encounter potentially dangerous situations, they avoid the problem area in any way possible. If forced to expose themselves to further risk, they will self-protect with an oppositional response.

The duration of oppositional states varies significantly, depending on the situation. Oppositional states stemming from natural maturation tend to resolve themselves readily, as long as parents avoid pushing the children. Oppositional states stemming from prolonged exposure to unreasonable expectations last until the expectations become reasonable. Oppositional states that come in response to trauma, or fear of trauma, can last indefinitely. They require a resolution of the impending threat and the assurance of future safety. Children who have been severely traumatized will take longer to outgrow their oppositional states.

RESOLVING OPPOSITIONAL STATES

Oppositional states tend to resolve themselves, given sufficient time and reasonable expectations. The key is to prevent in the child a developmental fixation that would lead to ODD and to identify any hidden sources of trauma.

Natural development is often interrupted by obstacles to growth that bring on temporary regressions. Typical examples include perceived dangers (such as bullies), situations where children feel set up to fail (as in divorce or school burnout), and excessive parental protection (as in spoiling or excessive controlling tactics). When children encounter an obstacle to growth, they regress to earlier levels of functioning. This retreat is rewarding at first because it creates a feeling of safety. However, stagnancy soon becomes painful. To alleviate the pain, children try to face the obstacles that have been standing in the way of growth. We can look upon this cycle—from facing an obstacle to growth, to regression, to reaching a painful stagnation point—as a developmental detour.

Once parents recognize the developmental detour, they realize that, at certain times in their children's development, change may not be possible, but that growth can eventually occur. Abilities develop at their own pace. Some children are precocious and others are late bloomers. This variation occurs in many areas of development, including weight and height, social skills, sexuality, and intellectual pursuits. Children who have not developed an ability cannot derive a sense of pride from it.

Many children are deeply entrenched in behaviors that worry their parents. These habits persist despite efforts to modify them. The parents' worry only causes the unwanted behaviors to intensify. Children abandon their problem behaviors when they mature to the point where these behaviors no longer meet important developmental needs, or when the parents stop efforts to control them. The attitude of parents is a determining factor in the strength and duration of oppositional behavior.

Gratifying the needs of oppositional youths can foster their growth and security. But parents and teachers should encourage them to meet their own needs. Children should be put in charge of correcting their own problem behaviors, and adults must have faith that natural consequences will force the children to self-correct.

A 1-year-old boy had developed a peculiar self-soothing habit. He simultaneously inserted the index finger of one hand into his mouth, and shoved the other hand down his pants. He walked around like that all day. The practice was of major concern to his parents. His grandmother and others who knew the family demanded that the parents do something to change their son's behavior. People would approach the parents and ask, "Do you realize what your son is doing?" as if the parents hadn't noticed.

The parents received a great deal of unsolicited advice on how to rid their son of his habit. The boy's uncles are dentists, and warned of what might happen to his teeth if it continued. But nothing the parents did could stop it. I advised the parents not to worry much about it because it wasn't worth jeopardizing their son's emotional security just to avoid orthodontia. A few years later the boy's habit began to threaten his social standing. This was the low point in the developmental detour. The boy asked to have his sucking finger taped so it "won't taste right." He then conquered the habit in a couple of weeks.

Other examples of natural developmental detours occur in middle school and high school students who are so burned out that they feel traumatized. They drop out or they just barely graduate. Their first job in a fast-food restaurant provides relief but soon the tedium of the job sets in. Suddenly education seems more appealing and many former burnouts return to their studies with newfound maturity.

Parents can cause oppositional fixations if they try to push their children past obstacles to their growth and can traumatize them. Without pushing, these developmental detours will most likely resolve themselves. If they don't, it can be assumed that the children either lack important abilities, or are facing unreasonable expectations. If their families seek help, the clinician must determine what are the unreasonable expectations, and must keep the parents from exerting too much pressure on the oppositional child.

Each step in a child's development presents unique emotional needs. When these needs are not met, growth is interrupted and resistance sets in. A child who becomes oppositional can upset the whole family. Individuals who work with the problem are likely to end up committing an inordinate proportion of available resources to the most difficult children, but children indulged in this fashion will drain their parents and remain developmentally stuck, despite the provision of structure, the use of punishments or rewards, or the lowering of expectations.

THE NEEDS OF THE OPPOSITIONAL PHASE

Children in oppositional states are negative, irritating, obstinate, and explosive. They are stubborn and draining. They criticize and blame others for anything that goes wrong. They don't want to get up in the morning, get dressed, eat breakfast, or go to school. They ruin the family atmosphere until they get their own way. They enjoy the sense of power that comes from having spoiled matters for everyone else. Oppositionalism is maintained by a hunger for power.

Oppositional states quickly become unbearable for the parents, but the more they clash with oppositional children, the more power they are handing over to the children. Children can display oppositional traits for a decade or more, during which time the oppositional states come on like moods, with increasing frequency, severity, and duration.

There are two things parents and teachers must do to deal effectively with a child going through an oppositional phase. First, they must isolate the child from the rest of the family, possibly by a time-out. For example, the child violates the rights of others in the family. When reprimanded, he stages a tantrum. He is then removed from the family, loses his sense of belonging, and is forced to fend for himself until he regains his perspective. The time-out reduces his entitlement. This device, however, will not work with older children and adolescents, who are often too big to be forced into a time-out room. Second, parents can allow the child to fail, which helps to deflate the overbearing preoccupation with self that he presents before becoming oppositional.

Clinicians can support parents by exhibiting confidence in their child's ability to outgrow this phase and eventually succeed. Clinicians can suggest to parents that permitting children to fail without interference allows them to complete the entire developmental detour. Children will regress, avoid exposure to challenging situations, and find temporary relief, only to reach a stagnation point, become tired of the rut into which they have fallen, and finally abandon the oppositional phase. The clinician's input eases the parents' anxiety, helps them gain confidence, and encourages them to assume an effective, kind, yet neutral attitude in relation to their children's tantrums and failures.

To have a therapeutic effect, failure must mean something very special to the child. He must feel caught up in the activity involved and responsible for what transpires. Failure at a trivial matter that the child cares little about does not have much impact. Sometimes the wonderful impact of failure does not take place until a year or two after the initial intervention. The ODD child craves success but has no immediate challenges providing opportunities to achieve it.

"I think I finally understand the meaning of failure," Carl's mother wrote to me. "You have always underscored the value of failure to these kinds of kids. What I've learned through Carl is that the key to failure is to ask, 'Whose failure is it?' Flunking over and over again does not count as failure to these kids. Getting in trouble with the system is not failure to them. They have not failed at something that matters to them. The failure has to be in something that matters to them. Failure is an important part of engaging these kids. I'm sure of it. But it must be their failure. It must be a failure in something that matters to them, not just to us!"

Providing failure opportunities for the oppositional child, and—as in the case of the mother's decision to go off-duty—isolating the child, will not come easily to the parents. However, these functions are vital to the resolution of the oppositional phase of development and the resumption of the maturation process. Parents who separate their oppositional children from the rest of the family and allow them to fail are sending them a strong signal, and have met the needs of the oppositional phase of development. The parents are saying to the child, in effect: "Your needs are not that important," and, "I am confident that this is a simple developmental detour and you will soon enter a stage of self-sufficiency and mastery." The proper response of authority figures dealing with the oppositional phase is to allow it to run its course.

THE NEED FOR A PARADIGM SHIFT

The change to thinking developmentally in our culture will require a paradigm shift. Stagnant thinking about children is pervasive and deeply rooted. Our task is to uncover the limitations that lurk beneath many of our old child-rearing assumptions and introduce a new philosophy that bypasses them.

A paradigm is a set of beliefs, accepted without question, that guide mass behavior. People believed, for example, that the earth was flat until it was discovered that it is round. People also believed that God created the world in seven days until for the overwhelming majority this concept was replaced by the theory of evolution.

Many good parents believe they must pressure their children to do well throughout their development. They say, "I want to be able to say to myself when he grows up that I tried everything possible to secure his future and make him successful." They believe their teenagers adopt a poor attitude because it's natural for them to do so. They believe it's their duty to keep their teenagers from making irresponsible choices. They believe teens need a mother around to tell them what to do.

We need to address the paradigm that children are simple creatures of habit who can be molded like clay into perfect little adults. Parents who believe this notion try to force their children from an early age to conform to the standards of full-fledged maturity. They demand mature behavior regardless of whether the children possess the required neurological maturity, or whether engaging in mature behavior meets the youth's developmental needs. Parents who practice this mode of child-rearing seldom feel the needs to question their beliefs. It is assumed that children will adjust to mature behavior and then effortlessly behave like serious little adults. This assumption ignores the need to promote real growth by gratifying basic developmental requirements.

The assumption that children can be molded like clay encourages coercive child-rearing tactics designed to force conformity with an established norm. Difficult children instinctively resist authority based on coercion and conformity. Clinicians can introduce a paradigm shift in therapy to counteract this assumption, engage the attention of the disruptive child, and encourage hope in the family. Clinicians can explain to parents the limitations of creatures-of-habit thinking and suggest a new and developmentally sound paradigm.

When clinicians work with older disruptive children, they find the parents more motivated than the children. But the parents are still committed to the mistaken principles of child rearing that caused their children's problems, the principles that society encourages to foster compliance in children.

Disruptive teenagers are reluctant to see a therapist because they think therapists serve as vehicles for conformity who will make the same demands on their behavior as their parents and teachers do. They think a therapist will try to reason with them and orchestrate yet another attempt to mold them. They think a therapist will shame them by exposing their disrespect and abusive feelings for their families. But if older disruptive children sense that the therapist understands the mistakes the adults in their lives have been making, they will bond with him. They will see him as a powerful ally, especially if they see that their parents are receptive to the therapist's explanations of the flaws in their child-rearing tactics. These children cannot articulate the problem they have with how they are being raised. But they know intuitively that something is wrong and will welcome the therapist's putting it into words.

Clinicians can forge a strong alliance with parents and their disruptive children immediately by clarifying the need to drop their struggles for control, and support natural development instead. The children will find relief in the realization that adult disregard for natural development has caused their deviant behavior. Parents will find hope in the notion that a different approach will allow their children to outgrow their most troublesome behaviors.

To introduce families to a shift to developmental thinking,

clinicians can instruct parents to picture their children at age 25. What do they envision for them? What education and choice of career do they foresee? What choice of spouse? What values? Do they picture them as intelligent, well-adjusted people? If they are like most parents, they will want to believe in their children's character and abilities and in their prospects for success. But they still question their children's abilities. Somehow, they assume, their children will manage in the long run, and find it difficult to accept the fact that the children can adapt to failures and make their own way right now without constant guidance and correction. This exercise exposes the contradiction that exists in the parents between their faith in their children's long-term development and their lack of faith in the short-term. Parents are ignorant about how children develop, a fact that robs them of their confidence and undermines their ability to cultivate natural development. They feel helpless and fall back on the only thing they know—the pressuring, molding, and controlling of the outdated creatures-of-habit paradigm.

THE SHIFT TO A PARADIGM OF NATURAL DEVELOPMENT

A shift to developmental thinking will free parents from feeling an obligation to micromanage the day-to-day lives of their offspring. The children will be fine, whether or not their shirts are clean, their socks match, and they eat all their vegetables. Who the parents are and what children inherit from them, genetically and otherwise, largely determine what the children will become. Parents who want to influence their children positively should live as they want their children to live. They can expect their children ultimately to turn out much like the example they set but better, because evolution suggests that each generation takes a small step forward. A child's potential is determined at the time of conception. All that parents can do is help their children realize the full extent of their genetically given abilities. Parents cannot change a child's essential disposition.

Faith in the rightness of children's natural development and acceptance of their innate abilities frees parents to make loving their children a top priority. The energy that once was spent trying to mold and shape their children can now be devoted to spending time with them and appreciating and enjoying them.

A true grasp of the natural development process allows parents to accept and have faith in the following tenets of contemporary child psychology:

1. Failure is a vital part of the growth process. It should not be feared or prevented. Failure breeds necessity, and necessity yields growth. The most powerful way to induce confidence in children is by maintaining faith in them, especially when they begin to mismanage their affairs. Parents should be present and ready to comment. Indeed, their absence would constitute neglect. However, they should allow their children to self-correct whenever possible. Paradoxically, children need their parents' faith in them the most when they seem to deserve it least!

2. Good deeds must be freely chosen if they are to yield growth. If we force goodness on them, children may comply and may appear successful. However, forced goodness will yield minimal growth.

3. Laziness and overindulgence are enemies of growth. However, we don't fear laziness. A certain amount of lethargy is an integral part of normal development, and children fluctuate between high-energy and lazy phases. These are natural occurrences in their journey toward adulthood.

THE NEEDS OF THE MASTERY PHASE

Meeting the needs of this phase of development is a central goal in the treatment of children. The mastery phase involves putting children in charge of themselves and offering them the chance to belong and the opportunity for success with little or no parental assistance. Recognition of their accomplishments, however, is extremely important to these youths. The role of those who deal with children in the mastery phase is to allow them to be independent and to appreciate their efforts, regardless of the outcome.

Children in the mastery phase need to handle their affairs in their own way. Even if they know a better way, the adults who work with them should support the children's decisions. They should demonstrate confidence in their children, whether the children succeed or fail. They should not teach, lecture, or take charge. Rather, they should be willing to learn, and to allow the children to become the teachers when they have made a discovery or accomplished a task.

ENCOURAGING MASTERY STATES

An understanding of developmental dynamics prepares the way for realization of the central treatment goal, which is to induce a shift to the mastery phase of development and help children attain it. Any approach that fosters dependency in children diverts them from the quest for mastery, and doing things for youngsters fosters dependency. Dependency fosters regression and, ultimately, oppositional tendencies. Parents need to minimize unnecessary rescuing and doing for children, especially when such assistance allows them to maintain unhealthy behavior patterns.

Parents and teachers can promote the mastery phase by challenging children. Mastery comes from having to face consequences, feeling responsible for the outcome of an endeavor, being in charge, pursuing genuine interests, and having the opportunity to teach others. Adults can induce mastery states by performing three key functions: (1) allow failure when children behave irresponsibly; (2) provide opportunities for success, giving youths as many chances as they need; and (3) establish challenges children can handle. Children must be allowed to experience developmental detours in order to let go of dependency and oppositionalism. They need to taste failure when they don't try. However, they must experience a generous measure of success when they do apply themselves. We must structure challenges so youths can succeed most of the time.

The essential factor in mastery learning is to allow children to take charge and to feel in charge. Parents, nevertheless, must continue to perform some functions for their children so as to buffer at least some of the difficulties of life. This is a way to make life's challenges reasonable. Teenagers must feel sufficiently in charge to keep them striving to overcome challenges. They also need to experience enough failure to help them recognize their weaknesses and learn in what areas they need to improve. They need to have sufficient opportunities and successes to keep them feeling confident in their ability to manage their own affairs.

The treatment approach I present in this book is designed to achieve states of mastery. It allows and encourages the ODD child to develop along ways that satisfy his inner urges, the imperatives of his life, and his quest to find a way to be himself.

ENTERING MASTERY STATES

Daniel Goleman, in his groundbreaking book *Emotional Intelligence* (1996), describes mastery states as expressions of emotional intelligence that involve a specific mindset sometimes referred to as *flow*. According to Goleman, individuals operating in mastery states can be identified by the ease with which they handle the most challenging tasks. While this is going on, there is a lessening of cortical arousal and, in effect, their brains "quiet down," he writes (p. 92). People enter flow states when the expectations of others around them are just high enough to force them to invest themselves in a task requiring more effort than usual. Goleman describes the flow state as "that delicate zone" between having too little to do or too much, between boredom and anxiety (p. 92).

In sports, a player may be criticized for trying too hard to achieve a quick victory, rather than taking his time, establishing a relaxed pace, and letting the big plays come to him. For example, when a well-coached baseball player is at bat, he will try simply to meet the ball, and the home runs will come. Overeager fighters go for the early knockout, rather than work combinations and let the knockout come in time. Coaches try to counter these tendencies by urging their athletes to stay within themselves. These examples involve reducing excessively high expectations to eliminate anxiety and facilitate entry into flow states.

This efficiency of flow states yields maximum absorption and satisfaction. The uninterrupted flow and abundance of energy yields optimal performance, with bursts of brilliance to accent a solid, sustained effort. We can achieve the same engaging, productive, and energizing mind states in any activity, including basic education or countering academic weaknesses.

EDUCATION AND MASTERY STATES

Educators and clinicians training students in how to achieve mastery states should choose an activity that the student likes and for which he has an aptitude. Individuals involved in such activities are much more likely to feel challenged and practice the required moves. Component skills required to perform the task should be practiced to the point of fluency. It makes sense that well-practiced moves will require much less brain effort than unfamiliar ones. As the training progresses, expectations should be gradually increased to keep the students challenged and to offset feelings of boredom or anxiety.

Teaching youths the process of entering mastery states in any subject matter provides them with the motivation to get better and better at it. The experience of entering mastery states is intrinsically rewarding. Once the student learns to enter a flow state in a given task, he will want to enter it in other tasks.

Ideally, we would teach children to achieve mastery states by allowing them to pursue activities that spontaneously capture their interest. The children would develop a passion for their chosen body of knowledge that would provide high levels of achievement while they were enjoying mastery states. Since they would have to push themselves to the limits of their abilities in order to sustain mastery states, the children would be motivated to get better and better at what they do. This quest for mastery would transfer to other bodies of knowledge because learning this way would make them happy. According to Goleman (1996), such a model of education is very different from the traditional one in which children find themselves enduring long periods of boredom (underchallenged) followed by bursts of anxiety (overchallenged).

SUSTAINING THE GAINS

The most frequent cause of relapses in children's ODD symptoms is the parents' ineffective use of expectations. The parents combine the strong limits that the clinician teaches them with inappropriate, unreasonable, and unhelpful expectations and fail to provide sufficient opportunities for growth-related experiences. The absence of helpful expectations and opportunities causes a recurrence of the children's symptoms, which happens frequently in ODD children. To attain a lasting resolution to the ODD psychopathology without recurrence, all areas of conflict must be resolved and follow-up must be provided. In addition, the ODD teenager must have opportunities to strengthen developmentally related abilities.

Only the growth process of the mastery stage of development can replace the draining dynamics of ODD. Only the correct expectation levels can replace stagnation with growth. Challenges must be difficult, yet fun to pursue. Learning must be useful. Restriction should be minimal and usually arranged with the consent of the child. This is the real challenge presented by ODD youths. It is the challenge addressed by this book.

THE KEY TO HEALTHY DEVELOPMENT

Cognitive learning theory has demonstrated that the key to healthy development is establishing the right expectations. Yet the expectations applied to children frequently fail to present developmental challenges. Parents assume that children's problem behaviors accompanying the developmental changes will last forever, and, as a result, they battle their children endlessly to curb behaviors that would otherwise fade away naturally on their own. Unwittingly through this practice they compromise their children's development.

Children's mental states change position continually according to natural tendencies. Their attitudes vary dramatically with these changes. Their needs change, as does the nature of their responses to the demands of parents and teachers. Unaware of the process of change, however, parents and teachers expect all children to respond consistently to a single approach. Clinicians give parents and teachers a series of interventions and naively expect these to work all the time. When the children fail to respond as expected, most parents and teachers attribute this failure to flaws in the children. They do not consider that children respond differently in different developmental states. The possibility of shifts in tactics in order to deal with these changes does not occur to them. Parents and teachers would increase their efficiency in dealing with children markedly, however, if they learned to identify different developmental states, and were equipped with strategies appropriate for dealing with them. They would not blame children for failing to respond as desired but would simply switch tactics to elicit different responses.

THE GOODNESS-OF-FIT HYPOTHESIS

The studies on the goodness-of-fit hypothesis demonstrated the weighty impact of expectations of psychological development. Chess and Thomas (1984) conducted research that fundamentally altered how we deliver mental health services to children. They were interested in the construct of goodness of fit, and its counterpart, poorness of fit, as they pertain to a child's abilities (in this study as determined by temperament) and the corresponding expectations in the environment (in this study, the parenting style of the mother).

A good fit with a difficult child is a patient and flexible parent. A poor fit is a demanding, aggressive, and controlling parent. A good fit with an easy child is a parent who is reasonably easy to satisfy. A poor fit is a parent who is excessively difficult to satisfy.

The study sought to determine whether temperament would predict outcome, or whether goodness of fit would. The results were clear and surprising. Goodness versus poorness of fit predicted outcome. Difficult children turned out just as healthy and successful as others when raised in an environment that provided goodness of fit. The study shows that all one has to do to optimize a child's development is provide goodness of fit. Developmental forces will take care of the rest. Goodness of fit can be used to overcome weaknesses, optimize pride, and foster healthy involvement in life. Poorness of fit yields the opposite. A poor fit causes children to escape from reality and live in a fantasy world. The victim of poor fit is the lost teenager who plans to be a rock star but never takes a music lesson. He listens to rock music and watches music videos all day. Any attempt to force this child to recognize reality in his approach to life only stirs up resistance and rebellion.

GOODNESS AND POORNESS OF FIT

For several reasons, including the folly of lowering expectations in areas of little interest to the student and the constant changes in developmental dynamics, it is not as easy as it may seem to optimize development by adjusting expectations.

Some school programs lower expectations for developmentally challenged children, at the same time requiring these children to perform in environments that expose their weaknesses. The children are expected to sit still and learn through perceptual channels that are constitutionally impaired. Such a classroom environment constitutes a poor fit and may lead teachers to soften its effects by giving the student full credit for doing very little. The softened poor fit, however, does not offer the same growth opportunities as the good fit, in which children get to exercise their real strengths and interests in the pursuit of challenging expectations.

In the case of AD/HD children, we often medicate them, lessen their work loads, and ask teachers to watch them closely to make sure they conform to the demands of the traditional classroom. We have them sit quietly, be prompt, be prepared, follow instructions, and conform to rules. This kind of program gradually strips AD/HD children of their pride and it is only a matter of time before they lose motivation, lose respect for authority, and burn out. Eventually, school becomes so traumatic that they drop out.

We can prevent such problems by offering high-risk children the correct blend of soothing and challenging. This can be achieved by supplying proper levels of opportunity and family support, accompanied by developmentally sensitive expectations. It is essential to familiarize families with developmental thinking so they can adjust their expectations to meet their children's varying needs. Parents and teachers who have come to understand the dynamics that occur as children reach developmental milestones are able to remain calm and handle themselves effectively at those times when the children become most unstable. Equipped with such awareness, they can help their children grow and mature.

An Illustration of the Difference

Consider what you would do if you were a parent who believed that children are simple creatures of habit and your job is to mold them into proper little adults. You would think in metaphors like molding and shaping. You would structure, command, control, demand, insist, protect, lecture, and limit. You would expect your child to absorb your teachings and conform to your demands. You would supervise your child's actions and intervene the moment your child began to stray. You would make your child be good so your child would become accustomed to goodness. You would avoid errors. You would consider your children's errors as blemishes on your parenting skills. You would fret and worry about any bad behavior by your child for fear of that behavior becoming a habit. You would feel a need to nip such behaviors in the bud. These tendencies would make you a surrogate adaptive brain for your children and you would be likely to fall into the ODD trap.

Consider, on the other hand, what you would do if you believed that children are programmed to unfold according to a genetically determined blueprint, and your job is to nurture their development. You would think in metaphors like growing and gardening. You would nurture, feed, support, protect, expose, allow, listen, and observe. You would expect your children to discover things for themselves, learn from experience, and teach you what they have learned. You would monitor your children's activities, and allow them to self-correct as much as possible before you intervened. You would not allow a child to be traumatized by situations, but would permit the natural consequences of that child's behaviors and choices to have their impact and influence. You would welcome errors and enjoy watching your children self-correct. You would feel proud of your children whether they were doing things right or wrong. You would feel confident that your children would outgrow unwise behaviors. These tendencies would make you an encouraging ally who would allow the oppositional phase of development to resolve itself naturally.

Disruptive disorders can be evaluated in a way that circumvents the resistance one will face in working with ODD adolescents (see Chapter 3). There are stunning repercussions to subjecting AD/HD or ODD children to the behavior management strategies commonly practiced in our society. These tactics obstruct development and leave children prone to oppositional fixations. The poor fit between molding tactics and the needs of AD/HD and ODD children is the primary reason why behavioral methods designed for AD/HD children have failed.

The molding paradigm differs from the developmental in two ways: in the level of responsibility and freedom it grants children, and in the source of the consequences children experience. A developmental paradigm emphasizes trial-and-error learning from real-world consequences. The link between natural consequences and growth makes sense to parents who adopt a developmental paradigm.

Parents who operate from a molding paradigm strive to control and protect. They deliver all the consequences themselves. If the child won't do his homework, the parents punish him. If he bullies the neighbors' child and the neighbors call to complain, the parents punish him. If he won't wear a coat, the parents go through a prolonged battle to force the issue, solely to protect him from exposure to the cold.

Families that operate from a paradigm of natural development allow natural forces to act upon their children whenever possible. They allow their children to respond to situations independently of their advice, and then evaluate the results. They know natural consequences will challenge children to utilize hitherto latent strengths. They protect their children from harmful exposures that could traumatize and debilitate them, but allow modified versions of the same consequences to strengthen and inoculate their children against future exposures.

Inoculation is a construct derived from cognitive behavior therapy for stress disorders (Meichenbaum 1985), in which exposure to manageable levels of stress-inducing experiences helps the individual build up resistance to future traumatic responses to similar stresses. Consequences that don't traumatize will build tolerance and adaptive strengths. I elaborate on the concept of inoculation as it applies to child rearing in Chapter 6.

For now, let's look at how parents who operate from a natural development paradigm would deal with the situations just reviewed. The child refuses to do homework; the parents request a meeting with the teacher and obtain an agreement on what consequences the teacher will mete out in school. The child bullies the neighbors' child; the parents apologize privately to the offended family, and discuss with them the consequences they will administer.

One of the key problems clinicians must address is how parents of AD/HD and ODD children become surrogate frontal lobes for these youths with one adult frontal lobe managing one or more juvenile brains. The ensuing appearance of harmony secures the approval and support of the extended family and the school. The children are spared cold and hunger. The family benefits from a more pleasant household in the short run but only until the children become oppositional and learn to exploit their parents' dedication.

2

ODD as Two Minds at Odds

J ack was elated about his school performance in this, his last semester of high school. He had always been brilliant, but lacked motivation, and had struggled with school failure for years. He had been socially isolated as well. He was clearly different and had always felt misunderstood. He had learned to lie, manipulate, and hide his true self. He had seen the depths of despair. However, Jack had recently achieved a dramatic turnaround following two years of intensive treatment for ODD, AD/HD, and drug addiction.

Jack had found a new level of honesty and the inner strength to conquer all of the obstacles that had weighed him down. He felt confident because he had experienced genuine motivation and social success for the first time ever. He attributed his remarkable accomplishments to an integration of two very different parts of himself. He didn't need to see me anymore, he claimed, but had come in bursting with pride to tell me about what he considered a thrilling discovery.

"The reason I was able to keep my head above water this semester is because I became in touch with my body by working out," he said. "I've gotten big! I didn't need to see you as much because that's the function you perform. You connect me. Anyway, the thing that worked was a connection between my head and body. Well, that's not quite it, because that doesn't say anything. I mean a connection between my thoughts and what I am.

"Before I had a dissociation to my body, a contempt for it. I had a tendency to hide it under clothes. I was just a head, with a life support system, instead of one connected unit. I also realized how split I was, and how everybody is split to some degree. and that's what we all have to get past, especially AD/HD people.

"This semester I got in touch with talking to my hands. Know what I mean? This is what got me through all the hard times. Now I'm addicted to it [exercise]. My next step is cardio. When that happens, I don't know what will follow, because that connects everything. It works out all the muscles that you can't get to in a gym. I'm also connected to truth and people. It doesn't have to be exercise that connects you, but for me that's what made the difference."

There should be nothing difficult about treating adolescent ODD, provided the clinician enters the therapy room with a proper understanding of this condition. In fact, given the right support, the process can be manageable and predictable as well as gratifying. Prevailing wisdom has it that treating acting-out, oppositional adolescents presents the psychotherapist with a difficult and undesirable challenge. The poor prognosis reported in the literature supports this notion (see Appendix A). However, experience has shown me that this misconception stems from the way that established treatments have used sound psychology to impose the wrong agenda on these youths.

This chapter introduces the view that persistent exposure to unreasonable expectations (see Goodness and Poorness of Fit in Chapter 1) eventually freezes the development of the child at the oppositional phase, and produces a split in the youth's psyche. Continuing efforts to enforce a developmentally insensitive agenda simply entrenches the natural oppositional response of the youngster and furthers the split.

The end result is the developmental fixation we refer to as ODD, a persistent pattern of negativism, hostility, defiance, frequent arguing, loss of temper, rule breaking, externalizing blame, spoiling, hurting others, irritability, spitefulness, and vindictiveness (*DSM-IV*). This pattern, which initially comes about to conceal the youth's weaknesses, eventually becomes a mental disorder that thrives from continued efforts to enforce the very agenda that triggered it. Thus, ODD only grows stronger—and the underlying schism only grows wider—as parents and teachers attempt to fulfill their responsibilities and maintain consistent expectations.

The subtitle of this book suggests that a lasting resolution of ODD can only come about by what I have referred to as *finding the real child*. This chapter argues that the clinician accomplishes this task by establishing an alliance between two opposing sides of the youth's mind, and reintegrating an exiled part of the self that is referred to in the literature as the *emotional mind*. In other words, the emotional mind is, in a very real sense, the real child. The challenge is to accept, attach with, and facilitate the reintegration of the emotional mind with its neighboring brain region, the *rational mind*.

The notion of two divided minds has been thoroughly addressed in the literature from a variety of perspectives. At one end of the spectrum lies the purely scientific, neurophysiological school of thought (Bogen 1985). At the other extreme lies Eastern philosophy, with its body therapies, holistic remedies, and meditation (Bierman 1998, Griffith 1998, Locke and Colligan 1986, Pelletier and Herzing 1996). In between lie the psychoanalytic thinkers (Grotstein 1997, Hepburn 1997, Schachter 1997) and those who integrate traditional psychology with the neurosciences (Goleman 1996, Joseph 1992, Pally 1998). I base my exposition on the underpinnings of ODD on these latter two schools of thought.

The neurophysiological school of thought emphasizes brain anatomy and split-brain phenomena, based on case studies where the corpus collosum has been severed. Investigators from this field address dichotomies between the two hemispheres of the cortex (Bogen 1985). They discuss right-brain–left-brain phenomena, cerebral duality, hemispheric specialization, and convergence, among other topics.

Psychoanalytic schools have long studied the phenomena of mind–body splits (Hepburn 1997, Schachter 1997). Psychoanalytic thinkers address a series of subtleties related to such schisms. They explore the relationships between the body (the peripheral nervous system [PNS]) and the emotional mind (the unconscious), as well as between the emotional mind and the rational (conscious) mind.

Hepburn (1997) explores some of the ways in which body functioning, feelings, and cerebral activity may be split. He describes the mind–body split as a fear-based defensive maneuver, and warns that psychotherapies that ignore body memories prolong the split. Schachter (1997) adopts a developmental perspective to trace the gradual differentiation of the mind and body, and establishes the importance of body experiences in the formation of a sense of self. He traces the origins of psychoanalytic thinking on mind–body phenomena to Freud's original studies of hysteria, where Freud described syndromes in which the patients' bodies exhibited unresolved conflicts, yet their conscious minds remained oblivious to these dynamics. These cases suggest a schism between the head (conscious mind) and the body (self, or unconscious mind).

Grotstein (1997) uses the term *humanity's odd couple* to describe problems of the mind and body. He argues against artificially separating these two entities, and proposes viewing them as a fundamental unity that is either cooperative (integration) or uncooperative (split). Investigators from the behavioral medicine and medical psychology tradition present similar arguments (Bierman 1998, Griffith 1998).

Investigators who integrate the neurosciences and psychology address the dichotomy between the conscious and unconscious mind in a more objective and scientifically precise manner. Joseph (1992) and Goleman (1996) represent good examples of the integrationist model. Their work clarifies the underpinnings of the unconscious mind. Both emphasize the powerful influence of the right brain and limbic system on human behavior and our fundamental lack of awareness of this influence. Joseph explains how the left brain devises rational reasons for our choices and behaviors, without realizing the powerful influence of the unconscious.

Pally (1998) outlines the brain circuitry of emotion and shows how these circuits apply to a range of important phenomena. She introduces evidence from the neurosciences to demonstrate that emotion plays an important role in judgment and reason, and supports the notion that patients can benefit from learning to experience their feelings and express them to others. Emotions facilitate adaptive behaviors, contribute to problem solving, and facilitate social relationships, as long as their intensity is controlled. Conscious awareness of emotion plays a key role in helping to regulate its intensity level, a capacity that is critical to healthy emotional expression.

The fields of medical psychology and behavioral medicine have produced a movement known as psychoneuroimmunology (PNI) (Locke and Colligan 1986, Pelletier and Herzing 1996). These investigators describe PNI as a model of mind–body–environmental interaction that emphasizes the relationship between the emotional mind and the body. PNI sees the disconnection (split) of these two entities as the cause of many illnesses, and their integration as the key to healing.

Another body of literature spurred by interest in head/body phenomena involves the integration of verbal and body therapies (Mueller-Braunschweig 1997, Saggino 1996). Body-oriented psychotherapy methods argue that verbal psychotherapy (especially cognitive psychotherapy) impacts the processing of cognitive information, whereas body psychotherapy affects the perception of internal and external stimuli.

This chapter argues that, by the time an adolescent presents the full-blown ODD syndrome, the poorness of fit situation has become traumatic and has left the ODD youth in the passive and helpless position of a victim. Deprived of legitimate opportunities to exercise their innate quest for mastery, ODD youths express this need in its most negative and deviant form. They master the art of bringing significant others down with them. Their motive becomes jealousy of those who enjoy life. As the ODD progresses, we see the deterioration of many of the youth's vital emotional abilities, including self-awareness, self-restraint, confidence in decision-making, motivation, empathy, moral intentions, and the ability to persevere through difficult times.

This chapter outlines the process necessary to reverse the dichotomy between the two minds that constitutes the fundamental pathology in ODD. The key is to turn passive into active, victim into fighter, failure into mastery. To refer to the language of Chapter 1, we want to move the child from the oppositional to the mastery phase of development. However, before addressing the steps necessary to reverse this dichotomy, we must understand the two minds and how the dichotomy between them takes place.

OUR TWO MINDS

> In a very real sense, we have two minds, one that thinks and one that feels. . . These two fundamentally different ways of knowing interact to construct our mental life. One, the rational mind, is the mode of comprehension we are typically conscious of: more prominent in awareness, thoughtful, able to ponder and reflect. But alongside that there is another system of knowing: impulsive and powerful, if sometimes illogical—the emotional mind. [Goleman 1996, p. 8]

Goleman explains that emotions have a mind of their own and can form opinions quite independent of those of the rational mind. Yet the two minds are designed to join forces with remarkable skill. The rational mind offers the sophistication of analysis, while the emotional mind contributes a deeper kind of certainty. This deeper kind of certainty allows it to override the rational mind.

The independence of these two faculties, and the dominance of emotion over reason, leaves the two minds prone to conflict with each other. Children are particularly susceptible to this kind of internal conflict. All you have to do to engender such states of conflict is have their caregivers impose an agenda on them that betrays the wisdom of their emotional mind. The youth's rational mind will side with authority and the emotional mind will rebel against it.

Like Goleman, Joseph (1992) has integrated the latest findings from the neurosciences and clinical psychology to renew old constructs like conscious and unconscious and bring to them a new level of precision and sophistication. Like Goleman, Joseph divides the mind into semi-independent entities but takes this distinction a step further.

The first distinction that Joseph makes is between the conscious and unconscious operations taking place at the cortical level. He describes both sides of the neocortex as highly developed and relatively accessible. The left hemisphere performs the functions of the conscious mind, including the ability to talk and think in words, and to listen to and analyze spoken and written language. By contrast, the right half of the brain cannot read or write, nor understand human speech, except for a few simple emotional words.

The right brain performs the functions of the unconscious mind, since its operations are nonverbal. The right brain can use language to express itself, but only through singing, swearing, or crying. It expresses and comprehends best through body language, which conveys and detects intent, attitude, feeling, context, and meaning. Without input from the right brain, language becomes monotonic, bland, and impersonal.

The second distinction that Joseph makes refers to a deeper, less accessible level of the unconscious mind. He associates this level of the unconscious mind to the limbic system, a primitive region of the brain. Joseph calls the limbic level of the unconscious the *primary unconscious,* because its operations precede and override all other aspects of mental functioning.

THE WISDOM OF THE EMOTIONAL MIND

Feelings play an indispensable role in decision making. Our emotional mind stores memories that it associates with either pain or joy and references these at key times to steer us in a given direction. Thanks to the emotional mind, we can make key decisions automatically, without conscious awareness of the factors that swayed us in a given direction. To a great extent, our gut tells us whom to marry, what social group to join, what land to settle on, and what career to pursue. The certainty of emotions provide us a sense of security and confidence.

Feelings also drive our behavior and are ultimately responsible for motivation. All emotions are impulses to act, and each one reflexively launches a form of behavior that has worked well in the past given similar situations. Through evolution, each feeling has been imprinted in our nervous systems and been associated with a mode of perception and a series of behaviors that unfold automatically (Ekman 1992).

Feelings also provide the raw material for empathy, which in turn becomes the building block of moral development. Empathy is the ability to perceive the experience of others. It is an innate capacity that stems from the awareness of one's own emotions. The more open we are, the greater our capacity for empathy. Empathy, in turn, serves as the building block for essential social competencies. "All rapport, the root of caring, stems from emotional attunement, from the capacity for empathy" (Goleman 1996, p. 96).

The capacity for empathy develops in reverse order, from too much awareness of the feelings of others to just enough. Most abilities unfold in gradual increments from nonexistent to fully developed. Empathy, on the other hand, begins with a lack of awareness of the difference between one's feelings and those of others. The classic illustration of this phenomenon is the way infants become upset when they hear the cries of other infants. Gradually, through differentiation, the infant learns to distinguish between his own feelings and those of others. It takes about one year for them to realize that the cries of the other babies do not come from their own distress.

There is an inbred connection between the body and the capacity for empathy. In fact, the emotional communication that results in empathy only takes place when two bodies are in synch— a process called attunement. This means that the capacity for empathy decreases whenever the person loses sensitivity, whether this happens in response to previous trauma or insensitive treatment of another sort. "Empathy requires enough calm and receptivity so that the subtle signals of feeling from another person can be received and mimicked by one's own emotional brain" (Goleman 1996, p. 104).

Finally, feelings supply the raw material for moral development, since morality results from empathy. Martin Hoffman (1984) argues that morality stems from empathy, since sharing the feelings of victims genuinely drives us to want to help them. This in turn invites certain moral principles, like sensitivity, caring, equity, and forgiveness.

Healthy moral development requires striking the proper balance between one's personal needs and those of others as perceived through empathy. One must maintain a strong sense of one's own needs and feelings to strike this balance. Devoid of self-awareness, the capacity for empathy can lead to a false sense of morality and to social success at the expense of personal development and genuine satisfaction. Individuals who fail to establish this balance will suffer from either insensitivity or falseness. They become social chameleons who adopt whatever stance or opinion they assume will gain them approval and help them fit in. Psychoanalytic authors have described such individuals as false-self disorders.

TWO MINDS AT ODDS

The two hemispheres of the brain may reach very different conclusions given the same information. This can happen because memories and perceptions are represented separately in each half of the brain. Since the two hemispheres of the brain can support very different agendas, they can selectively perceive different aspects of experiences. This selective inattention can yield a significant degree of conflict between the two halves of the brain. The different perceptions of the two brains will trigger different memories and then act in opposition.

Based on the different way in which a single event may be perceived by the right and left brains as well as the different memories that may be triggered, each half of the brain may then act in an oppositional manner, one half attempting to do or believing one thing, the other half attempting to accomplish (or believing) something entirely different. In such circumstances, the person may feel in conflict, confused, mistrustful, or even paralyzed by indecisiveness, since certain memories cannot always be shared or transferred from one brain half to the other. [Joseph 1992, p. 61]

Joseph explains how, whenever there is conflict between the right and left brains, the efficacy of overall information processing suffers. In most people, the left brain dominates and tries to perform the tasks of the right brain. This is unfortunate because the left brain will suppress and inhibit the abilities of the right brain, yet has difficulty processing social and emotionally laden situations, particularly those that are negative. Such individuals appear socially inept, have problems in relationships, and deny painful or upsetting information.

Everyday situations can easily trigger intrapsychic conflicts in youths who face unreasonable expectations. The youth's rational mind will demonstrate loyalty to the demands of adult authority (for example, homework), but the emotional mind will demand loyalty to pressing emotional needs (for example, a video game). The right brain dominance of many immature youths will yield a rebellious response. Such intrapsychic conflicts are quite normal.

However, as unreasonable expectations become conditioned with fear or associated with trauma, the danger increases that the youth will develop a clinically significant schism and ODD. The resulting schism is due to the raw power of the emotions involved. As memories triggered by related perceptions become emotionally traumatic, the response to such memories is likely to remain unconscious because of the left brain's difficulty with processing negative emotions.

Without a resolution to the threat of further trauma, the memories grow painful, and eventually leave their indelible mark in the limbic system (the primary unconscious, to use Joseph's term). They remain inaccessible to conscious awareness, impervious to reason. Once memories become painful, they are instantly imprinted, yield rapid learning, and become prominent in their influence. They are stored in the form of unconscious opinions that govern decision making, even when defying logic. They lie there dormant, but able to generate intense emotions given the slightest provocation.

Goleman uses the term *emotional hijacking* to describe how emotion manages to overrides reason. He bases his explanation of this construct on the work of Joseph LeDoux on fear conditioning. According to LeDoux, memories of painful events are stored in a site within the limbic system called the amygdala (AL). The amygdala "is a focal point in an emotional learning network. It is interconnected with sensory (thalamic), perceptual (neocortical), and higher cognitive (hipppocampal) processing areas" (LeDoux 1992, p. 468).

According to Goleman, each incoming sensory signal initially travels to the thalamus, a switching station in the lower brain regions. From the thalamus, the signal is duplicated and routed to two different sites in the brain. One is sent to the emotional brain for immediate screening out of emergencies and one to the rational brain for more sophisticated analysis. The signal sent to the emotional brain is relatively inaccurate. It is rapidly deployed and transmitted directly to the amygdala. Meanwhile, the second, more detailed signal is routed to the neocortex for more elaborate processing. This puts the amygdala in the position where it can respond before the neocortex can even complete its rational analysis of a given situation.

Under normal circumstances, the amygdala does not trigger its alarm and the sensory signals travel to the neocortex, where they are processed. The neocortex then signals the amygdala, which imbues the signal with the appropriate emotional charge that will in turn trigger the necessary action.

However, the amygdala can interrupt this slower, more sophisticated process at any time, and not necessarily because a given event presently poses a real threat. The amygdala works by association, meaning that it will call anything that contains one key element of a past event a match. If so, it takes over in an instant, acting before it can fully determine the rational importance of that similarity.

Goleman explains that this puts the amygdala in the privileged position of a *psychological sentinel*, scanning every experience for possible trouble, and sounding off an emergency alarm every time it detects anything that even remotely matches the memory of a prior bad experience. The feelings that stem from this neural alarm system can overwhelm the rational mind. Once alerted, the amygdala will trigger the same behavioral response that was utilized when the distressing event was initially imprinted.

THE IMPACT OF DISTRESS OR TRAUMA ON THE MIND

The wounded mind has difficulty entering states of serenity and surrender or facing situations that resemble the original trauma. It can use distraction to escape the memories of disturbing experiences during the hustle and bustle of daily life—out of sight, out of mind. However, any time the individual attempts to enter a restful state, or encounters a situation that the amygdala can associate with danger, the amygdala hurls a vivid recollection of the trauma at the neocortex. It is as if the amygdala were dropping the gauntlet on the rational mind. "You're going to rest? In this unsafe world? What if this were to happen again? What would you do?"

Ordinarily, when an individual learns to be frightened by something the fear subsides with time. Otherwise it becomes posttraumatic stress disorder (PTSD). Fears subside through a natural relearning process, as the feared object is experienced under safe and pleasant conditions, allowing the amygdala to alter its associations, and the neocortex to deal with the object intelligently. However, when an individual is forced repeatedly to encounter the feared object under unpleasant circumstances, the mind is fundamentally altered.

Thus, with its unexpected recollections, the emotional mind

continually tests and challenges the rational mind to provide it with effective solutions to disturbing memories, and the answer of the rational mind will determine the coping style of the individual. If the rational mind remains passive, and fails to provide an effective solution, the amygdala uses primitive defenses to cope. The objective of primitive coping mechanisms is to adopt a passive, helpless stance, and repeatedly endure the traumatic experience, each time with less pain. This is the victim mentality.

Key biological changes take place in the victims' passive response that explain their tendency to prepare to endure further trauma with less pain. Goleman (1996) explains that these changes occur in the brain's opioid system, which becomes hyperactive. The opioids are brain chemicals that act as powerful numbing agents, like narcotics. "When experiencing high levels of opioids ('the brain's own morphine'), people have a heightened tolerance for pain" (p. 206).

If, on the other hand, the rational mind can respond to the emotional mind with an effective strategy, the individual will learn to rely on more sophisticated coping mechanisms. The amygdala will challenge the neocortex with a vivid recollection of a traumatic experience, and the active rational mind will respond with a plan of action that should effectively protect the individual. This will establish a level of trust between the two brains, and the effect will be a quieting of the amygdala, the restoration of the capacity to enter states of surrender, and the effective management of situations that resemble the original stressors.

Nonetheless, as soon as the rational mind passes one test, the amygdala will present it with another, and then another, until every possible disturbing scenario has been mastered. The amygdala will scan its extensive memory and consider all possibly threatening scenarios. It will find a scenario that is not covered by the previous solution and present it to the rational mind in the same startling manner. The emotional mind will repeat this procedure until it has exhausted every possible scenario. Once the rational mind has passed all of the emotional mind's tests, the disturbing episode has been put to rest for good. The key ingredient in the relearning process involves an active, problem-solving approach to old traumas. Once more, the key to well-being is to adopt an attitude of mastery.

"Helplessness as the wild card in triggering PTSD has been shown in dozens of studies," Goleman (1996) states. "The operative word is *uncontrollable*. If people feel there is something they can do in a catastrophic situation, some control they can exert, no matter how minor, they fare far better emotionally than do those who feel utterly helpless" (p. 204). It is the helpless person who becomes susceptible to developing a mental disorder.

Milder hardships leave their imprint on the emotional brain and have a similar impact on development as the more dramatic traumas. Young children who are continually exposed to harsh criticism and shame, or who persistently encounter poorness-of-fit situations, tend to manifest low-end versions of the callousness and transmission of cruelty seen in abused children.

THE DECLINE OF MORALITY

Abuse is self-perpetuating, and individuals who have been consistently mistreated as children may behave similarly toward others as children and adults, their capacity for empathy thwarted by their own victimization. In fact, Goleman says, "this failure of empathy is sometimes, if not often, repeated over generations, with brutal parents having themselves been brutalized by their own parents in childhood" (p. 199).

The dichotomy between the limbic system (emotional mind) and the neocortex leads to emotional brain dominance that renders the ODD teenager susceptible to addiction and a host of relationship problems. These youths fail to develop many of the abilities that emerge when higher centers for reason govern emotional life. They are often lost in their emotions, overwhelmed by impulses, and unable to reflect, empathize, or cooperate successfully with others. They struggle with communication and motivation.

In addition to its influence on the rational mind in response to trauma, the amygdala plays a key role in the formation of addictions. This is because the limbic system mediates all drives, including the need for human contact. Hence, it can generate a feeling of satisfaction in a lonely person who eats. The person feels pleasure, and relief from the pain of loneliness. Soon, the person eats when not hungry to avoid facing the emotional pain of loneliness.

Similarly, a person who is experiencing difficulty in meeting a pressing need can find relief from the resulting distress by involuntarily activating other limbic drives. An individual who is sexually dissatisfied may take to gambling or drink excessively. A person who is bored may decide to get high on drugs. These subterfuge indulgences lead to addictions because they never address the primary unmet need, the underlying tension never subsides, and the urge to launch another cycle of drive and indulgence never ceases.

> If the original need continues to go unmet, the limbic system will again motivate the person to take some action, any action. If a wrong action satisfied the need just hours or days before by reducing the level of tension and inducing feelings of pleasure, this same erroneous behavior will be engaged in again and again. The person may eat to the bursting point or may choose to go out and fight with anybody who looks at her or him cross-eyed. [Joseph 1992, p. 136]

ODD represents nothing less than an emotional mind lost in a nightmare, a mind constantly overwhelmed by emotion and devoid of reason. ODD youths rely on outdated instinctive responses that may provide security by concealing its weaknesses, but simply don't fit in with society at large. They operate in a single-minded manner that routinely leads them to misunderstand situations and pit them against loved ones. Along the way they unwittingly harm those who care for them most. Unable to satisfy their innate drives for belonging and success, they become susceptible to a host of addictions, including spoiling and fighting. They shut doors to their own futures and fail to learn from their experiences. In short, because of the dichotomy that marks their lives, ODD youths fail to develop essential levels of self-awareness, and miss out on the wisdom of emotion.

THE IMPORTANCE OF INTEGRATION

The integration of the two minds affords us a series of essential skills that yield emotional intelligence. These competencies facilitate moral development, will, and character, including self-awareness, self-control, empathy, and the ability to resolve conflict and practice cooperation. Youths possess an unusual capacity to learn these skills with relative ease until their late teenage years.

Self-awareness becomes the basic building block for all other emotional abilities. It represents the linking together of the limbic system and the frontal lobes of the neocortex. The processes serve to bring intelligence into emotion, allowing us to master life's greatest challenges. As Goleman (1996) puts it, "Bringing cognizance to the realm of feeling has an effect something like the impact of an observer at the quantum level in physics, altering what is being observed" (p. xii).

Self-awareness provides us with a surer sense of how we really feel, and guides us in our lives. This aptitude provides the capacity for empathy and affords us a grip over our emotions that allows us to manage them effectively. Those who can manage their emotions are able to express them in interpersonal and social situations in appropriate ways. The ability to manage emotions yields the capacity to self-soothe and to recover quickly from disturbing emotional states. This capacity in turn yields the ability to motivate, to inhibit impulses, and to delay gratification. Finally, the ability to motivate leads to the state of mastery.

The clinician's goal for the ODD teenager is to arrive at what Goleman refers to as the *master aptitude*, the ability to turn adversity and failure into a growth opportunity. The ODD youth presents a series of defense mechanisms that stem naturally from the developmental phase in which he has become lodged. These mechanisms are manifestations of the dichotomy between the emotional and rational minds—the mind–body split. However, they interfere with the capacity for self-reflection, and it is imperative that the clinician find a way around them.

Given the central role that self-awareness plays in mind–body integration and emotional development, the denial of the ODD teenager represents a major obstacle to the process of mind–body integration. These youths externalize blame for all of their short-comings and refuse to accept responsibility. They must disconnect themselves from all self-reflection to maintain this defensive posture. The impact on the acquisition of emotional intelligence is, of course, devastating.

Following is an overview of the treatment steps necessary to achieve integration of the two minds. I explain how the two minds come to trust each other and reach a healthy state of integration. Subsequent chapters of this book guide the clinician through the process necessary to achieve these ends with ODD teenagers.

TREATMENT TO INTEGRATE THE TWO MINDS

The key to integrating the two minds involves exchanging the ODD youth's passive, defensive, victim stance for one of mastery over adversity. The clinician must assist the ODD teenager in modifying painful associations imprinted in the emotional brain that stand by, ready to trigger shutdowns and states of alarm. The process involves (1) desensitizing anxiety-laden perceptions that trigger dysfunctional behavior, and (2) training the neocortex to override the emotional triggers that are automatically set off during anxiety-laden situations, and to respond effectively.

The treatment can involve a variety of steps, among them establishing trust, acceptance, and safety; empowering the individual by putting him in charge; and encouraging responsible action and the adoption of a self-validating perspective. The teenager must be encouraged to exhaust every possible option to recapture losses and build a positive life, and to develop self-awareness, a new understanding of his past, and a new plan of action. This last step usually requires continued individual therapy with the adolescent.

The first step involves establishing certainty that distressing situations will be resolved and traumatic episodes will not recur. This assurance calms the emotional circuits enough to allow therapeutic relearning to begin. The clinician begins this process with ODD teenagers by focusing on issues dealt with by the emotional brains, as discussed by Goleman and by Joseph. Not only does such a focus foster trust and a sense of safety, but it also facilitates fulfillment of therapeutic tasks.

ODD youths will not attempt the activities prescribed for them in therapy unless the clinician has earned their trust and has motivated them to want to please him. Thus, it is imperative for the clinician to become a true friend of the emotional side of the schism. This means doing playful and pleasant things together and not just talking, because action is the medium of communication of the emotional mind. The therapist should find out what the ODD teenager loves to do and then join him in the closest approximation possible to that activity. The clinician wants to form an indelible imprint on the ODD teenager's emotional circuitry so that the teenager associates him with safety, trust, understanding, advocacy, play, and the youth's most impassioned activities, whatever they are.

Play yields soothing properties that can assist the relearning necessary to transform imprinted distressing memories into pleasant ones. Youths can use pretend play to reexperience the disturbing past safely, rehearse different approaches to managing threatening situations, and imagine a positive outcome to each problem event. The clinician who has been associated with friendship and healing can use his influence to make the therapeutic context a place where this level of transformation can take place.

Another quick way to bolster an alliance with the ODD youth involves normalizing any deviant or dysfunctional behavior presented. The clinician can increase self-awareness and promote self-acceptance by framing humiliating symptoms as normal responses to an abnormal history. ODD youths can utilize this reframe to normalize aberrant behavior patterns and attain a sense of mastery over emotional memories that have haunted them. Rather than adopting their usual passive and helpless stance, these teens can learn to become active observers. Rather than thinking of themselves as defective, they can feel validated and understood. In short, this reframe makes the intrusive memories and the hijacking process less toxic and frightening.

The next step involves utilizing the sense of safety and therapeutic influence that the clinician has established to promote responsible action. This will prevent the spread of trauma or dysfunction on to significant others.

The use of distress as an excuse to escape responsibilities tends to create a vicious cycle that magnifies addiction. This is because each escape sets up the need for another. Each escape from pain that involves an abrogation of responsibility provides a brief period of relief followed by an experience of greater pain. The individual returns from the escape to face the original unresolved source of the pain, plus the stress of all the additional unfulfilled commitments. This leaves the youth with an even better incentive to repeat the escape into indulgence. This cycle violates trust and closes doors to opportunity, leaving the youth in a growing state of dependence on the indulgence.

The clinician needs to explain the danger of this cycle and encourage the youth to fulfill his responsibilities, despite the pain, and indulge in escape only after the responsibilities have been met. This will break the addictive cycle, prevent harm to others, preserve trusting relationships, and leave doors to a fulfilling life open. It is essential to place the distressed teen in charge of this responsibility to empower himself, and prevent the helpless, passive stance that leaves him vulnerable to the formation of a mental disorder. This intervention to counter addiction is discussed in greater detail in Chapter 11, dealing with negative peer influences.

The next important step in reintegrating the two minds is adoption by the teenager of a self-validating attitude. This translates into doing what is right because it is the right thing to do, in contrast to external validation, which is approval extended by others. Adoption by a teenager of a self-validating stance is his investment in what he will become. He asks for help or offers forgiveness, not because these gestures will be accepted by others, but because he knows it is important to become the kind of person who takes responsibility and forgives.

Adopting a self-validating stance allows distressed and fragile individuals to take risks in pursuit of recovery, and benefit from their attempts whether these yield the desired results or not. It protects the individual from becoming risk-aversive and adopting the passive-helpless stance of a victim who refuses to try for fear that failed efforts will worsen his already precarious state. The well-being of the externally validating individual depends on factors such as the generosity and kindness of others. The well-being of the self-validating individual, on the other hand, depends solely on his personal efforts. What he accomplishes that way cannot be taken away from him.

The clinician can help the ODD teenager utilize self-validation to view failure as an opportunity for growth. The self-validating individual does things his own way and does what he thinks is right, whether he succeeds or fails. Since ODD youths utilize failure to manipulate others, this intervention becomes central to their treatment. It takes the sting out of failure, leaving the teenager with nothing to hold over his family's head. It frees the family from its perennial struggle to prevent failure and renders the ODD teenager's manipulation efforts ineffective.

The clinician can explain to the youth that, in the journey toward self-actualization, it is essential to view each failure as a learning opportunity, each weakness as a strengthening exercise. One can derive just as much benefit, if not more, from bolstering a weakness than from developing a strength. Since we are all blind to our weaknesses, we need some vehicle for uncovering them. Failure can become this vehicle. In this way, youths can come to view adversity in a positive light and attempt to master it.

The clinician can readily foster the right kind of attitude toward failure in ODD teenagers when preparing them to manage increased freedom, anticipate new challenges, or process recent failures. ODD teenagers will be most open to influence during these times because of the uncertainty they present.

The next important step in achieving integration involves

exhausting every possible option to replace the losses incurred as a result of hardships endured in the past. Taking steps to retrieve what was lost increases confidence and faith in oneself. The end result should be a happier life.

Nagy and Krasner (1986) argue that true forgiveness entails restoring one's life to at least as good as it was before troubling experiences left their mark. Individuals can lose physical or mental abilities, confidence, trust in the safety of their world, material possessions, friends, loved ones, and social opportunities. Living a life without these attributes serves as a constant reminder of the hardships endured.

The hurt individual must exhaust every possibility to replace losses and restore happiness to his life. For example, if the individual has lost the use of his right arm, he can learn to use his left. If a material possession has been lost, the individual can strive for a better one. If the individual loses a loved one, he must mourn that loss and find another to love, or dedicate himself to a cause in memory of the lost loved one. Grieving families often do this by taking up causes that prevent others from falling into tragedies similar to their own.

The end result of this step is a life that youths can look forward to, care about, and see meaning in. This step represents the antidote to self-destructive behavior. Youths who do not care about what they do with their day end up not caring about themselves. Youths who do not care about themselves are prone to self-destructive behavior. On the other hand, those who care about what they do with their lives end up caring about themselves. They maintain strong self-preservation instincts and avoid harming themselves. This is the reason why, in my work with adolescents, I challenge them to fashion lives that will make them glad to wake up in the morning.

The process of replacing losses involves asking for help from anyone able to give it. It also involves considering all possibilities for procuring the resources necessary to repair one's life. Every effort must be expended, every request made, every risk taken. The journey of a thousand miles begins with one step. It is the inching forward that does the healing. The journey restores hope, allows distressing memories to fade, and provides the individual with a sense of confidence that he can master future adversity without reverting to the position of the helpless victim.

The final step involves developing self-awareness, a new understanding of one's past, and a new plan of action. This stage represents the individual therapy work. The previous interventions for establishing safety, remaining responsible despite pain, adopting a self-validating perspective, and exhausting every option to recapture losses pave the way for this ongoing relearning process. This treatment component involves retelling and reconstructing the story of the disturbing past, of acknowledging one's own contribution to the problem, and allowing the emotional mind to acquire a rational understanding and adaptive response to the distressing assumptions stored there.

The only way to overcome distressing circumstances is to learn a different way of living. However, it will be difficult for the individual to learn new behaviors if he does not understand the ways in which he can fall back into the old patterns that oppress him. Thus, the individual must be able to look at his own life to identify his own maladaptive patterns before he can consider new alternatives.

In his discussion of treatment methods, Joseph (1992) stresses the value of helping the client to make conscious choices and accept responsibility in attaining mastery over unconscious forces, which he calls the *stranger within*. He stresses the importance of developing self-awareness as the essential first step in this process. "Admittedly a person is capable of choosing only what he is able to conceive. One cannot explore a road he does not know exists. . . . Such an individual may be incapable of choosing to live his life any differently. . . . It would be as alien as living on the planet Mars" (pp. 367–368).

Joseph acknowledges that it is difficult to look at oneself and learn new behaviors, especially for people who have been programmed by fear or trauma to fall into a symptom pattern passively. However, he says, most people retain the capacity to make these changes throughout their lives. "The tape recording can be turned off, and a new one can be put in its place; the brain can learn new patterns of responding and thinking and can reorganize itself in the process" (p. 368).

To rework distressing memories with teenagers, the clinician often has to rely on unconscious expressions of the old memories as they manifest themselves in the reenactments of daily life. Simply retelling and reconstructing tales of old experiences, as when working with adults, would quickly become awkward and grow old with ODD teenagers. The clinician must find manifestations of the old memories in current situations, especially in their setbacks, failures, and expressions of ODD symptomatology. Many of the interventions I introduce in this book are designed to promote these experiences and facilitate the resurfacing of buried material.

The successful completion of these treatment steps will yield mind–body integration. Only this level of in-depth work will truly resolve the root of the disorder and yield lasting benefits. The process leaves the ODD youth with a life of responsibility that satisfies him, plus a fuller understanding of himself and his past experiences. This may seem like a lot of work, but the treatment need not be completed all at once. Many youths drop in and out of treatment, allowing the clinician to accomplish a few of these steps at a time. They return when they are ready to outgrow their old problems and reach greater levels of integration. The benefits of relearning and reintegration make the entire effort worthwhile. The positive outcomes in youths who have been taken through these steps stand in marked contrast to the terrible long-term prognosis that accompanies unresolved ODD.

The next chapter shows clinicians how to accept the ODD youths' defense mechanism of using failure to conceal weaknesses and how to turn this defense against them for their own betterment. The intervention will temporarily resolve the ODD stance and expose the hidden problems of the ODD youth. Things appear to worsen before they improve. However, the clinician gains the youth's cooperation and places himself in a position to assess properly the needs of the child. In the next chapter I present the reframe of ODD as two minds at odds in the way a clinician would when addressing a family. I demonstrate a method for interviewing ODD youths and describe a variety of ways that facilitate the integration of the two minds. This set of interventions makes it only a matter of time before the youth's emotional aptitudes unfold naturally.

Part II

Assessment

3

Evaluation: A Strategic Approach

Tom, a strikingly handsome 15-year-old high school sophomore, sat sheepishly in my office. It was his fourth session, and I could sense a new level of resistance. This was a dramatic change from a few weeks before, when he had been eager to see me. I had asked his mother to bring him to my office despite his newly acquired negative attitude. I now knew that I needed to prime him for a more comprehensive evaluation. I needed to rule out AD/HD, LD, and emotional disorders before I could discover what lay at the bottom of his difficulty.

I had gone through my routine admission process for an ODD adolescent. I had met with the parents to take a history, gather other details about Tom's presenting problem, and arrive at a preliminary hypothesis about the case.

Tom had been refusing to do his schoolwork. He was also violating curfew, lying, defying his parents, and taking personal belongings from family members without their permission. He had become irritable and would lose his temper with his parents at the slightest provocation. He stopped participating in activities that formerly were important to him, including sports, and his circle of friends changed from wholesome to unwholesome. He wanted to spend all his time with his peers. He was using drugs and telling his parents that marijuana was good for him, and that all they needed to do was leave him alone and "everything will be fine." Tom's parents were conscientious. They sought to enforce firm but reasonable limits. Tom, however, would either defy them or lie to avoid complying.

My preliminary hypothesis was that Tom had developed an addictive relationship to his peers and to drugs. This addiction was his reaction to family standards for conduct and education that were too high for him to manage. He was secretly nursing a depression stemming from the loss of friends who had moved away.

I tested the accuracy of this hypothesis with a trial intervention designed to determine whether Tom's problem could be resolved easily without further evaluation. Perhaps, after all, his escape into the peer world contained an element of wisdom. He lacked motivation to do well in school. It was natural, then, for him to discard the false motivation of having to please his parents, and turn to his peer group to satisfy his need for social interaction.

The goal of the trial intervention was to alter the addictive cycle of escape and indulgence, of feeling bad and using this as an excuse to shirk responsibilities. The cycle provided short-term relief for Tom. Soon, however, he would experience greater pressure to discharge his obligations. He would feel guilty about his shortcomings and the stage would thus be set for another spin through the escape cycle.

The way to improve Tom's conduct was to change the order of events and offer him a structure that made peer contacts a reward for responsible behavior, rather than an escape from it. The new cycle I recommended was for him to feel bad, fulfill key responsibilities, and then indulge in peer involvement. Tom readily agreed because he understood the addictive nature of his old cycle, and realized the new structure meant earning permission for sleepovers and access to peers with an ease he had never experienced before. I had thus arranged for Tom to have the opportunity to prove his contention that his parents were mistaken in their refusal to go along with his assertions that all they had to do was let him have his own way and everything would turn out fine.

By design, this trial intervention created a special therapeutic alliance. Tom finally had a taste of the freedom he so desperately wanted. The intervention was calculated either to resolve the case very quickly or expose the deeper nature of Tom's problem. It turned out to be highly informative. But, despite some early signs of progress, its success was short-lived.

Tom failed to observe the terms of the new cycle for long. This is why he now sat so sheepishly in my office. He had quit his job and had deceived his family in numerous ways. He had lied about where he had spent a night, claiming he was at a male friend's house when actually he was staying with a girl. He was often at the homes of friends whose parents were out of town. Worst of all, the extent of his involvement with drugs was now clear. This explained his resistance.

During the previous meeting, we had discussed Tom's misuse of his new privileges. As agreed, he would have to forfeit his privileges temporarily. He would have opportunities to try again. I had no time in the previous session to speak with Tom alone, no chance to restore my alliance with him. He had felt exposed and ashamed and had given up on therapy.

GETTING PAST THE *ODD* TO ASSESS COMORBIDITY

With a disruptive adolescent, the only thing one can assess at the outset is the ODD. ODD symptoms mask other underlying conditions, and undermine assessment efforts. The parents describe the child as lazy, apathetic, uncommunicative, and deceptive. They complain about his selfishness, negative attitude, and tendency to spoil things for the family. They report his tendency to externalize blame. Teachers report he does not do his schoolwork and disrupts classes. His oppositional tendencies keep him from communicating openly with the therapist and facing up to his problems.

ODD symptoms make it difficult to evaluate AD/HD or LD symptoms. The tests for these conditions depend upon the child making a determined effort to do well, thus giving the clinician the opportunity to observe the effects of these disabilities. However, when the ODD child is not making an effort, it is difficult to tell what factors might otherwise influence his behavior. The rating scales that measure AD/HD and other emotional problems will point strongly to ODD, and it will be hard to detect any other underlying condition.

ODD also makes the child unresponsive to any remedy for AD/HD or LD, even if those conditions are diagnosed. Dealing effectively with AD/HD or LD requires, in fact, the same kind of dedicated effort by the child as seen in individuals who overcome the effects of other types of limitations by perseverance and efforts of will. The ODD child avoids and procrastinates, and does not work hard to take advantage of the remedies available. In short, ODD undermines the effectiveness of multimodal evaluation and treatment. It is essential for the clinician to circumvent the ODD before attempting to complete an evaluation that can provide the child and his parents with new understanding and win their cooperation.

The first step in setting up the preevaluation trial intervention alluded to above is winning family cooperation, which involves reframing ODD as two minds at odds. An introduction to a reframe of ODD explaining how this dichotomy takes place follows. This reframe will help the family view the condition in a positive light. The new perspective also prepares the clinician to deal with the adolescent more effectively. This reframe of the problem is the cornerstone of treatment and the basis for all the interventions that follow.

REFRAMING *ODD* AS TWO MINDS AT ODDS

The process I refer to as a split between two minds involves a growing dichotomy between the emotional and rational minds. These semi-independent minds lose their integrity once the youths encounter a poorness of fit between the expectations they face and their genuine needs and abilities. Parents and teachers habitually unite to demand compliance with these expectations, yet the child's emotional mind knows they are dead wrong. This set of circumstances leaves the two minds at odds.

In the absence of an emotionally laden situation, the youth's talk reflects the perspective of the rational mind, that is, the voices of authority and society. However, when the threatening situation presents itself, emotional hijacking takes place, and the behavior of the child reflects a very different agenda—the fight-flight response of the emotional mind. Instantly, the emotional mind commandeers the rational mind, which accommodates the emotional mind by using talk in the service of manipulation—for either avoidance or attack. In the end, the youth's talk and walk do not match. The youth loses integrity and the split grows.

The Source of the Split

It is a central hypothesis of this book that behind each case of ODD lies a misunderstood child, one whose natural essence differs from that of the norm, and whose special needs have gone undetected. Although they may not know it, ODD youths develop their symptoms as a last-ditch effort to conceal and protect their natural but hidden essence. Their combative tendencies also reflect a desperate attempt to gratify the needs associated with a different course of development, one that would help them actualize their unique potential.

There are differences among individuals in the timing of when different developmental needs become pressing. Some youths become social, athletic, intellectual, or sexual much earlier than others do. Some become academically oriented at age 10, some at 20. Some become sexual at age 12, others at 19.

Well-intentioned adults often misinterpret the special needs of ODD youths and impose on them the normalization agenda of our institutions. The efforts of these authority figures will further alienate youths who are ashamed of having special needs. This is especially the case with youths who suffer from AD/HD, physical handicaps, or learning disabilities. The unreasonable expectations of misguided adults cause these youths anxiety, and make the normative agenda seem repulsive. The children's rational minds get the message that the activity is good and necessary, yet the emotional mind feels violated and assumes that the opposite is true. This experience leaves the two minds at odds and lays the foundation for a dichotomy between the rational and the emotional minds. From this point forward, use of controlling tactics by parents and teachers subvert the child's natural cycle of motivation, and risk turning the child off to that activity for a long time to come.

I illustrate this process to my clients with the metaphor of force-feeding peanuts into the alimentary tract. I then discuss the forcing of knowledge through the auditory and visual tracts (the knowledge acquisition system as it pertains to school). The metaphor works best if the ODD teenager's least favorite food can be determined.

In this scenario, the opening of the alimentary tract is dormant. However, I explain, it's lunchtime, and I have a bag of peanuts that I want to feed to the children, even though they would prefer something else. The emotional brain responds with distress and distrust when I try to arouse it. I offer it peanuts and it rejects them. I try to force it to open up and it fights me. To overcome the opposition, I threaten the children with unpleasant consequences. No TV until all peanuts are gone, and no spending time with friends. The children choose the lesser of two evils and eat the peanuts.

Forcing an unwanted energy source on the body tampers with nature's instinctive motivational cycle. The effect is one of repulsion. If this occurs, the experience will be categorized as disturbing and imprinted that way in the amygdala. The child will respond with alarm to any situation reminiscent of the original episode, his sensory system closing involuntarily when it is confronted with a similar stimulus.

Human sensory systems can open fully to create a satisfying experience, however. Such experiences are rich and full of energy and the individual involved feels very much alive. Yet, when an organism is open, it is also vulnerable. The delicate sensors that process the experience are equally sensitive in generating pain when violated or betrayed. The senses subsequently attempt to shut down on any experience reminiscent of the initial forcing. They adjust to force by losing sensitivity.

Parents and teachers establish routines for children early in their lives, force on them experiences the parents and teachers believe are beneficial, and insist that the children continue to participate in activities they dislike—all in the interest of teaching them to make good on their commitments. Parents who have adopted the creatures-of-habit paradigm (see Chapter 1) and believe they must mold their children's lives may force them to take music lessons, participate in a sport, join the Scouts, or attend Sunday school. They may insist that their children stick it out even after they tire of an activity because "they must learn to follow through on their commitments."

It becomes impossible for children to satisfy the desires they develop naturally if their parents and teachers think these desires are not wholesome. Parents use coercion to make their children try new things, avoid dangerous situations, and fulfill obligations. Coercion can keep children out of trouble and help them achieve the success they otherwise would never know. However, it can also deprive them of the opportunity to exercise the wisdom of the emotional mind and can interfere with their development. The more unwanted the experience forced on a child, the more irritating it will be to the body's nervous system.

The response to being force-fed unwanted experiences is disconnection. After sufficient unwanted ingestion, the person feels violated. In an attempt to escape further violations, the emotional brain learns to shut down the sensory system involuntarily in recollection of the event. However, if it cannot escape further forcing, it gradually disconnects enough to make involuntary ingestion less uncomfortable.

People who learn to disconnect themselves from their experiences lose wisdom. They don't realize how their emotional minds distrust their own logic, and how their rational minds lack clearcut signals from their emotional minds about what is right for them.

The experience of being coerced into opening up and engaging in unwanted experiences produces unfavorable symptoms if the coercion persists, even though the human nervous system is quite malleable, and an individual can tolerate a considerable amount of forced experiences and remain healthy.

The Symptoms of School Aversion

Our society places so much value on formal education that it thinks nothing of forcing it on children year after year. No mechanism is in place to reduce the pressure on the children to take in unwanted knowledge. In fact, during the period when the students' learning systems are suffering most from the dulling effect of what amounts to force-feeding, our culture increases the pressure to learn. The pressure is greatest during the adolescent years and its impact on the emotional minds of many teenagers is substantial.

Psychoanalyst and object relations theorist Wilfred Bion was the first to address the striking parallels that exist between the way the alimentary tract digests food and the mind digests elements of experience. Bion derived this parallel from his analysis of the work of Melanie Klein and based much of his thinking on this model.

In his paper, "Learning from Experience" (1962), Bion addresses the emotional impact of experiences and how these influence capacity for thought: "It may be useful to suppose that there exists in reality a psycho-somatic breast and an infantile psycho-somatic alimentary canal corresponding to the breast" (p. 34). He argues for the use of the alimentary system as a model for understanding the processing of experiences. In his words, "There is reason for using alimentary system as a model for demonstrating and comprehending the processes involved in thought" (p. 62).

Based on this alimentary tract model of the mind, Bion advanced the construct of containment as a central therapeutic activity. The patient imbues the analyst (the container) with intolerable parts of himself, which the analyst ingests and digests to make tolerable. These disavowed parts of the self become the contained and are fed back to the patient in a palatable form that facilitates integration.

There is growing scientific evidence to support Bion's assertion that the ingestion of food and the ingestion of knowledge have much in common. Shadmehr and Holcomb (1997) employed recently developed technology to scan the brain after the learning of a motor skill had taken place. The study showed that during the learning process a pattern develops first in the front part of the brain. It takes five to six hours for the new knowledge contained in the pattern to travel to the back of the brain, where it is stored in a more stable form. The scanning showed increased blood flow while this process was taking place, just as in the digestion of food. If a person learns a new motor skill before the previously acquired knowledge reaches the back of the brain, however, the earlier pattern is erased. Scientists suggest that learning sessions should, therefore, be five to six hours apart for knowledge to be retained.

This observation of how the brain processes knowledge strongly suggests that traditional learning practices sour children on school and are inefficient. The proper mission of our schools can be viewed as twofold: (1) preparing students through the acquisition of a series of academic skills to research, apply, and report on a given body of knowledge; and (2) teaching specific content areas to produce well-rounded, well-informed citizens. Viewed from the perspective of learning academic skills, this approach has merit because it teaches the motor skills involved in researching, organizing, memorizing, and articulating new information. It makes sense for students to acquire these skills while dealing with subject matter they find interesting and applicable to real-life situations. It also makes sense to encourage students to make their own choices of the bodies of knowledge they will pursue to practice these skills.

Viewed from the perspective of producing well-informed citizens, the traditional approach to education is inefficient. Students are called upon to learn one item but quickly crowd out this knowledge when they are required to learn something else. Because the process stops with the articulation of the knowledge, they never apply what they learn to real life and often fail to realize the relevance of what they learn. They rarely experience the complete cycle of knowledge acquisition. The students learn and forget, learn and forget without the knowledge becoming part of them. If a student were doing the same thing with food, and not absorbing the nutrients, he would be diagnosed as the victim of an eating disorder.

An efficient approach to producing well-informed citizens would require teachers to demonstrate the relevance of what the students learn. The students would be granted opportunities to apply the knowledge and integrate it into real life. In fact, the grading system would reflect the extent to which the student has completed the cycle of learning, with the highest grades reserved for those who have applied the lessons to real or imagined life circumstances.

The child who develops a strong aversion to further academic learning shows symptoms of (1) low energy states, (2) proneness to loss of temper, and (3) increased resort to deception. In some cases, there are signs of substance abuse.

Lethargy is the first symptom exhibited by a child who has reached a point of serious aversion to academic learning. The sensory tracts involved will involuntarily shut down upon exposure to cues that remind him of past unwelcome experiences. A cue can be as simple as sitting down to do homework. Nothing can pass through after the sensory tract closes. The child's experiential capacity is deadened. The student feels incapable of working the moment he sits in front of his homework. Drained of energy, he procrastinates, discouraged by the mountain of work piling up.

The low energy state the student experiences when he must read a book can be limited to a particular subject or teacher, or can generalize to any class he is required to attend, or to any subject matter he is supposed to study. I have seen children who are alienated the moment they set foot on school grounds. They are repulsed not only by the curriculum, but also by the presence of other children with attitudes and tendencies leading them to attempt to dominate and violate others.

It is unwise to apply pressure to a child who is turned off by a particular subject. Many students develop anxiety focused on specific subjects. Math and test anxiety are common. Such anxiety is evidence that the emotional brain is struggling. Students affected by it are at risk of being turned off to education.

Another and more dramatic symptom of rejection by the emotional brain is triggered by parental response to the problem. Once students shut down and begin to procrastinate, their parents and teachers exert pressure on them to complete their work. The entryways involved are closed, however. The flow of energy is dammed up. The prodding, nagging, and threatening build up pressure for which there is no outlet. The teenager hangs his head, drags his feet, and expresses himself with terms like, "I don't know," or "Whatever." The nagging parent prods, coaxes, and cajoles. Then comes a blowup. This can take the form of a tantrum, a fit of tears, slamming the door, or acting out.

Lying is the third symptom. Teenagers in this state of mind say, "No, I don't have any homework," when actually they do. Or they say, "I did it during study hall," when they did not. Their emotional minds do not trust the wisdom of those in authority. The child wants to be left alone, free of parental pressure, and he lies to escape responsibility. When the lies are exposed, the parents begin to mistrust their child and are always uncovering deception. They confront and punish the teenager. The teenager blows up and learns more sophisticated ways to deceive.

Many teenagers closed to academic learning seek other forms of satisfaction. This is the fourth common symptom of school aversion. The sensory tracts are closed. The lack of energy creates dysphoric states. The ability to distinguish right from wrong, which is part of a happy life, is dulled. Under these conditions the child tries anything to feel alive, anything to open the energy tracts. The deadened child soon discovers harmful substances or practices that restore the experience of energy flow. He forms addictions to foods, sex, alcohol, and drugs. The experience of hating his everyday responsibilities creates a need to escape and even self-destructive urges. Drugs can seem to make life worthwhile again, and, at the same time, can satisfy the child's craving for self-harm. By creating pressure, parents and teachers drive children to seek companionship on the streets.

To summarize, the symptoms of repulsion to academic learning can become serious. The experience of school can become traumatic. Students under pressure to succeed manifest signs of lethargy and apathy when facing schoolwork. They become explosive and increasingly disrespectful to their elders. They lie and otherwise violate trust. And they may become addicted to substances and unwholesome peer-world activities. This book covers interventions for all of these problems. It also discusses a model of learning based on meeting developmental needs and providing opportunities for mastery in learning.

Adults may prefer to assume that the symptoms of aversion to school are part of normal adolescence. But they may be normal only in those cultures where forced learning is the norm. Our norm includes an alarming decline in the emotional intelligence and moral fiber of our youth.

The Cost of Alienated Youth

Society's unwavering efforts to enforce the normalization agenda of our institutions prevent a significant portion of our youth from achieving emotional integration. Increasing numbers end up alienated, traumatized, and programmed to lash out at members of mainstream society who remind them of the distressing agenda imprinted in their emotional brains. The destructive acts of these alienated youths in turn traumatize others, and contribute to a spread of harmful behavior that reaches epidemic proportions.

Goleman (1996) uses the expression "the cost of emotional illiteracy" to describe the decline of our youth. He reports that in 1990 our country suffered the highest juvenile arrest rate for violent crimes ever. Up to one-third of teenagers manifested clinically significant symptoms of depression, and the frequency of eating disorders in teenage girls has soared. The dropout rate from high school approximates 11 percent (Office of Education Research and Improvement 1997).

Compared to the previous two decades, teenage arrests for rape doubled, murder rates quadrupled, and suicide rates tripled. The number of murdered children and the rates of venereal disease also tripled (National Center for Education in Maternal and Child Health 1991, Zaslow and Takanishi 1993). The rate of drug use among whites has tripled, and in blacks it has increased by thirteen times the rate of twenty years before (Goleman 1996).

It would not be fair, however, to attribute all of this moral decline among our youth to school aversion. The true cause of these problems, Goleman suggests, is emotional illiteracy. Forcing educational experiences upon children may not cause these problems directly, but for a sizable portion of the teenage population it interferes with the integration of minds and the development of emotional intelligence. School aversion creates the dichotomy between the two minds, and, if nothing is done about it, the criminal element of the streets completes the destruction of our youth.

Talking to Families about Mind Splits

The clinician may prefer to use a variety of interchangeable terms to refer to the two minds that are at odds, like old brain and new brain, heart and head, or emotional mind and rational mind. The key to the reframe is to define ODD as two minds at odds, a developmental impasse that produces a growing dichotomy. The clinician must stress that the integration of these two minds is the principal goal of treatment.

The medium of the rational mind is talk. The medium of the emotional mind is action. Youths can relate easily to the notion that there is inherent wisdom in the emotional mind. It seems to them that sensory systems reflexively know whether an experience is right or wrong, desirable or repulsive. These sensory tracts know instantly when to open and when to close.

The distinction of rational-emotional/talk-walk is not so simple as it may appear, but the trained eye of the clinician can readily discern the possible complications. When the emotional mind, or body, dominates the rational mind, reason becomes the servant of emotion. Talk becomes a variant of acting out, as in manipulating, deceiving, or attacking. The clinician can detect this state of mind by the voice intonation, attitude, and body language of the teenager. When the rational mind, or head, dominates the emotional mind, emotion conforms to reason, talk becomes a true vehicle for communication, and walk becomes an expression of reason, even if rigid or disconnected.

In a treatment setting, the clinician can employ different terms to clarify the youth's present state of mind and increase his self-awareness, by saying, for example, "That's your rational mind talking," or, "You're talking purely from the rational mind," for instances in which the youth's words represent the agenda of a disconnected head (reason) without input from the emotional mind. Usually this involves youths talking without emotional intonation about their need for limits, the importance of school, their willingness to do homework or chores, or criticism of the notion of abrogating responsibilities.

"That's your emotional mind talking" can be applied in instances in which the youth's words seem to betray the agenda of the emotional brain, but are in fact setting up an escape through deception. These are instances in which language is used for manipulation rather than communication. Examples include promising to complete chores or homework later, or readiness to get out of bed or to interrupt a favorite game "in a minute." The term also applies to instances in which the youth's actions reveal the agenda of the emotional mind, as in verbal attacks, externalizing blame, or rationalizing acting-out behavior.

The clinician determines the presence and relative influence of each component of the rational-emotional mind split before completing his evaluation and selecting a treatment focus. This helps to authenticate his reframe. To succeed, he needs to communicate in a way that engages the teenager's emotional mind. The clinician who adopts the traditional agenda of the rational mind and disregards messages from the emotional mind, appearing as symptoms, ends up allied with the rational part of the child's split but alienated from the emotional mind. However, the teenager's peers instinctively ally with his emotional mind and its self-indulgence agenda.

In situations where the rational mind alliance prevails, therapy sessions become duller and duller. The child seems to agree with the clinician's suggestions for restoring healthy functioning but the sessions continue to deteriorate. The child responds with "I don't know" because the emotional part of his mind is closed. The therapist has become just another lecturing adult; resistance grows and the therapist has no leverage.

The clinician who has reframed ODD as two minds at odds will still have to forge a strong alliance with the youth's emotional mind. This will require a novel way to interview the adolescent, the subject of our next segment.

A NOVEL APPROACH TO INTERVIEWING *ODD* ADOLESCENTS

It is possible to interview ODD teenagers in a way that allies the therapist with the emotional mind. When this approach is working, the teenager comes to life and demonstrates emotion, intensity, and appreciation.

Tom, introduced earlier, complains about the difficulties he is experiencing in his chemistry class. His tone is resigned, his attitude one of helplessness. I interrupt him: "Why go to school at all? Quit tomorrow! You sound like a wounded cow." Tom laughs, a sign of emotional engagement, but he is obviously confused. He is animated in his protest, not realizing that I'm addressing the agenda of his emotional mind.

Communication with the emotional mind of the teenager can be established in a variety of ways. One way is to talk about the shortcomings of the rational mind, and the normalization agenda of the institutions that misunderstand the emotional brain. The clinician talks about society and the part of the rational mind that conforms to society's demands, as if the rational mind were not present during the discussion. For example, "You mean that your rational mind couldn't find a way to get you to your friend's house even when your parents were enforcing such a stupid rule? That's retarded!"

A second tactic for talking to the emotional brain is to imply an awareness of the hidden value in the ODD youth's symptomatic behavior. The clinician speaks to the emotional brain like an insider, one who is privy to an inside joke or story. Those who are not in on it (i.e., society and the rational mind) find the meaning obscure. They have no clue why others may be responding with greater insight. Questions such as "Why go to school at all?" confuse the rational brain, but suggest familiarity with the inside story on the intentions of the emotional brain.

The most powerful way to communicate directly with the emotional brain is to comment on or emulate the adolescent's body language. Body language is a direct, nonverbal transmission of feeling, attitude, or intention stemming from the emotional brain. It is powerful because it bypasses reasoning altogether. Words similar to, "You sound like a wounded cow," accompanied by appropriate body language will make a strong impact on an apathetic or resistant teenager. The emulation of the youth's style mirrors the body language, while the verbal statement articulates it. The combination integrates the messages from the emotional brain with the rational mind, and raises these to the level of conscious awareness. (My mentor in brief therapy, Robert Mendelsohn, used to refer to similar strategies as mirroring or "talking to the unconscious.")

The tactic of talking directly to the emotional brain (talking to the unconscious) is the antithesis of the established psychotherapy construct of interpretation. The distinction between these two forms of intervention is in the choice of which brain the clinician forms his primary alliance with. Talking to the emotional brain involves establishing a principal affiliation with the emotional brain, initially at the exclusion of the rational mind. Interpretation, on the other hand, seeks to clarify and make sense of the irrationalities of the emotional mind (unconscious) for the benefit of the patient's rational mind (ego). For example, a clinician may interpret the resistance involved in a missed appointment. "Perhaps the reason you forgot our last appointment was that I wasn't responsive enough to your wish for . . ."

Interpretation tactics works well with motivated adults who come into therapy seeking insight, meaning, and mastery over their unconscious drives. The rational minds of such adults dominate their intentions. However, ODD teenagers do not seek insight. In fact, their rational and emotional minds are conflicted and disconnected; they identify clinicians as authority figures and come programmed to rebel against them. With them, the challenge is to connect first with the emotional brain and then to help it accept the rational.

As expected, Tom responds to my talking directly to his emotional brain with intense protest from the emotional mind but with bewilderment in the rational mind. "I have to go to school! What are you talking about?" Tom's rational mind has revealed its agenda. I make Tom aware of the two sides that are speaking in the room. I inform him that his words reveal the passivity of his rational mind, "I have to go to school." Yet his intonation and body language register the complaint of his emotional mind.

I raise Tom's awareness of the conflict within him by questioning his use of "I," and challenging all of his assumptions. I ask, "When you say 'I,' what part of yourself are you talking about, your rational or your emotional mind? You speak as though you represent your entire self. But I doubt that's the case. The fact that you assume you're in control probably means this is your disconnected rational mind talking. No offense. People who use the word 'I' to explain themselves or make excuses are usually talking from the rational mind. The rational mind is usually so disconnected that it doesn't realize that it represents only a very small part of the entire self."

Tom protests, "My parents would never let me drop out. What about my future?"

"This is definitely your rational mind talking. Your head is working," I say, referring to the thinking part of his brain, "but its arguments are weak. Actually, if I may be frank with you, they're pathetic." Once more I'm siding with the emotional mind, throwing reason to the wind. I let him know I'm speaking for the emotional mind: "If I were your emotional mind, I would decide you're hopeless and go to sleep, because you hide me, you make excuses for me, and you give me no hope. You're passive, and you sound resigned to my having to endure a tiresome life. You have no confidence in your ability to meet my needs. So much so that you don't even bother to represent me! If I were your emotional mind, I'd be dead. No energy for you." Again, Tom protests: "What do you want me to do!"

I respond, "It's not what I want you to do. I don't matter. It's what your emotional mind wants you to do. The job of your rational mind is to read what your emotional mind asks you for, and then figure out an adaptive way to get it what it wants, or to get the closest thing possible. You can stop going to school tomorrow and have a fine future. Your parents will have to accept you. All you have to do is regain the trust of your emotional mind and you will have motivation, confidence, and energy. You can eventually end up at Princeton or MIT, even without finishing high school. Tell me if this is what you want and I'll back you."

My suggestion that Tom consider leaving school is to make the point that mind–body integration is much more important than any diploma. I am addressing Tom's unconscious here, attempting to gain its trust by demonstrating my awareness of its worth. I am telling the emotional mind that I know it is okay for him to sacrifice short-term success for long-term integration, because, given a healthy state of integration, he will know what path to pursue and have the mental energy and perseverance to succeed.

Tom wants to know how he can go to college without suffering through the high school curriculum. I rush through some alternatives, making it clear, however, that they are not for him. I know that it's best for Tom to remain in school and I want his rational mind to respect my thinking. I renew the pressure on the rational side of the two-mind split. "The only person who makes you do what you don't want is you," I say, and the rest of the session is a discussion of this theme.

Tom is accustomed to assuming that all answers to choices and opportunities must come from his elders, acting as surrogate frontal lobes for him. This spares him from taking responsibility for the direction his life takes. He believes there is no way for him to fashion a satisfying life for himself. This conviction reduces his adaptive functions to exploiting, deceiving, and escaping responsibility.

The key to interviewing ODD teenagers successfully is to side with the emotional mind and then challenge the rational mind in a way that will strengthen it. Cognitive dissonance theory has demonstrated that weak arguments in the wrong direction strengthen conviction. For example, saying that a good slap in the face is the best way to deal with a crying child bolsters a parent's argument for soothing instead.

The therapist challenges the rational mind by asking why the teenager doesn't do more of what he's already doing to satisfy his desires, even if this behavior is considered wrong. This may seem absurd, but the therapist asks, "Why don't you drink more?" "Why do you go to school at all?" "Why didn't you hurt him more in that fight?" "Why didn't you have five hundred people over when your parents were away?" "Why didn't you have sex with everyone you could?" "Why didn't you steal more money?"

Besides allowing the clinician to join the youth's emotional brain, questions such as these activate his rational brain. When the teenager tells you why he hasn't carried his behavior to these extremes, he has begun to listen to his rational brain—the voice of reason. He has admitted the problem with his current behavior. If he has been drinking too much, he won't drink more because, he says, that would make him an alcoholic and destroy his health. If he has been cutting classes, he won't drop out of school altogether because, he tells you, he wants a diploma. Whatever the teenager says amplifies the voice of his conscience. This provides evidence of the logic of the adaptive brain, and offers the therapist an opportunity to influence it.

The therapist can work to justify the rational agenda where it differs from the emotional. The therapist can assert that the emotional mind, as opposed to the rational mind, is demanding a form of satisfaction that is destructive because more attractive options are not being offered. It sees no hope of finding more satisfying options because of the passive, childish operating mode of the rational brain. Once this weakness is exposed, the teenager will open up to the therapist's influence, and the therapist can begin to offer illustrations of how the teenager can improve his life.

Because the emotional brain has learned to rely on addictive and escapist behaviors, the therapist must concentrate on removing boredom from other parts of the teenager's life. For example, if the teenager is escaping to drink, the focus should be on what he does when he is not drinking. The objective is to make the youth aware of the unmet needs that drive the limbic system to produce substitute drives that can be easily gratified again and again. And that when satisfied these substitutes provide momentary relief from the discomfort created by the unattainable, unmet needs (see Chapter 2 for a discussion of drive substitutions in addictions).

The therapist directs attention to the unmet needs and challenges the child to take the steps necessary to satisfy them. Gradually, as the youth develops greater awareness, he learns to identify the unmet needs himself, and the problems they cause. He then can begin to invest his energies in addressing these needs and resolving the problems. The clinician should encourage the teenager to take the initiative in pursuing the unmet needs so the youth can take pride in being the originator of his own drive toward health.

The clinician must be active and in charge while teenagers are in deadened and disconnected states, and receptive and supportive when they come to life. What it is that attracts the attention of the emotional brain and brings about a change in attitude is irrelevant. What matters is the openness and expression of needs and wants, because this allows the clinician to form his primary alliance with the emotional brain. It is not important whether the teenager's interest is in sports, weapons, music, sex, or drugs. What matters is that he feels free to be open and confiding and that the clinician form an alliance by joining the youth's world without reservation or judgment. There will be ample opportunity later to bring this buried and alienated aspect of the ODD teenager back into the fold.

Glenn, who was in his late adolescence, was extremely closed off, but became animated when we hit upon the subject of cheating in school. He had left a private school after just six weeks. He entered therapy, but quit after one session because he found it dull. Glenn and the psychologist had hit it off only on the level of the rational mind.

Now I explained to Glenn how young people tell me the most incredible things when I side with their wants and forget their rational agendas. For example, I said, I've heard about the most ingenious efforts to cheat on exams. Glenn interrupted me: "That's right. Some of my friends and I worked harder at cheating than we would have had to work to learn the material. We were geniuses at it." He went on for at least fifteen minutes about the cheating tactics employed. Once he became open with me, trust had been established, and we could then get to the important agenda of the emotional mind, which had to do with his obsession with a girl. This, it turned out, was the cause of his departure from prep school.

Properly implemented, this method of interviewing turns the tables on the ODD teenager accustomed to the promotion by adults of the rational mind agenda, including logic, thought, and sense of obligation, and his disregard of the agenda of the emotional mind. Clinicians do the opposite by siding with the emotional mind agenda, and challenging youths to explain why it must be rejected. These youths must be encouraged to recognize and correct their erroneous belief that freedom comes as a dispensation from others, and realize that freedom is within their own power to grasp. It is easy to show them, once they are open, that they also must be responsible and ethically motivated in order to enjoy the benefits of freedom, because freedom depends on trust. ODD teenagers respond in a strong and positive way to therapist's siding with their emotional minds.

The ODD teenager may leave the session believing that the message the therapist imparted is a license to rebel against all conventional agendas. The rebellion, however, is not to be feared, because it is an integral step in the mind–body integration process, and can be used as an opportunity to unmask deception and weaknesses, and for the teenager to learn valuable lessons. Parents and teachers can be warned that the teenager may become temporarily rebellious. But the hope that teenagers feel as a result of the emotional brain alliance reverses the self-destructive tendencies that place them at serious risk. Their behavior may be selfish, but it is benign, not aggressive or self-destructive.

Sometimes during a session I speak sharply to the child: "You became passive, and now you're using excuses to avoid facing how pathetic that was. This is the problem. Your rational mind is weak." Or, "You may not know it, but you're setting things up to keep yourself exactly where you are, hating your life and hating yourself. You're trying to prove that you were born perfect and don't need to improve, because you're afraid to face your weaknesses. But until you take some risks, and accept your failings, you won't grow."

To defend the child's emotional brain, I am sharply critical of the rational brain. This does not hurt the child because the criticism is well intentioned, conveys a message of hope, and is not aimed at the child's emotional being. It is aimed at the rational mind, which does not have feelings and, unlike the emotional mind, can change. The rational mind can marshal advanced abilities and apply sophisticated methods to improve adaptation.

Some level of well-placed criticism (putdown) couched in the lingo of the youth culture (often with gruff or crude language) earns the admiration of the typical ODD teenager, as long as it's clever, humorous, and done with caring intentions. The reason for the positive impact of what could be construed as insulting is obvious from the perspective of the emotional mind. As long as the clinician is comfortable with the language, the emotional brain of the ODD teen will associate this kind of criticism and language with the peer world, where trash talk and personal affronts are the norm.

It often helps to couch playful insults in the form of challenging questions inferred from the material the ODD teenager presents. For example, the clinician may ask questions like: "So does that make you a flake?" The question can end with a variety of labels derived from the youth culture: a liar, a wimp, a bully, a user, a druggy, a nerd, a loser, a pervert, a retard, pathetic, the man, the bomb, the shit.

If this is done properly, the teenager gets the message that his heart is in the right place, and that he is in touch with his body, which possesses great wisdom. Essentially, he is fine, but is struggling because he has been programmed to distrust his deepest source of knowledge in society's misguided attempt to make him like everyone else. He has learned to go along passively with an agenda that betrays what is best about him—his natural but hidden essence. Therefore, he cannot trust his rational mind to pursue what his instincts know will allow him to realize his full potential.

This criticism increases trust and fosters hope, because it implies there are better ways to support the emotional brain. My presentation is purposely playful, for play promotes cohesion, it is the language of the emotional brain, and the emotional mind needs acceptance. I also speak sharply about misguided authority figures everywhere. I criticize the controlling institutions and the individuals within them who simply don't understand, and who insist on adherence to the norms that impose the stresses causing the ODD. I then move on to use the influence I have earned over the emotional mind to promote integration, and invite healthy adaptive functioning. Anyone can criticize society, but the task is to win over those in charge and learn to share the best they have to offer. I model an integration of the rational and emotional minds. I earn the trust of both minds.

The ODD vanishes once I align myself with the child's hitherto unrecognized desire to satisfy the needs of the emotional brain. I have reframed the youth's ODD to gain the cooperation of the teenager and his family. I have interviewed the youth in a way that makes me an ally of his emotional mind, challenges his rational mind, and begins the process of integration by fostering self-awareness. Now the stage is set to implement the preevaluation trial intervention. This intervention will allow me to conduct a resistance-free evaluation to rule out comorbid conditions that may lurk beneath the ODD, such as AD/HD, LD, and mood disorders.

A PREEVALUATION TRIAL INTERVENTION

As discussed in Chapter 2, I view ODD as a widely misinterpreted effort by the child to actualize his natural but hidden essence. Often, this involves a need to follow a course of development different from the one his parents and teachers seek to impose. Children with special needs experience greater alienation from the normalization efforts of our institutions. They encounter poorness of fit and obstacles to development more frequently than other children (see Chapter 1). They hide their shame about their AD/HD, LD, or physical handicaps behind their ODD.

I suggest that the family give its ODD teenagers an opportunity to demonstrate how well they can manage their lives if they are allowed to unfold in their own unique ways. Sometimes this trial resolves the behavior problem, a sign that the youth was ready to function on a more mature level, but that parents and teachers were being too controlling and held him back. At other times, the trial reveals more serious problems, and this helps the teenager see the need for testing and further help. These problems can be dealt with more effectively once they are out in the open. This was the case with Tom. In his case, I had to reestablish my alliance and get past the ODD.

Tom seemed to be secretly nursing a depression stemming from the loss of friends. He had exhibited all the symptoms of ODD, including academic difficulties and addiction to drugs. As part of my attempt to prime Tom for a full evaluation, I had arranged for a trial intervention offering greater freedom of action. The trial offered Tom the opportunity to prove his contention that all his parents had to do was let him have his own way and everything would turn out fine. The trial turned out to be highly informative.

Tom was to balance indulgence with responsibility by reversing the addictive cycle of feeling bad, escaping responsibility, indulging until feeling good, and then returning to a life that made him feel worse because of all the obligations piling up. He had been willing to shift to a cycle of feeling bad, fulfilling key obligations while he felt bad, then indulging himself as a reward. This cycle can help reverse addiction.

Despite early signs of progress, the success of this attempt was short-lived. Tom had sat sheepishly in my office because he had failed to observe the terms I had prescribed. He had quit his job, and had deceived his family in numerous ways. He had lied about where he had spent a night, claiming he was at a male friend's house when actually he was staying with a girlfriend. He had been socializing frequently in the homes of friends whose parents were out of town, and his involvement in drugs had increased.

Since Tom was resistant to seeing me, I adopted an active, no-nonsense stance. I needed to reconnect with the emotional brain. "I asked your mom to bring you here because I don't think you have a clue as to the nature of your problem. Do you know what's happening to you?" I asked. My body language was challenging but playful. Tom warmed up a bit and tried to be friendly. He was looking for support. "It's my parents. They won't let me do anything. My dad pisses me off," he said, referring to his recent loss of privileges.

I dealt with Tom's resistance by confronting him with observations designed to promote self-awareness, and expose him as an active participant in a complicated family dynamic, rather than a helpless, passive victim of unreasonable parents. "And so you retaliate by taking it out on your mom, his wife," I said. Tom was amused by my observation, and seemed impressed by the accuracy of my guess. I was able to make this observation because it is a common dynamic in ODD family systems that when one parent is tough, the other is empathetic and needing to feel connected to the child. When the tough parent, the father in Tom's case, attacks the child, the child retaliates by cutting off the other parent, as if saying, "Choose between him or me!"

Oppositional children often find satisfaction in realizing their ways of getting even with authority. "You get mad at your dad, and cut off communication with your mom, who needs to feel close to you. Then your mom resents your dad for having been so hard on you, and they don't talk to each other." Tom's body language conveyed agreement. "This is serious stuff," I said. "You make your dad pay, and your whole family pays. Parents can be driven to divorce this way." Tom had a grin on his face by now. However, he was facing what he was doing to his family, and seemed ready to accept what I was saying.

I challenged Tom's rational mind. "I didn't ask you what your parents' problem is," I said. "I asked if you knew what your own problem is, because I think you have a problem, and you don't even know that you do. This family control battle is so lousy that it keeps you from seeing what you're missing." Tom became pensive and more receptive. I continued, "I just want to tell you what I think your problem may be. Then if you don't want to come back to see me, it's your business." It is very important to let the teenager know that he has the freedom to leave. Otherwise, he perceives the clinician as controlling, and shuts down. ODD thrives on control.

At this point, I reminded Tom of the conditions of the trial intervention, and how his problem was demonstrated by his forgetting of our agreement. "Do you recall our agreement?" I asked. Tom had obviously forgotten. "Do you remember that we had an agreement at all?"

"Yes," responded Tom. "I'm just not sure how, right now." Tom was thinking hard, struggling to recall the terms of our trial intervention.

I refreshed Tom's memory. "I set things up to put you in charge. I told you this was a test to expose your weaknesses, so you could see them and do something about them. I suggested that I might want to run some tests on you if you seemed to have problems once you were doing things your own way. I warned you that you would fail, and you agreed to learn from your failure, and not feel bad about it."

"Yeah, I remember," Tom said, his attention now engaged.

I interrupted: "You agreed that you would not feel shameful and hide, but would look at your shortcomings in an accepting way when you failed. Am I right?" Tom agreed. "But the first thing you did when you failed was run and hide. You aren't doing what you promised.

"Now, the way you promised to deal with failure and the way you dealt with it shows us the nature of your problem—the problem you have but aren't aware of. You see, the problem is that you don't do what you say, and a lot of times you don't say what you do [this alludes to the two-mind split]. I believe that the reason you promised what you did back then is because it was an easy way to get yourself some freedom at that time. Talk is cheap, so you promised. Maybe you didn't even expect to fail. But once you got your freedom you forgot the whole thing. Out of sight, out of mind. Now that you failed you forgot the deal, your parents forgot the deal, and everything we did back then becomes a joke.

"All of this may sound critical, but it's really very common. I set you up to do things your own way and, in that way, set you up to fail. My job now is to show you how to turn this failure into a positive. I think we can use your failure to make you much more successful."

Tom invited me to tell him what I thought, and I took this opportunity to ally myself with his emotional brain, rather than with all the "shoulds" of normalcy. "Kids like you," I said, "often endure a mind–body split that is very common in our society. Your rational brain, says, 'I will have a good school year.' Or, 'I have to do well to graduate and have a future.' However, your emotional brain says, 'I hate school and I just want to be with my friends.' So you speak 'graduation' and enact escapes with your friends.

"I'll be very up-front with you. If I side with your emotional brain, and help your rational brain gain its trust, I will be in a position to truly help you put the two parts together. If I side with your rational mind and use psychology to help you please everybody, your emotional brain will distrust me as much as it does you. Meanwhile, the only allies of your emotional brain will be your friends, and the lures of the streets. My job is to assist you in getting your family and the school into a position where they can help you to drop your oppositional state, and find a way to enjoy your life."

Clinicians can align themselves with the hidden agenda of the emotional mind by finding the positive intent in the youth's oppositional tendencies and his acting up. This is how I accomplished it in Tom's case:

"I think your real problem is that you sell out," I told him. "You're not true to yourself, to your genuine desires. You try to play goodie two-shoes and promise to do too many good things that you don't really want to do." This is not what Tom expected to hear. He expected me to discuss his lying and drug use. I had the sense that he didn't think my argument was sound. He may have been saying to himself, "Me being too good?"

I continued: "I've seen you betray yourself this way with your girlfriend and with your parents. You want to play with your friends, but you talk with your girl on the phone for hours so she'll feel secure. Then you avoid her for days and lie about why you haven't been in touch. In general, when you get sick of trying to make good on all your promises, you break down and do all the things you just did."

This apparently made sense to Tom. "I know what you mean," he said. "I've been telling my girlfriend what I want more and more since we talked about it, and it's been better between us." His body language changed to a plea for help. He adopted a whining and complaining posture. "But my parents are impossible!" I wanted to let Tom know that his mistakes were understandable, and that he should have more chances to prove himself. I invited him to tell me the details of his wild weekends.

My challenge was to provide Tom with an opportunity to be completely open, and not have to practice deception. I told him stories about the excesses of my own teenage years, and explained how my mistakes had made me a better person. I bet him that we could find wisdom in even his most bizarre behavior. I allowed him to entertain me with tales about himself and his friends, and was fascinated by the scenarios he described. The stories portrayed him as interesting, daring, and smart. I viewed them through the eyes of a peer. In the end, I thanked him for being so interesting and honest.

"In a way, I'm glad you did all these things," I said, referring to how he lied, quit his job, and smoked too much. Tom was surprised. "Now," I said, "we can find out what led you to screw up the freedom trial (trial intervention) we set up for you. This is how we make you a better person. At least you're not one of those boring kids. Nothing worse than a boring teenager to work with!"

He relaxed. I had acted as his rational mind and performed analytical functions for him. I found a way to accept and understand the actions of his emotional brain, and in doing so, launched the process of mind–body integration. I reframed his failure as a learning opportunity, an intervention of critical importance in dealing with these youths.

"You see, when you first try to be free to do things your own way, you're going to fail," I said, "You're going to cause problems. If you allow your failures to bring you down, and you give up, you lose confidence. But if you use your failure to identify your weaknesses, you learn from them, and you strengthen your weak areas. You grow every time you fail.

"Your ultimate goal, whether you know it or not, is to grow into the most complete human being you can be. How are you going to do that if you don't welcome discovering your weaknesses? Or are you going to be like those kids who just want to prove they were born perfect, and don't see any reason to change?" Tom was quiet, but his body language was asking for more. He was paying attention, and seemed visibly hopeful.

"Most really successful people use failure to develop themselves," I said. "I needed to see what you would do with your freedom so I could learn about you. Now I invite you to learn from this discussion, decide what you need to strengthen yourself, and then try again. But you can't do this if you continue to lie to yourself about your shortcomings."

"My parents won't let me try again," Tom insisted. "They figure I blew it for good." I reminded Tom that his failure had come about in response to a trial intervention designed to expose his weaknesses, and was based on an agreement that he would get another chance, as long as he demonstrated that he had learned something from the last attempt.

Tom is impulsive, and shows signs of AD/HD. AD/HD and impulsive children act on their immediate urges, and are unable to consider the long-term perspective. However, these factors are not addressed at this stage of treatment because these children will feel they are being criticized, and will become more resistant. Instead, I challenge the passive-victim stance. I considered Tom's complaints about his parents as resistance, and confronted him on the issue. I pointed out how he frequently uses his parents as an excuse not to deal with himself.

"You keep using your parents as an excuse for not looking at yourself. Take a minute to deal with yourself. Let's not talk about your parents. You can master your own problems. Then we'll be in a position of strength in dealing with your parents," I said.

My explanation left Tom confused. He had expected me to focus on the irresponsible quitting, the lying, and substance abuse, because everyone else did, although to no avail. I didn't want to spend time discussing what he did wrong each day, for this would be siding with the rational mind and against the emotional mind before I achieved the alliance with the emotional mind. I wanted to help him look at more promising areas of focus in which there was an opportunity to improve the quality of his life. It is easier to drop dependencies and bad habits when you have a better life to turn to.

I explained that young people who don't care about what they do with their time end up not caring about themselves, and engaging in self-destructive behavior. Tom's parents and teachers were focusing on a control battle over his acting up. They were preoccupied with the disturbing methods he was using to escape from a life he disliked. They were not looking for underlying causes, and Tom couldn't correct a problem that he himself didn't understand.

Tom had a significant substance addiction problem. This was the reason he had failed the trial intervention. The tactic I was using here would pave the way for later work on the addiction. However, for the moment my intention was to offer him a fresh perspective and some hope, and to engage him in the evaluation process. Tom was now ready to be tested for AD/HD and LD.

WORKING WITH THE ABSENT ADOLESCENT

Some ODD adolescents refuse to see a therapist. They are succeeding too well with their current behavior to agree to the need for an intervention. Often, they are getting their way with parents who are inconsistent in limit-setting, or who are otherwise unable to deal with child-rearing responsibilities. The parents are worried, and the family is dysfunctional. When this occurs, I treat the parents, using the ODD adolescent's behavior as the focus. My objective is to get the parents out of the controlling trap and allow the ODD to resolve itself naturally with the passage of time and the impact of the consequences that ODD behavior inevitably engenders. I established in Chapter 1 how ODD resolves itself once the individual reaches a stagnation point, where the deadness of the ODD outweighs the difficulty of the developmental obstacle creating the poorness of fit that gives rise to the symptoms.

I teach parents to view ODD as the child's need to take charge, and his failure in school and life as the best remedy for the condition. I show them how to soften the consequences imposed by the outside world so that the process will not traumatize their child. I support the parents in allowing their child to experience sufficient failure and stagnation to bottom out and move to the mastery stage of development. I allow the child to do things his own way. This meets the needs of the emotional brain, with the result that we gradually build trust with a child who is failing.

In the case that follows, the parents and I waited two years before it was possible to do a full evaluation. But finally failure came, and Mark was willing to accept help.

Mark, a gifted and fearless athlete, was in my office with his parents. He had been caught smoking marijuana, and lost the possibility of getting a driver's license and a car. He loathed his parents. The impact of therapy I had previously done with the mother had yielded slow progress. In keeping with brief-therapy guidelines, I was seeing her intermittently as needed. The benefits of the therapy were increasing gradually. The slow rate of progress was due in part to the difficulty of dealing with the child. Mark was adopted, and suffered from AD/HD. Progress was also slowed by lack of support from Mark's father, who systematically undermined most of the tactics I recommended.

Mark's mother was generous, patient, consistent, reliable, and hard working. As is the case with many parents, nevertheless, she had been misguided in her approach to raising her

AD/HD children. She had used structures and other controlling methods to mold them into normalcy. They didn't trust
or respect her, and they challenged her at every turn. Her
husband's attitude was that she knew nothing about child rearing. The husband and wife hardly spoke to each other.

With my help, Mark's mother learned how to ally herself
with her son's real wants, and how to be true to her own
emotional mind. This meant that she no longer allowed him
to mistreat her, violate her trust, or take advantage of her. She
positioned herself to be enough of an ally to help her son. Dad
was left alone in his daily battles for dominance over Mark.
Mark could see the difference between the approaches used
by his mother and father, and sensed the positive impact of
my work with the mother. This made him amenable to visiting
my office. I had used the mother to get past the ODD.

The Assessment Proper

COMORBID CONDITIONS

The attitude of disapproval in Larry's father was palpable. Such an attitude needs to be recognized early, for it conveys a negative message to the child's unconscious and affects his behavior. This undermines any new approaches to behavioral problems. The father was friendly as he reported the evidence of Larry's deviant behavior. However, everything he said was directed toward establishing a united front with his wife to teach Larry that "no" meant "no." His wife resisted his efforts, and he hoped that my support would change her mind. He wanted to control Larry in his own way, but needed his wife's backing.

The father made it clear that things were miserable at home since he had grounded his son. The distance between him and his wife was looming large, and Larry was defiant and doing whatever he wanted. Dad wanted to involve law officers in handling the discipline, but did not follow through because Mom objected.

Their disagreement prevented the parents from developing the tools they needed to stop Larry from acting out, and Larry had called their bluff. Both parents worried constantly. Mom was visibly dysphoric. Dad was short of temper.

I questioned the father's attitude when he began to speak angrily about Larry's lazy, self-centered, manipulative attitude toward an undemanding school curriculum. Larry's father believed in the creatures-of-habit paradigm discussed in Chapter 1, and would not attempt to understand goodness of fit or other developmental needs his son might have. He was convinced that his duty as a parent was to make his son accept his responsibilities.

I listened as Larry's father complained. Then I asked what he was going to do to solve the problems. The question took him by surprise. "I don't know. What can I do? I thought you would tell us," he said. "Maybe you can convince him that he needs help; that we as his parents know what's in his own best interests. He should know that 'no' means 'no.'"

"To be frank," I said, "I can tell that you assume your son is lazy, and believe he could do the work if he wanted to." The father agreed. I continued: "If laziness is the problem, then all you have to do is force him to do well, however much he rebels, and it will resolve itself. However, if your assumption is wrong, your decision to apply force will only make your home life worse, and your son won't do any better in school. As long as you cling to this assumption, I can't help you. But let me know if you find reason to believe that your assumption is wrong, and I will be glad to help you consider different solutions to your son's problems."

I reminded Larry's father of our agreement regarding the trial intervention. I was purposely granting Larry excessive freedom to do things his own way so that I could (1) form an alliance with his emotional mind, (2) expose Larry's weaknesses to accurately assess the factors that lurk beneath his ODD, (3) motivate Larry to cooperate with psychological testing, and (4) give Larry reason to appreciate the support that his parents and teachers had been providing. Like many ODD youths, Larry maintained a negative attitude toward those who attempted to support him. He took their help for granted, because he couldn't imagine what life would be without it. Larry would, however, come to appreciate the help he got once he experienced the hardships of life on his own.

Dad soon asked me to tell him about other possibilities for handling his son. "The problem with your son begins with procrastination," I said. "He just can't get started on the work. He doesn't know why he can't, but sooner or later he stops working, and then promises to finish later. You ask him whether he is done, and he lies to you. He'll say anything to escape responsibility. He'll go out with his peers, and the escape will alleviate the bad feeling caused by leaving work undone and lying to you.

"There is a restlessness that occurs in children who lie. They don't have true peace of mind. Yet, they can escape this restlessness easily. All they have to do is become engaged in peer activities, drugs, sex, and drinking. However, the good feeling soon passes. The bad feeling sets in as a consequence of the misbehavior. This sets the stage for another escape. The child has entered an addictive and destructive cycle—bad feelings, escape, and short-term good feelings, then bad feelings, and a constant need to escape.

"Our question is, Why the procrastination? It could be that Larry has a negative, immature, and selfish attitude, just as you describe. In this case, he needs a structure that compels him to do his work. For example, you might arrange it so that he cannot go out and join his peers until all his obligations have been met. You could use the courts to enforce this structure if you had to."

The courts can prove useful as a last resort with youths who are too difficult for their parents to manage. They can implement the necessary structure and enforce it with stern consequences. The courts can set a curfew, monitor school progress, enforce the fulfillment of domestic responsibilities, and set limits on aggressive behavior. They can limit contact with peers who are a negative influence.

I explained to Larry's father. "If structure was all your son needed, then your assumption that he's capable of getting the work done would be appropriate. He would respect you and feel thankful once you had implemented this structure, and he had become accustomed to success in fulfilling his obligations.

"Another possibility, however, is that the mechanism in the brain responsible for shifting from one activity to another is immature, or somehow weak. This problem typically manifests itself in attempts to shift from a desired activity to one that is less desirable, like going from watching TV to doing homework. The difficulty in getting started would suggest a neurobiological cause. Medication could help, and so could breaking down the work load into manageable parts. You could accomplish the latter by engaging a tutor to get your son started, and help him keep going. You could gradually lessen the availability of this support and encourage your son to initiate his own activities. This would help him develop a sense of responsibility.

"If incorrect, however, your assumption that your child is lazy and doesn't care can cause serious problems for him. If he is suffering from a neurologically faulty shifting mechanism, he will not be able to meet your demands. And you will remain convinced that he's lazy and doesn't care. You will not accept the reality of his handicap, or be able to encourage him in his activities. Your son will learn not to try. You will pressure him, he will lie, and the dysfunction will worsen in your family. The battle surrounding your efforts to force your son to comply with your wishes will occupy all your attention, and, as a result of this failure to understand, you will not be seeking other ways to help him.

"Yet another possibility is that Larry's knowledge-processing pathway is slow and doesn't allow him to enjoy schoolwork. This is the pathway through which numbers and words travel. Slow progress of learning would make academic work tedious, and Larry would feel school was being forced on him. A form of cognitive-learning theory–based mastery training could correct this problem. It could sharpen your son's brain so it can enjoy the learning process a great deal more.

"This form of training would also give him a taste of success in school, and thus increase his confidence. His emotional brain could associate learning with enjoyment and success, rather than tedium and failure.

"A final possibility is that your son is going through a phase in which his emotional brain is rejecting acquisition of academic knowledge, even though his shifting mechanism and pathways for the processing of knowledge are perfectly good. Sometimes children go through phases in their development when they're repelled by certain activities. They've been forcing themselves to study and have reached the point where they burn out. Suddenly they can't force themselves to sit in front of a book. A student who sits in front of a book unable to study demonstrates the quintessential manifestation of a mind–body split. The rational brain directs him to complete the assignment, while the emotional brain resists, and exercises conflicting behavior.

"The more someone else tries to force them, the more traumatized the children become. A youngster in this situation requires relief from pressure. It often helps the situation to remove the pressure to do well in every class and encourage the student to succeed only in classes he likes. In severe cases, it becomes necessary to reduce pressure to graduate from school and to permit the student to attend only classes in which he is interested. Children usually regain their motivation within one year.

"In all of the scenarios I've described, your assumption—that your son is simply lazy and doesn't care—would cause problems. You wouldn't be of much help to him, unless the root of his procrastination was, in fact, laziness and an uncaring attitude. I won't be able to do much for you until you recognize that your assumption isn't going to help you save your child, which I am sure is your genuine intention."

Larry's father wanted to know how we could determine the cause of his son's procrastination. I explained that we could evaluate his son in a systematic way so that we could most likely identify and remedy the cause of his inability to get his work done. To help, however, the father would have to enter into a learning and accepting mode, and stop pressuring the boy to improve his report card.

The next step was Larry's evaluation.

A Problem with the Brain's Shifting Mechanism

I don't say to a patient, "You may have AD/HD," because the label may mean nothing to him or his family, or it may trigger problematic misconceptions. There has been so much publicity surrounding the AD/HD label that families will come with a host of misconceptions. For example, some families will resist the diagnosis, citing their child's ability to sit glued in front of a TV for hours, or they may protest that their child is perfectly calm. Others will have formed negative opinions about medication for no good reason.

However, to picture the brain as having a physical shifting mechanism that may be faulty may make understanding easier. The diagnosis of AD/HD is a complex matter. The disorder often has little to do with attention or hyperactivity. Patients suffering from this malady can be very focused and hypoactive. A characteristic that many have in common is an inability to shift between activities. This frequently manifests itself when the AD/HD individual is engaged in a preferred activity, and is expected to concentrate, instead, on one less interesting.

AD/HD individuals frequently suffer from boredom. The boredom magnifies whatever symptoms the afflicted individuals have been exhibiting. If the child is hyperactive, boredom will make him fidget more. If the child is inattentive, his mind will wander more. If the child tends to procrastinate, he will procrastinate more. If the child is anger prone, he will have more outbursts. If the child tends to be late or is accident prone, these events will happen more often.

Children who procrastinate may be suffering from AD/HD. Specific instruments can be used to help establish this diagnosis. Some continuous performance tasks (CPTs) can serve the purpose. To date, the most sophisticated of these CPTs is the Test of Variables of Attention (TOVA).

A CPT is a computerized task that presents the student with many trials of two different stimuli that require a differential response. The student presses a trigger when one stimulus appears, and refrains from pressing it when the other appears. Failure to press when the stimulus calls for it represents an error of inattention. Pressing when the stimulus calls for restraint represents an error of impulsivity. These two measures provide the accuracy portion of the CPT. Excessive errors suggest AD/HD. In addition, the computer keeps track of the student's response time, and steadiness of response time versus variability. Response time and variability represent a measure of the effort necessary to complete the task. Too much effort in the form of slow or highly varied response times suggests AD/HD. The TOVA is much longer than most other CPTs, and it has been suggested that longer trials make CPTs more reliable.

All CPTs are limited by the problem of false negatives. The child can score in the normal range on a CPT and still have AD/HD. However, if the test indicates AD/HD, the diagnosis is probably correct.

Other instruments can be used to complete a diagnosis with or without a CPT. These involve rating scales like the Conner's, the Achenbach Child Behavior Checklists, and Barkley's Home Situation Questionnaire and School Situation Questionnaire. Using norms, these measures compare the respondents' descriptions of the children's behaviors to descriptions of the population at large.

One problem with rating scales, however, is that they tend to measure emotional problems more accurately than they measure AD/HD. These are measures of disruptive behavior disorders that are sensitive to emotional factors. The external oppositional attitude will tend to conceal underlying problems like AD/HD and LD.

Nonetheless, rating scales can provide much useful information. The clinician can use them to determine the presence and severity of symptoms seen in a significant portion of the AD/HD population, like impulsivity and hyperactivity. They can also detect other problem symptoms, such as anxiety, withdrawal, deception, depression, and social difficulties. Such symptoms often complicate treatment or warrant additional diagnoses.

If the brain's shifting mechanism doesn't work well, medication can help. So can coaching and support from tutors and teachers who can help AD/HD youths get started on work on a daily basis. Over time, supports to encourage the child to exercise these brain functions can be reduced. The key is to have the child himself want to get past the procrastination problem so he can pass in school, and to have him participate in making the arrangements for these supports. Once the child gains the support he needs, he should be provided with reasonable expectations and a genuine opportunity to achieve goodness of fit (see Chapters 6, 8, 10, 11).

Sluggish Information Processing

I don't say to clients, "You may have a learning disability." This label would offend them and invite their resistance. For many youths, the LD label is synonymous with dumb or retarded. I have heard many students use the term "SPED-head" to ridicule those who receive special education services.

However, youths become receptive and hopeful if it is explained to them that the brain has physical pathways through which information travels that may be slow and make learning boring, but that can be made to pick up speed so that learning becomes fun. A diagnosis of learning disorder is indicated when information cannot travel to the working memory (short-term) and active processing centers of the brain efficiently enough to make learning interesting. This condition is worsened by the problem of boredom in the dual-diagnosis child with comorbid AD/HD and LD.

Modern cognitive learning theorists say that, for learning to become interesting, several items of information must be fed into working (short-term) memory within a brief period (Royer and Sinatra 1994). If sufficient information reaches working memory all at once, the student will be rewarded with positive stimulation, the feeling that "I get it!"

The problem with short-term memory is that if the bits of information fail to arrive quickly enough, all will be lost. If a student's retrieval process lacks fluency, the mechanics of reading or math will require excessive effort. The student will become distracted, fail to absorb the material, and associate learning with tedium and fatigue at the emotional brain level. For such students, the prospect of finding school traumatic is significantly increased.

Children use play to blunt the harshness of reality, and to rehearse skills they seek to master. The process of developing fluency can become very painful unless children can exercise these capacities in a playful way with materials they find interesting. It takes hours of practice to establish the kinds of pathways in the brain that provide fluency in numbers, words, writing, and organizing. Without sufficient play to soothe the process, and without an efficient system for developing fluency—like the Computerized Academic Assessment System (CAAS) (Royer and Sinatra 1994)—children will suffer through the learning process and fail to develop the necessary tools.

Specific instruments can be used to help establish the diagnosis of LD, as I am using the term here. The kind of learning problem I am describing should not be confused with the traditional learning disability diagnosis made for special education services. This latter diagnosis is made with elaborate tests like the Wechsler Scales and the Woodcock Johnson. However, this type of LD diagnosis has been politicized. It is defined as a gap between scores on achievement tests and the child's potential in an IQ test. To be diagnosed, the child has to score below grade level by a specific amount on achievement tests.

The established approach to LD diagnosis does not take into consideration the effort required by the student to complete academic tasks. Some students complete tasks with high degrees of accuracy and little effort. Others perform equally well, but must struggle hard to succeed, like someone maneuvering a car through a snowstorm. I look at learning deficits as problems of excessive effort and tedium based on the ease and speed of information processing.

Specific instruments can be used to diagnose the lack of fluency learning deficits. I use the CAAS, which has proven to be highly effective. Royer has developed a protocol to remedy the deficits that the instrument detects. Most academics in the field of cognitive learning theory can offer access to a variety of scientifically valid instruments.

Numerous centers across the country offer remediation for lack of fluency. They supplement traditional education by filling in the academic gaps in the minds of students who missed parts of their education. They make the process playful and fun. A growing number of colleges and universities offer their own version of those cognitive theory-based programs to promote fluency. It is important to be able to make such referrals once clients who have academic deficits become motivated to overcome these weaknesses.

Overcoming weaknesses is a central goal of the treatment program presented in this book. Parents often have to give up on school struggles in the early phases of treatment with these children, especially if the children keep putting things off and develop a strong aversion to schoolwork. I discuss this condition next. I emphasize for parents of these children the need to understand and accept the wisdom of the emotional brain in triggering this aversion.

Assessing Involuntary Aversion to Learning

The problem of aversion to schoolwork can be identified through direct interviews and observation of the child, although there are no established instruments to measure the condition. See Chapter 2 for a complete description of aversion to learning, and the reframe of ODD as two minds at odds. A child can develop varying levels of involuntary resistance without suffering from any of the diagnoses discussed above. The condition can range from a fleeting and harmless aversion to academic work to a full-blown syndrome that can lead the teenager to varying degrees of trauma and psychopathology. I describe this syndrome in Chapter 8, which deals with failure in school.

Larry's Test Results

Larry's evaluation revealed a problem with the brain's shifting mechanism—AD/HD. Medication, a self-imposed structure, and the support of tutors made the demands of getting started on work manageable. Larry chose the structure gratefully once he understood his condition. I offered him the option of managing school in whatever way he wanted. He could choose to do as well or as poorly as he wanted, in whatever classes he wanted. Once the element of compulsion was removed, he decided he wanted to perform well in most classes. He wanted Bs and Cs. Making this choice empowered him and made all the difference in the world.

The tests showed that Larry's information processing system worked flawlessly. He tested in the ninety-ninth percentile for numeracy and almost that high in literacy. Larry was not repulsed by schoolwork, except for two classes that he found irritating. One involved a teacher who penalized students heavily for minor errors stemming from faulty frontal lobe functioning—Larry's area of disability. In this class, a student who was thirty seconds late would be given a zero for the day. An assignment paper that failed to follow the approved format for name and date also earned the student a zero. Although unwittingly, the teacher was in effect punishing Larry for manifestations of his AD/HD.

With my help, school authorities, Larry's parents, and Larry himself fashioned a plan to keep him from being unfairly penalized for his AD/HD-based disability. This empowered him, and, with the cooperation of the school, he dropped one class and straightened things out with the teacher of the other class he found irritating. He then began to enjoy his day, and the problem of involuntary school aversion never again reached clinical proportions.

Similar help for parents and children seeking to modify school requirements is available under a federal law dealing with the educational rights of the disabled. Assistance is provided under Section 504 of the Rehabilitation Act, and the Individuals with Disabilities Educational Act (IDEA). The force of federal law may be more effective than informal agreements between school and parents in making sure disabled students, including those with AD/ HD, are treated on the basis of their special needs.

The clinician should attend meetings the parents have with teachers to ensure that the teenager's case for special treatment is properly presented. The teenager himself should be asked to join in the discussion, and to approve or initiate any adaptations that will be made on his behalf. Failure to include him in negotiations and to win his support may destroy the effort and promote ODD. Chapter 8 deals more fully with methods for creating goodness of fit for the AD/HD child at school.

CASE CONCEPTUALIZATION

To select the correct combination of interventions, the therapist must determine the true basis for the child's behavior. A thorough evaluation is essential, because comorbid conditions are common among disruptive disorders. Use of the acronym BETS (biological factors, environments affected, sources of trauma endured, and types of symptoms manifested) helps recall the various factors to consider during interviews with the parents and the ODD teenager. The clinician should inquire extensively until he can rule out the relative contribution of any or all of these factors to the syndrome. He should survey teachers and significant others if he suspects that their reports may provide a useful perspective. Once the evaluation establishes the presence of these factors, an appropriate protocol can be launched.

Biological factors tend to involve frontal lobe deficits, as seen in AD/HD, and biochemical imbalances, as seen in mood disorders. The presence of these conditions will hinder the benefit of psychotherapeutic interventions. On the other hand, these conditions respond to medication. Frontal lobe deficits diminish a child's capacity for adaptation. They interfere with his functioning in school, and require a different child-rearing approach.

Frontal lobe functions responsible for adaptations include sustained attention, sustained effort, consistency, inhibition, delay of gratification, frustration tolerance, impulse control, mood control, planning, organizing, attention to detail, the ability to anticipate problems, problem solving, double-checking, moral judgment, and moral behavior. Individuals with impaired frontal lobes are error prone, inconsistent, excitable, impulsive, inattentive, and unmotivated, and often have difficulty conforming to rules. They lose things, have trouble shifting from one activity to another, are habitually late, are easily bored, and plan poorly, leaving many details for the last minute. AD/HD does not mean that all of these frontal lobe functions are impaired all of the time. Rather, it means that one or more of them impede normal functioning to a degree that causes problems.

Children who suffer from AD/HD need (1) medication, (2)

information about their condition, (3) structure to help them perform these brain functions with reasonable effort, (4) a different parenting approach, and (5) modifications of the disciplinary code to create goodness of fit at school. There are abundant resources for AD/HD education. However, most adolescent patients will not read the material, and some oral instructions may be needed.

It is nearly impossible to treat AD/HD effectively without first resolving ODD. The structure necessary to help AD/HD individuals succeed must be imposed and directed by the individuals themselves. It may include tutors, reminders, or contingencies such as not going out with friends until homework is done. Tutors may help the teenagers organize and prioritize their work, or help them get past procrastination. The purpose of the structure is to assist them in exercising the limited frontal lobe functions they can perform, and to supplement them with the mental capacities of those who are helping them, so that success is possible. AD/HD individuals must welcome this help. If it is imposed on them against their will, it will simply foster ODD.

Parents can play a role in facilitating treatment for their teenage ODD children. Clinicians learn how to use the influence of parents to reverse ODD and strengthen AD/HD-related brain functions over time. *Parenting the AD/HD Child: A New Approach* (Bustamante 1997) describes a detailed program in language that parents can easily follow, and is a useful adjunct in clinical work employing this model. Parents should be encouraged to follow a parenting program that reinforces the work being done in therapy sessions. Most parents need professional assistance to implement the program successfully. The science behind this parenting program will be published elsewhere (A. M. Bustamante in press).

The Role of Environmental Stressors and Trauma

Two out of three possible spheres of functioning must provide goodness of fit for a child, or development will be arrested and symptoms will set in. The spheres of functioning are home, school, and peers. Children need to experience a feeling of being wanted and appreciated by family, teachers, and friends, and be given reasonable opportunities for success in these settings if they are to undergo healthy development. These settings must offer acceptance, autonomy, positive regard, and reasonable expectations. A child who endures poorness of fit in two of these settings will reach a developmental arrest, and become easily wounded by events. A child who is traumatized in one of these settings may struggle in all of them.

Developmental arrests secondary to unknown sources of trauma abound in cases that involve ODD. It is a critical factor to consider when conceptualizing ODD cases, yet it is easy to overlook its presence and importance. Children have a difficult time recognizing the effect that these experiences have on them. It is very hard for them to admit the experience, even to themselves. It is hard for them to report it or articulate it. Their instincts tell them to avoid dealing with it.

Clinicians must be particularly sensitive to low-level trauma related to stress. I refer to the phenomenon that takes place when a situation produces significant distress for a child, yet remains undetected and unresolved over the long run. Such situations do not qualify as events capable of producing formal posttraumatic stress disorder (PTSD), since to fulfill the criteria for this class of event the individual must endure a near-death or a severe violation, as in torture, rape, or aggravated assault. Nonetheless, the stress that results from ongoing, unresolved distress can have an impact on the emotional brain that parallels a low-level version of trauma. Following are typical situations that tend to go unnoticed, yet can pose serious obstacles to the treatment process.

Home

The home environment is usually the most affected by trauma, even if the source is outside the home. Youths often inflict on their families the trauma inflicted upon them by others. They also enact with siblings the traumas they witness in their own parents. Hence, if a parent abuses a spouse or a child, the child might reenact this trauma with another sibling or with a peer outside the family.

The term *family dysfunction* refers to ways in which families create emotional problems for their members. Family dysfunction usually involves difficulties in attaining closeness, effectively helping each other, or adapting to situations as a group. Often observed as well are the inability to communicate effectively, a tendency to blame, and violations of trust.

Family dysfunction is beyond any individual's control and less dramatic than outright abuse. However, long-term dysfunction can eventually become a source of trauma. Individual attempts to control the dysfunction can lead to extremes in dysfunctional behavior that can become imprinted in the amygdala (midbrain) as emotional wounds. The dysfunction makes it difficult for family members to trust anyone. The dysfunction becomes a matter of concealment, ultimately ruining the chances of family members to achieve satisfying relationships. It grows, the children become accustomed to it, and distrust and dysfunction become part of their behavior.

School

Much of the trauma inflicted in the domestic and peer worlds has a subtle but significant impact on the learning environment. Traumatized children often lose much of their learning capacity. They develop resistance to experiencing positive emotions, and act out their oppositional tendencies in ways that spoil the learning environment for others. Their acting-out tendencies represent the emotional brain's last-ditch effort to communicate its distress without words. Their actions draw attention to their distressing situations.

As discussed above, school failure can become traumatic. The compulsory and competitive nature of scholastics can become exceedingly stressful for some students, especially when a formal labeling process that predicts failure in life is involved. Scholastic trauma is common in younger children with neurological involvement including AD/HD or LD, and in mid- to late-adolescents without neurological problems. These teenagers tend to "burn out" because they have not developed mature motivation for schooling, yet are pressured to act as if they had. In the process, they are further traumatized and weakened by harmful labels applied to them by others, among them underachiever, lazy, ADD, LD, dropout, delinquent, and drug addict.

Social psychology has documented the destructive power of labels. Labeled individuals gradually adopt the characteristics that the labels suggest for them. Random assignment of IQ scores has had the effect of improving or diminishing student grades. People have been tricked into administering what they thought were devastatingly cruel shocks to innocent experimental subjects. Normal college students have been admitted to a mental hospital, labeled schizophrenic, held against their will, and made to develop psychotic-like symptoms by being kept there. College students have been made to act like sadistic jailers. All of these strange results were accomplished by placing people in roles that labeled them, and thus determined their behaviors.

Since trauma and stress have cumulative properties, school failure makes its victims more vulnerable to other stresses, and moves them closer to the threshold of symptoms. Thus, children who struggle with school are at much greater risk of succumbing to mental disorders than those more comfortable with the learning process. By the same token, children who suffer alienation from peers or experience family dysfunction are more prone to school failure, and the traumatic labeling process that ensues.

Peers

The peer world is the least affected by outside sources of trauma (those occurring at home or school). The clique that adolescents form considers family and school stresses unimportant. These issues are all but forgotten when these youths gather. In fact, school failure and family dysfunction can become the very issues around which they bond. For peers, being with each other usually means relief from the pressure of home and school. This aspect of the peer world is healthy.

On the other hand, the peer world can inflict some of the harshest treatment that children encounter. Peer pressure can expose youths to some of the most dangerous and cruel influences imaginable. Brutal reenactment of trauma takes place between cliques, and among peers. Children humiliate each other through dominance ("Pick that up or you're dead! Good, now kiss my feet."). Through exclusion, they deprive each other of growth, and they bully each other for pleasure. PTSD secondary to peer trauma is common though often undetected.

Peers are able to traumatize each other through violence, teasing, labeling, and involving each other in illegal or life-threatening events. Whatever adults have done to children, the children do to each other. One adult sexually molests one child, and that child sexually molests many children who will in turn molest many children. This is the nature of trauma. Parenting and educational demands create stress in children, and they in turn coerce each other to the point of trauma. Some adults mistakenly consider the cruel practices of children normal and part of their nature.

Attributing the callousness of minors to their nature, however, is the same as saying that trauma is natural. Molestation is natural, war is natural, oppression is natural, sexism and racism are natural, and deviance is natural. In fact, trauma spreads. Mankind has never been free of it. However, children are not born with a disposition to destroy each other. They at times lack empathy for others when they're very young. They bite their mother's breast because it feels good to do so. They display territorial instincts and a tendency to hate newborn siblings. However, there is a genuine innocence in these aggressive tendencies, and children outgrow them naturally.

Once we coerce and push our children past emotional brain aversion, they become more callous, lose their capacity for empathy, and spread trauma unconcernedly. Many victims do this. Perhaps peer pressure and peer cruelty are not normal, but simply the natural response of youths to excessive pressure and control.

TYPES OF SYMPTOMS

Implications for treatment are contained in the type of symptoms that youths exhibit. Children manifest two kinds of symptoms when their stress reaches a critical threshold: internalizing and externalizing. Internalizing symptoms include different manifestations of anxiety and depression. Externalizing symptoms involve acting out. The internalizing child suffers quietly, the externalizing child makes others suffer. Many children exhibit both types of symptoms.

Anxiety can take on the classic worry manifestations, psychosomatic manifestations, or posttraumatic stress manifestations that embody characteristics of both anxiety and depression. Psychosomatic symptoms typically involve stomachaches, dizziness, or headaches, often before going to school. Posttraumatic symptoms typically include withdrawal, irritability, moodiness, covert repetitions of the trauma, sensitivity to surroundings reminiscent of the trauma, and a tendency to become uncommunicative.

The externalizing disorders include oppositional defiant disorder, conduct disorder, and social skills deficits—all of them disruptive. Children with biological, frontal lobe deficiencies (AD/HD) tend to externalize their problems once they reach the symptom threshold. Children of difficult temperaments tend to do the same. Children who experience moderate attachment problems (i.e., trauma, stress, loss), and who have learning problems tend to internalize their symptoms. Children who experience severe neglect early in life may fail to form a conscience, and develop serious antisocial tendencies (conduct disorder).

A deficit in social skills causes a poor fit with peers and invites trauma. The absence of a social life significantly retards emotional development. This factor places youths on the verge of symptoms. The clinician must determine the different sources of distress by interviewing the adults involved in the children's lives. Most children will not speak of their pain. Secrecy is part of the trauma syndrome. Youths suffering from ODD or conduct disorder tend to underreport their problems. Denial and externalizing blame are part of their conditions.

From this very basic information on diagnosis, I derive a series of questions that I use to determine which interventions to prescribe.

KEY DIAGNOSTIC QUESTIONS

What Are the Age Considerations?

While the teenager in the family may initially present as the identified patient, his siblings may develop symptoms of their own along the way. This tends to occur once the clinician begins to tamper with the family system. For these reasons, the clinician must be prepared to apply the protocols presented in this book to children of different age groups. The following guidelines should be kept in mind. For older children (14 and up), the clinician should follow the protocol of the next three chapters, and then refer to later chapters that address complications, such as school failure, excessive aggression, peer problems, and drug involvement. For children in middle childhood (between 11 and 13), the ODD protocol is usually used. For younger children (usually 10 and under), reliance should be primarily on a parenting protocol (see Bustamante 1997). For families that have younger children, the parenting tactics presented in Chapter 6 (Turning Failure into Growth) should be emphasized with the young ones. Older children may be enlisted to help younger children in the parenting efforts.

Does the Child Have AD/HD?

If he does, he will do better on stimulant medication. The clinician should take the following steps: (1) Make a preliminary diagnosis by taking a history and looking for a lifelong pattern consistent with *DSM* guidelines for AD/HD. (2) Implement the psychological interventions presented in the chapters that follow, and monitor the response (children with AD/HD will respond only partially). (3) Prescribe Ritalin (or whatever other medication is recommended). Once a child is on Ritalin, the clinician should look for a notable improvement in the response to the interventions. If Ritalin helps, it should be administered after school and on weekends, so the children will derive as much benefit as possible from the psychological intervention with which they will be presented. If a child responds to Ritalin, but continues to be difficult, the interventions in this book for ODD should be emphasized.

Does the Child Have Problems with Information Processing (Fluency or Automaticity)?

Automaticity is a cognitive learning theory term for the ease (speed, accuracy, and effortless retrieval of information) with which a student can read, compute math, or write. If school performance is a problem, it is best to test for automaticity problems during the diagnostic period. If the child's retrieval system is slow and labored, there are systems for diagnosing and remedying the problem (see Royer and Sinatra 1994). However, if automaticity is a problem, it is likely that the child has been turned off to education because of the tedium endured over the years. (See Chapter 8 for more information on scholastic trauma.)

I recommend to the therapist the following remedial steps: Establish the problem of automaticity and make the child and family aware of it. It may help to have the family and child read the section in this book on academic failure and scholastic trauma. Next, explain that it may take a while with lessened school pressure before the child is ready to do the exercises necessary to correct the problem. Temporarily, school grades must become unimportant. The protocol for school failure discusses how to make scholastic matters unimportant without undermining the child's confidence. The interventions presented in Chapter 8 can be used to reverse the family dysfunction that stems from school pressure, give the child confidence, and eliminate the harmful label he has endured. Refer the child for remediation once he regains his natural desire to achieve in school. The motivation will return.

If There Is ODD, Against Whom Is It Directed?

If the child is disrespectful toward a parent, the clinician should look for a controlling parent clashing with a rebellious child. Such children resist being controlled. If this is the case, the interventions that involve the parent as described later in this book should be implemented. If the parent is unable to implement them, the clinician should follow the protocol for parental neurosis in Chapter 9. If the parent follows the prescribed protocol but the child is too difficult, the protocol for "Countering Narcissistic Rage" in Chapter 10 is indicated. If the child is disrespectful to both parents, and to authority figures outside the home, but not to others, it should be determined whether the parents are forcing the child to yield to the wishes of an adult the child does not respect. Such an individual may be intimidating or somehow unreasonable. If this is the case, the clinician should implement the protocol described under "Parents as Allies and Protectors," Chapter 6. Otherwise, he should follow the protocol for "Countering Narcissistic Rage." If the child is disrespectful toward specific authority figures outside the home, the clinician should look for a controlling adult (teacher, administrator, or caregiver), and, if this is the case, use the protocol under "Parents as Allies and Protectors" to safeguard the child against an unhealthy power struggle with a controlling adult.

If There Is ODD, Are the Parents Pressuring the Child to Study?

If so, the clinician should turn to Chapter 8 on academic failure, and try the recommendations under "Addressing Developmental Needs to Counter Scholastic Trauma." If the child remains oppositional once school pressure is reduced, the clinician should use the protocol for "Countering Narcissistic Rage."

If There Is ODD, Are There Signs of Involuntary Aversion to Academic Learning?

Signs of involuntary aversion to scholastics include an unwilling-ness to do homework, procrastination, deception, angry outbursts, drug use, significant underachievement, resistance to help, cheat-ing on exams, and concealing report cards. The clinician should ask the family to offer a valuable reward for doing homework and getting good grades for one entire marking period. If the child does not do the homework, his inability to study can be attributed to involuntary aversion to scholastics (see The Consequences of Scholastic Trauma in Chapter 8). He should be tested for auto-maticity. I recommend the CAAS. If automaticity is a problem, the clinician should consult "Addressing Developmental Needs to Counter Scholastic Trauma." Once the child has regained confi-dence, and family dysfunction has been reversed, the automatic-ity problem can be corrected. Cognitive psychologists at local universities may offer protocols that can help.

If There Is ODD, Are There Signs of Peer-Related Trauma?

The child may be identifying with the aggressors, taking the stress out on younger siblings, and picking up a bad attitude from bul-lies. This attitude may be directed toward parents. If this is the case, the protocol for "Countering Narcissistic Rage" is indicated. Access to peers should be made dependent on whether the child treats the family with respect. If the child is being victimized by someone else, it is essential to empower him. This can be accom-plished in several ways. Sometimes the child will want to stay at home on a given day to escape a frightening situation. It is desir-able to allow this, as long as the child has a counseling session to process the episode. The relief from the pressure will ally the parents with the child's emotional brain. Sometimes the child is excluded by his peers. In this case, to make up for the loss of the peer world the child can be granted special privileges (more TV time, new video games, more quality time with the parents), and encouraged to participate in special activities, including teams and clubs. A possible remedy for the trouble is a direct challenge to the tormentors. This can involve help from the parents in bringing legal charges against them, or arranging for authority figures like school administrators to confront them. The child must approve of and welcome attempts to protect him, and be encouraged to believe that in some way he is standing up for himself. Otherwise he will feel victimized while placed in a passive position, fearing that increased attention to the problem will only worsen the torment from his peers. Whatever is planned, the family should support the child in any way possible. Scars inflicted by episodes of peer-induced trauma can last for years. Counseling to back the family intervention is critical for peer aggression.

Does the Teenager Smoke?

It is safe to assume that most children who are smoking cigarettes are also involved in smoking marijuana, drinking, or negative peer influences. These teenagers are at risk and must be handled carefully. Trying to control them only drives them deeper into secrecy, and makes them more susceptible to the lure of the streets. Lecturing them about stopping smoking leads to distrust and resistance. However, by earning their trust, and understanding their dilemmas, the therapist can help them focus on the quality of their lives when they are not using illegal substances. Over time, they may see the danger in using drugs. Chapter 11 provides more detailed direction on bad peer influences and drug dependency.

Clinicians seldom encounter instances in which ODD is the sole and primary diagnosis. The ODD cases I have presented thus far involve a natural response to unreasonable expectations, an overcontrolling caregiver, trauma, or an underlying attention deficit or learning disability. The youth faces an unreasonable situation that triggers the natural oppositional response in the service of self-protection. The misguided caregivers attempt to force the youth to engage in the unwanted activity, which exacerbates the oppositional defiance and brings about the mind–body split that will cement the ODD.

Occasionally, an ODD child presents a long-standing and persistent pattern of oppositional defiance, yet the clinician will fail to detect underlying disabilities, trauma, controlling caregivers, or unreasonable expectations. The next section discusses how the clinician arrives at a diagnosis of ODD. It also presents considerations for effectively managing these youths through the intake process.

DIAGNOSING *ODD*

Charlie's parents saw me as a last resort in their search for help for their ODD son. A chubby 8-year-old, with a round face and dark hair, the boy seemed pleasant enough on the surface, but his parents were plainly worried about how to control other aspects of his behavior.

Charlie was an adopted child. His parents were delightful—patient, dedicated, responsible, and hard-working. They had followed without success every recommendation given to them by professionals, including medication, token economies, parent training, and counseling.

In my office, Charlie couldn't conceal his oppositional defiant tendencies even for a short time. His parents said he had an explosive temperament and a short fuse. In fact, he seemed to live only to wear his parents down. He would gladly give up a desired privilege in exchange for the pleasure he derived from not doing what his parents wanted. He thrived on the power he got from threatening self-harm. He became vindictive when he didn't get his way, and would retaliate with a vengeance. Sometimes he would hurt the family cat to retaliate against his parents. His father had given up on him. His mother was desperate.

Charlie sent me a note through his parents when he found out they were coming in for a consultation. The note read, "Dr. B.: Fuck you! You can't help me." I sent a note back saying, "Charlie, fuck you, too! Who says I want to help you?"

Apparently challenged by my message, Charlie now insisted on coming to my office. He wanted to meet me so I could witness his defiance first hand. My office is stocked with games, toys, and snacks that most children enjoy. Charlie noticed and even asked some questions about these attractions, but was careful not to display a desire for any of them.

While he was in the waiting room, some older teenage clients of mine entered and attempted to engage him in conversation. They told me later that Charlie refused to tell them his name or shake hands. His negativity was so apparent that the teens wondered what was wrong with him. They were prepared to like him and include him in their discussion, but Charlie was not interested.

I gave Charlie a couple of chances to turn down some treats, but let him know through my words and body language that I couldn't care less about what he chose to do. I said that I wanted to watch him cheat himself out of chocolate, video games, and the money I might have given him from a small supply I kept on hand for my clients to spend on snacks at nearby food stores.

Charlie attempted to disrupt our first session five minutes before it was scheduled to end. I was talking privately with his parents when he knocked on the door and barged in from the waiting room, asking when he was leaving, and announcing that time was up. His parents began to object, but I asked them to let me handle matters. I turned to Charlie and said, playfully, "We still have time, plus sometimes I just run real late anyway. Bye!"

Charlie lingered in the doorway, but I suggested that I could turn his presence into a psychoanalysis session very easily. This presented the threat of exposure, which he wanted to avoid. I intrepreted his standing at the door as an attempt to gain attention, yet protect himself from rejection by claiming not to care. I adopted his body language to reflect it back to him. Charlie promptly left the room.

I gave the parents some strategies for managing Charlie along the lines I discuss in Chapter 6, dealing with how to turn failure into growth. I helped them adjust their expectations to challenge Charlie, see to it that he faced consequences for his misdeeds, and yet protect him from unreasonable consequences outside the home. I showed them a method for communicating with Charlie that would defuse the power he wielded through his rudeness, unreasonable demands, and refusal to cooperate.

I made it clear to the parents that they would have to take dramatic measures to help turn Charlie's type of ODD around. His mother's expectations would have to change. She would have to abandon many of her wishes for her son, including good grades and participation in social activities. She would have to choose her battles carefully in areas of contention with her son, and empha-size safety, respect for parents and property, and contributions to the family as standards for behavior. She would have to learn how to talk to Charlie differently, avoid the role of the rescuer, and refuse to succumb any longer to the power the ODD behavior had often exerted over her in the past.

The week following his first visit, Charlie and I ended up in my office eating chocolates and playing video games, while he vented his complaints about his teacher, and agreed with his par-ents on the importance of family friendship. I established a strong and unique alliance with Charlie.

The turning point came when I offered Charlie some really good chocolates, and he turned them down, only to change his mind later. When he refused my first offer, I invited his mother to have a chocolate, but she declined as well. I expressed delight in not having to share my treats, but as it turned out, I had spoken too soon. The father accepted one of the chocolates, and I com-plained playfully: "I love offering really good things and watching people cheat themselves out of a golden opportunity. But Dad got me this time!"

Charlie obviously enjoyed my complaint about his father, and said, "On second thought, maybe I will try one of those." As he approached me, I acted as though I felt I had been misled. Charlie relished the moment and took two chocolates. Before long, Charlie and I were role playing, which consisted of extremely rude remarks to his parents, while they practiced deflecting the insults. Charlie found the exercise of defiance exhilarating. Yet he agreed with the limit-setting his parents were learning how to apply.

I established in Charlie's presence that he was simply a different kind of boy who was attempting to satisfy a different agenda, and explained to his parents that I was not surprised at how well he responded to my recommendations. In three weeks, I had diffused Charlie's struggle for power, eliminated his defiance as a means of getting attention, and demonstrated an understanding of, and a generosity toward, the agenda of his emotional brain. I had established that Charlie was primarily an oppositional child, and this knowledge enabled me to take the steps required to address his needs effectively.

When the primary diagnosis of a child is ODD, the condition requires special consideration. Such youths can damage a family. However, the protocols outlined in this book work with them. Charlie was such a case. The child-rearing methods that his parents had learned only fed the ODD. ODD youths are stubborn, resistant, and uncompromising. They persistently test limits, yet deny their oppositional and defiant tendencies. They see themselves as victims of unreasonable demands or circumstances. In adolescence, ODD is equally prevalent in both genders. However, males are more confrontational and manifest more aggressive and entrenched symptoms.

The approach to making the formal diagnosis of ODD must be cautious, especially during early childhood and adolescence. Oppositional and defiant behaviors in these age groups often result from normal attempts at individuation. According to *DSM-IV*, it is also easy to misdiagnose ODD in cases of language impairments that interfere with the ability to follow directions. A key distinction is whether the misbehaviors occur in response to unreasonable expectations, or are driven by the inner tendencies of the child. The diagnosis of ODD proper demands that the cause of the misdeeds be rooted in the child. The distinction is not easy to make. For example, according to *DSM-IV*, there is a greater prevalence rate of depression in mothers of ODD youths. However, it is not clear whether the depression in the mothers causes the ODD in the child, or whether the child's ODD causes the depression in the mother. Similarly, cases of entrenched ODD usually present with a long-standing history of bringing out the worst in authority figures who have, in turn, brought out the worst in them.

ODD symptoms are directly related to familiarity. ODD youths are more oppositional and defiant with those they are closest to. The symptoms almost always occur in the home, but not necessarily in other settings. The condition originates in the home and remains most oppressive there, only gradually spreading to other settings.

According to *DSM-IV*, at least four of the following tendencies must be present for at least six months to make the diagnosis of ODD: (1) frequent loss of temper; (2) frequent arguing, defiance, or refusal to comply with the commands or rules of adults; (3) deliberate spoiling to annoy others; (4) externalizing blame for mistakes or misbehavior; (5) a tendency to be easily annoyed; (6) anger and resentment; (7) spitefulness or vengefulness. To qualify for this diagnosis, these symptoms must interfere with social, academic, or occupational functioning.

It is imperative to establish the history of the ODD's progression in order to establish an accurate diagnosis. The prognosis of youths with ODD is far worse than that of youths who manifest developmentally appropriate oppositional tendencies or become oppositional in response to unreasonable demands. ODD with a history of certain predisposing factors often progresses to conduct disorder. Such cases warrant more extensive treatment efforts. And, in preparation for these efforts, it behooves the clinician to rule out factors that expose these youths to the risk of more serious psychopathology.

To make the formal diagnosis, the clinician should look for difficult temperaments after the preschool years, including difficulty with self-soothing, undue reactivity, or excessive activity. He should also inquire about emotional difficulties during the school years, including moodiness, low self-esteem, low frustration tolerance, swearing, and substance use. The classic ODD syndrome has become evident by middle elementary school, and certainly by early adolescence. The syndrome unfolds gradually over months and sometimes years.

High-risk factors include families who employ harsh, inconsistent, or neglectful child-rearing practices. There may also be a history of serious marital problems. At least one parent may present a history of mood disorder, AD/HD, ODD, conduct disorder, antisocial personality disorder, or substance abuse. Finally, the child may display a tendency toward physical aggression.

The form in which the negativity expresses itself serves as a clear indicator of the severity of the ODD. ODD youths tend to express their anger verbally, or manipulate to induce feelings of anger in others. Although there is significant overlap between ODD and conduct disorder, the misbehavior of ODD youths rarely includes physical aggression or serious violations of the basic rights of others. Theft, deceit, and physical aggression directed at people, animals, or property may be present in cases of ODD, but are usually characteristics of conduct disorder.

As many as possible of these predisposing high-risk factors should be addressed in the initial treatment plan. There is a delicate balance to be maintained in the evaluation process. On the one hand, the clinician must identify the environmental factors that may be causing ODD symptoms by creating poorness of fit, as well as the underlying comorbid conditions making it unlikely that the child will meet the expectations set forth for the norm. On the other hand, the clinician must determine whether a long-standing and complex case of ODD is the result of constitutional factors. Such cases are more difficult to treat, and probably require medication in addition to most of the interventions for special problems presented in later chapters of this book, especially the protocol for excessive narcissism in Chapter 10.

In his accumulation of observations, the clinician may also use the ODD youth's reactions to certain interventions as evidence contributing to a diagnosis of ODD, particularly positive responses to his own mimicking of the youth's oppositional mannerisms, and his seeming indifference to his chances of success with the youth's case. Charlie's responses confirmed the primary diagnosis of ODD. My handling of the case incorporated the core interventions of this approach, including detaching from the outcome, encouraging failure, and demonstrating the capacity to relate to the youth's emotional brain agenda.

I demonstrated my detachment, and joined Charlie in his oppositional defiance, initially with my who-says-I-want-to-help-you note, and later with my feigned delight in his turning down of my proffered treats.

I rejected his request that I end our sessions at the scheduled time, and told him I run over the allotted time whenever I like. I role-played a defiant child using profanity, and spoke of school failure as a matter of little concern. I was also able to establish my expertise by exposing his attitude when he attempted to interrupt my session and refused to leave the room. This earned his respect. Obviously these tactics differentiated me enough from traditional authority figures to allow me to form a positive alliance with Charlie's emotional brain. The effectiveness of these interventions was reflected in Charlie's remarkable turnabout in general attitude and his attendance at our sessions. In a relatively short time after he first appeared in my office, he was willing to accept my help. It is in the nature of ODD to respond positively to the tactics I have outlined.

Chapter 5 emphasizes the inducing of therapeutic failure to resolve ODD symptoms, and to pave the way for selection of a treatment focus. The teenager and his family are shown in active work on problems with the brain's shifting mechanism (AD/HD), the information processing pathways (LD), and involuntary emotional brain resistance (ODD). Specific interventions for these different problems are discussed in subsequent chapters.

Part III

Treatment

Step 1: Taking Failure to the Limit

Highly regarded authors in the fields of cognitive psychology and AD/HD, including Donald Meichenbaum and Robert Brooks, have written extensively about the positive side of failure. They have described how certain people become very successful once they learn to turn failure into growth and into a valuable learning experience. The process of turning failures into positive learning experiences is of quintessential value for those who struggle with handicapping conditions. It is uniquely effective for those with ODD.

By inviting failure, the trial intervention described in Chapter 3 enabled me to get around the ODD so I could complete an evaluation and form a therapeutic alliance. The next step in such cases is to reverse the ODD teenager's natural tendency to use failure to control other adults in his life and to derive secondary gains from being negative. The goal is to remove the influence of the ODD from as many significant relationships in the adolescent's life as possible, especially family and school. Failure becomes the child's problem, not the problem of his parents or his teachers. The ODD teenager can be taught to learn and grow from failures. He gains strength from his struggles with consequences.

From the perspective of two minds at odds, inviting failure alters the associations that have been imprinted in the emotional mind about the adult world. The emotional mind has a "most wanted list" of adults who prescribe unreasonable expectations. The teenager's emotional brain is predisposed to placing any adult who enters his life on the list, which includes teachers, administrators, parents, counselors, and other authority figures. These are the adults who join forces to present the teenager with a united front and a consistent message that fitting in with society's normative agenda is good. By prescribing failure in the way I recommend in this chapter, the clinician dissociates himself from this group, and opens the door to integration and adult influence.

Parents need to devote themselves wholeheartedly to the construct of therapeutic failure. This resolves the ODD in the family setting and turns it into a positive influence in the child's life. The parents need to encourage their children to take charge of activities that expose them to the risk of failure. The intervention will work best if the parents manage to arrive at a positive, yet pro-failure disposition, and are willing to accept the results. By involving the parents in the construct of therapeutic failure and having them put the teenager in charge of his own life, the clinician also dissociates the parents from the emotional brain's most wanted list.

In the interviews conducted in this and the next chapter, the parents and the ODD teenager are in the interview room at the same time. It is the parents' outlook on failure that ultimately yields the intended therapeutic impact. Yet it is the adolescent who keeps the parents honest. Very difficult teenagers welcome a thorough understanding of the intervention program, and quickly point out any deviations by their parents from the spirit of the prescribed course of action. There is no better source of information on parental habits and tendencies.

During the early phases of treatment, the ODD teenager or a parent may decide to withdraw from the therapeutic process in reaction to the group setting. It is important in such instances for the clinician to meet with alienated family members individually to provide them with an opportunity to express their concerns and to bolster his therapeutic alliance with them. It is often unsafe for the alienated party to express his feelings in front of other family members. Encouraging him to make such disclosures can expose him to attack. When this occurs, he may think he has been ambushed by the rest of the family, and refuse to participate in future group meetings.

This phenomenon occurs most frequently with teenagers after they have met with their parents and the clinician in the same room. Even if things go well, it often irritates an ODD teenager to listen to his parents express their annoying ideas, supported by the very same therapist the teenager has come to view as a strong ally. However, a conversation with the alienated teenager alone restores the bond with him, and helps allay his concerns.

THE THERAPEUTIC SIDE OF FAILURE

I first considered the notion of "therapeutic failure" when struggling with a particularly difficult case that involved an oppositional, acting-out 17-year-old named Jimmy and his headstrong and powerful father, who insisted on running the boy's life. Jimmy's parents were caring, honorable, and successful people who had been taken aback by their son's sudden and serious misconduct. They had made great sacrifices to help Jimmy, but all of them had involved enabling him and running his life. The harder I worked to help the father give up his controlling role, the more controlling he became. The more controlling the father became, the more intense became the conflict between the pair. The father would appear to think over my recommendations, then predict they wouldn't work and refuse to try them.

Authority figures who refuse to change their tactics have often fallen into an oppositional state themselves without realizing it. Despite the constant and draining battles that take place, they maintain a controlling stance vis-à-vis the oppositional teenager. The resulting dysfunction may lead them into the quagmire of clinical depression. Yet they do little to change their behavior. There is nothing rational about the ODD process.

Eventually matters become intolerable for the controlling adults who resist the therapeutic failure intervention. Their struggle against natural development is proving futile. The battle grows more intense, but suddenly they relinquish control and become open-minded. This holds true for parents, teachers, or anyone else in a position of authority who is interfering with the process.

I believe the rightful aim of the oppositional stage (see Chapter 1) is to bring controlling authority figures to the point of surrender, where they will allow their children reasonable autonomy.

Controlling adults feel it is the parents' job to keep their children succeeding at all costs. They resist granting them any sense of autonomy for as long as possible. They insist on having their children do things in just the "right" way, no matter what the cost, and they encounter oppositional behavior all along the way. However, once they allow their children the freedom to fail, they resolve the ODD and restore natural development. There is no way around this process.

It took months, but the ODD finally got the better of Jimmy's father. The battles had become intolerable. The family sought a second opinion from a physician, who recommended a temporary separation of Jimmy from his parents, a course of action I had been suggesting for some time. The family decided to lodge Jimmy with his paternal grandfather. This would give him the chance he needed to run his life his own way.

I spent, it seemed, hours on the phone one night listening to dire predictions from the family. The parents predicted their son would commit a dozen depraved acts. They resigned themselves to his death or imprisonment. As if to give substance to their forebodings, the grandfather called in the middle of my conversation with the parents to attack his son. While I was on call-holding, the parents told me, the grandfather threatened to kill himself, reported numerous deviant acts on Jimmy's part, and said these were evidence of the terrible job Jimmy's parents had done in bringing him up.

Jimmy did have some minor accidents and got himself into a bit of trouble, but nothing on the scale the parents had predicted. For example, his car broke down and had to be towed, and he was robbed in a downtown area. This relative he was staying with lived near an area where such holdups were common. The incident occurred in the parking lot of a restaurant during peak business hours, and could have happened to anyone. Jimmy was blameless in these mishaps.

It wasn't long before Jimmy had established the groundwork for a productive life. His success seemed limited at first, and the parents remained skeptical. However, one could sense the change in Jimmy's intentions. I knew the ODD had been resolved, and I expected to see the mastery stage of development next (see Chapter 1). I expected a short burst of accomplishment, followed by a few minor regressions, and then slow, steady progress, three steps forward, one step back.

Jimmy returned to his family after two months. He missed the creature comforts of home. He had accomplished much of what he wanted without his father telling him what to do. Jimmy behaved responsibly for a short while. His parents enjoyed two months without conflict. Then, however, Jimmy became demanding. The father sought to impose his own rules again. I predicted the return of full-blown ODD. But that did not happen.

There was a diversion. The failure had led to growth for the father just as much as it had for Jimmy, and he changed his tune. He and his wife developed new interests and adopted a completely different attitude toward their son. I remember the father's words: "I'm detached. If he wants to get high and be a bum, that's fine with me. If he wants to freeload here at the house and make nothing of his life, that's his problem. I'm just not going to make it too easy for him by giving him a lot of extras. I don't know what other words to use, other than I'm detached."

Once I heard the father say this, I knew the case was on its way to a successful resolution. Jimmy, in his typical impulsive style, had been demanding that his parents buy him a fancy car. He was going to need transportation to work, and they had given his brother a car. This is the kind of request the parents might have honored in the past. But they didn't indulge Jimmy this time. He protested strenuously when his parents refused to accede to his wishes, but they had become detached. He had to settle for no car. He continued to look for work, and remained productive at home. Before long he was in college, holding a job, and gratefully and respectfully accepting reasonable support from his father.

The content of my conversations with the parents about Jimmy changed dramatically after this turnaround. The parents spoke of how they had always known what a great heart their son had, and how he had it in him to succeed in life. Everyone in the family began to make constructive life changes. One could see they had all been missing important growth-related opportunities for some time.

After seeing the resolution of this extremely difficult case, I experienced one of those rare panoramic views of something that had been staring me in the face for a long time, but that I had never recognized. I looked back on my many years of working with ODD youths and saw a clear pattern. The majority of the important breakthroughs I had achieved with cases that involved difficult family situations and disruptive teenagers had followed on the heels of significant failures.

NATURE'S REMEDY FOR *ODD*

Failure is nature's remedy for ODD. It can teach vital lessons and promote growth. Inducing failure early in treatment exposes key problems for all to see. It exposes areas that need development in the teenager, and key family dynamics that may otherwise go unnoticed. Over the years, I have learned to use failure to resolve problems that appeared overwhelmingly difficult. I have learned to invite failure intentionally and to use it therapeutically.

I have found that inviting failure is an effective way to begin therapy in cases that involve ODD adolescents. The tactic energizes the treatment right away. The family arrives at my office expecting me to make their child conform to their standards, and, as a result, to succeed. The last thing they expect is for me to extend to their teenager every opportunity to fail. A teenager typically is convinced that he can handle things his own way without failure, and thinks of the permissive therapist as a genius with whom he can ally. He will summon every skill possible to succeed, just to prove that he was right all along in resisting his parents' wishes. This kind of attitude fosters growth.

By allowing their children to struggle against failure, parents will gain an immediate respite from the draining battles they have been engaged in for as long as they can recall. Their changed attitude will put them in a learning mode, open their minds, and give them an opportunity to question important assumptions about child rearing.

Parents generally assume that most of what they already do is correct. They will filter the therapist's suggestions through this lens, and view them as only a slight variant of what they are already doing. They will, thus, end up doing the same old thing, and getting the same results. They will expect the therapist to change their child, with no contribution from them toward solution of the problem. Despite this attitude, the therapist should prescribe failure every time he encounters a new problem area or when things go badly.

WHEN TO PRESCRIBE FAILURE

If the parents resist letting the teenager fail, a guideline for winning the point is for the clinician to allow the control struggle with the ODD to proceed until, worn out, the parents finally surrender. If they support the idea of allowing the experience of therapeutic failure, then a broader range of freedom to induce failure can be used, as described in this chapter.

In the event that parents resist allowing their child the freedom to fail, the clinician goes along with their decision and invites them to continue their struggles. He commiserates with them, and commends them for paying such a high price to ensure the success and safety of their child. He helps them see their efforts in a caring and positive light. However, he also makes sure they understand that there is another option—therapeutic failure.

He must never, however, push his recommendation to let oppositional children fail or become a party to the parents' decision to adopt another approach. If he remains detached, calm, and confident while they struggle unsuccessfully with ODD, the parents will come around in their own time. The same holds true for teachers and anyone else who resists this intervention and is wedded to a controlling stance in relation to the ODD teenager.

In most cases, treatment will progress quite nicely despite difficulties with individuals who insist on control methods. The battle against authority harms mostly the adults involved and the environment that the ODD teenager disrupts. It does minimal harm to the ODD teenager himself. The defenses of the ODD child against the demands of unwelcome authority are effective, and he emerges relatively unscathed from his struggles with it. In fact, the consequences an unpopular authority figure doles out motivate the ODD teenager to develop new skills for coping with the conditions thrust upon him. The ODD teenager, at the same time, grows to appreciate the therapeutic alliance he maintains voluntarily with the sympathetic and understanding clinician.

It is easy to induce failure in a creative and constructive manner by offering the teenager some opportunities to do things the way he thinks is best. This responds to his need to express his true desires, and pursue his own unique path to maturity. He will most likely begin by taking advantage and making mistakes. However, the lessons learned from these choices, including those taught by the unpleasant consequences experienced, will encourage him to pursue more realistic objectives.

In extreme cases of ODD, it is best to remove all restrictions from the teenager at once and simply invite him to pursue a life that he likes. I challenge these teenagers to stop doing anything they hate, including going to school. We have developed in my community a home schooling center that offers opportunities for self-directed education, opportunities to socialize, and a safe and legal option for stepping out of coercive battles with school authorities without involving law enforcement personnel and penalties for truancy.

I have been surprised by how few ODD teenagers accept a placement outside of school. Yet having that option available gives them a choice and allows them to experience the desire to go to school. Most of the time we negotiate modifications to the student's day that lessen the drudgery of school.

With these options in the back of my mind, I present to the ODD teenager the opportunity to do things differently and learn to welcome failure as follows:

"Nothing else matters," I say. "School, a career, a future, money, your property, it all means nothing. Once you mature and grow into the best version of yourself, all those things will come to you very easily. You'll have all that, and more. I believe in you. We all do."

I then remove all unnecessary support that has been extended by parents and ancillary services. I ask the parents to meet with school personnel and other authority figures in their child's life to alert them to what is going on, and instruct them on how to handle the teenager's failures. I stand behind the parents any time they encounter problems with authority outside the home. I help them plan ways of intervening with which the teenager will feel comfortable when intervention becomes necessary in order to prevent traumatic consequences.

I then wait for the failure. I schedule regular appointments in my office to prevent unnecessary last-minute urgent requests for my time. Setting up appointments sends the signal to the teenager that the stakes are high. It also signals to the parents that the clinician understands their concerns and will stand behind them for support. Failure provides precious opportunities to encourage and accept the teenager as he is. It also entails consequences that can be used to challenge and promote the development of new brain functions in the teenager.

HOW TO PRESCRIBE FAILURE

My experience with Paul, another teenager, demonstrates the technique for using failure as a means of making progress. I met with Paul to prepare him for the undertaking. Our objective was to discover areas that he needed to strengthen before he could manage freedom responsibly. I wanted him to understand the spirit of the challenge he was about to encounter. I wanted him to look at failures as learning opportunities and find ways to strengthen his abilities.

"I would like to run some tests. These tests are unlike anything you've ever seen. You don't have to take these tests. In fact, you shouldn't take them if you're afraid, lazy, or lack the desire to learn the results. These tests will not help you if you don't want to take them. These tests can also change your life for the better, in ways you could never imagine, if you take them because you want to.

"They are failure tests. I would have you do in your own way certain things that other people now tell you how to do, and when. I will take some supports away from you, like your mother waking you up in the morning, that currently make these tasks easy for you. Then I get to see how well you do without them.

"I want to find out what you fail at, and how badly. The test will show you what you want to get better at, and show me what you need to do to become better.

"The method I use is one that turns failure into growth. The goal is to make you the most capable, well-rounded person that you can be, and to do it the fastest way possible.

"Most kids spend their lives trying to prove they were born perfect, that everything they do is right. For them failure leads to shame, discouragement, and setback. Kids like this always want to win. The first time they play something, they feel bad if they make a mistake. They make fun of anyone who makes a mistake, and so on. Do you know what I'm talking about?" Paul said that he did.

I continued: "The problem with this mentality of always wanting to be right is that it keeps you from getting better at what you do. It stops you from learning. You see, if you always want to win and prove you're already perfect, you only exercise your strengths. You know what happens to your weaknesses then, right?"

"Yeah," Paul replied. "You never practice them, so you don't learn how to improve."

"Right," I said. "And how far could you go just by using your strengths? Furthermore, if you always need to do well, and you begin to fail, you start to freak out. You get all serious and upset, and you get into a negative state, a losing mentality.

"Now, let's say that instead of trying to prove I was born perfect, I just wanted to become better. Say I figured I was born weak and I have years to get strong at what I like. I would be able to laugh about my shortcomings. I would take my time about learning. I would put most of my time into working on my weaknesses. I would let others win with their strengths, figuring I would eventually become more than they could handle. They would be using their strengths all the time, and I would have time to develop a way to play them. Eventually, I would be able to expose their weaknesses and surpass them. My investment would be in becoming as whole, well-rounded, and capable as possible, and not by proving that I'm the best.

"This is how I want you to look at the new freedom you're gonna have. Do things your way. Don't worry about winning. Just try to uncover your hidden weaknesses, and see if you can improve on the ones that matter, one step at a time. Your failures will tell you what to work better at. Be proud of failing and then learning. Don't expect to do well, like you're an experienced grown-up. Lighten up about the failure. You'll have many chances to do right over the years. What could you possibly do now that would be so bad?

"Whether you know it or not, you need to do more and more of your life in your own way. You're asking for a certain level of freedom. You'll need to have certain parts of yourself developed to truly thrive and live well with adult-like freedom.

"I'm certain that you'll figure out how to grow strong if you're put in charge. Even if your ideas seem retarded to the adults around you. They'll need to respect how you want to do things.

You'll work hard at the things you want to do. The hard work will give you experience and greater strength to pursue dreams. The mistakes will show you how you want to do things differently. Every dumb project you engage in will lead to a smart project. Eventually, you 'll find a way to succeed. You'll be awesome.

"The list I have here will show me what parts of you are not ready to handle grown-up responsibility. Of course, once I ask you to operate with the responsibility and freedom of an adult, you'll show all your weaknesses. And you'll fail at some things. That's inevitable. But you'll also get credit for all the adult things you can do. You can decide if you want help with the areas you find weak, like having your mother do things for you until you're older. Or whether you'd like to remain in charge of the activity, and continue to fail until you can master it on your own.

"Grown-ups have many freedoms and privileges when it comes to their lives outside of home. They get to make many life choices. But then they must struggle with their choices and live with their results. They get to eat what they want, do what they want, sleep when they want, be with whom they want.

"Grown-ups also have a lot of responsibilities to manage at home. They have to clean their own toilets, do their own laundry, pay their rent, vacuum their own carpets, pay their own bills—you name it.

"So greater freedom for you means being capable of managing a full life. You plan your day outside of home, you get freedom, protection, support, and opportunities from your family. In return, you give friendship and cooperation, and do a fair share of the work.

"'Fair' means that you fulfill all your individual duties and I manage mine. In addition, we each fulfill half of the communal duties. You do your laundry and I do mine. You clean your room and I clean mine. You manage your job and I manage mine. We both clean bathrooms, kitchens, and common living and play areas. That's fair.

"If you can do your share in a home like this, you'll have things go well with any family you live with. You can move in with a best friend, live with your parents, move in with a girl, get married, or live alone. The same abilities would make you very valuable to any company or work group. It doesn't matter what your situation, you'll enjoy living, and get along with the people who matter to you in your life.

"Once you've matured to the point where you've mastered these obstacles, you'll have true freedom. It will be easy for you to have fun and succeed. It might take years, but you'll end up an extremely valuable person at a very young age, too. Our goal would be to get you to this point by the time you're 21."

I showed Paul the following list of possible obstacles to managing freedom, along with the skills he would have to develop to overcome them. I asked him to anticipate how many of these obstacles he thought would challenge him.

Obstacles	*Solutions*
Dependency	Decide and do for self
External control	Choose how to spend the day
Judgment	Expose weakness
Selfish urges	Put fun last
Perfection	Appreciate error
Weakness	Demonstrate discipline
Addiction	Break cycle and lead full life
Unskilled labor	Work to accomplish dream

Paul saw dependency, external control, addiction, and unskilled labor as problems. These became treatment goals. I notified him that I would consider it my business to challenge him on these areas if I thought he was hiding his weaknesses. I emphasized that I did not want to hear him pouting, being defensive, or being too serious about failure because of these weaknesses. I informed him that I had methods to strengthen all these areas, but I didn't want to share these with him yet.

Paul was to try to overcome these challenges on his own before learning how from someone else. He was to avoid letting others do things for him, or letting people tell him what to do. I explained that addiction and unskilled labor would be things he shouldn't expect to master until he was able to establish a life that he liked better. However, he would be able to manage these problems down the road, once he had matured and developed other basic skills.

Paul was psyched, ready to test his new freedom. He looked confident. He probably did not expect that his first major failure was right around the corner.

RECOVERING FROM LARGER FAILURES

I was surprised to learn that Paul had scheduled a family session all on his own, a significant benefit from his greatest failure ever. Paul's parents needed to adjust their outlook before a family session could yield anything positive. They had called in a state of alarm to request a meeting. They had caught Paul red-handed, smoking marijuana again. And there were more serious problems, his mother had hinted. I am accustomed to oppositional teenagers taking advantage of situations and acting out their wishes. However, I would never have anticipated what had taken place.

I could sense that the situation was bad, but I could also see that it was bolstering my therapeutic alliance with Paul.

"My parents were out of town, and I had about fifteen people over for a . . ." Paul stopped here and caught himself. This was the beginning of the story he had cooked up for authority figures who were pressuring him. He recovered rapidly. "Well, not true. Actually, I had the whole school over at my house." Paul laughed, and I cracked up in genuine disbelief, not about what he had done, but about his unmistakable sincerity.

"You didn't!" I responded, almost falling off my chair.

Paul's openness was a sign of real trust. It was a testament to the strong bond that can be forged with oppositional teenagers by forming an alliance with their emotional brains.

"We bought a keg of beer. We went all out. But I kept things under control. I kept everyone in certain parts of the house, and we cleaned up everything before my parents got back. But my mom is so anal that she still thinks the house was trashed. Nothing is ever clean enough for her. My dad was fine with it, except for the lying."

Happily, Paul's emphasis was on the positive side of his deeds. In the past, he would have left the post-party mess for someone else to clean up, but this time he had taken care of a difficult situation himself. In part, he wanted to prove that he could handle the responsibility of the house on his own in his parents' absence. He had taken our conversations about accepting responsibility to heart. It would be easy to emphasize the defects in his thinking, such as blatant violations of trust and inappropriate risk-taking. However, Paul will grow more from emphasizing his improvements achieved despite his failures, no matter how small.

This party would assure Paul a place in his peers' hall of fame. Paul's home was in a quiet neighborhood populated by well-mannered young children and parents, but because of the party, the block was packed with cars and music blared. Some of the partygoers roamed around the block, smoking and drinking. Inside, couples were using all the beds in the house. Condoms were left in the trash bins where Mom would find them, despite Paul's strenuous cleaning effort. Teenagers were sprawled on the floor of every room in the house.

Paul's parents had given him permission to have two friends at the house while they were gone. It was a major step for them to risk allowing him to stay in the house without adult supervision for two days. They were certainly not prepared for their son to host the kind of event that actually took place.

I had explained the process of addiction to Paul, the need to have a full life, the need for him to be evaluated so I could find out why he was procrastinating. We had worked on the need to establish trust so he could be in a position to open up to me. We had established the importance of his developing a life that he liked, so he wouldn't have to escape into the night to do drugs or anything else that attracted him.

I had met with the family, hoping to gain their approval for my plan. I had explained that Paul needed permission to change his entire life as often as needed until he reached the point where he could be satisfied with how he lived. We had set the stage for a successful start of treatment, but this last episode cast doubt on everything. Paul had revealed his true colors.

My objective with the parents would be to negotiate a fresh start, and use this event to show Paul and the parents how to position themselves to realize benefits from the failure. Needless to say, most families are ill equipped to cope positively with this level of adversity. It was important to interrupt the destructive cycle that Paul had set in motion here.

Large failures require a return to the assessment data and the evaluation process. Times like this either support validity of the previous diagnosis or require a search for a new one. I focused the family on the original data, and discussed with them the implications of Paul's latest difficulties. I also arranged for proper support and protection for Paul so he could afford to look at his failure and learn from the experience. His parents understood his mistakes, and declared their intention to let him stay home alone again in the future. They also explained the unintentional nature of Paul's loss of control to the school's band director so that he would not be ejected from the band in the event that word of his bash were to reach school personnel.

The second step of the therapy involves turning impending failures into growth, and is the subject of the next chapter.

6

Step 2: Turning Failure into Growth

"You know, Dr. B.," Mary said to me, speaking about her experiences as a parent, "every important accomplishment by DJ has been something we've struggled with for years and gotten nowhere. Then one day he decides to do it because he wants to, and the problem disappears. I remember the long fights over wearing a seat belt. Then one day he just did it without a word, and he's done it ever since, without missing a beat."

"Yeah," DJ said, "I just suddenly wanted to. It was easy to do, it was safe, and it seemed stupid not to."

"Now DJ is the one who bugs others about wearing their safety belts," Mary said. "The same thing happened with homework, helping out around the house, making friends, touch typing" (DJ had major graphomotor problems and we had tried in vain to get him to touch type). Mary sighed as she looked at her son admiringly. The two were in my office to discuss the current state of DJ's case, no longer requiring frequent visits.

I had seen DJ off and on for approximately five years. He was now 16, stood six feet tall, and weighed 190 pounds. He had been weight lifting to prepare himself for varsity football and it showed. He had recently stopped saving up for Nintendo games and toys and was putting all of his money into a watch and a Gucci bracelet to decorate the body he was so excited about molding for himself.

This was the same person I had met when he was a pudgy, insecure, passive, quiet 11-year-old, long before I had developed the treatment method I describe in this book. He had a diagnosis of AD/HD and LD, and suffered from significant anxieties. He was withdrawn and hardly spoke at all. Now he was outspoken and had an abundance of friends. DJ had been successfully managing by himself every responsibility related to school and home for almost two years. He took pride in accepting only minimal help. Like many of the teenagers with whom I have used this method, he was drug free, honest, communicative, and close to the parents, who had learned to believe in him.

DJ's was one of ten landmark cases in my practice that entailed the removal of all unwanted supports. The students involved were told they could pass or fail in school, whichever they chose, with no penalties attached. DJ had no visible reaction when I introduced the failure-for-growth intervention. He was unmotivated and seemingly had no opinions about anything. He was easily bored and was struggling to pass in school. He had received special education services for about six years to no avail, and felt stupid as a result. For years it had been Mary's painful ordeal to force DJ to do his homework. DJ procrastinated and avoided concentrating on anything that was difficult.

When I advanced the notion of putting DJ in charge of his education and his life, his parents were alarmed. Indeed, he failed in school briefly, but rapidly developed a more mature attitude. DJ was affronted by his parents' lack of faith. They were betting that deprived of their assistance, he would turn out to be a depressed ne'er-do-well. He, on the contrary, was confident that given the right to make his own decisions, he would succeed in school right from the start. The realization that now he could eliminate from his life some of the elements he didn't like brought his emotional brain to life. He felt empowered and set out to prove his parents wrong in their belief that he could not handle freedom. Under the new circumstances his growth was steady. Once he was placed in charge of himself, DJ accomplished things his parents never would have dreamed possible.

Mary continued: "Everything worthwhile came after he decided one day that he wanted to do it, and then it was perfect. There was no turning back. The funny thing is, if I had known this would happen, I would have been so different as a parent, so much calmer. I would have enjoyed him so much more."

Mary's story illustrates a subtle but important distinction between two forms of behavior change. One change takes place in response to conscious effort or external force, the other as a result of natural maturation. Sometimes a person can change a problem behavior, other times not, no matter how great the effort. However, he eventually outgrows the behavior.

The tactics employed to promote a mechanical behavior change are different from those used to foster maturation, and the two, in fact, often conflict. An attempt to achieve behavior change can stifle growth. Likewise, making growth the objective can interfere with the change process. It is vital for families to appreciate the difference between these two processes so they can learn when to adopt the right kind of growth-inducing attitude toward their children. This is vital to the process of turning failure into growth.

THE DIFFERENCE BETWEEN CHANGE AND GROWTH

I attended a family therapy conference in the late 1980s in which the theme was the need to eliminate the placing of blame in efforts to change behavior. Experts in the field described how change in symptomatic behavior is not possible without acceptance of the problem behavior. This insight called for methods to help families view problem behavior in a positive light. A reframe is a classic example of an intervention designed for this purpose. It offers a new meaning, a new perspective, and a positive outlook on problematic behavior. The term *reframing* has since become a common term among clinicians, but was relatively new in those days.

At the conference, the abundance of videotaped material demonstrating this device was convincing. I could see the practical value of the method, but its lack of logic bothered me. Why can't a person simply be criticized, feel bad about harmful behavior, and derive from the experience the inspiration to change? To me it appeared that this was the proper and logical way to correct maladaptive patterns. It seemed to me that I changed my own behavior that way all the time. In fact, simple observation shows that adults often criticize and seek to bring about change in the problem-causing behaviors of others.

The key to understanding this paradox eventually became clear to me after years of witnessing the process of natural development in difficult children. Somewhere along the line I realized that people cannot be changed, nor can the fundamental behaviors that stem from their basic being. However, problem behaviors do change eventually through natural maturation. In other words, it is not always possible to achieve mechanical change in individuals with behavior problems, but the problems can be outgrown.

We know that 20-year-olds do not wet their beds, and we know that many of these 20-year-olds had parents who tried and failed to resolve their incontinence mechanically when they were 10. These individuals needed a chance to mature. I discussed the difference between change and growth in theoretical terms in Chapter 1. Here I present a simple explanation of the difference and an illustration of how the details can be communicated to a family.

Once families understand the nature of conflict that occurs between change and growth, they are ready to abandon the critical, punitive, and controlling tactics typically used to induce change. Instead, they derive confidence from their knowledge of natural development, adopt an encouraging attitude, and arrange for a series of consequences to take place that will foster genuine growth.

Seeking change involves pointing out the difference between the misbehavior displayed and the desired, normal, or good behavior. The emphasis is on what is missing or deficient in the individual's behavior. The attitude toward the deficiency is negative. The wish to escape the negative experience motivates the individual to change the behavior. Most parents rely largely on this critical attitude toward unwanted behavior to run their households.

Professionals often try to train parents and teachers to utilize a different approach. This one emphasizes a positive attitude toward the new and desired behavior, purposeful disregard of the unwanted behavior, and systematic rewards for occurrences of the desired behavior. This is behavior modification in a nutshell.

The problem with behavior modification is that it requires a professional with patience, proper attitude, and proficiency to deliver it. Parents simply cannot deliver it successfully if they share the popular impression that compulsion is the best method of dealing with problem behavior.

Children who are able to execute a behavior that they do not like respond well to tactics for inducing change. Those lacking maturity find themselves unable to accomplish the target behavior. Behavior modification proves futile in these cases, except in the very short term. The child manages to feign the desired behavior for short intervals but won't be able to maintain it.

Fostering growth involves accepting the child's present limitations and believing that maturation will eventually yield the desired behavior. Acceptance of a child's existing capacities makes it possible to appreciate his efforts to improve. Paul, the young man whose story was told in the preceding chapter, did host a party bordering on debauchery, but tried to clean up the mess it left, and did, in fact, tell his parents the truth about the episode. Their attitude toward his deficiencies remained positive.

Acceptance gives rise to a sense of belonging, which means an attachment founded on mutual trust, openness, and the intent to cooperate. This is in contrast to the lack of understanding and the criticism of the mechanical change process, which leave the individual feeling excluded.

The interactions that come from belonging yield growth in the attachment realm (the emotional brain). The energy exchange that comes with the openness feeds the attachment regions of the nervous system. Growth in this emotional realm yields happiness, fulfillment, generosity, and a wish for a better life. A negative reaction to flaws, however, leads to blaming, distance, distrust, and loss of energy. Children who feel disconnected also feel self-destructive. Those who feel they belong want to live more fully.

Maturation in the attachment realm yields increased dependency, which does not necessarily foster adaptive capacities. However, the wish to develop those capacities will be there. The intention will be to do well.

Once a child wants to live more fully and improve the quality of his life, the right consequences can stimulate the development of adaptive capacities. Here, the parents need to allow the child to struggle with consequences in order for these new capacities to develop and strengthen. The parents need to maintain a growth-inducing attitude, while at the same time fending off attendant dependency needs, with the result that the child's adaptive brain is challenged and forced to work. Children who remain in an isolated, self-destructive state won't even try to develop these capacities when challenged.

Of course, expectations must be reasonable when the child is attempting to succeed on his own. The goodness-of-fit concept (Chapter 1) applies here. Children can tell us accurately how much opportunity, support, and protection they need to manage their affairs. They may take advantage of their freedom for a while by seeking to gratify all their desires. However, the wish to grow is strong, and once they come to trust their parents' growth-encouraging attitude toward failure, they enjoy facing challenges on a more realistic basis. They welcome consequences. And finally, they develop a sense of pride in their accomplishments.

Parents can assist the process by manifesting a positive outlook toward failure, and maintaining a balance between a supportive attachment and freedom to exercise adaptive capacities so that the child develops a sense of belonging and a love of life. He will eventually get things right, so he can be permitted to do things his own way even though failure is the temporary result. Parents must accept weaknesses and maintain loving intentions, leading to maturation in the realm of attachment. In this atmosphere, the child develops strong adaptive capacities as well as confidence. He derives strength from the right amount of anxiety, struggle, and hardship. He fails, and tries again. This produces maturation in the adaptive realm.

Children may develop separation anxiety when success in life becomes important to them and they realize that the helpfulness formerly exhibited by their parents will be sharply reduced. This anxiety sends a signal from the attachment (emotional) brain, calling on the adaptive (rational) brain to utilize its own resources. The brain will begin construction of appropriate neural networks as life makes increasing demands on the individual's ability to cope on his own.

ENCOURAGEMENT AND DETACHMENT

The remedy for ODD involves a basic attitude on the part of parents that combines encouragement and detachment, especially in the event of failure. An encouraging voice expresses confidence in the natural growth process and in the ability of the child to realize his potential. It says, "Child, don't you worry if this goes wrong. You may have failed, but all of this will pass, and ten years from now you'll laugh at what happened. One thing is for sure: you will eventually grow strong and succeed at whatever you want. That's how this world works."

When failure occurs, this level of acceptance feeds and strengthens the bond with the child. It breeds confidence. This kind of attachment yields growth in the emotional realm, and with this growth come joy, the abandonment of self-destructive behavior, and the birth of new interests.

From the perspective of the two minds, the parents feed the emotional mind of the child a healthy dose of faith, an essential ingredient for its growth. Faith fosters trust, upon which all successful relationships depend. In response to this feeding, the emotional mind associates the parents with allies.

All that remains is for the child to learn to escape from traps and avoid falling into them—situations from which it is difficult to extricate himself. A child doesn't learn to escape from traps by reading a book on the subject. It takes direct experience with falling into and getting out of traps. However, they must be traps from which the child can free himself relatively unscathed with reasonable effort.

The parent must allow the child to fall into traps and then struggle to get out of them. This is where the detachment vis-à-vis the outcome of the day's events comes into play. It doesn't matter what the child did today. What happened won't change how he will eventually turn out. If the child chooses wisely, he will have taken another step in learning to succeed. If the child chooses unwisely, he will learn from the consequences and do better next time.

The chances of poor judgment leading to significant and lasting harm are small in a child who cares about himself and his family. Very destructive outcomes usually take place in the midst of desperate and misguided control battles. Destructive behaviors stem from the wish to call attention to one's suffering and to have an impact on someone who is important to the child, but who doesn't understand him. Unfortunate incidents take place under the cloak of deception, under strong peer pressure, and in a child who lacks self-confidence.

What matters is that reasonable consequences be arranged ahead of time, so the parent can detach from the child's choices, confident that learning will take place and the child won't be traumatized.

ARRANGING CONSEQUENCES TO PROMOTE GROWTH

A caterpillar struggles to break from its cocoon. A youngster sees and sympathizes with the caterpillar's apparent plight. He says to his friend, "I think I'll cut that cocoon open to set the poor caterpillar free."

"You do and you'll kill it," his friend warns. "The caterpillar needs to develop the strength it takes to break out of its cocoon before it can survive in the outside world."

The lesson of this story for human development is that nature's harsh consequences force children to become whole, to adapt and grow strong. A child senses an attitude of encouragement, light-heartedness, and acceptance from his elders. He develops a positive outlook on weakness and failure. He experiences significant growth in the attachment realm (emotional brain). He responds to challenges with constructive intentions. His encounters with hardship can then forge greater determination. His struggles lead to valuable lessons. Magnificent pathways are formed in the brain (neurological networks) to ease the struggle for survival and bolster the child's sense of worth.

A cocoon is a temporary home for the caterpillar, a source of nourishment and security that, like all homes, may become a trap. As the caterpillar grows, the home becomes an obstacle to realization of the opportunities presented by the world at large to the wider-ranging adult butterfly. Home stands between the caterpillar and its desire to fly in the wilderness. The need to break out of the cocoon challenges the caterpillar to exert those abilities important to his free-flying future.

The same holds for children. Home is their cocoon. Home should nourish and protect, but it should also allow reasonable obstacles to stand in the way of the children's pursuit of their dreams. This forces the children to struggle, gain strength, and develop useful abilities. In other words, home should protect but not allow children to get away with stupid behavior without consequences. Home should insist that children earn what they want with demonstrations of abilities that will make them effective in later life. For example, a child who wants a new guitar should demonstrate willingness to practice and to do some work to earn the instrument. A child who wants a new style of clothes should show that he can take proper care of his clothing.

Home should present challenges that lead wherever the child wishes to go. The challenges should strengthen the abilities he needs to follow his dreams. However, the parent must not tell the child what choices to make or what dreams to pursue. The initiative for these developments must come from the child and must follow a natural course. Forcing these functions on the child is tantamount to taking the nourishment out of the cocoon and interferes with the natural growth process.

The nature of home for a child depends largely on the child's current growth needs. These manifest themselves largely through his primary interests and need to be adjusted for his weaknesses. Nature creates cocoons that are just resistant enough to strengthen the caterpillar for its impending transformation. The cocoon prepared for a child must take into account his areas of interest, challenge his weaknesses, and emphasize his abilities.

The objective is to have young people pursue their interests in whatever way they choose, yet experience reasonable consequences at every turn. They should receive fair consequences for every choice they make. The more natural the consequence, that is, the more closely it resembles what happens in the outside world, the better. The only reason to alter a consequence is to prevent excessive trauma.

THREE SOURCES OF CONSEQUENCES

Three possible sources of consequences are biology, society, and family. Examples of biological consequences are the following: If you don't bathe you itch. If you go out into the cold undressed, you freeze. If you don't eat, you go hungry. If you don't sleep, you become tired. In contrast, neglect of responsibilities to school, work, or friends has societal consequences, such as rejection and failure. Finally, tormenting a sibling, refusing to help out around the house, being disrespectful or abusive toward others, disrupting family outings, misusing family property, violating curfew, and lying have family consequences. I instruct parents to deliver family consequences only when none come from the other sources. If the child's infractions precipitate biological or social consequences, the parent should play the role of ally and friend. The parent is present, positive, encouraging, and helpful at every failure point.

To prepare them to accept consequences, children should be instructed as follows: If you misuse a privilege, you lose it, and you must demonstrate respect for that privilege to get it back. This is a commonly recognized principle of behavior modification and is part of most parenting programs. Loss of privilege gives the child a taste of real-world consequences and invites moral reflection. This is the same principle used in time-outs with younger children. The need to demonstrate respect for the privilege lost will help the child develop a conscience. This means performing a reparative activity that initiates a cycle of respect, rather than simply doing time or enduring a punishment.

A child deliberately spills milk on the kitchen floor. To teach a lesson, the parents say that the child is no longer welcome there. He has lost the privilege of using the kitchen. However, if the child cleans up the kitchen and goes to the store to buy more milk, trust and the use of the privilege are restored, and the child feels welcome, knowing that he has made up for his mistake.

The same reparation principle fits most infractions. If a child mistreats a family member, the consequence is to engage in an activity with, and act like the best friend of that member. Create a mess, clean it up. Misuse the computer, demonstrate proper use of it. With this system, reparations become positive and potentially enjoyable acts that teach important lessons, restore trust, and initiate positive cycles of respect. Each consequence can be delivered to the child in a friendly, positive, and encouraging manner.

In the traditional deterrent system, however, the child is treated with a critical, punitive attitude to discourage him from repeating an infraction. The child is punished by loss of privileges and either does a time-out or is grounded. If the child must perform some act to make up for misbehavior, it's usually an unpleasant one, like paying money or cleaning a toilet. In theory, the unpleasant consequence makes the infraction not worth repeating.

The deterrent system initiates a negative tit-for-tat cycle of distrust between the child and authority. It works only for those mature enough to behave properly. ODD children often see the deterrent as unfair. They tend to externalize blame, be vindictive, and lie to escape consequences. The child does time-out or cleans a toilet but doesn't necessarily demonstrate proper use of the privilege. The child rarely sees the positive side of discipline and authority. He never sees the positive side of respecting privileges to increase his sense of belonging and trustworthiness. The deterrent system simply does not work with ODD teenagers.

The alternative is for parents and school officials to impose on an ODD teenager a system of consequences that incorporates the loss of privileges followed by reparations. The parents deliver consequences for infractions that have no consequences from other sources. School authorities deliver consequences for infractions that affect the child's functioning at school. Still other infractions have natural biological and peer-related consequences.

The clinician's job is to train parents to deliver the right consequences at home and consult with teachers so they will deliver the right consequences at school. The family buffers excessively harsh consequences from biology and peers (society). Infractions related to school, biology, or peers are, in effect, off the parents' plate. Once parents and school officials reach an accord, the parents can allow their child to decide how to handle things and avoid further conflict.

The knowledge that other sources will deliver appropriate consequences will free the parents to become friendly allies of their offspring and to focus more on their own personal lives. They can emphasize the importance of a happy home life, something over which they have more control. The knowledge that sources outside the family will deliver consequences will force the ODD teenager to utilize his own adaptive brain functions to avoid traps. This will foster maturation in the adolescent.

I offer families the following guidelines during my training sessions with them. The teenager, the parents, and the therapist meet to discuss a new way to parent the emotional brain-dominated teenager, and start with situations in which the parents function as allies when the child faces consequences from biological and societal sources.

PARENTS AS ALLIES AND PROTECTORS

The clinician has introduced the family to the steps of putting the teenager in charge, emphasizing the positive side of failure, and adopting an encouraging stance. (See A Preevaluation Trial Intervention in Chapter 3, and The Therapeutic Side of Failure in Chapter 5.) Once these elements are in place, the parents build upon them to set up a home situation in which they can walk away from conflict, with appropriate buffers from trauma in place for both the parents and the teenager.

Step 1: Define Freedom

With the parents present, the clinician defines freedom and its limitations this way for the teenager: "We expect you to take care of your responsibilities at home, even if you are busy elsewhere. The freedom of grown-ups means you handle your life your own way outside of home but take increased responsibilities at home. Adults pay rent, clean, and cook. Your rent for living at home will be to help with a fair share of the housework and to contribute to the quality of family life, in addition to taking care of the responsibilities in your own personal life."

The amount of work the parents assign varies, based on the child's maturity and ability, but the learning principle remains the same. Each individual is required to manage his own responsibilities, including his room, laundry, social plans, and work obligations. Each individual takes responsibility for a fair share of communal obligations, including kitchen duties and maintenance of common living areas, including living room, bathrooms, den, and the grounds around the house. They also include contributing to the atmosphere of the household by maintaining a good disposition and displaying a positive attitude.

Increased responsibilities in the home have a stabilizing effect on the teenager's life outside. He can now focus on friends and de-emphasize studying. He and his friends can plan a day that makes them happy, but he still must shoulder a significant load of responsibility at home. He can earn money with extra work. Completion of tasks creates a positive attitude toward family. It also prepares the teenager to live successfully outside the home. It promotes respect, appreciation, and social skills.

Step 2: Arrange Home So Parents Can Walk Away from Infractions

In a plan of action calling for assistance from others, the parents walk away from infractions calling for consequences by persons outside the family. To make the tactic effective, they call on neighbors, friends, relatives, baby-sitters, school personnel, truancy officers, youth workers, church members, and house-sitters for assistance in watching little ones, providing transportation, locating temporary storage and living space, and enforcing rules or laws.

Each family's support requirements will be different, as will the availability of people to help out. The clinician asks the family to prepare for walking away by listing sources of support as well as possible consequences for the youth's infractions. Most families will be able to assess the possibilities for assistance realistically and will find some support sources available.

It is important for the clinician to keep three factors in mind when he instructs parents on how to arrange their home life so they can walk away from their child's infractions. (1) It is essential for parents to keep the number of battles with their ODD teenager in which they are willing to engage to a minimum. Thus, it is wise to have adults outside the family administer consequences. (2) It is better for families to make whatever sacrifices are necessary to secure the resources needed to resolve a problem than it is for them to attempt to manage without them. (3) ODD youths tend to escalate misbehavior in the presence of their parents, and, conversely, to de-escalate in their absence. Parental absence invites reflection and self-awareness in the teenager and helps induce in him a critical shift from an emotional to a rational-mind dominance.

A central theme in Ross Greene's book, *The Explosive Child* (1998), is the importance of minimizing the need for parental control and authority. The lesson is simple. By their nature, these teenagers are different. Their level of frustration tolerance and control over emotion is deficient, so parents can't afford to get involved with them in the struggles typical of traditional parenting. They must choose their battles carefully and be willing to sacrifice input on many issues so they can focus on the few issues they select that are worth enduring a "meltdown" over (to use Greene's terminology). These include safety and respect for the basic rights of family members.

Most conflict-laden scenarios thrive on parental presence and emotional-mind dominance. Once the parent leaves and the youth is left alone reason tends to take over, and the situation de-escalates. From a legal perspective, these youths are old enough (after 12) to be left alone at home for substantial periods of time, though it may be prudent to ask an adult to monitor the situation from a distance. Many, however, cannot be trusted to remain at home alone because of the possibility that they will use the chance to undertake an inappropriate activity like hosting a party and serving alcohol. Nevertheless, if left alone unexpectedly while they are angry, many will cool off, reflect, and regain control. While the popular view may be that they are likely to blow up and retaliate against whoever is in the line of fire when the parent is absent, this does not occur in the overwhelming majority of cases.

It may be more costly to employ a decisive intervention to resolve a situation rapidly than to endure daily battles without taking corrective action. But in the long run the investment proves cost effective and clinically prudent. Long-term struggles with inadequate resources result in impasses that confirm and strengthen the ODD symptoms. These situations will drag on and on and thwart development.

I have found that it is often necessary to fashion an extensive support network in order to maintain an intervention for several months to resolve a specific type of infraction. Such might be the case with an intervention to prevent a teenager from falling prey to the influence of a drug-involved peer group now, rather than to pay for residential drug treatment later. Children whose violent outbursts are not contained often become abusive and face problems with police, and those who have their entitlement catered to without intervention tend to develop serious psychiatric problems.

It should be kept in mind in connection with the withdrawal of parental presence that conflicts take place when the parties involved fall into states of emotional-mind dominance. The very presence of the parent triggers an emotional response in the youth (See Chapter 2), and the presence of the youth triggers the same response in the parents. This translates into a fight-flight state and a re-enactment of old battles. The way to regain rational-mind dominance is to take a time-out and invite reflection.

To repeat the principle, when an emotion-dominated teenager is threatening aggressive behavior, the best way for the parent to cope is to leave the scene, irresponsible though this may seem to others. In fact, the teenager is not likely to act out his aggressions in the parent's absence. Experience shows that any form of parental attention fuels the oppositional display. When the parent leaves the scene, the fueling effect is gone, and in the overwhelming majority of cases the teenager experiences a rapid shift to rational-mind dominance. He becomes a different person.

In those rare instances where the teenager seeks to "get even" by damaging the property after his parents walk out, prompt correcive action is necessary if this tendency to violence is not to progress. Police may have to arrest the teenager for commitment to the court probationary system as a strong warning that this behavior will not be tolerated. The alternative to such stern measures to stop the violence may be long-term psychiatric care, with a consequent heavy financial burden on the family. I address the issue of violence later in this section, and then in greater detail in Chapter 10 under "Countering Narcissistic Rage."

Without involving themselves directly, but taking pains not to seem neglectful, the parents make sure that if the teenager fails to fulfill a responsibility he endures a reasonable consequence imposed by others. The teenager ends up in a position where he can make stupid choices but grow from the experience. Following are examples of how parents can walk away from situations knowing that their children will experience logical consequence for their choices.

*It's time for the parents to go to work, and the child is
not ready for school.*

The goal of the intervention is to have an alternative mode of
transportation in place for the day and have the school administer a consequence for lateness that will motivate the teenager to
be ready on time in the future.

The transportation problem can be handled in a variety of ways.
Each family will know what is possible in its own situation. The
child can walk or ride a bike to school if this is a reasonable option. His tardiness will trigger a consequence from the school that
will motivate the youth to be on time in the future. A parent can
provide the youth with a ride but take his time, so the child is late
and receives the planned consequence. This option would require
the parents to have sufficient flex time in their jobs to allow them
to be late for work. Sometimes a friend, relative, or church member can offer transportation if the youth lives some distance from
school and has missed his ride.

If the parents anticipate lateness as a problem, they should have
back up transportation in place and not be taken by surprise. They
should arrange it with their employers so that they will not be
penalized for being late for work if this is necessary to transport
the student to school. Teachers should be asked to provide a significant consequence for the teenager, such as detention, loss of
credit for the first class of the day, or loss of the privilege of participating in a valued extra-curricular activity for the day.

When he misses his early ride and knows he will arrive at school
late the desired response from the adolescence is anxiety. While
leaving the youth primarily in charge of how he gets up and read-
ies himself for school in the future, the parents offer supports to
help him avoid any more consequences. They may offer wake-up
calls, reminders, and help with preparations, stipulating only that
the youth must welcome and respect their help.

It is possible, however, that the youth will refuse to serve his
detention or respond with apathy to whatever privilege loss the
school may administer. He may let his grades drop or lose credits
altogether. The parents can respond to the adolescent's miscar-

ried response in one of two ways. They can invite more severe consequences by allowing the lateness to accumulate to the point that a truancy officer or youth worker is assigned to the case. A truancy officer can arrange transportation and administer serious consequences for failure to attend school.

The alternative is for the parents to reduce the pressure and sanction the lateness. This scenario has proven effective with youths who lack motivation for school and are extremely difficult, yet are improving and responding well to treatment in other ways. The school can schedule an open first period in the morning, and the parents can provide an alternative mode of transportation on the days that the teenager oversleeps. This works when the youth can walk to school, a parent has flex time, or a friend of the family provides transportation on a regular basis. This kind of support can make a positive difference in the disposition of an otherwise very difficult child.

The child acts up in public places

The primary goal of the intervention in this situation is to interrupt the emotional-mind dominance of the moment and invite rational-mind dominance, employing the principle that ODD youths who are misbehaving shift to a state of reflection and rational-mind dominance when their parents leave.

A second goal of this intervention is to invite consequences from sources outside the family. The objective is to influence the youth through what he believes is the pressure of public opinion. This allows the parent to adopt the role of ally more often and to reserve his role as limit-setter for the situations that require parental administration of consequences.

The first step in this intervention, which is performed in public, is for the parents to separate themselves from the child by going to the family car without him or moving away in another direction. Later in this chapter (See Managing the Teenager's "In Your Face" Tactics) I introduce a more sophisticated protocol for handling aggressive demands. That protocol culminates in the parent walking away from the situation anyway. I skip this level of detail for the purposes of this discussion. However, both interventions are compatible.

The desired response is for the youth to become self-conscious and embarrassed by his childish behavior. I recall a graphic illustration of this response in the early years of my practice. My office is in a university town, and in the lower level of my building is a busy ATM machine. Every fall, a class of freshmen comes into town and many young students open bank accounts. On this occasion, a young man obviously new to his surroundings attempted to make a withdrawal, but the machine showed his account was short of the necessary funds. When he was denied his request, he banged on the machine. After a minute or two of this angry display he realized that he was getting nothing for his efforts and became aware that a long line of people were watching. The young man blushed, blamed the institution of banking for his problems, and stormed off. Weeks later I was on hand for a second time when the same young man stood in front of the ATM machine again. Once more there was a crowd of people. Once more he didn't have the funds he needed in his account. However, this time his reaction was markedly different. There was no violence. He mumbled, "Damn it, I thought I had put money in there," and walked away quietly. I remember thinking that the machine had taught the boy something that his parents weren't able to teach him before he came to college.

Once the ODD teenager who has been misbehaving in public becomes self-conscious and has stopped pressuring his parent, the parent can offer the youth the choice of either cooperating for the remainder of the outing, or loss of privileges. (See Parents as Enforcers of Consequences later in this chapter for a detailed description.) The youth who refuses to cooperate loses all the privileges usually provided by family. To regain them he must go on a similar outing to prove that he can behave like a model child.

A miscarried response from the adolescent might be following the parent to the car or making a scene in public. He might damage property. If the youth follows the parent, the parent would walk away from the public place, thus taking that pressure off himself. He would then administer a loss of privileges. If the youth causes a scene or inflicts damages, the parent should report the incident to the appropriate authority. In a store, for example, the manager or head of security would be notified. In a restaurant, notification would be to the öwner or manager. In making the report the parent would take pains to let the authority know that a responsible party who cares for the child is present and that the child needs the lesson imparted by the consequence that the establishment usually doles out to troublemakers. This intervention is similar to what parents typically do when they discover that their children have shoplifted, and take them to the respective stores to return the stolen goods and face the consequences of their actions. Such an intervention teaches many youths not to steal. Depending on the level of infraction and the consequence doled out by the store manager, the parent may decide to administer a consequence of his own. Once again, the youth loses all privileges and must behave like a model child in a similar outing in order to regain them.

The teenager is purposely making the family late

This spoils the family atmosphere and threatens to ruin the outing altogether. The goal of the intervention in this case is similar to the one above involving tardiness in going to school. It is to anticipate the situation by having a sitter watch while the family enjoys its outing. The anxiety caused by being left out of the activity should motivate the teenager to join the rest of the family in being on time in the future.

The parents can handle the need for a house sitter in a variety of ways. The process can start with removal of privileges like the TV, stereo, computer, and video game machines if the child dawdles or refuses to get ready for the outing. This serves as a nonverbal prelude to the impending consequence. If the parents anticipate the youth making the family late for his own selfish reasons they should not be taken by surprise, and should have the sitter ready to take over in case they decide to leave without the teenager. Such an episode may even be arranged specifically to teach the ODD teenager a lesson. Once the youth has endured this level of consequence, he will think twice before holding the family hostage in this way. A successful response from the adolescent would be a high level of anxiety about being left behind and losing privileges. To regain the lost privileges, the youth would have to be ready to leave on time and remain helpful and pleasant in a similar kind of outing in the future.

While leaving the youth primarily in charge of his own conduct, the parents can offer supports to head off situations in which consequences for being late would again become necessary. They can offer reminders and help in getting ready, as long as the adolescent welcomes and respects the help.

A miscarried response by the adolescent would be for him to remain unconcerned with the consequence of being left behind. In this case, he might refuse to support future outings and respond with apathy to privilege loss. He might seem depressed or become increasingly hostile.

The parents can respond in one of two ways. They can increase the pressure by locking the youth out of the house when they go on a family outing. They can, however, reduce the pressure by allowing the teenager to do his own thing when there is an outing. He can then make a choice between joining the family for the outing or being dropped off at a friend's house or at a preferred hangout like the mall or local youth club. The parents can even go so far as provide the youth with money for food and entertainment. He can work to earn this level of support. The family can also offer to take a friend on the outing.

Reducing pressure to conform with family objectives proves effective with depressed youths who constantly seek conflict and indulge in self-pity. The clinician must decide whether to pressure the youth or turn these outings into situations in which everyone in the family has a good time, even if they aren't together. Such positive experiences can make a big difference in the life of a depressed and self-destructive ODD teenager.

The child threatens to damage property

The goal of the intervention is to interrupt the destructive state of emotional-mind dominance and induce a shift to rational-mind dominance. The parents should minimize the possibility of destruction of property, yet teach the teenager that aggression will get him nowhere. This intervention is based on the same principle that applied when the teenager was making a scene in public. It is that the oppositional teenager shifts to rational-mind dominance and becomes a different person when the parents walk away.

The parents should plan ahead to encounter this behavior so they will be ready to cut off privileges and remove themselves from the situation, leaving the youth to reflect, but with a positive option for constructive action that would restore the lost privileges. To protect property, the parents place valuables in storage and take whatever other steps they find feasible to reduce chances of serious damage to furniture and other belongings in case of a tantrum. They announce a cut in privileges, and leave. This may be followed on the part of the teenager by a short outburst of anger and thoughts of getting even. For a time he may wait for the family to return to give them a piece of his mind. However, as the minutes pass he cools down and thinks better of what he's doing. He notices that the process for regaining privileges is positive and relatively easy. Reflection leads to remorse and the desire to make things right. The youth performs a reparative act and earns his privileges by the time the parents get home. This is a relatively satisfactory resolution of the problem.

The parents restore privileges once the youth has completed his reparation. The adolescent may become anxious when he is left at home alone not knowing where the family has gone or when they'll be back. He may complain about this when the parents return. The parents can then negotiate an honor system in which the youth is handed a written demand for reparation after the next infraction, and the parents do not leave the house as long as the youth refrains from threatening to damage property.

If they do leave, the family may feel the need for an ally to watch the house. The neighbor, friend, relative, church member, or youth worker performing this service should be given a telephone number to call in case something goes wrong.

A miscarried response by the adolescent may entail damage to property. He may, for example, put his fist through a wall. One did while I was conducting group therapy in my office. To emphasize the discomfort caused by such misdeeds, I made the group responsible for repairs as a condition for the continuation of the sessions. Parents can take similar action if their teenager damages property before cooling off. They can require the youth to repair the damage he caused in addition to performing the reparation prescribed for regaining privileges.

This intervention parallels what behaviorists do with children who trash their rooms while in time-out. Once they complete the time-out, they have to put the room back in order before coming out of it. Once they have gone through this ordeal, it is unlikely that they will trash their rooms again during any future time-out.

If the damage is severe, the parents should report it to the authorities and invite consequences from sources outside the family. The youth can, for example, be taken to court and forced to pay for the damages. Often a period of probation is required to help ensure that the youth does not resort to violence against his family.

Chances are that a youth who is this violent will terrorize and hold the family hostage. Experience has taught me that the clinician must eliminate the child's option of using physical force against the family or treatment will be useless, because every time a consequence is due for deviant behavior the youth will use physical force to get his way. (See Chapter 10, Special Problem 3, Excessive Aggression.) There is no way to counter a child's narcissistic entitlement if the child rules the family with brute strength.

The cost of some broken furniture, a broken window, or a hole in the wall is relatively small compared to the cost of allowing a child to grow up with the pathology of violating his own family. If the youth is this aggressive, the parent's presence will not stop the destructive behavior and may make it worse. The cost of this level of pathology can eventually become incarceration or psychiatric hospitalization. The family must do whatever is necessary to stop the threat of physical force used against family members or property.

The teenager is bullying or harassing others in the family

The goal of the intervention is to remove the targeted family member from the situation, invite reflection and a shift to rational-mind dominance, and get the family members to demonstrate respect for each other. Once more, the intervention relies on the walk-away principle for parents.

Again, the parents should plan ahead. They should be ready to remove the other party involved, usually a sibling, from the situation and curtail the offender's privileges for having harmed another family member and spoiled the family atmosphere. Both siblings must demonstrate willingness to work and play together like best friends for the culprit to regain privileges. They can fake the friendship if they like, but they must contribute to the family atmosphere and demonstrate respect for each other.

A somewhat successful response from the adolescent would be a short period of complaining about the sibling (or other party), and then a willingness to make things up. The youth may resist the reparation for a while, insisting that he hates the sibling. However, as time passes, he cools down and realizes it is better to be a friend with privileges than do without and forfeit the enjoyment provided by electronics, favors, money, or having friends over. The quality playtime gets the two parties together. Both have an excuse to act as friends, so they save face. Soon they forget their differences and genuinely begin to enjoy each other. The youths regain privileges and continue to play well together.

The parent may have to mediate the play in instances where siblings can't share a particular activity well. A coin and a timer will often settle the problem. The choice of activity and the length of turns can be decided by a coin toss. One child chooses the first activity, the other child chooses the next. One child chooses the duration of each turn for the first activity. The other child chooses the duration of each turn in the next activity. The parent uses a timer to inform the youths of when it is time to take turns. Refusal to follow this structure leads to a loss of privileges for the child who is unwilling to cooperate.

If the parents fear for the safety of one of their children, they may need to place him outside the home until his tormentor is ready to perform the reparation required. The parents place the vulnerable child in the custody of an ally who is able to help. The availability of this individual should be established ahead of time. After such a limit has been set a few times, the offending youth will learn to respond to the privilege loss, and the services of the ally will no longer be necessary.

A miscarried response by the adolescent may entail a serious attempt to harm the other family member. This rarely happens. However, if it does the parents should report the offense to the authorities and invite consequences from sources outside the family. The youth should be charged with abuse and taken to court. Once again, a period of probation is warranted until the adolescent realizes that harming another family member is unacceptable.

The parents arrange to go out with the teenager in the family car

The teenager misbehaves. Again, the goal is to interrupt the emotional-mind dominance of the moment and induce a shift to rational-mind dominance by inviting reflection. This situation also relates to the principle that ODD youths tend to escalate misbehavior in the presence of their parents and shift to a state of reflection and rational mind dominance in the parents' absence. A second goal is to ensure the safety of any younger siblings who may be in the car with the teenager.

The parents accomplish their goals by pulling over, walking away from the car, and, if necessary, calling to cancel an engagement or explain why they'll be late in arriving at their destination. The parents should take any vulnerable family members with them. Usually, when one child acts out the others cooperate with the parents by becoming helpful. In the rare case that a younger and vulnerable sibling volunteers to remain in the car with the ODD teenager, the parents should respect his wishes but be vigilant in the event that they are needed. If the pair stay together, chances are they will form an alliance. The desired response is for the offending youth to decide to behave in order to escape the boredom of sitting in an idle car by the side of the road. Once he has gained rational control and decided to respect the parents, they can continue with the trip as though nothing has happened or dole out the consequence of privilege loss. (See Parents as Enforcers of Consequences later in this chapter for a description of how privileges are removed and regained.) The youth would lose all privileges usually provided by family. To regain these privileges he would have to go on a similar car outing to prove that he can behave like a model child.

Often the problem that takes place in the car involves sibling conflict—who gets the front seat, who gets to listen to a favorite station, or who gets to place his legs where. The parent would handle this in the same way that sibling fights were discussed in the previous situation involving sibling abuse. The parent can use a coin and a stop watch to decide who gets a turn at a desired position in the car, who gets it next, and for how long.

A miscarried response from the adolescent might be jumping out of the car into traffic, taking the keys from the parent, or refusing to calm down when the parent returns to the car. In the event that the teenager jumps out of the car into traffic, the parent may have to give in to whatever the teenager wants to appease him. This may be the only option left for the parent if the safety of the child is at stake and the parent lacks the strength to restrain him, as is often the case.

Most teenagers know better than to jump out of a car into traffic. However, younger siblings may endanger themselves this way. If a younger sibling decides to pursue this course of action, the parent must use physical force to control the child.

In the event that the youth continues to misbehave every time the parents return to the car, the parents will simply have to wait out the crisis, no matter how long it takes. Once the ordeal ends, the parents administer a loss of privileges. To make up, the teenager will have to go on a similar outing and behave like a model child while the parents drive to their destination.

In all of these situations, the parents have the option of giving in to the teenager if the response of the youth is destructive and a threat to safety. The parents may bribe the teenager to temporarily defuse the situation until they have an opportunity to plan to administer a consequence under more favorable circumstances. This option is detailed later in this chapter.

Step 3: Arranging Buffers for Parents

The parents should anticipate the supports they will need so they may in turn provide their children with buffers that will allow them the freedom to make decisions and commit errors. For example, the parent may be late for work as a result of some involvement with the child. He may, however, be able to create a buffer by arranging for flex time with his company or a system to warn the boss of possible tardiness. The parents may have their social plans threatened. They may need to arrange for child care or place younger children in a safe place before they go out. They may experience a spoiled family event because of a badgering, dawdling, or destructive teenager. They may arrange with relatives to take care of the young ones, ask neighbors to watch the house during their absence, and then go for a walk or ride.

Parents expecting violent behavior from their teenager need to meet with the clinician separately to agree on measures to be taken in case it occurs. The parents may have to contact the police if the child is violent. They may need to arrange a preliminary meeting with a knowledgeable officer so that when a call comes in, the police won't respond too vigorously. It may help for the clinician to speak with law enforcement or court-appointed officials about the case. This will make it easier for the parents to call the appropriate service for help when they are confronted by violence.

The parents may also arrange matters so they can leave a scene of violence without, at that point, calling police. They can bribe the threatening teenager, or give in to his demands as a way to remove the immediate threat. This buys them time to arrange consequences from a position of strength. Once they are separated from the offending child, they can store valuables, remove younger children, arrange to have the house watched, decide on removal of privileges, and leave. It should be recalled that parental absence will invite reflection and facilitate a shift from emotional to rational mind dominance.

Step 4: Arranging Buffers for Teenagers

The first step in the process of providing buffers for the ODD teenager is to present him with a list of all the supports and protections the family can offer, and to tell him he has the right to choose his own consequences. Consequences that can be expected for various infractions are reviewed as well as possible buffers. Families can offer their children reminders; assist with planning, organizing, and completing a task; and provide or withhold permission to engage in various activities. Parents can also meet with authority figures to modify consequences or expectations. They can offer transportation or other resources. They can enroll the teenager in classes, clubs, teams, and other activities. And they can hire tutors and personal trainers.

The clinician often needs to arrange meetings with outside authorities, including teachers, so they will understand and deliver reasonable consequences. The child has selected the buffers he thinks will help from the list offered him.

It is clearly worthwhile for families to invest considerable resources for a short time to ensure a good fit between school expectations and the child's abilities. Children spend far too many hours in the school environment to allow a poor fit to continue. It makes no sense for a child to attend counseling sessions for one hour every week (or every two weeks), and then have to go for thirty to sixty hours between sessions with important needs neglected.

There are instances in which the clinician can prepare parents to advocate for their children during office visits. The clinician documents the youth's special needs and related recommendations. The parents can then attend the school meeting with a written agenda. Many cases can be resolved in this cost-effective manner.

However, there are instances when it becomes necessary for the clinician to attend a school meeting to represent the family. This requirement occurs when there are emotional complications along with learning and attention deficits. Matters of the emotional mind are not rational yet have a powerful influence on the youth's behavior and development. Because the emotional mind is not rational, the conditions to which the child will respond well are not logical. It is hard for schools to comprehend this. An additional complication is that by themselves, parents have difficulty advocating for a method as alien to traditional authority as this intervention. The parents' lack of professional credentials makes it difficult for them to convince school officials of the soundness of the approach, even if they are able to state the case well.

The attendance of a clinician does not guarantee that the school will heed his advice and properly address the child's legitimate needs. In such instances, the family may wish to hire a professional advocate familiar with the state education laws. Extreme difficulty in gaining acceptance of the program may call for the family to hire a lawyer to represent them and assert their rights.

Hiring a clinician or advocate to attend school meetings, or retaining a lawyer to advocate for the family's needs is in keeping with an important brief-treatment principle, namely that it is better to invest considerable resources in the short term to get at the root cause of a serious problem than to attempt to struggle with it over a long time with inadequate resources. At first glance, this course of action may seem prohibitively costly, but there are many instances in which major sacrifices by the family have been justified by results.

Sometimes schools do not provide services because they lack funds and feel they will not be challenged. However, families have extensive rights and considerable power to influence decisions that affect the future of their children. Problems arise when children are denied their rights because their parents do not realize the extent of their entitlements. With capable advocacy, families can expect to have their children's legitimate needs met.

Some ODD youths present with underlying learning, social, and emotional deficits that require costly interventions. Outside placements may cost as much as $60,000 annually. Even minimal intervention can cost $5,000 a year. Without correct support some ODD youths will remain virtually illiterate or emotionally disturbed. It is clearly worth hiring professional advisors when so much is at stake.

Economically disadvantaged families can seek assistance. I have been paid a number of times by schools to attend meetings and provide consultation for an acting-out ODD client of mine. Many schools find this option desirable, knowing that the families cannot afford my fee. Once a school has exhausted its resource, but remains concerned about the well being of the student, it generally becomes willing to pay for an outside consultant.

When dealing with uncooperative schools, however, low-income families can seek pro bono representation from law firms or legal agencies that provide this kind of service. Universities often offer legal support for those who need it. Parents can also study state education laws and represent themselves in arbitration with the school. I have worked with families who have documented their children's needs, have documented specific instances where the school failed to meet their children's needs, and have requested a formal hearing, in which they successfully challenged the school's attorney. Organizations like Children with Attention Deficit Disorder (CHADD) offer advocacy advice without charge to needy families.

Once the family determines who should be present to represent the child, the parties involved should meet with teachers to discuss the ground rules they will apply in the child's program and the standards for his conduct. The school has every right to turn down the proposals, and all parties involved should know this (especially the ODD youth). Teachers should be offered its rationale and asked how closely the school can match what the therapist and the family consider the best program for the child. However, the child's right to make choices when matters are decided should be established.

It should be made clear that the nature of the intervention is to provide the child with opportunities to make the choices and take the consequences, and not necessarily for him to make correct choices at this time. The aim of the procedure is to develop frontal lobe functions by creating the need and opportunities for the ODD teenager to make his own choices, and, in doing so, to determine his own consequences. The school must understand that this is a growth-based, not a change-based model.

The clinician and the family should hold a preparation meeting to agree on an agenda and discuss the intervention and the desired consequence adjustments. It is up to the family to schedule a meeting with teachers or others whose cooperation is necessary. It should be determined whether the family needs an advocate other than the therapist, such as a lawyer or a letter from the teenager's pediatrician. All those concerned should know the standard rules and consequences of the school or other organization involved and the rights of the child and his family.

It will help to create a summary sheet on which to organize items for an upcoming meeting, including the youth's special needs and the program requirements. The teenager should be prepared for the meeting if possible, since he needs to be in charge and must have the right to change his mind about the support he will receive. The clinician should, however, make it clear that neither he nor the family can guarantee a successful outcome of the meeting.

The consequences must remain reasonable. They need to motivate but not cause trauma. Worst-case infractions should be anticipated so that the school is prepared to deal with them. A written request for adjustments to consequences based on the teenager's expected needs should be submitted to the school.

The ODD teenager should attend the meeting. The clinician should tape record the meeting in case unreasonable obstacles emerge, but should explain to the child that he cannot expect to get everything he wants. The family should be urged to anticipate any difficulties they might encounter at the meeting, consider what the school offers in connection with the specifics of the program, but make no immediate decision on whether to go forward.

The meeting should be followed by a debriefing during which the clinician summarizes the outcome for the family and explains the choices left for the child. Consequences for anticipated infractions should be formulated in the light of the different options provided by the school. For example, if the pupil is late or absent more than ten times, but has a written excuse from his parents, he will fail to get credit in the subjects he misses but won't be punished through detention. Buffers should be adjusted to the consequences based on the choices the child has made.

The clinician may have to advise the family to request further meetings with teachers or pursue other avenues of assistance for his client if the plan does not work as intended. As stated earlier, the family may wish to hire a professional advocate familiar with the state education laws to demonstrate to the youth that every option has been exhausted to support their choices. The adolescent must request the additional meetings, participate actively, and take charge of the effort to gain empowerment. The key for participants is to gain the youth's trust in them as allies at the emotional-mind level.

The ODD teenager must decide whether to accept the options offered at the meeting or continue to advocate for different buffers. Interim buffers should be supplied until the issue is settled. The clinician should continue in his role as advocate for the child's emotional brain for as long as needed, while allowing others to challenge any unrealistic demands of the teenager. The long-term trust derived from this process will pay off handsomely in future crises. The clinician, and the family by association, will gain places as powerful allies of the youth's emotional mind, whereas his only allies previously were his peers. This places them in a position to positively influence the adolescent for a long time to come.

PARENTS AS ENFORCERS OF CONSEQUENCES

Certain infractions will not result in biological or societal consequences. Consequences must then come from the family, and the parents must be trained to deliver them. Fortunately for most clinicians, established limit-setting practices will work effectively. Many professionals who read this book will have training in non-punitive privilege removal and restoration methods. Time-out, tough love, and substance abuse treatment programs share the same psychological technology of privilege loss without resorting to unnecessary punitive measures.

Three issues must be kept in mind by the clinician when he is training parents to deliver consequences to seriously ODD youths: (1) the intervention cannot be negative, (2) the ODD child must perform some reparative activity to regain lost privileges, and (3) the intervention must be limited to specific infractions that do not involve consequences from outside the family.

ODD behavior thrives on negativity. The ODD teenager loses perspective, allows his feelings to overwhelm him, and becomes involved in a tit-for-tat contest with those around him that will eventually grow into abusive control battles. Under these circumstances, parents must maintain an encouraging stance, and remain ostensibly uninterested in the outcome of the child's choices. They must detach themselves from events while the child is choosing to earn privileges or lose them, enjoy success or experience loss, learn a lesson, and grow to appreciate the family. ODD teenagers instantly discern and take advantage of any sign from the parents that they wish for things to turn out positively. Spoiling the hopes of others is an irresistible temptation to these troubled youths. It is the signature, the sine qua non, of ODD.

Methods like time-out—isolation of the child and suspension of all his activities—often are turned into punishments by parents who can only think of deterrents. The psychology of deterrence aims to end unwanted behavior right away by making the consequences of the infraction painful. Parents have a hard time inflicting this level of pain on their children so they use threats. The threats ring hollow to the oppositional child once he has called his parents' bluff enough times. By failing or becoming self-destructive, the ODD teenager will retaliate for any deterrents imposed.

As a matter of course, parents may adopt society's attitude of approval for deterrence, and with it an aggressiveness that tells the ODD teenager never to repeat that infraction. Their need to control the ODD behavior will drive the parents to escalate the consequences from time-out to grounding. The consequence of doing a time-out to regain privileges has an appeal because of its simplicity and may be fine for younger children incapable of performing useful restitution. However, it doesn't do much to foster respect for privileges.

ENFORCER VS. ALLY: WHICH HAT TO WEAR

In their zeal to make their child succeed, parents often interfere with every choice he makes. This leaves them in a position of micromanaging every behavior, fostering dependency, and participating in exhausting control battles. Many infractions will elicit consequences from sources other than the parents. Consequences coming from outside provide the parents with opportunities to adopt the role of friend and ally described earlier in this chapter. Parents should limit their enforcer role to the following infractions:

- Spoiling the family atmosphere
- Refusing to help out around the house
- Hurting a sibling
- Launching personal attacks on a parent
- Showing disrespect for parents' help
- Misusing family property
- Embarrassing the family in front of guests and in other social settings
- Misusing freedom to go out—specifically, violating curfew in a way that causes anxiety in parents
- Violating trust through deception or theft of family property.

All other infractions will have consequences from society or biology, and parents should not adopt the role of enforcer in those cases.

The consequence for most of these infractions should involve loss of all privileges. This means access to electronics (TV, stereo, video games, computer), having friends over, favors, money, rides, parental help, and participation in family activities. The teenager who loses privileges receives only food, shelter, and medical care. Infractions that affect the entire family warrant this level of privilege loss. This is the equivalent of a time-out for those who are younger.

Other infractions require limited privilege loss. Disrespect for parental help warrants the loss of further help, so the parent goes off duty as a reminder service, a transportation service, a tutor, an ally against social consequences, and a source of income. Misusing family property means loss of the use of that specific item. If the logical consequence is not enforceable, such as loss of kitchen privileges, for example, and the kitchen can't be closed, the child is asked to follow the honor system. If the child uses the item without earning its reinstatement, the behavior becomes a violation of trust, and warrants full loss of privileges.

If the child violates curfew, he loses the privilege of going out. Parents can enforce this consequence by informing the families of peers that furnishing assistance to the child would be contributing to the delinquency of a minor. Court-appointed enforcement is warranted for children who refuse to yield this privilege and earn it properly.

The reparations required of the ODD teenager to regain the lost privilege are all positive demonstrations of respect. Samples of infractions with corresponding reparations are as follows:

- Spoiling the family atmosphere requires that the child become entertainment director for a similar activity.

- Refusing to help out warrants the completion of a work list.

- Hurting a sibling requires engaging in an activity like the one that led to the initial conflict and behaving like a best friend while engaging in it for an extended period of time. The siblings can take turns engaging in a series of enjoyable activities.

- Launching personal attacks on a parent warrants engaging in activities similar to those that initially led to the conflict and treating the parent as a model child would. Showing disrespect for parental help means collaborating with the parent on a project.

- Misusing family property warrants repairing it or paying for use of that item, or some combination of the two. It also warrants demonstrating proper use of that item.

- Embarrassing the family in a social setting warrants a new outing with the same people and demonstrating respectful behavior. The willingness to go on this outing and the planning for it can serve to restore privileges temporarily. The child can arrange family fun for a day in the meantime to demonstrate good faith.

- Embarrassing the family in front of guests warrants arranging another visit with the same guests with the ODD teenager this time acting as a host and demonstrating model manners. There is nothing wrong with having the teenager enlist a friend to help with the process. This makes it more fun for him. There is no need to be punitive.

- Misusing freedom to go out warrants a demonstration of the use of curfew in terms of the parents' knowing the youth's whereabouts and whether he is safe.

- Violations of trust such as deception and theft of family property require that the child learn about trust and demonstrate understanding. Therapy sessions constitute the best avenue for achieving this goal. The youth should emerge from them with an understanding of the value of trust to help the person open up and make life satisfying for the family. The child should demonstrate an understanding of how distrust creates negativity and boredom, with everyone remaining closed off at the emotional level.

The teenager has it within his power to regain privileges at any time. All he has to do is initiate the demonstration of respect.

This can take the child five minutes or five weeks. The key is for the ODD teenager to initiate the reparation process. This forces the youth to exercise self-soothing and mood-reversing abilities. The results of a successful try are no privilege loss for a week and no grounding for the weekend. It is all up to the ODD teenager.

When the offender does not initiate reparative action, it is then up to the parents to deliver consequences without enduring an emotional beating in the process.

MANAGING THE TEENAGER'S "IN YOUR FACE" TACTICS

I have found the following principles effective when dealing with defiant behavior directed at the family. A detailed description of a systematic parent-training program for this purpose is available elsewhere (Bustamante 1997) and can be used as a handout in conjunction with therapeutic efforts. Greene's *The Explosive Child* (1998), also makes an excellent handout. It is easy to read and presents the special needs of these youths and some very useful strategies for managing their outbursts. Clinicians who have not specialized in parent training will find these sources particularly useful, as they are self-explanatory and consistent with the interventions outlined in this book.

EMPOWERING PARENTS TO FACE PERSONAL ATTACKS

The most important skill to develop in parents is how to remain empowered in the face of personal attacks. The empowered parent is positive, encouraging, and detached from the outcome of the child's choices. The parent who gives top priority to the success of the child, however, is under pressure to control the outcome. An ODD youth can deflate and drain a parent in this frame of mind simply by threatening to make stupid choices.

The power of the parent comes from his willingness to walk

away from the situation and give up everything (the therapeutic use of failure). The parent removes privileges and establishes a condition for restoring them. The condition is always the same: demonstrate the respectful use of the violated privilege. The child's initial response is to refuse reparation, fail, abandon the parent, and engage in self-destructive behavior. This is a test. The teenager responds this way in retaliation and as an expression of rage. However, once the parent endures this retaliation period without surrendering, he passes the test, and the child gives up and accepts any reasonable, rational condition for regaining family privileges.

The parent should observe the spirit of the law, and not attempt rigid rule enforcement. The therapist can serve as a model for the parents by demonstrating faith in the child, offering encouragement, giving him opportunities whenever possible, and showing he knows how important it is for teenagers to gratify their personal needs. If the therapist does it right, the child will complain to him when the parents aren't behaving this way. The child will turn to the therapist when he is feeling misunderstood, and may even act out if the family fails to bring him to the office for a visit when things aren't going well. Authority figures dealing with ODD youths should never intimidate or try to overpower them. Instead, they should create a quiet space that invites reflection and helps the child choose his consequences.

On the other hand, the parent should never hesitate to deliver a consequence when one is warranted. An encouraging and understanding authority figure does not have to be lenient. A parent must not allow the child to take advantage of or mistreat him in any way. The parent's attitude should reflect a friendly willingness to exercise empowerment at any moment by relinquishing control and walking away from a disrespectful or uncooperative child. This leaves the child in a position of isolation, with most likely a sobering view of impending consequences.

It is essential to teach parents a specific strategy to avoid the tit-for-tat interactions that frequently take place in the dysfunctional families of ODD children. The clinician should role-play these steps with each parent until he is confident of the parents' competence.

They should demonstrate the method for handling each situation they routinely encounter with their teenager.

ODD teenagers seek to spoil the world around them. Their objective is to get under their parents' skin. If they can't have an emotionally spoiling effect on the family atmosphere and pull for negative attention, however, their oppositional behavior will vanish and they will adopt a humbled attitude.

ODD teenagers badger their parents relentlessly and mercilessly with their demands. They resist and dawdle in response to the parents' requests for help, and launch personal attacks on family members when they don't get their way. Parents must separate themselves from these kinds of interactions. A description of an effective technique to achieve this purpose follows.

BLUEPRINT FOR A SUCCESSFUL ESCAPE

The objective of a parent under attack by an ODD teenager is to remove himself from the struggle, take a personal time-out to assess the situation in peace and quiet, and then negotiate rationally with the youth or decide on a consequence for the infraction. The key to handling the situation is for the parent to remain calm and clear-headed and leave the child alone to make his own choice about his behavior. This will help the child shift from emotional- to rational-mind dominance and realize that his choice will have consequences for which he is responsible.

Children involved in a battle with a parent take it for granted that it is the parent's problem to make the interaction turn out right. The child assumes that the parent will protect him from any consequences. Parental absence, however, leads to a healthy level of separation anxiety and a sense of responsibility for the outcome. It certainly takes away the excitement of the battle and the fun of the momentary indulgence. For example, a teenager who is dawdling and insulting his parent, only to have the parent drive away in the family car, will pause to wonder what will happen next. His comfort level will diminish.

The technique that I find most effective in dealing with hostile teenagers entails not answering the teenagers' questions or responding to their comments, but, instead, asking them to clarify their intentions by telling me what they want.

The intention of the parent as conveyed by his body language is critical to the success of this intervention. The parent should listen to the youth's demands as genuine opportunities to make the child happy. It is imperative that the youth have as happy a childhood as possible. Parents often lose perspective with their concern for all the serious business of parenting, and forget the importance of investing in the accumulation of joyful moments that will someday add up to memories of a happy childhood. Young people who love life don't engage in destructive behavior. They don't blow up schools.

If the tone of the parent is sarcastic or dismissive, the approach that follows will do more to infuriate the adolescent than help. The parent needs to understand that the youth is dominated by the irrational emotional mind, and that the parent, too, will experience emotional-mind dominance as the aggressive demanding style of the teenager triggers associations of past hurtful events. The purpose of the protocol that follows is to help the parent induce a shift to rational-mind dominance so that logical compromise in the pursuit of happiness can take place.

A parent confronted with an attitude of belligerence answers a request from the teenager by asking him to explain more fully what he desires. The parent asks, "Is there something you want from me?" Or, "Is there anything more you want to say?" Or, "Anything else?" The parent ends this phase of the interaction with the statement, "I'll think it over." Or, "I'll keep that in mind." At this point, the parent takes a personal time-out, expecting that the exchange will have diluted the atmosphere of tension.

The time to think invites reflection and allows the youth to shift to rational-mind dominance. Once the youth has become distracted while waiting for the parent to consider his needs, the shift to rational-mind dominance will have taken place. The parent should then approach the youth with the result of his thinking, which will usually be a reasonable yet generous offer. The parent takes the distracted youth by surprise, and informs him that he has thought things over and is ready to get back to him. The parent will then be talking to a different person.

By the time he comes back to ask if the parent has thought things over yet, the teenager has returned to a state of emotional-mind dominance, and it would be a mistake to discuss the issue at this time. The result would simply be a clash of emotional minds and a reenactment of the typical battles. Should the child return to the parent requesting an answer, it is imperative that the parent state that he is not ready to discuss the matter and needs more time to think. He must then wait for the youth to become distracted with another activity, and then catch him off guard by announcing that he is now ready to respond.

The parent responds to insulting comments or innuendoes with the question, "What's your point?" The child may say, "You're a bitch! I hate you!" Or, "The food sucks!" And the parent simply responds with "What's your point?" This forces the child to explain and diverts him from his impulse to retaliate. Once the child answers what his point is, the parent can begin questioning to find out what the child wants, being careful not to provide any responses. Once more the parent asks, "Anything else you want me to know?" The parent ends the conversation by giving notice of a personal time-out, saying, "I'll think it over," or "I'll keep it in mind."

I teach parents to speculate about the child's intentions when he refuses to answer questions. The ODD teenager asks a question or makes a degrading comment: "You expect me to eat this shit you cooked?" The parent responds with, "Why are you telling me this?" Or, "What's your point?" The child refuses to answer. The parent begins to speculate aloud. "Let's see, why would someone ask that? Perhaps you think I can help you more than I do, and I'm not a very good cook. Is that it?" The parent speculates for a while and tries another angle, in effect giving the child a multiple choice: "You wouldn't be offering to help me with my cooking, would you?"

The parent can keep the speculation up for a while until the child begins to reveal his intentions or seems ready to drop the subject. He is apt to say, "Forget it!" This is intended to startle the parent into an attitude of helpfulness. The key is for the parent not to reveal any information about himself and his feelings and to offer no opinions and no advice. The parent must limit his participation to listening and speculating on the child's intentions. If no explanation comes after a while, the parent simply says, "I'll have to think that over some more," and walks away for that personal time-out.

I emphasize that parents must not answer any of the ODD teenager's questions or respond to his demands unless the youth's body language reveals honest intentions. I remind parents of the prisoner-of-war discipline of giving to the enemy only name, rank, and serial number. I make it clear that answering questions or responding to demands will only open them up to personal attack. The ODD child will have achieved his goal of getting under his parents' skin.

The approach of individuals who wish to abuse others and attempt to exert excessive control over them often begins with demands and interrogation. Abusers often ask questions or give commands that set a trap for their victims. When responses are forthcoming, they disagree and insist on having things done differently. I tell parents that once they answer their child's questions, they create an authority that tells them what to do. Personal attacks follow if they don't comply.

The statement, "I'll think it over" is an important benchmark in the escape process. Any effort by the teenager to deny the parent a time-out for quiet reflection is to be construed as a violation of rights, an infraction requiring consequences. If use of these tactics does not resolve the situation, the parents must take the interaction to the next level.

I stated earlier that Greene, in *The Explosive Child*, emphasizes the importance of picking the occasion for battles carefully. Parents should allow themselves to endure a "meltdown" only over the most critical of issues. Safety is one of them. I tell parents that the right to think things over falls into this category.

Once a parent announces that he will think it over, he walks away and the interaction is finished. It is the right of any individual to take time to digest situations before deciding how to handle them. If the child tries to deny the parent this time, the parent should tell the child directly why this is wrong. Clinicians will need to teach parents how to expose the unspoken attitude of the ODD teenager who refuses to honor a request for time to think things over. I begin with a specific definition of attitude.

For my purposes, an attitude is a nonverbal statement repeated over and over again through body language. It is a message conveyed by one emotional mind to another. A person can be talking about milk and running errands with body language that says, "It's because I live with a retard like you that we have no milk!" On the other hand, body language can say, "It's because I live with a generous person like you that I can get money for milk when I need it." People reveal attitudes without being aware of it. They also respond to attitudes without realizing it.

To expose an unspoken negative attitude, the parent should simply put the attitude into words—the language of the rational mind. By articulating an attitude, in essence, one is exposing it to the rational mind, which most often has been oblivious to it up to this point. The effect is often chilling.

The parent says to the teenager, "So let me get this straight. You're telling me that because you have a need you want satisfied you have the right to force me to decide things right away without thinking. Like I have no rights and you own me. Is that correct?" Or he says, "You believe that if you get loud enough, I have to do what you want, is that right?" Then, in a chilly and removed way, the parent says, "Well, I'll have to think about what to do with that as well." This said, the parent leaves.

A parent frightened by a teenager who adopts a threatening attitude, who is big enough or strong enough to cause injury, and who won't let him walk away should not hesitate to give in to the teenager's demands and even offer bribes. The idea is to prevent violence at that moment by gratifying the teenager's demands as completely as possible. The parent can deliver a consequence at a more opportune time. To settle present matters, however, the parent should be prepared to give the child the money he demands to finance, for example, a trip to the mall. The parent can also wait for the child to leave on his own or to become distracted by momentary indulgence.

Abusive youths will usually change completely once they've gotten their way. After the child leaves the scene, the parent plans consequences for the infraction committed, to be delivered at a later time that is both convenient and safe. It will be wise for the parent to seek the clinician's advice at this time. The parent should also take steps to protect the home so the child cannot destroy property or harm others through violent behavior.

Once the parent is ready to deliver the consequences he can make it clear to the teenager that his threats of violence forced the parent to give in temporarily to escape harm. However, the momentary escape tactic did not excuse the aggressive behavior or eliminate the consequences. Police involvement and court-enforced violence prevention treatment are often warranted in such cases.

After the parent has taken a personal time-out to think over the teen's requests, he returns with an offer of what the youth can do to have his wants gratified, or the closest thing possible. The parent should do this as quickly as possible and be as generous as possible with his offer. For every want there is an obligation. Some requests are more reasonable than others. If a teenager asks for an extreme like staying out all night, or getting drunk, the parent simply informs the youth of what it would take to earn such a privilege, for example, changing the local laws on curfew or alcohol consumption by minors. The parent closes the interaction by inviting the youth to think over the offer and get back to him with a better option if he can think of one.

I cannot emphasize enough the importance of role-playing by parents to demonstrate these steps. An intellectual understanding of the process simply will not do. The clinician should emphasize to parents that the following steps are their responsibility to carry out: (1) Question the child's demands or requests in order to find out his intentions. The parent himself does not answer any questions or reveal any personal thoughts or feelings. (2) Respond to insults with some form of the question, "What's your point?" (3)

Ask what else the teenager wants to say or wants the parent to do. (4) Announce, "I'll think it over." This is a crucial step in establishing parents' rights. (5) Walk away and take a personal time-out. (6) Comment on the teenager's attitude if he bars the way and tell him why what he's doing is a violation of rights. (7) Return to the teenager with a proposal for how he can earn his wants or the closest thing possible. This often involves a compromise. The parent should be generous with a demanding ODD teenager who suffers from poor frustration tolerance. Consider some examples:

Johnny looks his mother in the eye and shouts, "Dinner sucks! Why can't you ever make anything good?"

The first step mother takes is to expose the unspoken attitude of hostility. With a defiant tone of her own, she protests. "So what gives you the right to attack me like that? Just because you don't like food you have the right to be hostile? I'm on your side, kid."

Johnny denies his hostility, but feeling exposed, changes his tone. "I'm not being hostile, it's just that you never make anything good!" (His tone is now whiny and needy.)

Mother asks in a matter-of-fact way, "So what's your point?"

Johnny responds: "That you don't care about us. You're just too busy with your friends and your work, and you never get us what we want."

Mother, unaffected but warmer, "Is there anything else you want to say?"

Johnny, more demanding, "So what are you going to do about it?"

Mother, "Is this your way of asking for something?" (Here the mother's body language portrays confusion. She intends to satisfy her son's wants, yet doesn't see the need for the demanding tone.)

Johnny, now cheerful, "Order some pizza!"

Mother, "Anything else you want?"

Johnny pleads, "No, will you just please order pizza!"

Mother says, "Let me see what I can do. I'll get back to you in a little while." (She walks over to the dinner table in the room.)

Johnny attempts to continue the argument by threatening not to eat and to fail in school if the pizza is not forthcoming. But

Mom, refusing to be intimidated, never comments on the pizza. She sits down to eat with those who want the dinner she has prepared. Her response to Johnny's threats is a variation of "What's your point?" She asks, "So why are you telling me this?" She takes time to reflect and waits for Johnny to distract himself. Once Johnny has sat down in front of the TV, she approaches him, catching him by surprise.

> *Mother:* "I'm ready to talk to you."
>
> *Johnny* (surprised): "OK."
>
> *Mother:* "I've thought about your pizza request. I think if you want pizza you should earn it with some work. I'll pay half of it and your share would be six dollars. You can earn that by doing the dishes and folding the laundry. If I hadn't spent money on the food I made, I would gladly have bought pizza for the same money. If you give me enough notice, I can do that for you and you won't have to work for it. You don't have to eat what I cooked, but you may prefer to make yourself something and save the money. Think it over."

Mother then does the dishes, having served those who wanted the dinner she prepared. Johnny finally makes his own dinner. He asks Mom if she could order pizza another night this week instead of making dinner. She agrees to do so.

Had Johnny persisted beyond this point, his mother would have defined his attitude by saying, "I guess you think if you make enough threats I have to buy a pizza. Otherwise, you'll do poorly in life on purpose. I'll keep that in mind." Had Johnny made an insulting remark, like "I hate you!" she would have asked, "What's your point?" Or, for variety's sake, "Is there something you're trying to tell me?"

As another example, Peter approaches his mother and asks sweetly, "Can I go to the mall, please?"

"Want to tell me more about it?" she asks, with a body language that reveals true intent to understand and support his wants.

"There's not that much to tell. Bob invited me to go with him and all the kids are going to be there. Can I go, please!"

Mom responds, "Is there anything you want me to do?" Mother shows no reaction to the request so far, but is happy that her son is considering something that's fun. This is very different from the attitude of parents who dread their ODD teenagers' demands because they have a history of being badgered into submission.

"Well, I could use five dollars," Peter says. Peter assumes that Mom's questioning and calm demeanor mean she is going to say yes. However, she is planning to ask for a time-out to think it over after she finishes listening to Peter's explanations.

Mother: "Anything else?"

Peter: "Yeah, I need to call him back right away because they're leaving in a little while."

Mother: "Anything else?"

Peter: "No. Can I, please?"

Mother: "You want to go to the mall with Bob. You need five dollars from me, and you're in a hurry, which doesn't leave much time to plan things. Is that right?"

Peter nods in agreement. He feels listened to.

Mother: "Well, okay, I'll think it over."

Mother goes to a place where she can be alone and sort things out. She thinks about the trip and the responsibilities Peter may have trouble managing. Most of these would have consequences from sources outside the home. Infractions might include failing to complete homework, going to bed late, and missing soccer practice. Mother returns to her son with a brief summary of possible consequences and asks if she will need to provide any special buffers if he is penalized for his irresponsibility.

Mother also notes that Peter hasn't taken out the garbage or fed the dogs. Moreover, he needs to earn the five dollars somehow. These concerns have no outside consequences so they require enforcement from home. Peter decides to take out the garbage and feed the dogs. He promises to rake leaves for an hour for five dollars. If he doesn't do it by Sunday at 4 P.M., he forfeits his private phone until the work is done and the debt settled. He and his mother write this down. Peter wants a note to give to his coach explaining it was all right for him to have missed soccer practice. He leaves with Bob for the mall—happily.

Had Peter persisted in his entreaties without completing his tasks, his mother would have pointed out that he was failing to meet his responsibilities and would have walked away, leaving him with no decision made on his request and nowhere to go.

As another example, Ben sits in a stupor in front of the TV while the family hurries to get out of the house and into the car. "Dude, we're leaving. Aren't you coming?"

"In a minute. Can I wait for this show to end?" The family is late for a social gathering. His father decides to probe his son's intentions. "What are you saying?" he asks Ben. "Is it that you won't go unless you finish watching this show, which will go on for another twenty minutes at least?"

"No," Ben answers. "I'm coming, but I just want to see what happens next. Besides, this place will be boring." It's obvious to Dad that Ben hopes to get something out of the delay he is causing the family.

"Is there anything you want me to do about the boredom?"

"Maybe we can have some video game money or go to the new pizza place when we come back, or a movie?"

"Let me get this straight. You're coming, but you want to do some fun things to overcome the boredom," Dad says. Ben nods in agreement, and Dad says, "Sounds like a good idea, I'll keep it in mind. Meanwhile, we don't have time to watch the show, so, if you're coming, it's got to be now." Ben has some trouble getting up, but finally makes it to his feet. Dad helps by shutting off the TV and walking toward the car. Ben follows.

If Ben hadn't followed, Dad would have walked away saying, "These things have consequences." Ben's refusal to join the family would not be the basis for social or biological consequences and so would warrant a consequence from home. Dad would have left his son at home and arranged with someone to check the security of the house if he were going to be gone for a long time. The youth would have faced a loss of privileges and would have had to participate without delay in a similar outing to restore them. Parents dealing with the early stages of ODD need to have such backup plans always available.

HOW YOUTHS CAN HANDLE
UNREASONABLE AUTHORITY

Teenagers can be taught how to use the strategy employed in Ben's case should they become victims of excessive control at the hands of adults or peers. An opportunity to demonstrate the effectiveness of the process came with the appearance in my office of Susan. Susan told me she was having trouble with a controlling mother in a situation complicated by alcoholism. Here is what happened after I described to her the methods used by Ben's father.

Susan, 17, is at home, but planning to leave to keep an appointment for a job interview. Her mother is drunk and looking for a fight, part of their dysfunctional ritual.

Mom approaches. "And where do you think you're going, young lady?" In the past, Susan would have fallen into the trap and begun to explain. Mom would have used this opening as a means of interfering with Susan's plans and starting a fight. Susan would have ended up abusing her mother.

Armed with her new knowledge, however, Susan this time says, "I'm not sure where you're coming from, Mom."

"Just answer my question, and don't get fresh with me, young lady!"

"I'll be glad to answer your question, Mom. I just want to know what you need from me so I can answer better. I'm not sure where you're coming from. Is there something you want me to do?"

"You're not going anywhere!"

"Is there anything else?"

"Yes. If you go, don't come back!"

"You refuse to let me go to my job interview and if I go, you won't allow me back into this house," Susan says. "Do you have anything else to say?" The mother repeats herself and Susan decides to explore her mother's motives for her hostile behavior. She puts it on a positive basis: "You probably feel ignored by my giving you short notice but want to stop me before I make any mistakes."

"Darn right!" the mother snaps, but she is obviously bewildered by her daughter's open-handed tactics. She had been expecting Susan to fight or give in to her demands.

"Well, Mom," Susan says, "I'll keep that in mind." The mother responds with another "Where do you think you're going?"

Susan now voices some observations about her mother's attitude because she has already made the statement that she'll "think it over," only to have it fall on deaf ears. Anything her mother demands beyond this point is a violation of Susan's right to some time for reflection before she makes a decision. "So you think that I'm not allowed to take a moment to make my own decisions. Is that right?" she asks.

"You get over here right now!" her mother screams. Susan responds by walking into her room and locking the door. She dresses to go out, and after a few minutes she emerges and leaves the house quietly.

Susan must plan for these kinds of situations, just like a parent who expects to have to deal with an ODD teenager's tantrum. In fact, she has arranged to sleep at a friend's house if she needs shelter away from home. She goes to her job interview. Her mother sobers up and pretends the whole thing didn't happen.

Such instances of an irrationally controlling or incompetent parent provide an excellent opportunity to forge a strong bond with the ODD teenage client. In this case, Susan could have ended up in a legal battle involving abuse, guilt, and other complications if she had not developed the skill to handle the clash with her mother. Her rational mind's ability to meet the needs of her emotional mind would have been emotionally honest but hardly adaptive, for they would not have obtained for her what she needed. By using the method described, Susan was able to walk out, fully empowered and ready for a successful interview. Her confidence, self-trust, and trust in her therapist improve as a result of the method's success.

A similar tactic can be used to protect teenagers from controlling peers, boyfriends, teachers, and others in a position to influence their lives. Youths in this position will derive power from their willingness to walk away from oppression. The principle applies to parents who need to accept their children's failure. Controlling people won't become reasonable until they are convinced they will have no further control. This often requires a willingness to walk away, to take hands off. The principle holds for children as much as for parents.

The next chapter begins with a case that illustrates the long-term impact of parenting as a friend and ally, and delivering consequences when none are forthcoming from sources outside the family. The case proved very difficult, with extreme dangers and complications. The initial intervention dealt with removing the young man involved from school. It also entailed putting him out of the house for a time. Dramatic as these measures may seem, the outcome of the case is not unusual. It illustrates a pattern I have seen in my research and practice. Very difficult patients who would otherwise end up hospitalized or in residential treatment respond well to an approach that emphasizes personal freedom, welcomes failure, and turns the teenager's mistakes into growth opportunities.

The chapter also addresses the individual therapy work that becomes possible once an ODD teenager has been introduced to consequences that teach, strengthen, and promote growth. In the case discussed, the youngster has been evaluated, given the test of failure, and had his oppositional tendencies reversed. He has been left to face responsibilities and consequences, empowered to make choices, and challenged to create a day that pleases him. Once a child reaches this position, individual work will yield rich results, for the child experiences challenges no matter in what direction he turns. The youth feels uncomfortable if he becomes lazy and passive. He feels the need for advice if he takes the challenge seriously. The only way for the teenager to avoid therapy, however, is to work hard, enjoy life, and do well at it.

7

Step 3: Addressing the Two-Mind Split

ONE YEAR LATER: A CASE STUDY

"I have little to say today," Patrick announced when he arrived at my office. "I'm fine with my father. I have no beef with him. Things with my mom need a bit of ironing out, but that's fine."

I could hardly believe my ears. Patrick was describing his feelings toward his father in a mature, carefully considered fashion: "I have all kinds of appreciation for my father. I owe him in a big way, and I'll pay him back for everything he's done for me. I'll pay him back every penny. I owe him till I die. I took money from him. He paid for a lot of things. I have to pay him back."

Patrick was 17, tall, with a cute face, blue eyes, a light complexion, and a charming smile. He had a whaler's beard and long dark brown hair in dreadlocks, Rastafarian style. He was dressed in casual, baggy, loose-fitting, oversized garments. He was soft spoken, and presented a calm, confident demeanor. Patrick was obviously an intelligent young man. He was acknowledged to be one of the best athletes in his high school. He had become a mystery to his family, however, when he suddenly stopped doing any kind of work and began to break rules aggressively.

Patrick's father, who joined his son in the visit to my office, was dressed in business suit and tie. He was a pleasant man in his mid- to late forties, with neatly styled graying hair, blue eyes, and a dignified look. He was the father of four other children. Patrick was the youngest. The older siblings had been a source of family pride throughout their school years, and were leading successful lives as adults. School authorities held the family in high regard.

Patrick, however, had been a very difficult challenge to everyone around him for almost two years before I became involved. He failed at school and violated every behavior principle his family stood for. He launched merciless attacks on the adults responsible for him. He refused to work, help out at home, or complete schoolwork. He violated his family's trust in numerous ways—lying, stealing, disappearing without a word for days at a time, and then breaking into his own home when he needed something.

He had become resolutely hedonistic, with an unkempt appearance and a blatant devotion to marijuana. He was proud of his antiwork philosophy. He was not about to turn into a "working stiff" like his father. He flaunted his lifestyle of not spending money. His sole occupation was playing with a Frisbee every day in the park. He wanted everything handed to him and contributed nothing to the world around him.

Patrick sold and used illegal drugs and was deeply involved with a group of fellow users. He was placed in an inpatient drug treatment program. The benefits of the program lasted for two weeks after his release. He requested enrollment in a private school and his family made the sacrifice. It cost them $10,000 in tuition. Then, as soon as Patrick reentered his peer world, he regressed to drug use at a more furious pace than before. He stopped attending the private school abruptly, with the result that the family was forced to forfeit the tuition money. Patrick would not agree to placement in a drug treatment program again and refused all forms of treatment.

I started working on Patrick's case with the parenting interventions described in the previous chapter. The father told how, reluctantly, he had left his son out in the cold rain early one morning before going to an appointment. Patrick tried to break into the house because his parents had changed the locks. On this occasion, his mother returned home to see to it that he didn't get inside. His parents' determination to enforce the suspension of Patrick's family privileges yielded results. He began to soften and to demonstrate an interest in getting back into the good graces of his parents. As a condition for regaining privileges he agreed to see me.

My early work with Patrick had revolved around joining with his emotional brain agenda, which involved talking about the advantages of his unorthodox and unlawful lifestyle. Whatever he presented, I responded, "Do you have a problem with having done that?" Or, "Why didn't you do more of it?" He eagerly presented his views on marijuana and avoiding work. He could make all kinds of money if he wanted to, he said, and he could spend his life following his favorite rock groups. "Why haven't you done this already?" I asked.

Patrick soon started to let me into his real world. He made it clear that, in his own estimation, he was one of the most cautious and levelheaded kids I would ever want to meet. He described the drug and violence epidemic that plagued his entire school. He emphasized how many of the so-called good students in his school were deeply involved.

Patrick took pride in not drinking. Also, in a violent world he remained a pacifist. He told of violent fights and vengeful feuds between his peers and other gangs. He vividly described a gang ritual that he and his friends had witnessed. It was called "curbing." The rival gang members would beat someone into a state of helplessness. Then they would hold their victim's head at the curb of a sidewalk, mouth open, teeth biting the edge of the curb. They would then kick the person's head into the curb. The practice could fracture teeth and jaw and cause brain injuries, possibly fatal ones. Patrick wanted no part of this violence.

Once I had joined Patrick's emotional brain in all of his most unacceptable choices, I challenged his adaptive brain to come up with an alternative to his unlawful lifestyle—a second career, something to fall back on. I suggested he create a choice for himself that fell somewhere between selling marijuana and a paying job requiring only unskilled labor. We made boredom and deception our common enemy. He needed to work at something he loved besides selling marijuana and T-shirts at rock concerts. We discussed glass blowing. He rapidly developed the idea of making special pipes to sell at the concerts. The light would shine through them and create rainbow-like colors. There was magic in his dreams.

The purpose of these initial visits was not to provide him with realistic career options. Those would eventually come from his own adaptive brain, from his own need to overcome his personal hardships. I wanted to encourage him, and help him begin to understand his problem. I wanted him to know that his oppositional and antisocial behaviors were to a large extent an understandable but misguided effort to grow in his own unique way in body, mind, and spirit. I wanted him to see that I could know the worst about him, yet remain confident that he would eventually outgrow his current limitations and find a life he would enjoy. All he needed was an opportunity and support for doing things his own way. He knew I was right.

Patrick still had a lot to learn about trust and about earning the support he needed. This learning had to come from consequences meted out by parents and school and through his own trial-and-error process. Despite our agreement on his needs, Patrick's basic lifestyle and his philosophy of nonwork had remained essentially intact, as had his devotion to his peers.

The decisive lesson for Patrick took place after he was caught stealing $1,000 from his parents through unauthorized use of their bank card. This was a felony, and the bank, if alerted, would be able to produce evidence linking him to the use of the card. Patrick at first denied the theft, but his parents found a way of extracting the truth. If he swore to them that he had not taken the money, his father would ask the bank to investigate. Patrick was informed that the bank could easily review the video footage of the transaction and identify and prosecute the culprit. If, on the other hand, he admitted making the withdrawals his parents would absorb the loss to keep him from facing criminal charges. Patrick confessed to the theft.

Patrick had been struggling in a well-intentioned way to master the failure challenge. We had put him in charge of his education. He had earned family privileges. He had been contributing to his family in numerous ways, and was having productive counseling sessions with me. The topic of the session had shifted to earning trust. Things had been improving steadily for Patrick until the theft took place. Based on the enormity of his misdeed, the word *trust* took on an entirely new meaning.

Patrick's parents had followed the interventions prescribed to them faithfully, a testament to their solid family structure. He lost the privilege of living with his family for this latest violation. His parents rented a room for him, and gave him until his eighteenth birthday to prove himself trustworthy. He needed to find a job and join family activities in positive ways to prove that he had learned from the experience. He would, however, be required to continue living on his own in the room provided by his parents until he paid them back the money he had stolen.

The Lie That Maintains the Split

Patrick signed an agreement stating the conditions under which the room would be made available to him. Among these was the stipulation that he find a job and pay off his debt. Agreeing to this condition was a big departure from his customary point of view, although it did not occur to him at the time. The agreement exposed Patrick's two-mind split clearly, and would become a powerful learning experience for him. By agreeing to go to work, Patrick was allowing his rational mind to betray his emotional mind. He had begun to live a lie by feigning interest in job hunting, even though he in fact did nothing. For Patrick, finding a job would mean acting contrary to his basic philosophy of avoiding work that was boring and required only unskilled labor. Though he still failed to grasp the significance of what was happening, the consequences of his effort to deceive his parents were growing very real by the time of his latest appointment with me.

Patrick left home with many aspects of his life settled in productive ways. He was back in my office after three months of living apart from the family. He now understood the seriousness of his violation and wanted to demonstrate honor and integrity and be considered trustworthy. As a result, he agreed to formal testing for AD/HD. The testing showed him to be in the severe range. He accepted medication and a special-education program that relied heavily on a home tutor.

Patrick told me during his visit: "I want to have a relationship with my father. And let me tell you what I don't want to have to say to my kids someday. I don't want to have to say that I don't want to turn out like my father. I don't want to say that I was afraid of my father or that I didn't appreciate my father. I don't want to have to tell them that my father wasn't there for me or that I couldn't talk to my father."

It was the father's turn to speak.

"Let me report the positives first," he said. "Christmas went well. We had the best Christmas morning ever. Patrick was around. He went to church with us. We had dinner. He resolved conflicts among extended family and added humor to touchy subjects. He seemed wise beyond his years. He was unusually helpful to his mother in the first Christmas ever without her own mother, who recently passed away.

"Home tutoring has continued satisfactorily, although Patrick hasn't had to do schoolwork. He seems satisfied with the program. He's gotten very good grades." Here, Patrick interrupted to gloat, "I got a 93 in English, a 91 in Social Studies, and a 72 in math, but that 72 is bogus. I got a 95 in the final. I got penalized unfairly for losing some assignments."

Now Patrick began to talk about his plans for the future. I had heard reports from the school that Patrick was making a surprisingly good turnaround. The school was impressed after an initial, and understandable, period of skepticism about my approach. Patrick told me of his plans.

"I'm going all the way, a Ph.D. in criminal psych, or something like that," he said. "I'm golden. They can't stop me. Next year I'm going back to high school to play soccer, maybe basketball. Then I'm going to drop out and get my GED. Then I'm going to community college, or the UMass auto-acceptance program." He was referring to a University of Massachusetts program offering students an opportunity to prove that they're qualified and win acceptance into a degree program.

"I'll get my B.S., maybe my master's, and then my Ph.D. Even if it takes my whole life, I'll pay my dad back every penny I owe him," Patrick said.

The father asked some questions about these ambitious plans, then said, "Patrick has made good decisions about peer involvement. He has shown very good character." He explained how Patrick had kept one of his friends from getting in serious trouble by seeing him through a precarious situation involving the use of alcohol.

"We've also quit smoking together," the father continued. In my customary manner of questioning emotional-mind restrictions, I asked Patrick why on earth he had quit smoking. I indicated my surprise. He responded vehemently: "Buy a pack of cigarettes and you buy a pack of cancer! That's how I view it."

The one problem area his dad reported was that Patrick had no job, no source of income, yet seemed to have money. This is the first hint of the tragic flaw. Patrick's emotional mind was refusing to sign up for a job but was willing to do everything else. He had all kinds of excuses for why he couldn't get a job. There weren't any jobs available for a guy with hair like his and he would rather die than change his appearance. Once he turned 18 it would be easy to get a job. Patrick responded to questioning by insisting that he was dying to get a job and pay off his parents.

Though neither he nor his father could see it, Patrick's behavior was perfectly consistent with his anti–boring-work philosophy and lifestyle. He lived with only the bare necessities and dressed in a way that made him unacceptable to potential employers. It was as if his emotional mind were screaming, "I do not grow this way. You cannot make me do this. You are betraying me!" Yet, all his parents could see was a lack of follow-through on the agreement he had signed.

The father suspected drug dealing as the source of Patrick's funds. Patrick, however, gave ample evidence of how he was getting by. Mostly, he was learning to live without spending much money. Friends assisted by giving him movie passes and other handouts. His response to any kind of challenge was surprisingly reasonable. Unlike in the past, he was not abusive in his language when his motives were questioned.

His father was detached when he listened to Patrick's reasons for his failure to go to work. "That's your problem, not mine," he said. I could tell that Patrick needed to pursue his growth path without finding a job, and that he was making excuses to himself as well as others for the apparent blank wall in the employment market.

I felt trapped between Patrick's excuses and his parents' insistence on the binding quality of the agreement with their son. I felt I would never be able to convince the parents that they should lift the agreement's principal requirement—a job that would pave the way for Patrick to pay off his debt to them. No doubt I was in the middle of and sharing the ODD adolescent's dilemma, which was knowing what would work, but recognizing that there was no chance of being heard. I allowed myself to remain in this position for a while.

I was willing to end this session on a positive note and allow Patrick's attempted deception regarding his job hunting to remain undisclosed for the time being. After all, I asked myself, how much can you accomplish in one day? Before I could proceed in this direction, however, Patrick said he wanted to speak to me in private. He pointed out that he was about to turn 18 and wouldn't be able to continue on his wonderful journey of making his own decisions unless he got a job. He also confided in me that he felt his mother was the principal obstacle in his efforts to satisfy his needs.

I confronted Patrick on his self-betrayal and he denied it vehemently. I said, "Are you telling me you really want to find a job but can't?" His emotional mind leaped forward in protest and excitement.

"Yesss!" Patrick said animatedly. "I want a job so badly! It's just that there aren't any. I try to tell that to my parents but they won't listen. Would you hire somebody with hair like mine?" He didn't give me a chance to respond. "I know *you* would, but do you think people like my father would give me a job?"

I sensed Patrick's need to believe in the reasons he gave for not finding a job, and because the time for our session was running out, I simply listened, saying only that I would think over what he told me. I dealt with the trapped-adolescent feeling by detaching myself from the process, and telling myself that Patrick's ODD would soften the attitude of the parents, and that in addition, the pain of being homeless, in effect, would force Patrick to face reality. I approached his father and requested a meeting at which Patrick's mother would participate.

Patrick's emotional mind insisted on hiding, and his rational mind was busy generating excuses for remaining on his natural growth process without having to acknowledge that he had sold his own emotional mind down the river. He had signed a contract that went against his deepest philosophy in life, but didn't understand its implications. He couldn't see the distrust his behavior was causing among others.

I ended the session by keeping this to myself, yet mentioning to the father that I felt we might need to try some different approaches. I was vague about the procedure. The father agreed to a follow-up appointment in a month, this session to include Mom as well as father and son.

Exposing the Final Lie

The principal items on the agenda were the unresolved matters involving the mother. My goals were to (1) expose the lie, (2) restore Mom's trust, and (3) extricate Patrick from the agreement that had served to expose his lie.

"Actions speak louder than words. That's my motto," Patrick

said, as his mother smiled knowingly. "This is the advice my mom gave me in a situation involving a girl, and I applied it to myself."

The girl in question had asked Patrick to support her in escaping from a relationship with an abusive boyfriend. He did, but ultimately the girl turned her back on him and resumed the relationship. Mom had warned him previously, Patrick said, that the girl might let him down, and repeated the adage. Patrick remained friends with the girl but kept his distance. His handling of the affair prompted his mother to say her son had "done well." We joked about what my reaction might be to Patrick's connection with the girl, but I left any comments I might have until later.

The session resumed. "Things with my dad," Patrick said, "have remained okay since last time." Suddenly, he stopped himself. "No, wait. There was one episode. We went back to old days." This meant that his father lost his composure and became abusive in his language.

Patrick told how he failed to return on time a winter coat he had borrowed from his dad, who was flying off on a business trip. Patrick had left the coat at a friend's house. He had also agreed to complete several jobs around the house, including the chipping of ice from the outdoor deck. His intentions were good and he planned to get up early to start work. However, his father's patience wore thin, and he exploded with recriminations directed at his son when he learned the whereabouts of the coat. Patrick had been very good in many other ways and was completely surprised by the abuse. He responded by throwing an expensive set of headphones at his father, but with the intention of missing. The act was expressive though destructive. Patrick had been fond of the headphones. He sat on his bed after the incident and cried. In the days to come, his dad would telephone from out of town in efforts to arrive at reconciliation. Patrick at first refused to talk with his father during repeated phone calls but eventually changed his mind, and the two resolved their differences.

I explained to Patrick that every time I was successful in persuading everyone to open up and attempt to establish an air of mutual trust, I inevitably exposed the family to further trauma. Their emotional minds had traumatic memories of previous violations imprinted in them, and when Dad reached a certain threshold, he blew up just like in the old days. We established that Patrick's explosion toward his father was equally irrational and reflected past trauma. Relax and trust, then feel violated, as in the past. This was the pattern. The only difference in the two individuals was that Dad worked up to the point of explosion gradually, while Patrick arrived there quickly. Patrick could now see the significance of trust violations.

Dad said he was happy with my explanations and felt heard and understood. "I couldn't have explained it better myself," he said. Patrick felt reconciled with his father and eager to learn more. The time had come to address Mom's needs, and, once more, Patrick began, this time by telling a story of how resentful and stingy Mom had been with him. The course of events followed a familiar pattern. Patrick intended to help and cooperate, yet he encountered resistance and misunderstanding on the part of his parents. The story began with Patrick needing a ride to arrive on time at his session with me. Once more his intentions were good but his family didn't see it that way.

Patrick said, "I called and asked, 'Can you give me a ride?' She goes 'GRRRROWL!' She says fine, and hangs up on me before I can say anything. No ride? Fine! I'll walk and still be home at 4 P.M. like I said I would. But it's cold outside, and I have no winter coat. Then I'm getting into the car and she hits the gas before I finish getting in."

Here Mom laughed a bit and protested that she wouldn't behave that way. Patrick continued: "Next, she opens the window and it's really cold outside. I don't have a coat on. I know I smell but I froze my ass off. She has an attitude against me. Know what I mean? Oh, and she loves to hang up on me."

Mom responded, "He's right. He's done it to me many times so I like to give him a taste of his own medicine. I don't do it when he's nice, only when I feel put out. He's right, I do have an attitude. Ever since his last visit to you with his father, there have been enough little stings, and it's hard to close the old wounds." She relates how Patrick has violated the parents' private space, looking for money. He has taken money from his father's wallet. Plus, he is always begging for money. "This chicken-shit stuff gets me to blow up," she said.

The matter of money came up several times during our meeting, and I selected this as an area of focus. Both parents said Patrick sometimes asked them for money and was making no effort to find a job. The conversation turned to the contract Patrick had signed but not honored. Here I interrupted and asked Patrick for the truth. "Who made that agreement?" Patrick replied, "I did." I asked, "What part of you is I, the emotional mind, the rational mind, or both?"

Patrick said that he wants a job, badly. Under my questioning he explained that he needs the job to pay his parents back. He has, however, numerous excuses for why he can't get a job, including lack of transportation and the fact that most employers won't hire someone with long hair.

Conflicts in the family system often point directly to the lie that maintains the split between the two minds. And lack of honesty usually breeds distrust in the family. The individual practicing the deceit talks a lot but shows little initiative or productive behavior. Those who see the resulting behaviors become concerned and pressure the individual to follow through on his commitments. Such pressure increases the need to lie and otherwise dissemble.

Patrick's case illustrates how family pressure can force an individual to betray the emotional-mind agenda, which reflects his true wants. By agreeing to the contract, Patrick made an ill-fated decision that condemned him to dishonesty. Should he be disloyal to his basic philosophy of life and adhere to his contract commitment? Or should he be true to himself even though this would mean deceiving the family? That was his dilemma.

Interpreting the Two-Mind Split

"Face it, Patrick," I began, "you want a job only to make things right with your family. But if you really wanted a job, no one could stop you from getting it. Look at all the difficult things you've accomplished because you really wanted them. You took on your family and the entire school system. You managed to break into your parents' ATM account and withdraw hundreds of dollars. You've survived incredible difficulties with peers. No one can stop you!"

"That's true," Patrick admitted. "So what are you saying? That I don't want to pay back my parents?"

"I'm saying that if you really wanted a job, you would get a haircut and be working by next week."

"No way! I'll never cut my hair."

"Why not?" I asked.

"My hair is my hair. It's sacred to me. I'd rather cut my arm off."

"And it's a complete coincidence that your hair keeps you from getting a job, and not working at jobs you find boring is your fundamental philosophy of life. I'm saying you need to have long hair to keep you from betraying yourself and getting a job you hate. I'm saying learn to listen to your true self. Hear what your emotional mind is telling you. Then, don't sign up for obligations that go against your personal truth. Don't put yourself in a bind in which you either have to betray yourself or deceive others.

"Again, it's your rational brain [I point to my head] that needs work here. There are different ways to make things right with your parents. Your emotional mind is saying it wants to make things right with your family, but your philosophy won't allow you to work at something you hate. So you find another way? But no! You promise to get a job, and insist this is your true goal, only to say later that you can't find that job. And look at all the discord it causes in your family."

The parents were very quiet as I made these points with Patrick. I explained how they've wasted most of their money on seeing him get healthy and educated. They've paid for drug treatment, therapy, and a private school. They really want to see him fulfill his plan of doing well in school, going to college, and ending up a criminal psychologist.

"I see your point," said Patrick. "How else can I make things right?" I suggested to Patrick that he could do work around the house that won't require commitment to a steady job or a haircut.

This won't immediately pay his parents the thousands of dollars he owes them, but he can pay that off when he has more income, which he can achieve by getting a good education. For the present, he can make home a nice place for the family by becoming a respectful and positive influence.

I then addressed the parents. I restated the difference between change and growth, as described in Chapter 6. Growth takes place in small steps. I wouldn't expect Patrick to go from an anti–boring-work philosophy to becoming a routine worker. He needed to find work he would like, and that might require more education. The parents' true payback would be in seeing him develop.

Patrick's parents were surprisingly receptive. Patrick responded by saying he felt a huge load lifted from his shoulders. His change in demeanor was noticeable. He said, "Hey, how about I apply for that glass-blowing apprenticeship we talked about? That would be true to my philosophy."

The session ended with the end of the last lie. I didn't need to see Patrick or his family again for months.

THE TIMING OF THE INTERPRETATION: A CASE STUDY

The best time to interpret a two-mind split is when the youth is in a state of acute suffering. This is when the intervention has its most powerful therapeutic impact. Under these conditions, the therapist who has formed a bond with the emotional brain of the youth sees a child who speaks to him freely, as he might to a close friend. The teenager, now relaxed, reveals his most intimate secrets, as in good therapy with an adult. The words used by the therapist to produce this result would not register with a child not in an acute phase, or yield the same level of openness.

Nick, a 12-year-old very hyperactive boy, had been caught in his 9-year-old sister's room late at night. He was carrying a flashlight. Mom noticed the light, and called out, "What are you doing in there?"

"Nothing," Nick responded nervously, darting out of the room.

Moments later, Nick's sister emerged, groggy, rubbing her eyes, and asking, "Why was somebody touching me? Why are my pants down?"

The mother followed Nick into his room and reprimanded him severely. The climax was, "You have raped your sister's decency!" The father talked to Nick in an understanding way, but remained concerned with the boy's feelings of extreme guilt. He called my office the next morning requesting an emergency visit.

Nick seemed depressed and frightened when he came to my office that afternoon. I employed my usual tactics of siding with the emotional-brain agenda and asking questions that coincided with the patient's desires. "What's wrong with wanting to look at your sister?" And, "Why not do it every night?" This time, there was no visible impact on the patient.

Nick was crestfallen. My mental image of this normally playful, energetic boy was of a dark shadow engulfing him. In his effort to maintain a traumatic secret, he no doubt felt as though a ton of bricks was weighing him down. Nick's father looked at me knowingly and with deep concern. Nick asked, "Can I go outside and play a video game?" This was the best invitation available to yield to the dictates of the emotional brain, so I sent Nick to the waiting room where the Nintendo game was awaiting him.

When I resumed my conversation with the father, he reported that his son had confessed. Nick had been looking at his sister's body since she was 3. The story changed a few times, but the boy insisted that there had been no penetration. Despite the father's understanding and accepting attitude after the discovery of what had been taking place, Nick remained guilt-ridden. Dad was hoping I could help Nick feel better and recommend ways to help his son.

I called Nick back into the room, this time to see him alone. He hesitated, but I remained firm. He asked whether he could play with the sculpture, and I indulged him. This time I took a different tack. I asked Nick to reveal the rational-brain agenda by expressing his guilt. "I raped my sister's decency. That's what Mom said," Nick told me.

"I get it!" I said. "You have a fight going on. Your thinking brain says this is very bad. But your body thinks it's very good." At this point, Nick came to life. He interrupted me.

"Yeah! And the body always wins." Nick now confessed that he was engaging in all kinds of sexual activities. His presentation was animated. He was sneaking pornographic magazines into the house and masturbating regularly, though fighting not to do it. "Don't tell Dad I'm sneaking the magazines. He'll throw a fit!" he said. He explained that the magazines were hidden in a place dangerous to climb to.

I asked, "Why are these things bad if your body wants them?"

"Because I invaded her space," he responded. He elaborated on his inner conflict. "God makes it work this way." The statement caught my attention, so I asked him to explain. "On days that I don't masturbate and sneak the magazines, I get to see my sister. When I go into her room at night, she doesn't wake up and I can look at her. But on days that I masturbate, she wakes up."

Nick went on to reveal the entire history of his sex games with his sister. His tone was playful. He was obviously relieved that I understood the battle within him. There was the spanking game, the car-wash brush game, the doctor game with toothpicks, the naked machine, and the weird feeling machine. Nick told several dramatic stories that involved almost getting caught. He stopped in the middle of his stories and exclaimed, "This feels better, talking about the fun side of it!"

Nick's stories were revealing. His sister pretended to sleep when he entered the room at night and went along with the games. The games were creative play and fun. They all involved nudity and touch, but this was a relatively small part of the game, and there was never penetration of any kind. There had also never been any adult or older child who had violated Nick.

Nick frequently felt the urge to touch other girls but his rational mind had won the battle in those instances. Their parents wouldn't be very understanding. His sister was a different story because she had taken part in the games for years. It was very difficult to stop. This explained Nick's current dilemma.

I commented that it sounded as though he and his sister had really enjoyed themselves with these games. He responded, "It was fun. But now that she's old, she thinks it's yucky. Now she hates the night game so I have to go in when she's sleeping, and I can't wake her up."

Nick finally volunteered a memory of an event he now considered repugnant. They had kissed each other's privates. I would use this opportunity to show him the difference between harmless indulgences and those that did harm. I ended the session by asking him to think about how he wanted to manage the problem of access to his sister and to the magazines. When I offered to suggest to his parents that they lock her door at night, Nick protested that he did not want to lose access to his sister's room. I asked his parents, instead, to supervise him closely, but not to scold him if he were caught again.

Nick walked out of the office feeling, I think, like a completely different child. I had enough information to know how to proceed with the case. The incident had to be reported. I held several meetings with the parents to help them be effective in limit setting, yet understanding of Nick so they would not further traumatize him. I worked with the sister to empower her and help her process the trauma that this history of violations had caused her. We went to great lengths to rig Nick's sister's room so that he would be caught if he tried to enter it, and sure enough we caught him red-handed shortly thereafter. We used the incident to justify locking him out of the room. He never stood a chance of getting away with the entry, but the exposure of being caught helped his emotional mind accept the locked door and his rational mind realize that he had a problem. For over three years, Nick was never left unsupervised with his sister until it was clear that he had outgrown the problem.

THE PATH OF WANTS: KNOWING, VOICING, DOING, MASTERING

The first thing the adolescent needs to learn is that want equals truth. This is emotional-brain language. The second thing to teach the adolescent is that each *want to* relies on a *have to* for its actualization. The lesson for parents is that if their child doesn't want it, it isn't important. If he wants it, however, he must perform the *have to's* necessary to earn it. This is the only way that wants will lead to personal growth.

The *have to* process requires trial and error. The process begins with the individual taking a risk. Risk is essential to growth. The youth can be offered useful information but should be granted the right to think things over and make a personal decision on whatever undertaking is involved. He should be challenged to base his decision on his personal wants. This ensures that the individual's *want to* brain region (emotional brain) becomes a point of connection in the new neural network being formed. Next comes error and the pain of consequence.

Suffering after failure in the trial-and-error process is a necessary experience if the process is to yield adaptive wisdom. Suffering leads to wisdom, and a new trial takes place. After enough error a new capacity for adaptation develops. The clinician should remind families that book learning cannot replace experience when a youngster is confronted by the necessity of making choices.

Most families will seek to make a bored and dishonest youngster tell cognitive truth. The rational mind sides with an alien agenda and the emotional mind rebels, creating a need for the rational mind to use deception as a survival tool. The emphasis on cognitive truth exposes the emotional brain to further denial of true self and works against integration. Trial-and-error learning that is socially adaptive and genuine will either fail to occur, or will take place under the tutelage of peers.

I say to the youth in front of his family, "You lied and will continue to lie because you want to. Why don't you admit to yourself that you want to lie so you can remain honest at the emotional-brain level? You use storytelling to create opportunities to live out your personal truth and your real wants. However, you are not earning your wants, not taking the proper have-to steps to ensure full development. You remain untrustworthy, immature, and worth very little to society. Eventually you'll get caught at storytelling, and lose your right to pursue your wants." It is very useful to frame lying as storytelling for the sake of emotional-mind satisfaction in an attempt to engage in vital wants, and pursue the trial-and-error process without misguided interference from adults.

The key from this point on is to show the teenager how he is violating the family trust and causing himself major problems by deceiving and taking the easy way out. Once the clinician defines this dilemma to his patient, he engages him in the process of developing more sophisticated adaptive functions, integrating the emotional and rational minds with the family, and living an honest life.

CATCHING AND EXPOSING THE WEAKNESSES OF THE SYMPTOMS

It is often difficult to talk to ODD teenagers about their symptoms or other deficits because of their habit of avoiding responsibility and externalizing blame. They are ashamed of their defects, will deny them, and will avoid discussing them. For this reason, attempts during sessions to air matters involving anxiety, depression, addiction, explosiveness, deception, or school failure quickly turn awkward.

However, an effective strategy for countering the teenager's tendency to avoid criticism is to externalize and personify his problems or symptoms to assist him in exploring these areas without feeling self-conscious. The initial objective is to help the youth feel free of blame in whatever unpleasant incident took place. It wasn't he who set the fire, who started the fight, who ran away, or who did something to lose a girlfriend. It was the outside forces of temptation, anger, fear, or jealousy that got a grip on him and took over his actions.

The first step is for the clinician to ask the teenager to discuss the forces that brought about his symptoms. ODD teenagers are always eager to discuss these forces because it validates their perspective that whatever happened wasn't their fault. In fact, the involvement of others and of forces beyond their control is all that

ODD children want to talk about. It was the principal, the teacher, the parent, the coach, or the other guy who was to blame. It was bad luck or the rain that caused it.

The next step is to "catch" the symptom or problem and give it an identity. The clinician asks the teenager for his emotional and cognitive reaction to the pressure from the unwanted external force, putting the question in a way that places the teenager in the position of the innocent victim. The clinician asks, "So what did the situation make you feel?" The youth will usually respond with a simple comment: "I thought this was bullshit," or "I felt mad."

This is where the clinician catches this internal state and brings it to life by making a statement that portrays the youth's internal state as an independent force that has taken control. This force has a voice and a life of its own. For example, in response to the youth declaring that he was angry, the clinician says, "So anger got a grip on you." The youth agrees. Then the clinician brings this character called anger to life by giving it a voice. "So anger said, this is a bunch of bullshit!" And asks, "What did anger say (or do) next?" The greater the detail with which the youth describes his internal characters the better. To the anger, depression, or anxiety can be attributed characteristics like sneaky, intense, strong, unfair, powerful, and tenacious. Depression or anxiety can take the form of dwelling on the negative, berating oneself, or picturing gruesome scenes. The clinician asks the youth to describe his anger, depression, AD/HD, anxiety, or other disturbing mental state. The clinician begins by asking for a general description of the teenager's internal state: "Describe your anger." If the youth can't describe it very well, the clinician asks him if he thinks it would be important to know what his anger looks like, how it operates. He can offer the youth a choice of descriptors and modifiers that can help him flesh out the attributes of the character he is creating. The objective is to get the youth to focus on the nature of the internal state he has fallen into as he recalls a past episode that brought on the symptom.

Once the clinician "catches" the symptom and converts it into a character, the teenager feels free of shame or anxiety and begins to enjoy creating a drama from the behavior of this character as it interacts with forces from the outside world. The clinician asks how anger or another emotion chosen for personification manages to get itself expressed. "Where did it go?" "What did you do with anger?" The youth may say that he buried it, took it out on someone, or acted out. "Wow!" responds the clinician as he summarizes the sequence of events. "So the principal started to lecture your class about obligations, and you were struggling to keep anger from taking over and swearing at him in front of the entire class!"

Once the clinician has externalized and given life to an internal state, he proceeds to catch other internal forces and states until he exhausts all those that usually surround the symptoms. The clinician either tracks the path of the first symptom or exposes the process by which this internal state was controlled by or gave way to another mind state. The response to what anger did next can only be that it grew more intense or that it was controlled. If it escalated, then it is anger's fault and it becomes the prominent character in the play. If not, the clinician identifies the force that counteracted the anger and brings it to life. The clinician asks, "So why didn't anger just curse out the principal? What stopped it?" The youth says, "Well, I couldn't attack the principal. I didn't want to get kicked out of school." This means the youth used reflection or caution. The clinician asks, "So what would you call that force that stopped anger? Was it caution, or reflection? Help me out."

In this way, the clinician identifies different symptoms, resources, and solutions that unconsciously impact on the youth's mind as he deals with the pressures of life. The clinician asks, "So were you aware that at times you can use caution and reflection to control your anger?" And, "Where does anger go when caution comes in?" "How strong is the battle between the two forces?" "How often do you endure conflicts between these two forces?"

Now comes the critical step of identifying the weaknesses in the evil character that has been tormenting the ODD youth. The key is to find out why the symptom or problem hasn't completely destroyed his life. Whatever stops it is its weakness, its Achilles' heel. The clinician and teenager thus begin to plot against these sinister forces that have hitherto gone unchallenged. Once they have exposed and laid out all of the strengths and vulnerabilities of the characters that have plagued the youth, they will have a much richer and more productive perspective. The youth will be armed with awareness of the elements that trigger and maintain his symptoms and the tactics that can counteract these sinister forces. This elaboration not only adds insight—the source of two-mind integration—but also brings the sessions to life and exposes problems and patterns that can be identified, interrupted, or otherwise altered. The youth can consider a variety of possible solutions to problems that he has never before had an opportunity to consider.

It is important that the clinician help the youth realize what these characters have been doing to different aspects of his life, and what, if anything, he wants to do about it. The first step is to determine the cost to the youth of the symptoms. "So what does your anger do to your family, your friends, your girlfriend, your income, your peace of mind, your self esteem, your grades, or your future?" the clinician asks. The second step is to challenge the youth to do something about it. "So who's in charge of your life?" "Is that how you want it?" "Do you want to do something about it?" "Do you want to get your life back?" As always, the youth must be in charge of what is done about these forces that have been spoiling things without his permission.

Michael White (1995), one of the founders of narrative therapy, outlines four categories of inquiry for interviewing patients to externalize and enrich symptoms. Much like cognitive therapy, narrative therapy seeks to alter the toxic meaning of many of our culture's labels and in the process transform the patient's negative identity to a healthier and more constructive self-perception. His methods are powerful, creative, and entertaining.

White's first category of inquiry is negotiating a particular and experience-near definition of the problem or concern. The second is mapping the problem through the various domains of the person's life. How does it affect the person's home, friendships, school, relationship to self, purposes, dreams, or aspirations? The third category is evaluating the impact of the problem on these aspects of the person's life (i.e., the cost of the problem). The final category is what White refers to as justification of these evaluations (Why do you feel this way about this problem? Is this okay with you? Why or why not?).

White calls these four categories of inquiry his "Statement of Position Map," and he uses them to engage in sophisticated narratives that serve to externalize, expose, and redefine the person's problems, and to expose the weaknesses in the grip that these problems hold over the individual's life. The clinician can use externalizing conversations in the tradition of narrative therapy to catch and transform the symptoms of the otherwise resistant ODD teenager during the two-mind integration phase of treatment.

Alfonso called my office in a state of crisis, preparing to leave the prep school campus where he was living. An otherwise remarkable young man, he had been brought to my office because of his explosive tendencies. I had only seen him for a couple of sessions, but we had managed to get his outbursts under control. However, we were all surprised (Alfonso, his parents, and I) because he now complained of panic attacks and depression. He was desperate. He wanted medication to ease his problem and he wanted to go home.

Working together in earlier sessions we had identified anger as the culprit causing his problems and unfairness as the outside force that brought anger on. When Alfonso was denied what he wanted for no apparent reason, his anger created a mood that completely gripped him. It worked its way around him quietly at first, but soon had him bound and gagged. Once the mood took over, any trivial thing that anybody did caused him to erupt. He would go to his room and begin to abuse the walls and furniture.

We had found that Alfonso vented his anger only at home among people with whom he really felt comfortable. He didn't allow himself to blow up in front of his friends. He had learned how to control himself when he was with his girlfriend. It was concern that had stopped anger. He didn't want to lose friends. Alfonso explained that he buried his anger and it stayed there, ready to erupt, until he felt alone for too long. Then he would initiate contact with someone he had gotten upset with and had withdrawn from for a time.

We had identified two points in the pattern at which Alfonso could communicate his feelings about unfairness, or take time to reflect and cool down so he could get what he wanted, rather than blowing up and later regretting it. Alfonso was very sensitive to criticism, which suggested perfectionism. He tended to worry and to judge himself harshly. We had worked on getting him to go along with criticisms and put-downs using humor, rather than retaliating against his critics. He enjoyed identifying the different parts of himself that battled for control and generating strategies to counter these forces. However, a sudden bout of depression and an unexpected panic attack really pulled the rug out from under him.

During an emergency visit that he requested, Alfonso was able to identify clearly how the depression he felt was a recurrence of a pattern that developed when he stopped blowing up at others. He was entering the same angry moods in response to the same triggers, but was ending up depressed. His depression took the form of dwelling excessively on possible scenarios that he feared would come true. He would become captivated with mental videos of things going wrong. He couldn't concentrate and couldn't study. This went on for hours. When he saw that it was getting too late to salvage the night and his work might go undone, depression would give way to fear, and a panic attack would ensue.

Given this level of understanding, I was able to prescribe a remedy that interrupted his crisis right away. We had determined that his depression was very sneaky in the way it hypnotized him into dwelling on negative things that might happen. Hence, it was of the utmost importance that he learn to keep an eye on it, and cut himself loose before it could get its stranglehold on him.

I said, "For the next few days, I want you to forget about all the injustices in your life and all your obligations. Your life will revolve around catching depression in the act of playing you these terrible videos. I know school is very important, but it can wait a few days, because your mental health is more important, and you'll need it so you can study the rest of the year." The school year had just begun.

"I also realize," I said, "how important it is to address the unfairness that you've endured at the hands of your teachers. You will get to those next week when you can handle them rationally, and end up getting what you want instead of getting kicked out of school. Before you deal with injustice in the outside world, you must deal with the greatest injustice of your life. I'm referring to the way depression and fear take turns setting you up to fail and then beating on you till you fall apart and they destroy your life. They beat you to a pulp with judgment and terror, threatening you with scenarios that either don't really matter or are very unlikely to take place."

Like many victims of panic attacks, Alfonso was gripped with the fear that he was going to drop dead from a heart attack. He feared that his best friends and girlfriend would be kicked out of school and he would be left alone. He also feared that he would take courses where he couldn't understand the material ever, no matter how hard he tried. Alfonso agreed that he needed to dedicate his life to countering these forces for the next few days. His perspective was clear and he felt motivated to do something about this problem.

I prescribed two tasks for Alfonso. First he was to become a catcher of negative thoughts. He purchased a diary in which he would make a list of all the thoughts that depression tried to get him to dwell on. He was to place these in a column and write in another column next to it either "So what?" or "Unlikely to take place?". Alfonso was to bring me the diary with all the negative thoughts he had caught, and for each one we would come up with a plan of action that would not only counter the negative effects of the threatening event, but make his life even better as a result. I explained that by catching these thoughts and solving the problems they posed we were stripping depression of the tools it used to torture him. We were turning these possibly damaging scenarios into opportunities to improve his life.

The second prescription was for Alfonso to welcome panic

attacks, yet provide himself with a guarantee that he would not be trapped away from home when he had one. He was to telephone his mother and she would arrange for him to come home for a break from the pressure. This lessened the sense of dread that comes from being trapped in a setting likely to trigger anxiety attacks. I explained to Alfonso that fearing attacks invites them, while daring fear to attack usually made the fear cower and run away. I said, "It's very hard to have an attack when you're trying to have one. See if you can do it, but don't let fear steal your territory." This simple prescription stopped Alfonso's symptoms. He was then able to decide without pressure whether to remain at this school or move to another one that was closer to home.

The next section addresses the problem of resistance. Many ODD teenagers will adopt a resistant stance that must be dealt with before conversations like the one just described can take place.

GETTING AROUND THE RESISTANCE

I always look forward to facing resistance in my work with oppositional teenagers. My confidence grows when I detect it. I am confident that the resistance of the ODD teenager will offer me an opportunity to achieve a decisive breakthrough. Resistance marks a potential contact point with the emotional brain, and offers an opportunity to view the real person and understand his secret desires.

It is beyond the scope of this book to offer a complete description of techniques for managing resistance in therapy. I limit my discussion to the most common forms of resistance encountered with teenagers, and to the basic techniques that work well for them.

I tie in the tactics I present with the treatment model outlined in this book, that is, the work on the two-mind split and the reframe of ODD as a hidden but powerful drive to pursue a different developmental course. Individual sessions with teenagers produce the most resistance. They are also likely to roll their eyes during family sessions in another manifestation of their feelings. This happens most prominently in the preevaluation phase, before the clinician can establish his alliance with the emotional brain. The clinician will also encounter resistance during family sessions after key failures, or in cases involving parental neurosis, the subject of Chapter 9.

Resistance comes in a number of forms, including passivity, deception, negative attitude, shyness, and unwillingness to communicate. This last form of resistance is secondary to anxiety, and is most prominent in cases that involve buried trauma. A golden rule to follow in dealing with the ODD teenager's resistance is, DON'T BE FORMAL! The teenager has to want help more than the clinician wants to offer it, and this will only come after failure or when the clinician has something to offer.

The clinician should avoid awkward silences during sessions, for these will encourage a form of resistance that the teenager will not articulate. The resistance will increase with time, and eventually the teenager will stop attending sessions. I never get caught up in the desire to make my sessions more productive than I can realistically achieve. A clinician should let go of any preconceived notion that he needs to be profound, to have all the answers. If he does not, the teenager will soon see through the pretense and regard him as just another one of those pushy adults with neurotic needs for goodness.

Another common error in working with adolescents is the tendency to remain aloof, showing no signs of sympathy, and to side with the agenda of the rational mind. Therapy with adults calls for nondisclosure on behalf of the therapist, along with exploration of client feelings. For example, the adolescent early in treatment takes a risk and reveals some personal material. Then the therapist asks, "How did that make you feel?" The therapist says nothing else. Eventually the therapist asks questions that suggest to the teenager that he should do things correctly. Teenagers, however, want to hear what the clinician did when he was young, facing similar situations. They want to know how the clinician can help them and what he expects from them.

I keep a state-of-the-art video game system in my office for calculated time-wasting. This helps engage socially deficient youths and works well in instances when I must cover tedious material with parents. The presence of this game system presents direct and powerful evidence to the youth's emotional mind that I am enlightened when it comes to the special value of these games, and the crucial role of staving off unnecessary boredom.

With children who love video games, I get to my agenda in a no-nonsense way at the start of the session, and move ahead rapidly with the business of the day. Then, rather than prolong the session needlessly to use up time, I offer the teenager a game or a treat. As we play the game, I await inspiration. I think of where I want to take the session, interrupt the game, and work intensely for short bursts. Kids rapidly learn to feel comfortable in my office, and they tell me if they want to address a specific issue or play a particular game.

Besides avoiding what teens experience as a neurotic need to take therapy too seriously, the methods I present to circumvent resistance include (1) maintaining an active stance, (2) exposing the negative attitude, (3) mirroring the resistance, (4) confronting the deception, and (5) joining the resistance.

Maintaining an Active Stance

It is a general rule in working with teenagers that the clinician must not allow the session to lag. To avoid this, he must talk a lot and engage in activities that the teenager values at the emotional-brain level. A model like this that educates and reframes is ideally suited for the purpose. The clinician gets a chance to teach the teenager about the rational and emotional brains and his own hidden desire to pursue a different course of development. The clinician defines the challenge of taking failure to the limit. These teachings need introduction and then restatement throughout the treatment.

The sessions take on a different tone after failure takes place. The time then is filled with stories of what happened, followed by analysis of the emotional-brain need involved. The clinician joins the emotional brain in its desires, challenges the attempt at adaptation, and reframes it positively as a learning opportunity. All of these methods take time.

Exposing the Negative Attitude

The clinician seeks to reveal the hidden message of the teenager who displays a negative attitude or adopts a passive stance. The negative attitude represents the agenda of the emotional brain. Attitudes express central assumptions that the rational mind does not feel free to express. We convey these through tone of voice, body posture, and facial expression. An individual can be talking about an ostensibly neutral subject, yet, through attitude, convey the message, "You owe me," "I hate you," "I own you," "I am in pain," or "I love you." Teenagers are often unaware of the messages they convey and feel secure in the notion that their words conceal their attitudes.

It is important to expose the attitudes of clients by saying, "Regardless of what your words are saying, your body is telling me something else." Here, the clinician describes the attitude he senses. He might say, "This is a waste of time," or, "You don't want to be here," or, "You think I can't help you." Once the attitude is put into words, most teenagers feel an obligation to explain themselves. This is an opportunity for the clinician to demonstrate his acceptance of the emotional-brain agenda, and become a vehicle for two-mind integration.

The next step is to go along with the teenager's mood of resistance. It is best if the clinician can actually magnify the importance of the personal attack that lies behind each negative attitude, especially if the attack is directed at him.

Mirroring the Resistance

Sometimes it is best to expose resistance by imitating it. This tactic is powerful and must be used cautiously. I prefer to warn the teenager that I am about to emulate his attitude. I say, "Do you know how you said that?" Or, "Here's how you said that." Most teens will show an interest when you approach them this way. I show them how their tone and body language came across. Alternatively, I may sound like a teenager, and say playfully, "This is you." Then I imitate. This device, if properly used, makes a powerful connection with the emotional brain.

Once the clinician portrays the attitude correctly, he will be able to help the teenager understand the ineffective adaptation involved. Take, for example, a teenager who has been very passive, and for whom every answer is, "I don't know," or, "Whatever." To show that he understands what's going on, the clinician assumes a slumped, low-energy body position, sounds really dull, and repeats, "I don't know." Then he says, "We'll never get anywhere if that's all you do. There's no way you are like this all the time, wherever you are, because you would be really boring. So you must think this is a complete waste of time, or you must think that I'm going to do something to make things get better magically."

Questions to the teenager to make the same points might be: "What do you think will happen if all you ever say is 'I don't know'?" "Are you like this everywhere else?" "Are you afraid to come off as boring?" If the teenager responds, it's better. However, if he does not, the clinician should answer the questions himself. He will appear to be intimidating if he fails to do this.

Addressing their limitations boldly gives hope to patients. The clinician says he wouldn't call attention to the resistance unless he believed he could help the patient operate at a higher level, and challenges the patient to explain the reasons for his behavior. The youth's emotional brain will begin to notice the clinician. It is then up to the clinician to form an alliance and become a mentor to the youth's rational brain.

Confronting the Deception

It is essential to inform ODD teenagers when it is apparent they are lying, either to themselves or to the clinician. I am direct and specific when I do this. I include defensive tactics in the definition of deception, because they are designed by the teenager to make it sound as though he were on the right track, and may involve claims that are not true. A teenager who cannot force himself to attend class may, for example, say, "I like schoolwork."

Brenda came into my office to discuss taking medication. She was attending a community college after a disastrous high school career marred by behavior problems. She was, however, offended by her mother's suggestion that she was having problems meeting her responsibilities. She claimed that she loved reading, math, writing, and other subjects. She tended to externalize blame, and seemed ready to walk out of the office at any time. I confronted her defenses, calling them lies for dramatic impact. Brenda responded, "I love math." I said, "I don't believe a word you're saying, but I know that's what you believe." Brenda was outraged. "WHAT! I'm not lying." I said, "I could be nice and pretend I don't see what I see, but then I'd be useless to you."

Brenda insisted that she was not lying. I said, "You say that because you're used to adults judging you, so you are accustomed to protecting yourself. But you'll need to get past protecting yourself if you're going to learn something new about yourself." Brenda was quiet and seemed receptive. I asked, "How come you don't attend classes if you love reading and math?" She responded, "I don't know."

I said, "I know that you claim you love reading and math, but that's because you aren't listening to the part of you that fights doing them. You don't know that you're lying, but you aren't listening to the part of you that refuses to do the work. I have to help that side so it cooperates with you. Otherwise you'll sound good here today, but you'll never make it to school." Brenda responded by opening up and giving voice to some of her reasons for not studying. "I only like studying the material when I do it my own way, and go at my own pace," she said. "Otherwise I get bored."

Brenda realized that she didn't understand how she could love all these subjects, yet fail to attend class and complete her assignments. She explained that she liked listening to class material, but not taking it in visually. She gave me other useful information. When she sounded defensive, I pointed out that the last thing I wanted to do was make her uncomfortable, but hoped, on the contrary, that she could become comfortable when she recognized and began to deal with her weaknesses.

I criticized her playfully every time I had an opportunity in order to mirror for her the kind of attitude I wanted her to adopt. I would say, "I want you to get comfortable with weaknesses, since I'm sure you have tons of them that you're not aware of." She was a lively person, and welcomed the challenge.

Most youths aren't aware of these defensive operations, so I tell them they probably don't realize they're lying. This provides a face-saving excuse, yet invites them to experience the best part of therapy, which is self discovery.

Joining the Resistance

In dealing with ODD teenagers, it is generally a good idea to side with and even prescribe resistance to the demands and expectations of authority figures. The clinician asks the client to engage in resistance to a greater extent than has been his habit, then joins the resistance by citing the benefits it offers. Resistance usually provides safety, or at least the feeling of safety. The clinician justifies the resistance by pointing out its value. He sides with the desires of the emotional brain, which prompt the resistance, no matter how ill-considered and unwise the teenager's expression of these desires may seem.

Once he has framed the positive side of resistance, the clinician turns to the negative, and notes that there are limits to the expressing of needs this way. The key is to show teenagers that these tactics will not get them what they want. To improve their understanding they should be asked to explain whether, in fact, they end up getting what they want through the use of resistance, and whether this type of behavior seems to them to be efficient. The clinician compliments the intelligence of teenagers who claim that resistance pays off. For those who don't, he suggests other ways of remaining safe but having needs met effectively.

In Brenda's case, the clinician might join the resistance by insisting that she tell just how much she loves everything she does. The clinician explains that adults have judged her so many thousands of times for so many years that she has been programmed to defend herself. Then, every time she claims to love something that she's neglecting he asks her to elaborate on what she loves about it. Suggesting that she's holding back, the clinician asks, "Are you sure you don't love it even more than you're letting on? Maybe the reason you don't go to class is because you love it too much." If, instead, Brenda says she doesn't like something, the clinician asks, "Are you sure you don't love that, too? You're giving yourself permission to admit something isn't perfect. Are you sure it's safe to do that? Maybe you should practice saying you love it."

After a few sessions during which I joined Brenda's resistance, she made critical changes. She began to change her attitude toward failure, and became increasingly comfortable with her weaknesses. This allowed Brenda to reduce her tendency to externalize blame, which yielded increases in self-awareness—the key to emotional mind–rational mind integration. Brenda's increased self-awareness and self-accepance allowed her to make important life changes and gave her confidence. She signed up for services offered by the college for learning-disabled students. She arranged with her professors to complete her assignments in different ways and get second chances to meet course requirements when needed. All of this began with the process of joining her resistance.

Joining the resistance can prove extremely effective when combined with a review of self-deprecating beliefs that trouble the client. The clinician adopts a critical tone and body language and gives voice to the underlying irrational assumptions. The following case illustrates this beautifully, along with other techniques presented here.

Katie has been depressed for many months. She experiences states of acute identity confusion during which she can't think and can't remember anything. She labors to make decisions.

She pursues the same ex-boyfriend for months without success. There is a histrionic quality to these mental states.

Katie began the session in her customary state of conflict. She had so much to tell me but couldn't remember what it was. She had written down some important things that she wanted me to read but had left her notes at home. She had gotten mixed results from her attempts to implement some strategies that I had prescribed for dealing with her ex-boyfriend.

My first move was to confront Katie's tendency to hide behind her confusion: "You're afraid, admit it."

Katie's body language demonstrated protest and she said, "What! What do you mean? Afraid of what?" I responded, "Afraid of finding out what you're made of. The reason you say you can't make choices is so you can hide your true self. I know you're not aware of this. But this is how your rational mind protects your emotional mind from rejection. It doesn't know any better way to protect you." Katie said, "Hmm, so you think I need to just make choices, no matter what happens?"

I explained that failure is vital to the trial-and-error process, and that she was operating out of a need to prove she was already perfect, rather than accepting that we all start out incomplete and live to overcome weaknesses. She was hiding her weaknesses, which kept her feeling accepted but prevented her from developing a mind of her own. Katie asked, "So what should I do?" I responded, "The fact that you ask that question is a reflection of your problem. You want me to decide for you, because you're afraid that your choices will reveal your true intentions, and your intentions will reveal your flaws." I assured Katie that her problem was quite common, and that it had a sensible remedy: "At present, you ask others what you should do every time you face a life choice. You never check your own inner voice. You need to wait for your own decision to come from your own inner voice. Once you have an answer, you can confer with others and see if their opinion matches yours."

I also advised Katie to experience failure, to engage in trial and error. "God knows, you're not perfect!" I said. The confrontation I engineered during this session led her to consider taking risks, and risk-taking always intensifies the therapeutic process. Her risks made certain things happen. For example, she met a young man whom she liked. This gave her hope and confidence.

Soon after, the plot thickened. Much to everyone's surprise, Katie began to consider dropping out of school. This impulse seemed to come from nowhere. She met with school authorities and was told she needed to consider seriously the hardships she would encounter in life if she didn't graduate. The school seemed well intentioned and genuinely cooperative. Katie raised the question of her education during a session with me with her usual air of doubt.

I saw Katie's pending decision whether to drop out as just that—a decision. I wanted her to make a genuine choice and then reserve the right to change her mind, whatever the subject. Therefore, I didn't attempt to dissuade her from dropping out, as others were doing. Katie didn't feel very confident, so she engaged in her typical defenses. I took the tack of joining her resistance and this had a dramatic impact.

Katie began this session by declaring her disgust with school and sounding very confident. She had been a good student but reported that she had reached the end of her rope. She then shifted unexpectedly to her doubts: "But my counselor says that I'll never get a good job if I don't finish high school. Plus, I'm afraid that if I don't go to school I won't do anything, and it will be a huge waste of time. Tell me what I should do."

I articulated Katie's worst fears about herself in response to her request for advice. I first tried giving her some useful information, but we simply went around in circles. The next time she asked what she should do, I responded: "I have no doubt about it. You should stay in school and do whatever people tell you, because you lack personality. You would turn out a loser. You can't make decisions. You have no confidence. If you quit, you would probably just sit around and do absolutely nothing all day. You would end up illiterate, and no one would want you."

Katie delivered a letter to me later that night that illustrated the decisive impact these words had on her. They established an instant connection to her emotional brain. Katie would soon embark upon a journey that would begin with failure and end with two-mind integration. She wrote:

"I'm writing to tell you how I am so happy tonight, after my appointment. I <u>know</u> now, right now, that I believe I should do whatever my heart tells me to do no matter what the consequences are, because I will be happier regardless of the outcome. When you said to me, 'No you shouldn't drop out, it wouldn't be good for you. You don't know what you want to do—you'll never make it,' wow—did I understand! I told you that's not true, and decided right there and then that I was going to do whatever I wanted because it was the <u>best</u> decision I could make." Katie underlined a sentence in the middle of her letter that captured the essence of her message. She wrote: <u>"None are more hopelessly enslaved than those who falsely believe they are free."</u>

Since the day she wrote this letter, Katie, who ultimately decided to stay in school, has caused her family some problems. However, she has been steadfast in her determination to make her own decisions, and has become much more positive in stating her needs. She has, in short, taken over her own life at a cost no more serious than most families experience when they are dealing with normal adolescent children.

COGNITIVE THERAPY: PROBLEMS AS OPPORTUNITIES

One way to view this approach to treatment of adolescent ODD is to invite failure, deliver consequences and supports, and then promote two-mind integration with cognitive therapy. Freedom has been used to encourage the oppositional teenager to face his own deficits. Failure has been presented as a unique growth opportunity, and the deceptions causing family conflict and distrust have been exposed. All that remains is to promote a higher level of adaptive functioning.

Repeatedly, my clinical observations have suggested that the ODD syndrome masks a need the child has to express his true nature, which is found in the emotional brain. ODD youths know that following through on emotional-brain desires can eventually heal them. To do this, however, they must practice deception, because most of those around them are insensitive to their requirements for development. The result, when the deception is discovered, is the creation of an atmosphere of distrust that ruins the teenager's hopes of ever being understood. No one in the family will recognize his needs and the youth himself won't know how to get past his oppositional behavior. The victim will be condemned to live a duality—a two-mind split maintained by involuntary lies.

The emotional-brain agenda is natural. It just *is*. The goal in approaching it as a problem is to foster adaptive functions that allow the individual to be true to this agenda, yet honest with others with whom he must deal. I cannot emphasize strongly enough the importance of identifying and meeting the needs of the emotional brain, as opposed to use of the therapy to encourage the deceptive practices, which, in the eyes of others, make the ODD victim appear to be leading a successful life. These youths are developing at a dramatic rate. Hence, it is vital for the therapist to help provide for the child the experiences that will promote growth. It is the therapist's goal to clarify, amplify, and sanction the agenda of the emotional brain.

Established cognitive-behavior therapy approaches can serve well to develop the necessary adaptive functions. Cognitive-behavior therapy methods have been documented extensively. A few examples include Beck and colleagues (1993), Freeman and colleagues (1989), Meichenbaum (1977, 1990), Meichenbaum and Biemiller (1998), Meichenbaum and Jaremko (1983), Meichenbaum and Turk (1987), and Meichenbaum and colleagues (1989). The therapist invites the patient to tell his story, and learns from his response the kinds of metaphors people use to explain their

behaviors to themselves. The therapist then helps the patient re-
construct a more adaptive story.

The final step in cognitive-behavior therapy is to test, as a sci-
entist would, the new perspective on the problem, that is, handling
the problem is viewed as an experiment. If the new belief is correct, then a certain behavior will solve the adaptive problem. If
the belief is incorrect, the problem will persist. If the person continues to deal with situations the same way as in the past, the symptoms will persist. The therapist assigns as homework between sessions comparison of different ways the patient employs to handle
problems, and uses role-playing to prepare the patient to face
various situations.

An effective way to introduce cognitive work is to invite the
teenager and his family to view problems as opportunities. Resistance is opportunity. Families that feel defeated by their struggle
against the natural tendencies of the ODD teenager will often
respond well to this reframe.

The clinician asks the teenager if he thinks he has problems,
and then if he has sufficient opportunities to lead a happy life.
The teenager is asked to list his problems in order of severity and
his opportunities in order of importance. The more depressed
patients will report many more problems than opportunities, but
the clinician points out that each problem offers a unique opportunity for growth. The bigger the problem, the greater the promise it holds.

Many clients will find this advice confusing. The clinician tells
them, however, that the only way to see problems as opportunities
is to believe that the individual's purpose in life is to become a
better person through struggle. If, instead, it is believed that the
purpose of life is to be fair, feel comfortable, have fun, and be
successful, then problems will seem worse. But if the purpose of
life is to become increasingly whole through the development of
all the individual's abilities, then problems are seen as sources
of inspiration. A problem is a call from nature to develop a new
ability. The absence of a certain ability has caused the problem
and the ability must be developed in order to solve it. Once this

is done and the problem solved, the individual becomes the person he was meant to be at whatever stage of life he's in.

The remainder of this book addresses specific problems the clinician is likely to face in the treatment of ODD teenagers. It shows the presenting problems, exposes the underlying complications, and details the process of finding adaptive solutions to the two-mind split. In all instances, the protocol is the same—to take failure to the limit, turn the failure into growth by offering the right blend of consequences for privilege violations, and help provide opportunities for finding an integrated life. The final step is to interpret the two-mind split and find an adaptive solution to the problem. The next chapter addresses the problem of school failure.

Part IV

Special Problems

8

Special Problem 1: School Failure

James's grades have been consistently poor, and now he has a low D average in high school. But this year, his parents say, must be different. They insist that this year their son must "really apply himself" if he's going to try for college. James agrees, though he slumps in his chair, obviously unhappy with what is being demanded of him.

In his heart of hearts, James knows he is bright, but his dislike of schoolwork is discouraging. He knows that matters involving his education have gotten progressively worse and that he has missed the basics for many of the courses he will have to take if college is his goal.

However, because James is smart, highly intuitive, and creative, he has developed numerous ways to get around learning in the traditional manner. He has charmed his teachers into leniency. They have even padded his grades in recognition of his potential, and in the hope this will stimulate him to greater efforts to improve his work. His friends have given him the answers for homework. James's neglect of his schoolwork has given him plenty of free time to master his drum set and cultivate friendships. He has many friends and is well aware of his own charm.

As he begins his junior year, his parents have attempted to ensure that he has everything he needs—a new calculator, a computer, a set of encyclopedias, pens, paper, even his own new drum set. All these things taken together constitute a plea for him to complete his assignments. His parents don't expect A's or B's. They just want evidence that he's been studying. James feels guilty about his true state of mind—so much the opposite of what his parents want. He pretends to go along with his parents' wishes, but knows in his heart that the material items they have supplied cannot bring about the mental effort necessary for him to succeed in school. There will, however, always be time for the drums.

James knows only too well how to gratify his personal needs. He knows how to put aside his more serious responsibilities in favor of television, drugs, and drums. James has become famous in school for his ability to tap out intricate and beautiful percussion sounds in a style completely his own. Unfortunately, because of the decline in his academic performance, he has been forbidden to play his drums any longer in the school's practice rooms, but he does so on a few occasions. His parents are furious.

The mail brought the report on James's first-quarter grades. The impact on the family was described to me in detail later. That night, I learned, there were recriminations at the dinner table. James's mother asked her son to explain his abysmal record in school, and tell his parents why he could not do better. James had not been able to prevent the marks from reaching them because he was too busy smoking marijuana with his friends when the envelope was delivered. At the table, his mother finally controlled her sobs, and read aloud comments from teachers about her son's school record. James was still feeling the effects of the marijuana. "James's performance has gone from successful to stagnant," one teacher remarked. "I haven't seen him in months," another wrote.

James's father broke his silence to shout: "After all we've done for you! Look at all the equipment and supplies we bought you to help you succeed. You NEVER learned how to use the computer. The calculator was never even opened! All you ever do is bang away at those drums! No more friends! No more anything until you bring up those grades, James!"

Now James has lost all the outlets that formerly allowed him to enjoy some sort of success. It's happened before. James is back to having nothing on his mind of the slightest interest to him, and his drums are inaccessible, leaving him with no challenge and nothing to master. So he continues to refine what remains—ways to act out his deviance.

The deviance gets James deeper into trouble, but entertains him as well. At the same time, consequences mount, satisfying his unconscious need for self-destruction and providing an outlet for his growing bitterness. These consequences reinforce a blatant disrespect for authority, which James has developed over many months of educational boredom and humiliation. James has become a lazy and disrespectful child, whose only response to punitive action is to focus on a wider spectrum of deviance, and how to get the better of the system.

James's parents conclude that medications, including stimulants and antidepressants and the help of special tutors, are not enough to get him back on track in the classroom. A stronger, more consistent remedial structure is called for. James's parents find this solution a bit of out of character for him, but an attempt must be made. They are considering offering him a new car if he will agree to attend a one-year residential school that provides a program designed to teach the consequences of actions and to instill the proper study habits. However, James will not agree to enter the program, not even for a new car.

Because of the boredom, deception, and duality in James's

life, his parents have no clue as to the risks he faces. They have no sense of his true concerns. James has become more and more callous, more and more turned off to the belief that life can be made worthwhile. He has come to share his parents' unspoken fear that he will fail in life, the same way he has been failing in school. He doesn't see much of a future for himself. So he hides in a world of conflict and escape.

James's story illustrates the experience of duality and isolation that abounds in today's peer world.

Many cases the clinician encounters present with school failure or a serious decline in grades as the primary concern. The pressure to improve placed on these youths by teachers and parents is often overwhelming. The first step for the clinician in such cases is to negotiate a temporary reprieve from the pressure, and then go through the ODD protocol described in the earlier chapters of this book. This reprieve from academic pressure becomes the trial intervention, as described in Chapter 2.

Persistent pressure, however, invites an oppositional response from the teenager, which, in turn, invites disciplinary action by the school. The youth's resistance to authority will, more often than not, meet with strict authoritarian responses that antagonize him without achieving positive results. Resentment grows in the teenager and he seeks to take out the anger on himself and his peers. The youth is attracted to the worst peer elements and encounters the cruelest, most dangerous elements of that culture, which expose him to the risk of violence, drugs, sexually transmitted diseases, and other pitfalls.

My method has been to alleviate the academic pressure immediately, and then challenge the ODD teen to change his lifestyle, change his activities so that he looks forward to his day, and make honest disclosures of his real needs and desires. I offer youths three options for changing the school day to reduce boredom and decrease the need for escape through deception. The first option is to modify the curriculum. Sometimes dropping a particularly irritating class will make a big difference in the life of the student, as will help from tutors and other special services. The second option is for the teen to go to school with the idea of just getting by and giving socializing and extracurricular activities the highest priority—all with the family's blessing. The third option is a charter school or schooling at home.

Home schooling involves pulling the teenager out of school for an extended period without making him liable for truancy violations. The family plans a life full of special activities and academic skills training to prepare the adolescent for adult education—a community college or technical school. The family may choose from a variety of desirable activities, including college courses, apprenticeships, jobs, and athletic and fun activities. The child's goal is to become the best at the one thing he wants most.

My findings with this approach to school failure have been uniformly encouraging. I have treated severely disturbed children who were headed toward hospitalization or residential treatment and whose primary presenting problem was refusal to do schoolwork. I have removed them from school pressure, and taken them through the protocol for ODD to address the mind–body split, as described in the early chapters of this book. I have offered the youths an opportunity to select one of the three options I have developed to reduce academic pressure, and, within a few months, I have seen a significant improvement in their mental well-being.

I have carefully followed this protocol with at least twenty severely ODD teenagers who were failing school. I have seen the return of a healthy wish to learn and the active pursuit of a productive life within one year of the reduction in academic pressure. I have seen a restoration of trust and healthy bonding in the family.

The results of this method have proven superior to those of highly structured programs that force teens to study. Such programs induce kids to earn credits, but do little to restore the genuine wish to learn, much less to integrate the emotional and rational minds, encourage honesty, and reduce boredom.

The program outlined below applies to teenagers (middle and upper school students), and younger children who display an unusually adverse reaction to school demands. The road of education is long. It requires frontal lobe maturity. AD/HD children develop slowly. Many of them turn out to be late bloomers. It is senseless to make the learning process arduous for so many years.

This chapter describes ways in which school stress can reach traumatic proportions and result in a full-blown clinical syndrome. Clinical observation suggests that well-intentioned efforts to help academically deficient children often overlook the trauma that can result from scholastic pressure over time, or how scholastic pressure can exacerbate other sources of trauma. This chapter discusses the factors that can cause scholastic trauma, and introduces the safe home base agreement, an intervention designed to help these students recover from trauma, outgrow their oppositional attitude toward school, and come to appreciate education.

THE TRAUMA HYPOTHESIS

It is the hypothesis of this chapter that two critical factors can account for the development of resistant attitudes toward school in teenagers: (1) the impact of forcing children to learn in ways that go against their natural style, and (2) the use of controlling tactics with traumatized children who have developed oppositional tendencies in response to school-related stress.

The next section elaborates the process by which education can become traumatic for students who lack sufficient fluency, technically referred to as automaticity. It is followed by a description of how schools, by failing to meet the vital needs of certain students, can unwittingly obstruct emotional development and cause ODD in a portion of the student population. Then comes a description of the full-blown syndrome that results from excessive academic stress.

THE PROBLEM OF AUTOMATICITY

School systems offer training in the fundamentals of education during the elementary grades. They then expect students to apply these basic tools of learning to a long curriculum of studies during middle school, high school, and college. But students who reach middle school with gaps in the basics will struggle. There will be countless hours of tedious work to fulfill curriculum requirements. It is only a question of time before such students reach a burnout point and turn off to the education process.

AD/HD and other difficult children are more likely than others to finish elementary school with significant learning gaps in reading, writing, and math. They tend to be impulsive. These children, for example, try to assemble new toys without reading the instructions. It is characteristic of them to require an experience of necessity before welcoming education. They prefer to try life without schooling, experience their own shortcomings, and then attend school. Conformist children, on the other hand, prefer to be well schooled before facing life. The odds are against the AD/HD children. They often need a second chance to fill these academic gaps.

The focus of traditional education is to mold informed individuals by ensuring that children adhere to a well-rounded curriculum. Course material is often presented in a serious, competitive way. Students who completed elementary school with gaps in their learning, and lack automaticity, can rapidly develop a negative attitude toward school and sour on education. They will find school an obstacle to growth and will seek to protect themselves by entering the oppositional phase of development, as described above.

Cognitive learning theorists refer to the capacity to retrieve information quickly and effortlessly as automaticity. Researchers are developing fluency training protocols, based on speed and accuracy drills, that are yielding a significant positive impact in children who struggle with literacy, numeracy, and graphomotor skills (Johnson and Layng 1992, Royer and Carlo 1991, Royer and Sinatra 1994, Talbot et al. 1992). Although the need for and the benefits of this kind of training are gaining substantial attention, the emotional consequences of having gone through a competitive academic curriculum without sufficient automaticity has not.

Chapter 4 described the cognitive learning theory concept of automaticity, and made the point that one must get several chunks of information into short-term memory within a short time span for learning to become interesting. Once enough chunks of information reach short-term memory, the student is rewarded with positive stimulation. Conversely, if information fails to arrive quickly enough, the mechanics of reading or math will require excessive effort. The student will quickly find learning tedious and tiring.

It makes sense to use material that students find interesting to help them develop automaticity. This is particularly important for AD/HD kids who are prone to boredom and for students who have been turned off to education. An efficient computerized system for developing automaticity represents the best option for these students. This form of skill building can help these youths gain academic competence and prepare for higher education. I suggest using the Computerized Academic Assessment System (CAAS) (Royer and Sinatra1994).

LACK OF A DEVELOPMENTAL PERSPECTIVE

Schools can unwittingly join parents in adopting a make-sure stance that can cause AD/HD students to burn out, end up in an oppositional fixation, endure a lasting struggle, and stay turned off to education for years. The classroom environment was designed long before developmental psychology made its most important contributions, and the classroom has yet to adapt to its discoveries. Students are expected to move from grade to grade, year after year, each time displaying greater capacity for discipline, greater willingness to learn, and greater respect for authority.

It is noble enough to offer free education to all who seek it, at any age. However, our education system goes further and makes learning compulsory. Some educators assume that children can be made to succeed, even against their will. It is assumed that unmotivated students will develop a taste for success once they are made to study correctly. Educators who believe strongly in this philosophy can reach a point where they literally prohibit failure. They will go to great lengths to prepare a thorough curriculum, yet will fall into the trap of becoming surrogate frontal lobes (adaptive brains) for a bunch of resistant children. Parents fall into the same trap.

One can see here the danger of prohibiting failure, mandating compliance, and using special-education services to achieve involuntary success through medication, structures, tutors, and the like. These services can interrupt the natural detour from growth that is integral to the transition from a dependent stage of development to a more mature mastery stage (see Chapter 1). By attempting to control oppositional tendencies, educators unwittingly provide these children with the only thing they need to remain fixated at the oppositional stage—a worthy adversary. As the struggle for control persists, it will concentrate attention on the antigrowth behaviors and escalate the oppositional symptoms.

Administrators often believe that teenagers who become rebellious are simply testing the limits of the school's tolerance for their behavior. The customary reaction of school authorities is strong, consistent, and sometimes rigid adherence to the rules. In their zeal to enforce rules and curb adolescent rebellion, however, such educators overlook the problems of obstacles to growth. They can create a poor fit and can cause what I refer to as scholastic trauma.

Lack of automaticity creates a poor fit in competitive education and constitutes an obstacle to growth. As noted in the earlier discussion of natural development (Chapter 1), when children encounter obstacles to growth, they regress to earlier levels of functioning. Growth ceases. When this occurs, educators and parents join forces in pushing for involuntary success, and often traumatize the child. This is when oppositionalism, nature's protective mechanism, kicks in. Whenever children reach an oppositional stage and adults force them to comply with their demands, the results are developmental fixations and oppositional defiant disorders. The more adults push oppositional children, the more pronounced the symptoms become.

The developmental perspective I have just outlined suggests that dire consequences may result from trying to make all children in the class learn in the same way. Whenever a group of children is put together in a classroom there will be a subgroup in a dependent stage of development, another in an oppositional stage, and still another in the mastery stage.

Each developmental stage presents its own unique emotional needs. When these needs are not met, growth is interrupted and resistance to learning sets in. This spoils the learning environment for all, even if only a small portion of the population develops a resistant, disruptive attitude. Teachers allocate an inordinate amount of their available resources to the most resistant students. These students drain their teachers.

To summarize, any system that attempts to make all children operate the same way ends up neglecting the emotional needs of some of them. The teaching process grinds to a halt for the entire class because of the resistant, oppositional students.

I next look at the impact scholastic trauma has on children, their families, and educators, and describe a full-blown syndrome that can result in devastating consequences for everyone involved.

THE CONSEQUENCES OF
SCHOLASTIC TRAUMA

The description that follows breaks the symptoms of scholastic trauma down into biological, psychosocial, and systemic categories. This breakdown is made for heuristic purposes, and hardly does justice to the complexity of the phenomena involved. In real life, these elements interact with each other in complex ways and form a myriad of vicious cycles in which the different elements feed off each other. The description that follows is based on clinical observations, including direct experience with a severe case that contained many elements that I have found repeated again and again, even in more moderate circumstances.

Involuntary Shutdown: The Primary, Biological Symptoms

The primary, biological symptoms of scholastic trauma present as an aversion to academic activity. Clinical interviews with teens who resist school because of this condition find the following symptoms: (1) involuntary loss of energy when facing schoolwork, sometimes accompanied by procrastination, dread in anticipation of homework or cramming for exams, or, in severe cases, nausea and a strong feeling of revulsion; (2) irritability and explosive tendencies when urged by others to study; (3) noncommunicative tendencies toward parents or other figures of authority; and (4) callousness toward others and a willingness to control and force their wishes upon others in the same harsh fashion they have experienced as victims. These students often resent and feel animosity toward successful, popular peers. A fifth distinguishing characteristic is a tendency to ingest drugs and alcohol to escape or alleviate the stress.

These symptoms are present in most biological manifestations of trauma. The unique characteristic of scholastic trauma is its relationship to forced competitive schooling on an unmotivated student, as evidenced by aversion to academic material.

Students who suffer from these symptoms present differently from other disruptive and disordered children. A defining characteristic is that they remain unaware of their trauma. This is evidenced in the way they naively assume they can turn things around and do well at any time. They often start semesters optimistically by promising themselves good grades. They are often surprised when they shut down early in the year, their hopes unrealized. These students recognize the above symptoms in a dramatic fashion when being questioned about them. They admit their performance is strongly impaired by them.

Clinicians can make strong allies out of these disruptive, resistant teenagers by explaining their condition to them. The children are largely unaware of their own plight. Questions that reflect an understanding of their problem give them hope and a sense of having found an ally. They feel relieved when their parents begin to appreciate why they promise to work and then procrastinate, lose their temper when they are reminded of work responsibilities, and lie to escape obligations. At this point, they are ready to be helped.

ODD: The Secondary, Psychosocial Symptoms

The primary, biological symptom of scholastic trauma (involuntary shutdown) causes a series of secondary psychosocial symptoms. These behaviors stem from deviant motivation, based on fear of failure and coercive tactics. Symptoms tend to take three extreme forms: (1) rebellion, as seen in ODD, where the child becomes resistant, negativistic, moody, irritable, and even abusive; (2) violations of the rights of others in the tradition of the streetwise, as seen in conduct disorder (CD); and (3) living the dual life of the same mind–body split phenomenon described in Chapter 2, except that these teenagers tend to sneak and deceive, rather than oppose and defy. The dual life is the most common and worrisome manifestation of scholastic trauma because it is, to some degree, the cultural norm.

The potential for students to fall through the cracks is great here. The victims are students who give lip service to authority and may even perform well in school, but lead secret lives that compensate for the hardships they endure. They cheat, lie, and engage in high-risk behaviors like shoplifting, substance abuse, violence, and unsafe sex. They tend to binge to escape obligations and then to celebrate after cramming for exams. These high-risk behaviors reach their height during the college years. However, the behavioral patterns are deeply ingrained early in high school.

Parental Neuroticism: Tertiary, Systemic Symptoms

The tertiary, systemic symptoms of scholastic trauma affect the adults in the resistant teenager's life. The student's shutdown creates a significant amount of stress in teachers, who are caught between the state's compulsory education mandate and the resistance of turned-off, disrespectful students who cannot produce, cannot be motivated, drain the teacher, and spread their resistant attitudes to the entire class.

In attempting to explain the behavior demonstrated by failing students, teachers consider several possible causes: AD/HD, LD, ODD, CD, family dysfunction or abuse, and involvement with reckless peers and drugs. The school calls home and asks the parents to make sure their child produces. If this doesn't work, the school recommends a doctor who might be able to diagnose and medicate the child.

If the parents force children to work, the school will conclude that the children are from a good family, but seem to be suffering from some deficiency or disorder. If the parents are unable to force their children to study, some educators will conclude privately that the family is dysfunctional. This assumption colors how the school deals with these families.

During the call to the student's home, the teacher's evident state of stress will convey a sense of urgency and may induce in the parents a case of parent neurosis (see Chapter 9). The parents quickly develop a secret fear that something is wrong with their child. This fear will be conveyed indirectly every time they ask their children questions such as, "Did you remember to turn in your paper?" The children interpret this as meaning, "Do you have a brain?" The parents may engage in endless lectures about the possibility of their children ending up losers, grilling hamburgers for a living.

Parents blame themselves for their children's failures. They express their concerns at parent–teacher meetings. They state again and again their belief that their children could do well if they wanted to, thus revealing a fundamental ignorance about the involuntary shutdown that comes with scholastic trauma. They recall how smart the teachers say the children are.

The parents' reaction is a well-intentioned effort to build the child's self-esteem. However, they secretly convey a concern that the child lacks this quality. The child hears, "School is the most important thing in life, and something is seriously wrong with you if you can't do it." In a show of desperation, parents may spend considerable time and money procuring special help, developing activities, and hiring tutors.

These children rapidly come to view their parents as embarrassments. The parents offer all kinds of help but the youths react as though they are humiliated and insulted. The parents say, "You did so well, you have so much potential." The youths respond, "Shut up!" and storm off to their rooms, giving more proof that something is wrong with them. The children avoid being seen in public with their parents. The deception grows, and the parents become more and more disturbed by their children's prolonged silences and by the abusive language they encounter when they offer help or reminders of unfinished work.

ADDRESSING DEVELOPMENTAL NEEDS TO COUNTER SCHOLASTIC TRAUMA

Parents can make up for the stress they have induced in their children by sending them a different message about school failure. Rather than treating scholastics as the key measure of their children's worth, they can interpret lack of interest in school as only a normal stage of development. Instead of fearing a dismal future of burger flipping, they can send a message of confidence.

Most students who persistently fail in school possess the skills required to perform adequately, but suffer from significant emotional problems. Most are in denial about their conditions and reject the many offers of support they receive from parents, teachers, and tutors.

By the time a student is failing school, the aversion to schoolwork and the mind–body schism that underlies it have reached clinically significant proportions. Such students require periods of reduced pressure followed by opportunities to associate learning with interest, success, and gratification. The extent of reduced pressure can vary from lowered expectations and special help to a period of removal from studies altogether. The primary objective of reducing pressure is the promotion of emotional well-being by facilitating self-awareness and obviating the need for denial and deception.

Whatever happens, it is imperative that the student is given the opportunity to select his own remedy for the problem. School failure often becomes traumatic, and empowerment is critical to recovery from trauma. Empowerment requires that the victimized individual take an active part in decision making. In trauma, *passive* and *victim* are synonymous.

Dealing with Mild School Aversion

The key to helping failing students is to reduce expectations, offer greater supports, and encourage the teenager to alter his negative associations with school and homework. It is also essential to help the youth develop an increased awareness of his problem with school aversion, for this will keep the ODD teenager involved and motivated. The clinician can use a combination of parenting, school consultation, and counseling to achieve these ends.

Adjusting Expectations to Alter Negative School Associations

In cases of mild to moderate school aversion, the most effective way to adjust expectations and to modify negative associations is to enable students to apply themselves only in classes that inspire them. Students should deliver their best performances to teachers whose classes they like, and their worst to teachers they dislike. Many oppositional students target all teachers indiscriminately, despite the fact that only a few have been causing them hardships. Students can be persuaded to give each teacher his due, based on his performance, once the clinician points out the unfairness of this habit.

> Luke tried in vain to conceal his elation as he first pondered the notion of having complete license to perform poorly for his science teacher. He was already getting a D-minus in that class, so poor performance would be nothing new. The appeal was in having his parents sanction his poor performance. The move shifted the onus of responsibility from Luke to the teacher, and used Luke's tendency to externalize blame to form an alliance with him. There would no longer be an implication that Luke was an inadequate student. It was the teacher who was inadequate.
> Luke's surprising good humor marked the beginning of a

promising shift in attitude that would become as obvious to his parents as it would to me. This shift stood in stark contrast to his timid, anxious, nearly voiceless presentation of a few minutes earlier. From the moment that he understood he could behave as he wanted in his science class, Luke spoke with ease and certainty. He sounded confident and was able to be honest with his parents about how they could help him, and about how their demands that he improve his marks in school had been bothering him.

This session had started as a moment of truth for Luke when his parents handed me his report card and confronted him on his poor grades. Luke had promised to do well in school in exchange for privileges such as playing on several traveling sports teams, a new video game system, and a generous increase in peer activities, including sleepovers. These were the terms of his trial intervention (see Chapter 3).

Dad reminded Luke that he had wanted to get all B's at the start of the year. His father had wisely asked, "What grades would you like for yourself?" In response, Luke committed himself to a level of performance that belied his emotional mind's genuine lack of interest in school. He was speaking largely from the perspective of the rational mind, wanting to gain his father's momentary approval and express his gratitude for all the privileges granted him in the trial intervention. In the process, he had sold his emotional mind down the river.

Luke had told me in confidence that he could not care less about school, but had to convince his parents that he genuinely cared about it so he could gain privileges. I didn't argue with him at the time. In fact, I joined him and complimented him on how clever he was.

I used this situation to help Luke admit his true feelings about school to his parents, and to introduce expectations that were true to his emotional mind and would gain his parents' approval. I interrupted the session to confer with Luke in private when his dad reminded him of his wish to get straight B's. I knew that his parents were bright, and would understand

Luke's predicament. They would support the expectations that would eventually help him grow to love learning.

During our private meeting, I told Luke he should be honest about his feelings, and that I would get him the freedom he wanted without the need of pretending to like school. He agreed to try. He said, "Okay, but when we get in there, don't just ask me to tell you the stuff about my pretending to like school. First ask them a few questions and then ask me how I feel about school." I could sense that it was a big risk for Luke to admit that he didn't care much about school. I followed his request. He followed my lead and came clean.

I explained to his parents that I didn't want to see Luke reject the idea of learning, and I feared that continued pressure to pretend that he wanted to do well in all his subjects would eventually have that result. I explained that Luke should do well only for the teachers whose classes he really liked and perform poorly for those he didn't.

We put Luke in charge of how his school career would be handled and how his parents could provide support. We examined his report card. He rated the value of his classes and informed his mom of the kind of support he needed for each class. It turned out that he liked most of his teachers. He wanted a single reminder daily that he should start on his homework, and asked that Mom check to make sure the assignments were complete. He reserved the right to ask for help with difficult assignments and for feedback on his work. However, these supports were to be granted only if he asked. There would be no more bugging him about school. Once Mom agreed to provided these limited supports, the rest was up to Luke.

The science teacher didn't like him, Luke said. She graded him poorly no matter what he did. Luke cited an incident in which he and a favored peer had turned in the same answers on an assignment, and the other student was marked two grades higher than Luke. The teacher was critical and boring. She lectured extensively. Luke didn't want to fail her class because he planned to participate in school sports and failing could prevent him from trying out for teams. He would settle for a D in the course. This decision made all the difference in the world to Luke.

Once a student has taken the first step of performing optimally for select teachers, the clinician can challenge him to become his own special teacher, and learn to make boring classes more interesting. The student can attempt to inject life into one boring class on one day, and gradually broaden this skill to other days, and then to other subjects.

Chances that the student will actually achieve this lofty objective are slim, indeed, but this is not the purpose of the intervention. The suggestion that it is possible to make school stimulating sends a message of hope for the future. The assumption that the student can attain this objective makes a statement of faith in the youth. Finally, the mere pursuit of this goal, no matter how unrealistic, keeps the youth pointed in the right direction in relation to his education.

Offering Supports to Establish Goodness of Fit

In his recent book, *The Explosive Child* (1998), Ross Greene makes a strong case for justifying a variety of effective school modifications tailored to meet the needs of ODD youths. Greene supports the notion that it is imperative to establish goodness of fit with school (as described in Chapter 1) when dealing with this population. He refers to this process as "creating a user-friendly environment." The modifications that he prescribes for ODD youths differ from the typical ones for learning disabilities or AD/HD. However, they are uniquely valuable.

Throughout his book, Greene cites inflexibility and explosiveness (poor frustration tolerance) as the primary impairments of ODD youths. He is emphatic in justifying modifications to school demands based on these tendencies. "Inflexibility-explosiveness is as good a reason to adapt school work as is any other type of learning disability" (p. 200). In discussing poor graphomotor skills (handwriting), a common problem for AD/HD youths, he argues,

"Although it would be important to make sure that the student continued to work on writing skills, it would be even more important to make sure that our expectations took into account both the student's writing capabilities and level of frustration" (p. 200).

The best way to offer support to a teenager failing in school is to have him select his own forms of assistance. This puts him in charge of the process and counters the passive stance that failing teenagers tend to adopt. The imposition of an unwanted structure can aggravate a youth's anxiety or trauma. However, allowing the youth to choose his own structure facilitates the relearning process necessary to modify associations from past experiences.

The clinician can also increase awareness by putting a failing teenager in charge of his own school situation, even if this initially means failure. This is consistent with the core protocol for dealing with ODD as presented in this book. (See Chapter 6, Step 4, "Arrange Buffers for Teenagers," for a detailed description of how to provide support for a school failing teenager.) The procedure will fit mild cases of school aversion well. The process is as follows.

The clinician first presents the ODD teenager with a list of all possible supports and protections. The possibilities include reminders; assistance with planning, organizing, or completing tasks; and permission to engage in or avoid various activities. To make his school day better, parents offer transportation or other resources. They enroll the teenager in classes, clubs, or teams. They can also hire tutors or personal trainers.

When, with the parents and the student, the clinician attends the meeting at school, he advocates for whatever buffers the teenager has requested, whether he agrees with them or not, whether he expects to get them or not. In preparation for the meeting, the clinician familiarizes himself and the family with federal law regulating special education services, namely the Individual Disabilities Education Act (IDEA), so they can assert the youth's rights. The advocates for the youth present the requests of the ODD teenager in writing, and clarify for the teenager that there is good chance the school will turn down some of the requests.

Sometimes it is appropriate to have a meeting without the ODD teenager to agree upon the consequences that the school will administer for a given misbehavior. This allows the parents and the clinician to remain allies of the ODD teenager when the school turns down his request for unhealthy or unwise support. The clinician and parents adopt the role of advocate and the school becomes the contrary force in the mind of the teenager. Teachers will know that, at some level, they have the support of the family.

Some time after the conclusion of the meeting, the ODD teenager decides whether to accept the options offered by the school in response to the meeting or continue to advocate for different buffers. The clinician and family are prepared to offer the youth interim buffers until the issue is resolved. The problem of homework presents a good opportunity to illustrate this principle. Ideally, the clinician arranges for reduction or elimination of the homework load. If the teacher does not cooperate, the family hires a tutor to help with the homework. This serves as an intermediate measure until the proper arrangement can be worked out with the school.

Altering the Homework Experience

The role of homework in creating school aversion is common in cases of ODD but is rarely understood. Homework contributes to the emotional disturbance behind school failure and creates greater family dysfunction than any other factor I can think of. The reason for this is simple, as we will see.

It is essential to present convincingly to the school the ODD teenager's need for homework modification because, if left unexplained, the legitimate needs of the student will not make sense to the mainstream educator. The clinician must provide a clear understanding of the special needs and legal rights of youths suffering from this disorder. Only then do the modifications make sense to the educator.

Greene (1998) discusses modifications of homework demands that are consistent with those I have found effective, and that make a lot of sense from the perspective of scholastic trauma. He categorizes certain misbehaviors as important to deal with but impossible to modify. He emphasizes that consequences and motivational strategies make possible whatever is possible, but never make the impossible possible. He places homework in this category for ODD youths:

> Homework is often a good example of the second possibility— important but not capable and not possible to address. Many parents, teachers, and school administrators believe that homework is an essential component of a child's education. Which is fine, except that many inflexible-explosive children find homework to be remarkably frustrating because they don't have any brain energy left after a long day at school, their medication has worn off, they have learning problems that make completing homework an agonizing task, or because homework—especially long-term assignments—requires a lot of organization and planning. Thus, it's no accident that these children often exhibit some of their most extreme inflexibility and explosiveness while they are trying to do homework. [p. 198]

Greene argues that it makes little sense to force ODD youths to complete normal homework loads:

> Do these difficulties render some children incapable of completing the same homework assignments as their classmates? Yes. Is it always possible to address these difficulties effectively? No. Does having a child melt down routinely over homework help him feel more successful about doing homework? No. Are these difficulties a good reason to alter or adjust homework assignments? Yes. I've yet to be convinced that the best way to instill a good work ethic in a child—or to help his parents become actively and productively involved in his education—is by inducing and enduring five hours of meltdowns every school night. The best way to instill a good work ethic is to assign homework that is both sufficiently challenging and doable in terms of quantity and content. [p. 199]

From the perspective of scholastic trauma, forcing meltdowns over homework will only further the association in the emotional brain of books and homework with shame and evil. It will undermine confidence and respect for authority. The emotional mind will instinctively know that these expectations are wrong because they are unreasonable and even unhealthy. The rational mind will know that these same expectations are correct because one needs an education to succeed in life. Thus exist all the elements that cause ODD—the unpleasant association of books with upset and shame, and the conflicting message that increases the schism between the two minds.

Greene offers a series of commonsense modifications for very mild cases of homework-adverse youths. He suggests eliminating unnecessary repetition from homework assignments by, for example, completing a few math problems rather than twenty of them. He suggests placing limits on the amount of time a student spends on homework, and prioritizing assignments so that the most important ones are done first and there is no penalty for unfinished work.

More severe cases of school and homework aversion require the support of a tutor who can make the experience more pleasant and efficient.

> I often recommend that the child complete homework either at school, under the supervision of an adult whose feedback and assistance is less objectionable to the child (many schools have "homework clubs" that can serve their purpose), or at home, with the assistance of a high school–aged "homework helper" or hired tutor. Such assistance often improves communication between the parents and child and permits the parents to focus on the more important aspects of parenting. [p. 201]

A high school–age homework helper or hired tutor can perform wonders in modifying negative associations to homework. The system can resolve homework problems just as effectively as performing for selected teachers can resolve classroom problems.

Many ODD youths associate homework with adults and tedium. But they associate same-age peers with bonding, acceptance, and enjoyment. It makes sense that working on assignments with a teenager whom the ODD youth likes greatly increases the chances of altering the associations to the experience of homework.

It makes sense to hire these youths and pay them a decent fee.

The impact of a well-liked teenage tutor can be great if the ODD youth manages to have a good time, do the work effectively, and achieve success and good grades. By compensating the tutor, the parent will have more influence on the process, and increase the chances for consistently good work by the student. The parent can improve the relationship by offering both the student and the tutor a special outing together for achieving certain objectives. This will motivate the tutor to take the task seriously and the ODD youth to cooperate.

In some instances, a study group or a peer to do homework on the phone with, can effectively modify associations to homework, but are not so likely to produce lasting results. It is too easy for the participants to waste time through lack of concentration, since there is no accountability. The more effective students are likely to conclude that they're wasting their time with the slower ones and give up. It is important that the advanced student knows he is primarily there to help the other one.

The Need for Mastery States

The ideal way to alter the negative associations that accompany scholastic trauma is to interest students in learning by training them to enter mastery states, though this approach may not be practical in many school settings. It behooves clinicians, nevertheless, to begin to familiarize themselves with this form of learning. The process of entering these states requires tapping areas of interest, training key skills to the point of fluency, and setting the right expectations. Learning becomes addictive once these conditions are met (see "Entering Mastery States," Chapter 1).

Education and Mastery States

Educators and clinicians should keep two guidelines in mind in mastery state training. One is to choose an activity that the student likes and for which he has an aptitude. With those conditions satisfied, the student is likely to feel challenged and to work to improve himself. The other guideline is to encourage practice to a point of excellence of the skills required to complete a task.

Much-practiced moves require much less brain effort than those that are unfamiliar. Expectations should be gradually increased to maintain a sense of challenge and prevent boredom or anxiety.

Teaching teenagers how to enter flow states in any subject provides them with the motivation to get better and better at handling the task. The experience of entering flow states is intrinsically rewarding. Once the student learns to enter a flow state in any task, he will want to enter it in other tasks.

Howard Gardner, the Harvard psychologist who developed the theory of multiple intelligences, sees flow as the healthiest way to teach children because it motivates them internally, rather than by threat or by promise of reward. As Goleman (1996) writes, "We should use kids' positive states to draw them into learning in the domains where they can develop competencies . . . You have to find something you like and stick to it. It's when kids get bored in school that they fight and act up, and when they're overwhelmed by a challenge that they get anxious about their schoolwork" (p. 94).

A number of schools are putting Gardner's model of multiple intelligences into practice. Their strategy involves identifying a child's natural competencies and using them to teach the skill of entering the mastery zone. They also optimize challenges and present the material in a way that will assist the child in using mastery states to shore up weaknesses. "Knowing a child's profile can help a teacher fine tune the way a topic is presented to a child and offer lessons at the level—from remedial to highly advanced— that is most likely to provide an optimal challenge. Doing this makes learning more pleasurable, neither fearsome nor a bore," Goleman (1996) quotes Gardner as saying (p. 94).

The rest of this chapter emphasizes the special needs and interventions that can help alleviate the more severe cases of scholastic trauma.

Dealing with Severe School Aversion

Severe cases of school aversion require either school attendance with minimal expectations or a period of time away from school altogether. The decision is based on the extent of social involvement of the student. Teenagers who maintain strong ties to their peers will often elect to remain in school. They generally are willing to make extensive sacrifices to do so. Students who are less invested in their peers are more likely to accept a home-schooling option or time away from schooling altogether.

For older teenagers, trying life without education represents a valuable learning experience. It often leads to the development of a true appreciation for learning and for success later in life.

Time away from school while holding down a job can provide a valuable learning experience for the older adolescent. This works particularly well when the family manifests its positive regard for the enterprise entailed, and when the teenager takes advantage of the opportunities available to him to pursue genuine wants and comes to enjoy his daily activities. (See the protocol in Chapters 5 and 6.) Only in the worst cases of scholastic trauma should students withdraw from school altogether rather than learn to develop a different outlook on school, or attend a charter school or alternative learning center.

It is important for youths to have access to at least a modicum of educational opportunity in the unfortunate instances where they withdraw from school altogether. The worst consequence of dropping out of school is the emotional baggage and sense of failure dropouts carry with them. The clinician, wishing to avert the disapproval, lack of faith, and lack of opportunity that afflict dropouts, attempts to arrange consequences and opportunities so that the youths hunger for professional training earlier rather than later.

He wants to encourage his client to leave school, not to fail but to become the best at one thing that appeals to him, and maintain at least a minimum level of success in academic skill training. The family should be encouraged to view the youth as recovering from scholastic trauma and preparing for a positive experience of learning in real life. The clinician wants to help the parents see this as a transitional stage that will eventually lead to a quality experience in higher education.

Younger individuals who have not worked hard in school

should be made to work hard in their homes. They should have moderate help and support, but should not be given things they have not done anything to earn. Denial of special favors is the most effective precaution a parent can take against deviant development. It eliminates the possibility of the young person having an unrealistically easy life—the greatest danger to the maturation process. Working hard in the home approximates real life: responsible adults work hard to pay the rent and other bills, and they cook, clean, and do other household chores.

Once parents insist that their children make significant contributions to family life, the foundation is laid for them to develop discipline. The children may initially do very little. However, staying at home, doing chores and wearing outdated sneakers because they have not earned new ones will sooner or later create a feeling of stagnation. Then these children will want to find work, get a degree, join an activity, or do something else meaningful.

The key expression of family generosity is support of the teenager in any activity he wants to be the best at, regardless of what this is. The clinician should encourage the family to make the sacrifices necessary to provide the child with opportunities to pursue his most important dreams. It doesn't matter whether the avocation is pragmatic and likely to yield a career, or whether the teen's main interest is in skateboarding or music. The critical elements are for the child to have a vital activity on which, in order to achieve success, he will exert 100 percent of his energies, and for the family to support him. The youth will eventually apply the same dedication to more productive activities.

Once these new activities are added to the obligations of home, life becomes difficult enough to require the discipline that will lead to the development of adaptive brain functions. These same activities and efforts fail to produce adaptive functions if the child does little at home, or if the parents give him unearned gifts and in general make life too easy for him.

The taste for education eventually returns to a nonstudent who has had a difficult but rewarding life. First, the inclination to do very little gives way to a desire for a job—anything that pays but doesn't require schooling. Next, the low pay and lack of work satisfaction awaken a desire for education and training. The process takes from months to a couple of years, at most. If the process is properly handled, the end result will be a self-motivated young adult.

The precaution of requiring hard work at home is likely to go against the protective instincts of many parents. The more common scenario, however, is the lenient parent doing a lot for the child in the effort to help him succeed in school. Parents often seek to buy productivity by indulging the child and giving him what he wishes. These tactics tend to create feelings of entitlement and promote narcissism. Treated this way, the child who suffers from scholastic trauma will remain unable to complete his work but will lie to get compensation for having done it. The parent, understandably, will feel betrayed and worry about the child's character.

It is important to note that the goal of the intervention for severe scholastic trauma is to refer the child to a mastery-based school such as Gardner's, as described above, or to a cognitive learning approach to remediation. These programs are designed to fill academic gaps and create automaticity in the fundamental skills the child will need to succeed in a competitive curriculum, whether in high school or college. They work best in teenagers who have outgrown their oppositional phase and regained a desire to learn. This is the aim of the intervention presented next — the safe home-base agreement.

Severe School Aversion: The Safe Home-Base Agreement

Mickey was back for his second session. I had completed the intake process and determined that he needed relief from school pressure. It was time to explain the safe home-base agreement to him. His mother also listened.

"The safe home-base agreement gives you the rights of an adult. It works this way. Part one, your parents support and protect you. You make your own decisions about your education. You decide when you want to be in school, what classes to take, and so on. The school says you can't, but no problem. Your parents provide you with a note giving you the right to do things the way you want.

"Part two, I support and protect your parents. The school challenges your parents for allowing you to do things your own way. They claim your parents are neglectful. I use my professional standing to vouch for their case. They say they are writing these notes to the school because they are following my directions.

"Part three, you protect me. You use this freedom and empowerment wisely. You don't just break the law, and use this freedom in a destructive way. Otherwise, your parents would fire me. You make errors, but you learn from them. You show good intentions. Use your freedom wisely, demonstrate good intentions."

My source of inspiration for the safe home-base agreement is D. W. Winnicott's (1979) work on the maturational processes and the facilitating environment. The idea is to create a home base that will facilitate maturation.

The safe home-base agreement empowers students to handle their lives outside the home in any way they wish, free from coercion and the involuntary repulsion reaction to schoolwork. This intervention addresses the systemic pressures that come from failure in school and from teacher stress. The clinician notifies the teachers that the student has been granted a temporary reprieve from compulsory education. Thus alerted, the teacher will no longer feel pressured to pass the student.

In exchange for reduction of the pressure, the student agrees to respect the atmosphere of the classroom and the authority of the teacher. The teenager will neither disrupt the class nor show disrespect. This is a key condition of the safe home-base agreement. Teachers are informed that the student is stuck in an oppositional phase, and needs time to develop a true hunger for the privilege of education.

Students who have been seriously traumatized by scholastic pressure often need time away from their studies. The clinician should formally notify the school that the student is suffering from emotional problems. There are, to be sure, situations in which the clinician must document the severity of the condition for the child's physician. On the basis of this diagnosis, the physician can request that the student be given time off from school for health reasons. The laws and requirements surrounding this tactic, however, vary by state.

In some cases of severe scholastic trauma, a semester away from school has worked well. Other students have remained in school on the basis that they socialize and make a minimal effort for a full year. Some youths have been persuaded to contribute productively to the home, with very few other demands placed on them. In short, they have been offered opportunities without pressure.

Even the most traumatized and difficult of these youths develop the motivation to find a job after a few months of sitting around with little to do. When the root of the problem has been scholastic trauma, the difference in these children has often been striking once they are relieved of school pressure.

Among the youths I have followed, most of those who have been guided by the safe home-base protocol have developed an appreciation for education and a taste for learning within one year of the initial implementation of the agreement. Many were initially headed for legal problems or even residential treatment. Some failed to respond to the threat of judicial consequences. However, most have matured significantly as a result of the agreement. This is an excellent time to refer them for a mastery-based program of academic rehabilitation.

Many ODD teenagers initially see the safe home-base agreement as an opportunity to watch tremendous amounts of television. They will do this for several months at most. However, their refuge in the world of laziness and TV will soon became intolerable and the need to outgrow the oppositional phase and experience mastery will take over.

Successful in his efforts to work his way out of laziness, one teenager told me the reason for his accomplishment: "My motivation came from watching so much TV that I felt like a complete ass." He reported this after months of struggling to build a life, acquire a car, and attend community-college classes.

The safe home-base agreement grants teenage students many of the same privileges that adults enjoy, in effect making them emancipated minors. The teenagers are empowered to add and drop classes, change activities, and direct their own lives in other ways. Families are informed of their legal right to seek special-education status for their children if necessary. However, this option can be costly to the school, and is often unnecessary if the school is flexible.

If an individualized education plan (IEP) is needed, it should be low cost. Many schools offer an exploratory IEP to allow the child time to outgrow scholastic trauma and ODD, and find a higher level of motivation by entering the next stage of development.

The agreement focuses on how the child should handle life outside the home. It contains seven clauses and a definition of freedom. Obligations are (1) seeing failures as opportunities for growth; (2) practicing autonomy, which means complete control over self but no control over others; (3) participating in the belief that all family members are supportive of each other, and that this is the number-one priority in their lives; (4) respecting privacy; (5) obeying the law; (6) avoiding laziness at home; and (7) developing mutual respect for other family members.

The safe home-base agreement defines freedom as maximum independence outside the home, but maximum responsibility in the home. This approximates what occurs in adult life, as mentioned above. Adults are free to make their own decisions and run their lives their own way. They decide where to work, where to live, what activities to engage in, with whom to be friends, and what to spend their money on. There are, however, obligations to be met at home, such as paying the rent and other bills, and doing household chores.

The safe home-base agreement grants children the right to decide how to run their lives outside the home. At home, however, the requirement is that they take on an equal share of household responsibilities. This means the teenager will manage his individual responsibilities, including maintaining his own room, cleaning up after himself, doing his own laundry, paying for his own gas and insurance if he has a car, and managing his own work, school, and social relationships

I say to these teens: "You take care of you, Mom takes care of

Mom, Dad takes care of Dad, I take care of me. That's fair. It's also fair that we split communal areas more or less equally. If we all use the kitchen, living room, bathrooms, yard, and basement, we should all help to maintain those areas. That's fair."

This means the teenagers should take responsibility for a fair share of household responsibilities, including work assignments and contributions to a pleasant family atmosphere. They should perform a certain amount of the cleaning, food preparation, and outdoor maintenance. They should also help keep others company, help with child care, and participate in family entertainment.

The core of the safe home-base agreement pertains to school. However, the ideas embodied in the terms of the agreement also apply to peers, activities, sports, and clubs. The teenager is responsible for making the best use of it. The family supports the teen's decisions.

Teenagers participating in the safe home-base agreement are free to do poorly in any class. They are also free to fail at, or drop, any activity. This conduct is authorized in notes from parents giving their children permission to drop classes, add classes, arrive late, leave early, or be signed out of school altogether. However, students are never allowed to show disrespect for their elders or disrupt the learning atmosphere of others. To maintain their privileges, they must at all times carry out their responsibilities to the home and family.

The safe home-base agreement asserts the importance of the family over the individual. It states that the success of a family depends on its members agreeing to the following priorities: first, communal needs; second, personal duties; third, self-improvement; and fourth, fun and friends.

Stress is one factor that can make school a traumatic experience. Abuse by parents or other relatives at home or by punitive-minded educators at school also has traumatic effects and a deleterious impact on the psyche. Victims of trauma in one setting tend to become victims in other settings. What differentiates victims of scholastic trauma from the rest is the mind-deadening impact on them of textbooks, exams, or other academic assignments. This makes them vulnerable to other forms of trauma.

Students suffering from scholastic trauma feel stupid, regardless of what factors make school difficult for them—AD/HD, LD, limited intelligence, or an accumulation of burnout from excessive pressure placed on them by parents and educators. The students end up trapped in cycles of academic decline, failure, and increasing levels of shame and suffering. Gradually they become numb. They tell us everything is fine when they arrive home from school. They even accept the stigma of being considered inferior students. They comply with demands made on them, and on the surface they may seem fine. However, it becomes impossible to motivate them.

The Home-Schooling Option for Younger Teenagers

Finding options for younger teenagers who have become turned off to education presents a unique challenge. It is an opportunity for the clinician to resolve their problems and help them develop a mature attitude toward learning while they are still young, before they succumb to the temptations of the peer world.

There will be instances in which attempts to install the safe home-base agreement are rebuffed by school administrators who do not understand the severity of the ODD teen's condition, or the proposed remedy, and have a different philosophical outlook on how to manage adolescents. School, it will be held, is mandatory, and punitive measures should be employed to force the child to study. Educators with this point of view are programmed to view grades as the single most important measure of healthy adjustment in children.

Schools in such instances deny the options the scholastically traumatized teenager desires. This is a particularly difficult problem in the middle-school years, when the teen is too young to sign out of school and the entire day is rigidly structured.

The clinician's choices in such instances are limited. He can encourage the family to hire a lawyer to advocate for his client, and he can then serve as an expert witness in the case. Documentation of sufficient psychopathology to warrant the excusing of the patient from further academic pressure is required.

I have been developing options to traditional education methods and beliefs in my practice with teenagers for several years now. My interest dates from the time I began to recognize the presence of the scholastic trauma syndrome. I have seen charter schools work wonders because they are not bound by traditional concepts. I have recommended as options for older teenagers independent studies, work-study programs, and enrollment in community-college courses.

One of the most promising options I have found with seventh to ninth graders has been home schooling. The home-schooling option has worked well with severely ODD elementary school pupils as well. It is ideally suited for instances where the school system will not yield to anything nontraditional that the ODD teen is willing to try, and the family is not in a position to hire a lawyer.

So it was in the case of Gerry, whose problems with ODD were severe. Yet, the school would not support the process we were requesting. Gerry is the only patient whom I identify by his real name in this book. He insisted that I tell his true story using his real name, and said he wished his photo could appear in this chapter.

Gerry's Case

I knew what I wanted for Gerry, but wasn't sure the school would approve. It was worth trying, I assured Gerry and his parents. We were in my car on our way to a school meeting. We had just stopped at a Dunkin' Donuts. Gerry had a grin on his face. He wore a baseball cap, backwards, and shades. He was listening to a controversial radio show, holding a mug of coffee, and devouring a cream-filled donut. Mom was already at the meeting. We would be a few minutes late.

"I want to be in the eighth-grade class. Yeah. That would be cool," Gerry said, with inflections of Beavis and Butthead. This would be an unlikely event, since Gerry had just flunked the seventh grade. At last year's meeting, he had been put in charge of himself and subsequently was allowed to fail. Gerry had done no work for his teachers for a solid year, and this had upset some of them.

"We'll see," I responded. "Do you think you can do well in there?"

"Sure!" Gerry answered with enthusiasm.

"You'll do the classwork and the homework?" I asked, testing to determine whether he was being true to himself, whether he was speaking from the emotional or the rational mind, or possibly deceiving himself and setting himself up for failure.

"Not homework!" Gerry protested. His grinned more widely, obviously entertained by my line of questioning. Gerry is true to himself, I thought. No need to worry about phony tendencies here.

"I know what you mean," I said, "but they may not go for it."

My job as ally of Gerry's emotional mind is to advocate for exactly what he wants. It doesn't matter how ridiculous that may be. It doesn't matter whether I think his request is a good idea. My job is to (1) explain possible consequences, (2) encourage him to articulate what he thinks will help him, (3) prevent him from being traumatized by the consequences of misuse of privileges, and (4) give him opportunities to change his mind if consequences of another kind would help him resume his growth.

Gerry is trying to develop naturally. He is trying to disentangle himself from the complications of the life he has fashioned for himself. I felt it would be an improvement if he acted like a student and did everything but homework. Gerry had started his treatment by being hospitalized for threatening his mother and little sister with a kitchen knife.

His discharge summary described him as "a somewhat younger-appearing eleven-year-old . . . well groomed and sullen in manner. He made limited eye contact and said little. He tended to minimize difficulties, and was difficult to engage. There was no evidence of thought disorder. He continued to speak of intense anger and homicidal ideation toward his mother."

Following his discharge, Gerry was sent to live with his biological father in Florida. The father found him infuriating and abused him. I began to treat Gerry upon his return from Florida.

Gerry dedicated his life to getting under the skin of anyone in authority. He enjoyed tormenting younger children. He was extremely self-centered and unreasonable in his demands. He spent most of his days alone in front of a TV. For hours, he brooded and plotted revenge against any authority figure who tried to set limits on him. He took spoiling matters for others to the limit. He could sense what others wanted and took pride in making sure their wishes were thwarted. This aspect of his personality explained how it was that he did no work for an entire year in junior high school.

For over a year, Gerry had been unwilling to listen to anything I said. He refused to do anything positive for his family, yet demanded everything. He bullied his younger sister without mercy. This drive to a school meeting was the first time he recognized me as an ally of his emotional mind.

The year of inactivity at school yielded important gains. However, Gerry was not functioning in the normal range. The plan was not succeeding in the school's eyes, for he was still not working up to his potential. It was difficult for the school to see how far from normal Gerry had been just a year ago. This was the first time that Gerry was admitting he wanted something. I had no doubt it would work if the school would give him an opportunity. I felt that the granting of Gerry's request would be a significant step in resolving his core ODD.

His enrollment in the eighth grade, as he requested, would have left him functioning near the normal range. He was bonding with me, open to influence, listening to me on matters like the importance of being trustworthy. He had become reasonably affectionate with his mother. He had even been a bit helpful at home. The most acute problem that remained was his unwillingness to do schoolwork. His conduct had been fine at school, but he coasted through the day. This was also true at home. He had a limited peer life. But he was deriving a sense of belonging from interacting with the eighth graders he met at school.

Gerry was developing socially but had lost his place with his peers as a natural consequence of his lack of effort the previous year. His social need was to stay and function as a regular student. If he didn't, his attempt to fit in would nevertheless bring out some positive behavior, which would save the school system a lot of money on a special placement. If he were to do poorly, not much would be lost.

Based on this analysis, it occurred to me to propose a one-month trial without guarantee of credit. I said to Gerry, "I can ask the school to allow you a one-month placement and see how you do. But they may want you to do homework and pass your classes to stay there. You might be out, but if that happens, you always have the option of the home-schooling center."

Gerry and I had planned a placement that allowed him to gain peer access and develop a self-directed study program that could be requested under home-schooling regulations. This plan allowed him to feel that he had a legitimate option other than eighth grade, being locked up, or subjecting himself to endless control battles with authority as a seventh grader. Gerry could pursue a day he liked no matter how this meeting went.

"They'll never let me into the eighth grade," Gerry said.

"You never know," I responded. "You would become a better person, and it wouldn't cost the school that much money to let you try. Kids like you know what will work for them. I think it's a good plan."

"What do I say when I'm in there?" he asked, referring to the approaching meeting at the school.

My answer was to prescribe the turned-off behavior he customarily demonstrated involuntarily, only this time I wanted him to engage in it intentionally.

"Just say 'Whatever' or 'I don't know' about everything except what you want. If they ask whether you want an eighth-grade placement, let them know how you would handle it. I'll take care of the rest." Gerry typically would say nothing but "Whatever" or "I don't know." He would look down at the floor, avoid eye contact, and fail to express any interest. Behaving this way, but for a reason, could prevent him from entering into a genuinely oppositional state.

"Got it," Gerry said.

Gerry sat calmly through the meeting, even though it did not go well. I presented the results of a test for AD/HD (the TOVA) that I had administered recently, and that placed Gerry in the severe range for the disorder. I explained that Gerry had failed school over the last year, but his ODD, though lessened, was strongest in school. I explained that frustrating his teacher's interest in Gerry doing his work satisfied the spoiler side of him. I emphasized that Gerry needed the right blend of consequences for his violations, and opportunities to drop the ODD by demonstrating respect and regaining privileges.

I could sense this group of educators' resistance setting in as I spoke.

"The consequences should create necessity, but not traumatize," I was saying. Then, a teacher who could take no more interrupted me. She was obviously disturbed by the direction of the proceedings.

"You have just taken up fifteen minutes of this meeting to tell us that Gerry should have no consequences for last year's behavior. He has not done a stitch of work. He knew that if he didn't do his work he would fail, and now you want us to forgo the consequences and pass him. What will that teach him?"

"I understand that you're upset," I was saying when she interrupted me again to deny that she was upset. I could see no point in arguing. Instead, I adopted the position I always take on when one of my ODD patients faces the controlling influence of an authoritarian personality. I invite the authoritarian individual to control the ODD teenager and experience the struggle with increasing ODD symptoms first hand. The ODD protects the youth. It feeds his need for power. The ODD also becomes intolerable for the adult, as long as the other adults in the child's life refrain from enforcing the agenda of that individual.

The principal took over with a menacing tone and began to clarify the consequences for Gerry. She wanted him to know that he owed a detention and must serve it soon, or there would be further consequences. I repeated what the principal said, asked the principal what the next consequence would be if Gerry chose not to serve his detention, and then matter-of-factly repeated the consequence to Gerry. The principal clarified that a Saturday detention would be the next step. I then asked what would happen if Gerry didn't serve that one. Gerry could then be suspended for ten days.

"What happens after that?" I asked.

The principal became uncomfortable, and asked why things had to go so far. "I was hoping there would be some reasonable way to avoid this going further," she said. "It doesn't have to go that far."

When I addressed Gerry, I was detached: "You have to serve a detention. If you don't by the end of this week, you will have a Saturday detention. If you don't serve that, you will be suspended for ten days. After that there could be more consequences. The school would have to meet and present your case to the school committee. Are you clear about that?"

Gerry's response was right on cue. "Whatever," he said in a matter-of-fact tone.

The school psychologist, obviously a bright man, chimed in.

"We can't make further exceptions or consider other special-education placements unless Gerry agrees to be tested," he said.

I repeated this for Gerry, who responded with the same apathetic "Whatever." I then explained to the principal that this kind of pressure caused ODD. She seemed to get the idea, and became more helpful in her attitude. The teachers were now divided, and they had to leave soon.

I clarified that Gerry had been extremely ODD, and was now signaling his willingness to drop the struggle and become a productive student. He had experienced the consequence of being held back and removed from his peers, and was willing to regain the privilege with quality participation in the eighth-grade curriculum. I proposed that they let him try for one month without giving him credit. The teachers left and the school psychologist spoke for the group.

"Sometimes adults can be oppositional, too. Once you get under their skin, and they get to choose what happens to you, they will deny what you want."

There was an obvious lesson for Gerry here. However, he wasn't ready to benefit from it. The school agreed to consider the eighth-grade placement, but never followed up with the family. Gerry didn't serve his detentions but the school accepted a letter from me asking that disciplinary action for failure to attend school or do work be reduced.

The case stagnated for months. Gerry went to school two or three days a week, but only to flaunt his refusal to work. He considered numerous special-education placements, but, in true ODD fashion, he rejected them all. The family hired an advocate. Gerry didn't worsen but didn't improve much, either.

Turning Failure into Growth

Months later, Gerry was placed in a unique home-schooling center that offers a social group to enrollees and a variety of self-directed learning opportunities. Gerry lived some distance away, in another town, so had to take a bus several times a week to travel to the center. I recall his ear-to-ear grin when he arrived for his first day. He stopped at my office carrying a huge backpack full of books.

Gerry's mom took limit-setting at home to a new level at about this time. Gerry had been violating her space by taking her things. He had begun to irritate those around him and violate the rights of family members immediately after leaving his last session with me. He had dominated his sister, monopolized the TV, and refused to help out. Gerry's mother reported the following sequence of events.

1. Bored and desperately seeking stimulation, Gerry asked Mom to provide entertainment. She attempted to help, but he was tyrannical in making his demands and turned down whatever she offered.

2. Gerry then chose to derive stimulation from tormenting his sister. His continued requests for entertainment gradually became excuses for tormenting Mom as well.

3. Gerry exploded in a sinister laugh when his mother handed

him a list, or ticket, telling him what he must do to atone for his infractions.

4. Somewhat later, Gerry seemed to take the ticket a bit more seriously. He did some work for the family, though with a scornful attitude.

5. Gerry asked whether his meager attempt to regain privileges would prevent further privilege loss. "That's a start," Mom said, and went to her room, only to find out later that Gerry had a way of striking back.

The Ticket Pad

It is a standard practice for me to give parents a ticket pad (see Appendix B) that lists family privileges that must be respected to gain the support of the safe home-base agreement. The pad lists the privileges lost for infractions and the reparations (demonstrations of respect for those privileges) that the child must perform to regain them. Gerry's infractions included spoiling the family atmosphere, hurting a sibling, misusing parental help, and refusing to work. They were serious enough to warrant loss of all family privileges, including access to all electronics, phone, favors, money, and transportation.

Mom cut Gerry's privileges more drastically than she ever had before. She called the cable company and discontinued service. In preparation for this moment, however, she arranged to leave a TV in one room with access to a satellite dish and installed a deadbolt lock to keep that room off limits. To exact his revenge, and in true ODD fashion, Gerry stole Mom's key and locked the room so that no one could watch TV. He destroyed the key. In his mind, this evened matters up.

Mom borrowed a spare key from her sister, however, and stuck to her decision on the loss of privileges. Gerry became humble after about three weeks and was a very different child. The combination of limit setting at home and removal from the coercive battle at school opened the way for new progress. Gerry agreed to perform reparative activities for his family to regain privileges. At first he talked of plotting new ways to get even but within a week he sounded genuinely affectionate. He spoke for the first time of being ready to prove himself trustworthy.

The softening process that took place resulted from deflating the narcissism that develops in excessively aggressive teenagers. This is the subject of Chapter 10. In Gerry's case, Mom reported some important learning experiences. She concluded that it is impossible to resolve clinical levels of ODD without detaching emotionally and remaining detached while the youth is in pain. This is particularly difficult for mothers.

Gerry's mother put it this way: "What makes it hard is that I can't show him that I love him."

In my practice, I have repeatedly found a direct link between parental willingness to detach from a weeping, apparently needy child and the success of interventions for ODD.

Another observation Gerry's mother made was that she had to maintain a long-term perspective and ignore her son's immediate responses. This translates to another form of detachment. The emphasis, however, is on acceptance of short-term failure to diffuse the spoiling tactics of the ODD teenager.

I could tell at the session during which I heard about the loss of privileges that we had not seen the last of Gerry's vicious tendencies. His present loving attitude represented a significant breakthrough but was no more than a temporary cease-fire. Mom told how it took three weeks for Gerry to begin to perform genuine, loving reparations. She explained how he had been transformed into a completely different person. As I spoke with Mom, Gerry was listening quietly and playing a video game, as was his custom. Suddenly Gerry chimed in.

"The next thing I'm going to do is . . . ," his voice now became an inaudible mumble. I couldn't tell whether he was going to work harder on regaining trust and restoring privileges, or whether he was going to plot new feats of revenge. I prompted him. Gerry responded, "I haven't thought of anything good yet." I prompted him again. "I was considering cutting the satellite wires." Obviously, Gerry was responding in an affectionate way only because he saw no other choice.

Addressing the Two-Mind Split

The mind split in Gerry manifested minimally. Most ODD cases involve a rational mind that tends to side with authority, at least verbally, and an emotional mind that refuses to cooperate. Gerry could only afford a minimal alliance with his parents, school, or any other authority. The rational side of the split was largely subservient to the emotional side. His adaptive functions lacked the maturity to earn him social acceptance. He would spend hours with nothing to do, bored and lonely, and then, for stimulation, would torment family members.

Gerry's statement of retaliation revealed a glimpse of his mind–body state. Gerry's emotional mind wanted belonging and affection. This need was largely satisfied with his social life at the home-schooling center. However, he wanted the same friendly relationship with his mom, as well. The emotional side of the split also wanted to feel successful and have possessions. Yet his rational mind was too weak to earn the success and opportunities demanded. So it adapted by tormenting and manipulating to get him what he wanted without having to work. The aggressive acts also fed his need to feel powerful, and spared him the shame of facing his weakness.

Gerry's method of adaptation was to hide his shame about his adaptive deficits and a host of fears secondary to the vulnerability stemming from his weaknesses. Hence, when Gerry heard his mom describe him as having become loving after experiencing a limit, he felt exposed and threatened. His rational mind resorted to its established mechanism for concealing fear: he began to save face by plotting acts of revenge.

A couple of weeks after the appointment just described, Gerry showed up at my door with an unusual request. He wanted to buy a set of throwing knives and have me store them in my office so they would be easily available for his use when he was at the nearby home-schooling center. I had developed a reputation with local youths for my mastery with knives and specifically for my ability to teach knife-throwing. Gerry was fascinated by knives and fire, as are many children. By now, he had become familiar enough with me to risk asking me to mentor him in knife-throwing.

The knife-throwing presented me with a unique opportunity to make a strong alliance with Gerry's emotional mind. But it also revived memories of trauma and the distrust that accompanies such violations. Gerry had threatened to kill his mother with knives, and continued to threaten revenge, irritate his sister, and cause other disruptions. The key was for me to insist that he earn the body's gratification by contributing to his family more, and taking other steps to increase his trustworthiness at home.

Gerry confidently dismissed the notion that he would present a danger to the family if he had access to knives. "I'm way past that," he protested. "But they have to learn to trust me, don't they? They aren't ready." It was clear that Gerry understood the importance of trust and wanted to earn it. One could see how much happier he had become. His bitterness had dissipated with his release from the ODD cycle with school authorities, and the social belonging he was deriving from the home-schooling center. "I'm much happier now," he said.

I talked to Gerry about a safe way to arrange opportunities for knife-throwing with the approval and support of the home-schooling staff. I explained that his family had an obligation to allow him opportunities for reestablishing trust. They were having trouble accepting this. Gerry had to earn trust in routine ways with his family before he could expect to take throwing-knives to his home. However, if he demonstrated trustworthiness at home, his parents might allow him to keep knives in my office, under my supervision.

Shocking as it may seem to many readers, experience has shown me that teaching knife-throwing is a remarkably effective way of engaging ODD teenagers, who generally associate therapists with teachers, parents, and other unpopular adults who enforce the normative agenda. A therapist who, surprisingly, can throw knives and teach knife-throwing confounds the associations of conventional authority imprinted in the emotional mind of the teenager and is well on his way toward establishing a bond with his patient. Dart-throwing or finesse demonstrated with yo-yos might also, in fact, be successful in overcoming such negative associations, but the knife-throwing I learned from members of a street gang when I was young is, subject to parental approval, a skill that I can use with dramatic effect.

In this case, I called Mom and relayed Gerry's request. Understandably, she was bothered by its nature. It happened, however, that we had an appointment scheduled the next day. She promised to think over my proposal.

The session began with Gerry reporting that he was ready to earn trust, and Mom indicating she was afraid to let him try. Gerry's claim was that he would give up tormenting his family, and work to earn trust at home, which represented his central lie. This was a manifestation of his mind split. The commitment betrayed his emotional agenda of deriving stimulation the only way he felt competent to do, by tormenting and controlling.

I addressed the distrust in Gerry's mother. Her words were reasonable but her tone was one of desperation. Gerry responded to his mother's attitude with hostility. I interrupted the conversation and confronted Gerry's lie.

"The reason you guys are getting so angry is because you have no trust. Your mom can tell you're talking purely from the pressing perspective of the emotional mind, and that you're really lying. You'll say anything to get your knives, but you have no intention of respecting your sister." Gerry had a smirk on his face.

I now turned to the mother. "Listen to your tone [I imitated her tone]. Your words are very reasonable, but your emotional mind continues to convey the message, 'I am fed up with you. One little step out of line from you and I'm out of here!' This makes it very difficult for Gerry to feel safe if he becomes more honest."

Gerry responded by opening up. He reported that he had talked to his mom on the way to our appointment and she had been mean to him. He went on to describe the dialogue. Gerry had been talking about his insecurities due to his lack of adaptive abilities. The conversation went like this.

Gerry: What am I going to do when I'm older?

Mom: I don't think you can make a career of annoying people.

(Gerry had just spent thirty minutes in the car rapping in an annoying tone. He was singing, "Play that funky music white boy . . . ," and fidgeting excessively.)

Gerry: I'm being serious.

(At this point, Gerry stopped communicating. I proceeded to challenge his rational mind.)

Dr. B.:   Why were you bothering to be serious?

Gerry: I don't know, but I was talking about regrets.

(Under questioning, Gerry continued to reveal the insecurities that stemmed from his rational brain deficits.)

Gerry: I blew all my Bar Mitzvah money on candy—$150.

Dr. B.:   What else?

(It took some prompting from his mom, but soon she reminded him of his tendency to quit activities he liked.)

Gerry: Yeah, quitting everything I was ever good at. Yeah, that sucked.

It turned out he had given up on skating, karate, and playing the bassoon. He enjoyed all of them, and his teachers encouraged him to stick with them, but he quit, probably to be oppositional.

Gerry had revealed enough. He wanted to know about the knives, but Mom interrupted to report that Gerry hadn't been very helpful at home, and being in possession of knives required a lot of trust.

I specified for Mom three categories of trustworthy behavior that Gerry would have to demonstrate before he could take knives home. Gerry sensed that he was not going to have to face any difficult demands during this discussion, so he reverted to earlier levels of adaptation. He turned on the video game machine and began to play. He tuned out what was convenient, yet monitored our conversation while pretending not to listen.

The categories of trust were as follows:

1. *Insulting, violating, or forcing:* Asked to rate his conduct in this area, Mom said: "He gets off the bus, and he's an SOB. He nit-picks and drives everyone nuts." Mom said he had received a ticket for irritating his sister but admitted she failed to follow through and remove his privileges. This kind of inconsistency occurs frequently in families with ODD children. The parent would rather leave a child glued to the TV than put up with the tantrum that would accompany removal of the privilege.

2. *Following through on commitments:* Mom reported that at home, Gerry had been reasonable in this area. However, she also reported that he was doing absolutely no academic work. He wasn't following the academic plan that he had committed to in his home-schooling agreement with the superintendent of schools.

3. *Fairness—helping out when asked, and doing chores and other services:* Mom reported that Gerry rated a bare minimum in this area. Gerry did what he had to do to get by. My intervention was to have Gerry lose privileges for infractions in these areas of trust, but to allow him a grace period in which to make good once he was warned that he had violated trust. The warning would come in the form of a ticket. He knew what a ticket meant from the experience of privilege loss during the previous month. He would lose home privileges for a day after being handed a ticket. If he didn't perform reparative activities by the end of the second day, he would lose the privilege of attending the home-schooling center.

Meanwhile, there would be no knives for Gerry. They would be withheld until he managed to earn trust in the three areas of functioning described above. In the discussion, we were noting how Gerry had slipped from the high-level functioning he had achieved in the previous month. Gerry put down the video game controller, and chimed in.

Gerry: Exactly. If I don't get what I want, I have to control.

Dr. B.:   And if you get what you want?

Gerry: Then I'm nice.

(I felt this was a manifestation of the lie once more. He was willing to say what he needed to get the knives.)

Dr. B.:   Are you saying that if you get the knives to keep in my office, you will do all three things that earn trust?

(Gerry ignored me. I confronted him and let him go home to think it over.)

Dr. B.:   You've told me that you were past tormenting people, and you had been earning trust. But really you were just using words to get me to buy you knives. When you get privileges at home, you will earn your knife-throwing privileges here in my office.

(I was firm and slightly detached as I said this.)

Gerry's last words revealed his intentions to lie. He mumbled as he walked out of my office, "I'll get the knives one way or the other. You can't stop me." He wasn't angry when he said this. In fact, he was playful.

My response was equally playful. "Make my day," I said. Gerry knew I would play Clint Eastwood as cop and enforce the consequences. My detachment and willingness to face failure were sufficient to avoid the ODD response. My playfulness helped him save face.

Mom removed Gerry's privileges the day after he got home. He tested the limits until he missed going to the home-schooling center for a day. After that he did genuine reparations. Gerry didn't buy the knives. But by the time of the next session, he had earned trust by performing well in the three areas we agreed to. For the time being, Gerry did not need to lie.

The Problem of Drugs

The safe home-base agreement works best with drug-free children like Gerry. However, the agreement offers a great opportunity to abuse drugs. The teenagers can do their chores, engage in key activities, and use their excuses and family backing to indulge themselves in their addiction to drugs. This does not mean that the safe home-base protocol is contraindicated. The problem of academics remains very real for them. This program can help them become aware of their problem, and find relief from the cycle of escape, deception, aggression, and guilt.

These students can take time to get their motivation back and can be referred to a mastery-based academic remediation program. The drug problem can be dealt with separately (see Chapter 11) after they have abused the privilege of family support, and the ugly reality of the extent of drug abuse is exposed. The clinician can follow the protocol recommended in Chapter 11 once he has implemented the rest of this program and the safe home-base agreement.

The next chapter deals with the most obvious obstacle to the successful implementation of the safe home-base agreement: *parental neurosis*. Neurotic parents cannot let go of the need to control their children. Their fear of allowing their children to fail interferes with every protocol presented in this book. The treatment for ODD is based on inviting failure as a way to expose weaknesses, and then establishing the right blend of consequences and opportunities to promote honesty and integration of the two minds. This is not possible with a parent who is obsessed with preventing failure and controlling the teenager's behavior.

9

Special Problem 2: Parental Neurosis

I didn't feel very professional about it, but I was so frustrated that I was almost tempted to strike the whining but undeniably needy woman sitting before me. I couldn't reveal what was on my mind because her daughter was present. The fact was, however, that whenever I tried to address this mother's questions I was completely drained. It was as though I had explained my theories on managing oppositional teenagers once too often. The thought of discussing my approach for yet another time was exhausting.

I would find it difficult to sleep that night, I was so frustrated. I felt manipulated by this woman, my time wasted in a calculated way. I was already unacceptably late for the next appointment, and yet she wanted to prolong the session. I couldn't believe I had allowed myself to be drawn into this situation. It was almost 9:30 P.M., and I still had a session scheduled with another patient. It had been a very long day—and it was not over yet. I also had three emergency cases pending, awaiting calls from me. It happened that these crises were precipitated by my early interventions. The cases involved teenagers who were taking failure to the limit in entitled ways. Each call would entail dealing with parents plagued by neuroticism over their teenager. The acting out of the teenagers had been inspired by my challenge to them to do things their own way, and thus expose their failures. In a sense I was to blame for the current crises.

One teenage girl was very drunk and belligerent. Her retaliation for Mom's trying to set a limit was to go out with her boyfriend on a cold, rainy night, with soaking wet hair, and sleep in the woods in a sleeping bag. "It will be your fault when something happens to me!" she said as she left, complaining of a sore throat.

In the other case, a teenage boy was punching holes in the wall, threatening his mother and siblings, and, in effect, holding them hostage until he got money. He had mistreated the washing machine so badly and had been so irritating to his mother that she had finally thrown a frying pan at him, barely missing. He had retaliated by throwing dishwasher powder all over the floor, where he had tossed the family's clean laundry. He wound up this performance by emptying several buckets of water on the detergent.

While this was going on elsewhere, another was in my office asking seemingly innocent questions that were driving me into a mental rage. It wasn't long before I couldn't think. She would start making her points in a sweet, patient, and concerned manner, but then would shift to a whiny, demanding, and victim-like tone. Whenever Mom made a comment, her 17-year-old daughter, Elaine, would roll her eyes and insult her. "That's why I hate you so much," or, "Listen to yourself! I can't believe you. You're such an idiot." This kind of angry response from an oppositional teenager to a seemingly nice parent is a common indicator of parental neurosis. Another giveaway is when kids show they consider their parents a source of embarrassment in public places.

This awful night, I was in the worst possible position to face parental neurosis. I had the mother and daughter in the room at the same time, I was running behind, and the mother was unfamiliar with my treatment method. The conflict between them made it impossible to speak freely to either one. If I spoke frankly to expose the mother's neuroticism, I would undermine her authority with her child and stir up even more resistance. If I sided with her mother, I would lose Elaine's respect. So I spoke blandly, my remarks marked by hesitation. I could tell the mother wasn't really listening to me because of the difficulty I had explaining the elements of my approach.

I was trapped repeatedly into trying to bring the session to a close by summarizing, and I recommended a follow-up appointment. The mother would defeat my attempt every time. She announced that she didn't think she could afford to come back, interrupted my summary to ask about a specific application of what I was summarizing (which I said I didn't have time to offer), and then went into a long, tangential story about how some principle of parenting needed to be clarified. When I tried to stop her, she would plead, "Can't you at least answer this question, or write a report, or tell my daughter?" Meanwhile, the clock was ticking, and I was neglecting my other patients.

The mother had called me earlier that day, threatening a last-minute cancellation of the session that her daughter wanted and desperately needed. I was at a critical point in my therapy with Elaine. She had not been ODD, but depressed. As often happens, though, when the therapy became effective and she broke free of her depression, her previous attitude of compliance vanished also. This hitherto quiet and submissive girl began to challenge authority. Since the girl had never acted out before, and the sessions had been strictly one on one, I had not prepared the mother for the possibility of facing ODD.

Mom insisted during a telephone call that she be allowed to attend the meeting I had planned with the daughter—or it would not take place! Elaine, however, objected strenuously. She made it clear she did not want her mother present. I had recommended that Mom allow me this day's session to prepare her daughter—alone. My plan was that the following week I would work with Mom herself on managing her daughter's oppositional behavior.

I had people in the waiting room, and I needed to finish with Mom's phone call quickly so I could attend to them. Mom asked me why I needed to see the daughter separately and schedule her own meeting with me for the following week. She waited for my answer, then said, "I'm not sure I can afford to come in next week, because I've cut back on my work to be around more so I can guide my daughter. Don't you think that's a good thing?"

I tried to explain that her daughter's acting out was a sign of health, and agreed that it is good to be present to guide one's children, hoping that my assent on this point would be enough to get her off the phone. But Mom wanted me to explain my methods, and asked me to give her and her daughter some guidelines for managing the current crisis. It was the least I could do, she said, for a struggling single parent who had sacrificed so much to pay my fees for several months. The conversation got us nowhere.

Despite my recommendation that I see Elaine alone, Mom insisted that she at least be permitted to join us for the last fifteen minutes of the session. This was her minimum requirement. I couldn't repeat myself again so I agreed that she could come in at the end. My mission during the fifteen minutes that followed would be to give Mom and her daughter an overview of how I handle acting out. I would prepare carefully to summarize my approach in a short amount of time, and elicit Elaine's cooperation. I looked at my watch and took a deep breath as I assessed the impact of this call on my schedule. Fifteen minutes had gone by and my next family was still in the waiting room.

By the time Mom entered the room for her portion of the session, Elaine had virtually agreed to the method outlined in this book for turning failure into growth. I presented my summary and overview to mother and daughter. As I spoke, Mom would listen for a time, but would then interrupt with a question about managing a difficult situation with Elaine. I would dutifully explain that we didn't have time to address specifics, but gave her the general idea of how the situation she described would be handled. She then sought my endorsement of the view that "there is a point at which a parent has to guide her children, and help them make the right choices." She asked for advice on whether children of her daughter's age should be allowed to stay out all night on a school night.

Elaine would blow up and hurl insults at her mother when-ever she asked questions reflecting on her daughter's behavior. Elaine would say things like, "Oh my God, Mom, you're such a moron!" or "You're so retarded!" It took everything I had to calm the daughter and reason with the mother. Mom's look of pain and exasperation said "See what I have to put up with!"

Mom was showing classical signs of parental neurosis. The condition was revealed in a communication pattern. Mom wanted to have her cake and eat it, too. She wanted to control her daugh-ter but at the same time earn the daughter's approval. Outwardly, she presented a picture of reason, patience, and pleasantness. She wanted her daughter to go along with the need she felt to set lim-its on her behavior. She dreaded having to set the limits, however, so she took forever to get to the point and addressed only the most extreme examples of misbehavior to show that she had every rea-son in the world to take over Elaine's life. She maintained a sweet and loving tone throughout and would look wounded in response to her daughter's insults.

Mom had told me she wanted to hear my opinion on how to handle this situation, but didn't tell me she wanted me to side with her in the dispute with Elaine. So she asked me to explain how I would handle things. She paid little attention to what I said, but urged me to cite an extreme situation or an exception. Finally, she got to the point she wanted to make: "Isn't that just too much freedom?"

Numerous times throughout this process, I pointed out that I had done extensive research, developed a program, and written a parenting book specifically on how to manage situations like hers. Her response was to inform me that she had another book at home, and that book also discussed how to handle these difficul-ties. She had read this book and could use it as a reference if she needed to. I failed to see the point.

Finally, I announced that I had to end the session, whether she intended to come back or not. "Think about it," I suggested. Now Elaine was outside in the waiting room and I was having my last private words with her mother. She made a final plea, "Do you ever do half-hour sessions for needy parents without charge?"

"What do you think this was?" I responded.

"This was a paid session," she said. I pointed at the clock and asked if she had checked the time. It was now a quarter to eleven.

"Your session ended forty-five minutes ago," I pointed out. She looked at the clock and appeared to be surprised. Her fifteen-minute visit had turned into a wasted hour that had achieved nothing—except to alienate her daughter.

"We haven't communicated very well," she admitted. She asked me to write a report, asked me to make a differential diagnosis around AD/HD, and asked questions about billing and insurance for which I had no answer. She said she recognized that it would have been better to have spoken about these matters without Elaine present. I didn't bother to remind her that I had recommended that in the first place. I now had two emergencies to contact. Otherwise, I would have relaxed and called it a day.

THE MAKE-SURE BRAIN

The ability to make sure something is done properly involves adaptive functions, which help an individual adapt to challenging conditions. To make sure something takes place properly he must inhibit desires and emotions, curb arousal, plan a course of action, find motivation, initiate and sustain effort, sustain attention, organize, attend to details, anticipate and solve problems, choose an adaptive course of action, communicate with others, and double-check all aspects of the project at hand until success is certain.

THE HIDDEN CAUSE OF MOST
CHILD-REARING PROBLEMS

Society assumes that parents have an obligation to perform make-sure functions for their children. Make-sure functions are extremely important, and parents obviously are much more capable of performing them than their children. The children, it is assumed, will learn through the example of the parents how to perform these functions for themselves. This assumption, however, leads to a parenting method that is fundamentally flawed. It may work well with easy children who live for opportunities to please their parents. Parents who use this approach with challenging children, however, don't stand a chance. This chapter explains why.

The Two Commandments of Parenting

Most parents understandably regard the well-being of their children as of paramount importance. They dedicate themselves to this cause with an almost religious fervor and reverently adhere to what can be referred to as the two commandments of parenting.

The first commandment is "Thou shalt protect thy child" and the second is "Thou shalt educate thy child." The instinct to protect their children is so deeply ingrained and such a passionate concern for parents that the second commandment serves primarily to further the protective function of the first. Parents teach their children incessantly, hoping to spare them the harsh consequences of ignorance as they become adults.

Unfortunately, parents' teachings, their logical, well-constructed arguments, and their lectures all too often fall on deaf ears, because adults and children live in two distinct worlds and speak two different languages. Parents engage in folly when they attempt to speak the language of logic to children, who only desire immediate gratification. In pursuit of their own gratification, children, and especially those with AD/HD, systematically override all adult arguments and grown-up logic, hoping that this will cause their parents to give up their efforts to instruct and control.

The Philosophy of Make-Sure Parenting

The two commandments of parenting have given rise to the child-rearing philosophy I call make-sure parenting, in which parents strive to make sure their children do everything correctly. Their philosophy is rooted in the misguided belief that children can be molded into being good (see Chapter 1).

The wheel of life serves as a metaphor for how parents in our society are always on the go. Get up in the morning; make sure the kids are up on time; make sure they have their clothes ready, the right clothes; make sure they eat breakfast, a healthy breakfast. Once the kids are on the bus, the parents have to go on about their own affairs, put in a hard day's work, and, in addition to everything else, make sure that after-school child-care is in place.

After school, the parent must make sure the kids do their homework. There are always notices from school about all kinds of activities—Scouts, basketball, soccer, swimming, religious education. All of these entail transportation, practices, registrations, games, and parents' meetings. Parents must make sure all activities are well coordinated and successful. The kids must have snacks and dinner must be prepared. Of course, there is laundry, too, and other chores. Kids must be bathed. They must all eat a good meal—another make sure. Clear the table, do the dishes, clean up the kitchen, make sure the children get to bed on time. They all need a bedtime story. Teeth must be brushed, pajamas located and donned, backs scratched, and fears of the dark allayed. Once the children are asleep, the parent can finally open that letter from the IRS, maybe exercise, maybe even talk to a friend by phone.

In directing all this activity, the parent is exercising a series of vital brain functions that are weak in AD/HD children, including the ability to inhibit impulses and emotions, plan, prepare alternate plans to compensate for error, organize, make moral judgments, attend to details, and double-check to *make sure* everything went well. These mental abilities virtually define maturity, or emotional intelligence, and fostering their development in the child is the single most important objective in parenting.

Most parents want to see their children function in a mature way. Yet, by performing make-sure functions, many interfere with the development of the children's ability to satisfy their needs independently. Parents prevent AD/HD children from having to exercise and strengthen these functions. The end result can be children who achieve success in areas including academics, sports, and social relationships, but lack drive and remain weak in their ability to manage other essential aspects of their own lives. Such children lose confidence as soon as they must face responsibility without Mom being around. Their self-doubts stem from never having accomplished things on their own.

When stakes are high, it is hard for make-sure parents to place their faith in children who have not developed sufficient adaptive brain functions. They will worry excessively when their children take charge of their own lives. The make-sure parents' lack of faith will limit their ability to supply confidence for their children right when they need it most—when they encounter humbling and potentially traumatic failures.

Also, when parents do too much for their kids they foster oppositionalism. And when children enter oppositional states those make-sure points become hot-spots of conflict.

How Children Exploit Make-Sure Parents

Children with AD/HD and other behavorial problems discover how their make-sure parents have a mission to protect and teach them no matter what their behavior. They sense the pressures brought upon their parents by the wheel of life. As soon as children make these discoveries they tend to exploit them and turn them to their own advantage. Having realized that their parents will invariably take care of everything, they learn to live mindlessly. They realize that the more irresponsibly they behave, the more ardently their parents will work to solve their problems and gratify their desires. In short, the less they think, the more they force their parents to think.

This realization frees misbehaving children to pursue immediate gratification goals, whatever the cost. Exploiting the two commandments of parenting, these children become masters at a game of defiance I call *control poker*. Although no money is on the table, the stakes of control poker are high indeed. For in this game of winner-take-all, the children play for power.

A Quick Hand of Control Poker

Imagine yourself as the parent of a difficult AD/HD child, and judge whether this experience would make you a good candidate for parental neurosis:

You open the game by asking your child for obedience in the kindest possible tone. "OK, sweetie, time to take a bath and get ready for bed." Faced with the choice of either obeying or ignoring, your child invariably chooses to ignore you, not even looking up from the Nintendo screen. You repeat your command three, five, even ten times. But your child still ignores you. (Neurological factors in AD/HD children make it unlikely that they will inconvenience themselves just to gain your approval. This is especially true when control is on the line.)

As your child continues to ignore your opening moves, including appeals for harmony between you and offers of praise and affection, your frustration leads you to employ increasingly harsher tones. Like the former Boston Red Sox slugger Ted Williams, patiently fouling off pitch after pitch until he sees the one he wants to hit over the fence, your child waits out all your sweet requests until the punitiveness in your voice reaches a peak of urgency.

Just before you explode, your child smoothly defuses you with an appeal to the second commandment of parenting, your mission to educate your child. "But Mo-om," or "But Da-ad," your child whines, "why do I have to?" In asking why, he deftly shifts the conflict from the issue of disobedience to a philosophical argument. In compliance with the second commandment of parenting, you want your child to understand your reasons. So you attempt to explain. You may employ any or all of these arguments:

"You've been playing outside all day and you got pretty dirty. So now it's time to clean up."

"Remember, you promised you'd be good when I bought you that toy you wanted."

"Your favorite TV show is on in half an hour. If you don't get ready for bed now, you'll miss it."

"You asked to join the soccer team and you have practice to-morrow morning."

For the sake of gaining even a momentary indulgence, your child will then seize upon one of the reasons offered and shred it. "Oh, that toy stinks: It doesn't do any of the stuff you see it do in the commercials." "I hate that TV show; it's totally lame." "I don't want to go to stupid soccer practice anyway." Now, instead of battling over the question of obedience, your child has you debating the merits of the toy, the TV show, or soccer. Your child's strategy is simple and obvious. If he disagrees with your reasoning—and don't doubt for a second that he will disagree—voilà! he no longer needs to obey you. Indeed, disobedience becomes the only "logical" course of action. "So why can't I take my bath later?"

As you attempt to reason with your child, he may interrupt with whiny appeals to your nurturing, protective side. "Do I have to take a bath? Pleeeeeease!" Although these appeals for your "kindness," in reality your surrender, lack sincerity, the tone sends the message: "Please spare me this severe pain. Aren't you tired yet? We don't have to keep doing this, you know." This strategy is calculated to wear you down—and often is effective.

By now you are exasperated and bewildered. If your child had only taken a bath the first time you asked, you'd both be finished already. Yet, neither you nor your child may be ready to quit. Your child has two reasons to continue waging the battle. First, he wants to demonstrate that he has control. But this struggle for control points to a second reason. Your child's pride is invested in the outcome of this game of control poker. Unable to build pride and self-esteem through achievements of his own, your child boosts his ego through his victories over you. By now, you may feel thoroughly caught up in the effort to determine the outcome of this contest of wills. Your child's apparent uninvolvement in the game (a good poker face) draws you in deeper, making you more impassioned about winning. After eight gentle requests, one angry command, and an exhausting debate, you move on to threats.

"If you don't get up to the tub right now, I'll take your

Nintendo and throw it in the trash!" Unimpressed, your child may stick with the same strategy, asking yet again, "Why?" Or he may counter with his own threats. "You do and I won't go to school anymore! Ever! And you can't make me!" Your child may even decide this is the time to use his ace in the hole: threats of self-injury. Since they are in conflict with the first commandment of parenting ("Thou shalt protect thy child"), such threats as "I'm going to run away from home" or "I'm going to kill myself" are virtually unbeatable cards in control poker.

Eventually, once the coercive cycle of the game of control poker has begun, you will have to choose one of three alternatives: acquiesce to your child's stubbornness, use physical force, or punish. Each inflicts its own particular damage on both you and your child.

Those who ultimately acquiesce often do so with a bitter remark, such as, "Fine, stay dirty, stink up the place for all I care." Not only does such a comment damage your standing by denying the importance of what you want your child to do and implying falsely that you no longer care for your child but it wounds the child, as well. At the same time, such acquiescence reinforces the dysfunctional patterns of family interaction and the child's control over you.

Those who finally resort to physical force by, for example, carrying a kicking, screaming, biting, arm-flailing child to the bathroom, tearing off the child's clothes, and dumping him into the bathtub, end up with something worse than a flooded bathroom floor. Everyone involved feels demeaned by the experience. Your child, who invests so much pride in issues of control, feels severely diminished, his self-esteem damaged even further. And no matter how justified you feel at the moment, you also feel profoundly guilty afterward for physically overpowering him in a direct violation of the commandment to "protect thy child."

Those who administer punishments in anger and frustration often go overboard: "Fine, don't get ready for bed. But you're grounded tomorrow. And if you say one more word, I'll ground you for a week." This ending only lays the foundation for future trouble. The punishment will probably end up serving as just another source of defiance, conflict, and coercion—another round of control poker.

In this situation, your child counts on getting out of the punishment and chalks up another victory. The child understands that you're worn out for now, and that later you will feel bad. If you do not rescind the punishment yourself, your child will no doubt use it to start another game of control poker. Often, the guilt that both you and your child feel prompts a reconciliation, an agreement to forget the whole thing. You may do something special together to cement the reconciliation. Thus, not only has the child won the round of control poker, but he gets this additional treat of something special as icing on the cake. Dr. Russell Barkley (1987), the most esteemed proponent of behaviorist approaches to AD/HD, has shown that, since in essence the "something special" rewards defiance, this type of reconciliation reinforces antisocial behavior. Indeed, no professional could design a better training program to promote defiance.

To sum it up, once a parent enters a game of control poker with his child, the parent cannot win. Use of physical force would damage the child's self-esteem and some of the parent's as well. If the parent acquiesces or imposes punishment, the child knows he has won for now. "Wow," your child thinks, breathing a sigh of relief and returning to whatever he was doing before the incident began. "Good game!"

In the movie *War Games* the young hero uses the game of tic-tac-toe to teach an advanced military computer an important lesson about nuclear war: The only winning move is not to play the game. Just so with control poker. Allow yourself to be drawn into a game, and you've already lost.

Emotional detachment is the remedy for control battles that feed neuroticism in parents and the ODD in the teenager. Over ten years of trials and observation have made this principle crystal clear to me. A recent child-care situation involving the mothers of two teenagers illustrates this phenomenon more dramatically than any single episode I can recall in my history of treating ODD youths.

Ruth and Linda were neighbors, friends, and mothers of extremely difficult adolescents. They were both in treatment with me at the same time as well. This was no coincidence, as I had been working with Ruth's family off and on for a couple of years and things had gone well, given the extreme difficulty of the case. Linda, on the other hand, had her son in treatment with another psychologist who had engaged with him well enough, but had not been able to resolve ODD behavior at home involving abusive behavior. In fact, the condition of Linda's son had worsened over the two years of therapy.

Ruth and her daughter persuaded Linda to bring her son to me. I worked in collaboration with the psychologist already on the case to facilitate a positive transfer. It took three months of intense work before we had Linda's son failing and Linda turning the failure into growth. However, both teenagers remained extremely difficult.

About a week after Linda made her first breakthrough with her son she had to leave town for several days. The boy was still disrespectful, volatile, and threatening to his two younger siblings. Linda arranged for Ruth to watch her children while she was out of town. Ruth had just been through a horrendous struggle with her own daughter, and Linda worried about leaving the children there.

Her concern was needless. In fact, Linda experienced an intense feeling of guilt when she checked in with Ruth and heard how wonderful the children had been. "It's me that causes the problems. I'm a terrible mother," she concluded. Ruth tried to explain that she could utilize the approach I have outlined much more easily in dealing with Linda's son than with her own daughter.

The next day Ruth was in my office for her regular appointment. She was amazed by how well she had done with this very difficult boy. The first morning she had to wake him up twice. The first time she said, "Do you want to go to school today?" her attitude was detached. The boy assured her that he did. However, he didn't get up.

"I went back to bed listening for the shower and waited

about five minutes. But he didn't get up, so I said to myself, 'Darn,' and went over to give him a second chance. He got up right away.

"That night I said to him, 'You probably aren't going to want to go to school tomorrow. It was so difficult to get up this morning. Do you want me to give you a wake-up call anyway?' He was accommodating. He assured me that he would get up and asked me to please wake him. The next morning he got up right away. The kid has been perfect for me. He's done everything I asked. He cleaned his room, helped me with the little ones. He was excellent.

"I felt so bad for Linda. I told her I couldn't do it like that with my own daughter. It was so easy with her son because I couldn't have cared less what he chose to do. Even though I know this, it's so hard to do it with my own daughter."

My view of the issue of detachment is that ODD youths focus on the parents' emotional-mind state. I picture the teenager as having an electric cord and the mother an outlet right over the heart. The teenager plugs in and tests the voltage. If there is ample current, the teenager will engage in irrational control tactics. If not, the youth will settle for a rational connection to the parents' rational mind. The key to working with parents is to teach them how to put up a wall and remain emotionally detached from the ODD behavior. Parents must drop their make-sure role, put their child in charge of key obligations, and allow them to take responsibility for the consequences of not cooperating, as described in Chapter 6.

Parents who cannot detach will suffer from parental neurosis. They will require therapy for the condition. I would diagnose it as an anxiety disorder, and provide individual and family therapy. I recommend considering it a separate treatment from that employed in dealing with the ODD of the teenager. The content of the sessions will have to revolve around the interactions affecting the child. However, the clinician should go beyond behavioral counseling and into the deeper reasons for the parents' anxiety disorder.

The therapy with neurotic parents must eventually shift its attention to the parents' investment in their own lives. This will not be possible until they have learned to detach sufficiently to allow their children to fail, take the consequences, and demonstrate their ability to learn from the experience. The parent needs to invest the energy that is freed by practicing the detachment process into something else. The healthiest investment is in their own personal lives.

Emotional detachment is generally more difficult for mothers than for fathers. In my mind, this explains the clinical observation that the exhibiting of ODD symptoms is more marked when directed at those who are familiar to the child, and worse when females are the targets. Obviously, this places the mother in the worst possible position vis-à-vis the ODD teenager.

The implication is that parental neurosis occurs more often in mothers. The next section describes the dynamics behind the development of parental neurosis and the reason some parents cannot take this step despite the best of intentions. It will be followed by a protocol for eventual resolution of the problem.

DYNAMICS

Parental neurosis develops when, in the face of oppositional behaviors, parents mandate goodness and punish their children's failure-bound behaviors. The children dread and avoid situations that represent obstacles to growth. Make-sure parents respond with excessive efforts to counter their children's regressive tendencies. They try to make up for their children's deficient efforts and incessantly push them toward success. In return for their efforts, these parents encounter a draining impact from their children's resistance. Parents understandably worry and redouble their efforts to control and supplement. Yet, their efforts yield them nothing but poorer performance, more resistance, and more drain. It is only a question of time before this unnatural cycle will cause a form of neurosis in the parents and oppositional defiant disorder in the children.

Society routinely prescribes make-sure parenting as though one approach to child-rearing could prove effective with all kinds of children. Make-sure parenting, however, only works with certain temperaments. Prescribing a uniform approach to parenting creates serious problems for families with AD/HD and other problem children. To maintain a positive image in society, these parents will deny the problems they experience. They sacrifice chances of growth in order to keep the ugly secret of the jamming, for hours at a time, of their family wheel of life. Control battles are being waged over even the smallest details of life in the household. They don't acknowledge that it took three hours of hell and abuse to get the family dressed and smiling so nicely for church. This secret will grow increasingly burdensome until it becomes a full-blown parental neurosis.

There are frequent episodes of extreme and irrational outbursts when parental neurosis is fully developed. This is referred to as "losing it." Parental tantrums give oppositional children a message of victory. These children turn to self-pity and tears, and pull for a nurturance that has been lacking because of their spoiling tactics. They know that remorse, reconciliation, and leniency will follow. They experience a vicarious discharge of their negative energy, and feel justified in defying parental authority.

THE CAUSE OF PARENTAL NEUROSIS

I find it useful to introduce parents to the term *parental neurosis* because it forces them to own up to the problem, yet helps them externalize it and want to get rid of it. This is what psychodynamic theorists have termed making the symptom *ego dystonic*. Parents often feel guilty about their ODD children's misbehavior. They are convinced that it is somehow their fault as parents. However, instead of blaming their negative influence on a specific tendency that can be modified, they attribute it to their entire being. They are all wrong, they feel, and it is because they are what they are that matters get out of hand. Of course, they reason, they can't change who they are, so there is no hope. I find it necessary to help parents avoid taking offense at the label. I explain to them that this condition is the natural result of trying to enforce make-sure parenting for a prolonged period with an AD/HD or difficult child. I explain that neurosis is an old-fashioned name for an anxiety disorder, which is really a combination of excessive worry and irrational thought. One feeds the other. The irrational thinking provides greater cause for worry, and worry invites further irrational thinking as well as ineffective solutions. I explain that the term *neuroticism* has been used to refer to the irrational thinking process involved in anxiety disorders.

I use the following description to help parents understand how neuroticism grows, to identify the family dysfunction it has yielded, and to reveal the toll it has taken on their children's development. This perspective leads to a treatment protocol that can reverse parental neurosis.

Neuroticism occurs around issues of control. The less realistic or adaptive the attempts at control, the more likely they are to cause neuroticism. Classic examples include ritualistic behavior, superstition, or reliance on magic for results. Less adaptive behaviors provide short-term relief but do little to resolve the problem. Hence, the problem returns. The person responds with increased worry and an intensification of the unrealistic solution. The cycle goes on. Extreme cases of neuroticism reach absurd levels, as in individuals who wash their hands hundreds of times a day to prevent catastrophic events from befalling their loved ones, or who control food and weight until their relationships succeed, or they find great career opportunities, or they are finally appreciated by insensitive relatives.

Those who are in close contact with impulsive or compulsive individuals are very likely to develop neuroticism. Entering into a control battle—invariably futile—with an individual who refuses to be controlled but is unable to control himself is a leading cause of neurosis. Such a scenario is nothing to be ashamed of. It certainly doesn't mean that a parent is a neurotic person. Consider the family members of gamblers, drinkers, drug addicts, control freaks, and workaholics. They become enablers. They tend to play a critical role in allowing individuals who are out of control to maintain lives of indulgence.

Enablers tend to keep secret the troubling behaviors of those on whom they depend. They feel a need to protect the impulsive individuals they enable. They also strive to protect their families by presenting a positive image for all to see. They tend to struggle to keep those they enable from losing control. They may, for example, struggle to stop gamblers from taking trips to Atlantic City casinos. They may attempt to change the lifestyle of those with irrational eating patterns, or prevent alcoholics from drinking. Enablers become so wrapped up with those they strive to control that they neglect their own lives.

Impulsive individuals sense their enablers' need to keep them under control and take advantage of it: "If you don't cater to me, I may have no choice but to go on a gambling feast! So let me watch this show. Let me have this money. Do this for me."

There is no reason why parents responsible for the behavior of AD/HD children should differ in any way from those who deal with other impulsive disorders, including gambling and drinking to excess. AD/HD individuals suffer from impulsive behaviors that are nearly impossible to control, just as do alcoholics and drug or gambling addicts. Attempting to make sure AD/HD children do everything they are supposed to is an effort as futile as trying to persuade an alcoholic to stop drinking or an eating-disorder sufferer to eat normally. This is doubly true when you try to make the AD/HD individual fulfill the requirements of an environment to which he is not suited.

Adolescents with raging hormones and a need to question everything they have been taught present a profile similar to that of the AD/HD child. Attempting to make sure ODD adolescents do everything according to their childhood teachings is as futile as efforts to force the AD/HD child to live by the requirements of an environment to which he is not suited.

The answer to neurotic thinking by parents is to reduce the fear and increase the adaptability of attempts to control. The parents need to understand this process before they become free to challenge it. The adaptive solutions to the ODD teenager's challenges follow.

RECOGNIZING PARENTAL NEUROSIS

Parental neurosis can be recognized in the parents' persistent but unspoken worry that their children will fail if allowed to take charge of their own affairs. Parents in this state of mind assume that children's experiences of failure will trigger a persistent and escalating pattern of discouragement and a downward spiral into despair. Once this spiral is set in motion, the parents unconsciously anticipate an uninterrupted continuation of the downward trajectory, with disaster ahead for their children and nothing to stop it. These parents assume their children have no internal drive to succeed, no ability to overcome adversity on their own. The truth is, however, that the situation they worry about and struggle to avoid, which is putting their children in charge, is precisely the one that will save their children.

This fear of the children's inadequacy is kept secret, but comes out indirectly in the parents' attempts to praise and support. Pressure to reveal secrets that are either pleasant or traumatic has a way of growing within us. The principle of repression states that once something is experienced strongly but not talked about, it must come out one way or another. Without realizing they do so, some people behave according to patterns they keep secret. This explains how people who have been abused may end up abusing others, or become victims repeatedly of those with similar patterns.

The secret of parents who lack faith in their children's abilities is thoroughly revealed, through the nonverbal channels of the emotional mind, with visible signs of parental worry and concern, and the desire to protect conveyed through intonation and posture. The process takes place unconsciously. Parents don't realize they are communicating lack of faith, and children don't realize they are responding destructively to this unspoken message. Every time the parents ask, "Did you do your homework?" the kids unconsciously hear, "Do you have a brain?" Every time the parents say, "You were wonderful," the kids hear it as, "See, if you make an effort like this every time, you can be successful just like the other kids."

The children come to respond aggressively to their parents' hidden fear of their incompetence. This lack of faith creates a tremendous distance between parents and children. The parents praise their children and try to help and the children snap at them in response. These are children who do not want to be seen in public with their parents. These children fear that others will witness their parents' lack of confidence in them. Yet, no one seems to know why this is happening. No one suspects that make-sure parenting can have such an effect.

The content of the parents' dialogue with their children reveals their neurosis. The themes are always the poetic, romantic versions of the rightful place of the parent as the controlling and protective agent for the vulnerable and naive child. The teenager can have extended, civilized conversation about his needs and desires, only to have the parent say, "The answer is still no!" The parent knows best, so the child doesn't get to find things out first hand. The remaining choice for the teenager is to deceive, rebel, manipulate, and retaliate—control poker.

Rose sat in my office facing the fiercely negative attitude of her 14-year-old son, who was clearly going down the boredom/ deception path of the full-fledged mind split. Rose was a smart, confident, warm, reasonably playful and pleasant young mother. She could see no reason for her son's attitude. Her rational mind spoke eloquently as she defended her more-than-generous parenting and challenged her son's deceptive tendencies. Simultaneously, her emotional mind tended to surprise, clutch, and command. She was a strong presence. She was persistent in her relations with her son and forceful with her responses. She often confronted her son in front of his peers.

Rose simply could not fathom why her son saw her as a source of embarrassment. She began by saying it was her duty to get him safely to adulthood.

"Sure I have faith in you," she said to him, "but I've thought about this a lot, and when you get to be 25 I want to be able to say to myself that I did everything within my power to get you there in good shape. I couldn't forgive myself if things went wrong and I didn't try." Her son agreed with her general aims, but objected that, in reality, she didn't have to do much of anything to ensure his future, because he was fine.

"You don't know that," she responded. "All teenagers think that way." She mentioned an incident that he had mismanaged, and asked, "What about that?" He argued vehemently against use of the episode but Rose dismissed his objections. In such encounters her technique was to let him speak but look away with a knowing smile, her body posture saying, "Sure, sure, whatever you say." She would then close with sayings such as, "All kids have limits" or, "It's normal for teenagers to rebel."

During the current session, Rose went on the offensive. "I have very reasonable limits. Ken [her son] has plenty of freedom. I don't see why he has to lie," she said.

Ken pointed out the embarrassing standards his mom maintains, and the embarrassing way she has of enforcing them.

Rose was vigorous in her response. "I am not," she said, "about to let you just go to your friends' houses without knowing what parent is there or if there even is one!" She turned to me. "He doesn't even want me to know where he's going." Ken protested that this wasn't true. He just didn't want her to know whose house and who would be there.

Rose maintained her mother-knows-best attitude about everything Ken wanted to change in his life. These were the very things that Ken was lying about—homework, grades, curfew, and peers. Ken was deceiving himself into thinking that his grades were all B's. Rose pointed out how they were substantially below that level. Meanwhile, Ken was not doing anything to help the family out, wasn't spending any time with them, and seemed to be always locked in his room. When he had to be with the family he was belligerent. He was explosive in his response to maternal nagging. Whenever he attacked or complained, his mother countered with, "All kids have limits. You have a mother, it's that simple. Face it."

Rose's words fell on my ears like lead. My shoulders grew heavier and heavier. This was my introduction to her diatribes. My voice must have sounded distant and weak. I dreaded having to respond. I could hear my own self-propelled internal dialogue. "I can't believe I have to explain that whole paradigm thing again from scratch," I was thinking. "What kind of job have I gotten myself into?"

At the same time that I was having these thoughts, I was also busy keeping Rose's son from adopting a completely insulting stance toward his mother. Rose's habit was to listen to her son's shouts and objections long enough to detect a flaw in his logic, and then say demeaningly, "That's what I'm trying to tell you." You couldn't win with Rose. I could tell that Ken was concluding, on the basis of the way this session was going, that he didn't want to come back to hear this kind of thing again. It was a waste of his time.

I learned in this interview with Rose that the only reason to talk to parents in front of their children is to diagnose parental neurosis. The setting is not good for effecting any kind of change. I have made it my policy to first discuss cases thoroughly with the parents alone, then bring in the teenager. I also see parents alone after all major failures.

It is essential for the clinician to manage the interaction between neurotic parents and ODD teens, to expose it, and to channel it into a healthy direction. He must have both parent and child present in order to engage in this process. This type of encounter is more easily arranged after the clinician has demonstrated his professionalism at a meeting with the parents, has shown that he is courteous in his approach to them, and has a thorough understanding of their concerns and point of view.

The clinician's goal is the same with both parent and child— join the emotional mind part of the split. Attack the maladaptive rational mind agenda of the make-sure parent, but emphasize how the heart is in the right place. This means siding with the parents' desire to control and urging them on: "So why didn't you force him more? Maybe it's worth a try." "Why didn't you call all the parents who were attending the party?" "Have you thought of forming a committee of concerned parents that can spy on everthing the kids are doing and give consequences to all peers at the same time?" "No one should tell a parent how to raise his child. A parent should never betray his own instincts, because no one else has to live with the outcome."

The communication style of the neurotic parent can also be symptomatic of the condition. The case of Elaine's mother at the start of this chapter illustrates this beautifully. Years of training in the trenches of control-poker battles have programmed parents to commence their attempts to control sweetly. They combine their underlying need to establish control with an on-the-surface need to please their child, or at least gain the child's approval. These parents are often hurt when their children, sensing their insecurity, blame their own shortcomings on an alleged poor quality of parenting: "It's your fault I've turned out this way. You're a horrible parent!"

Parents of ODD teenagers often fear their children's defiance or the withdrawal of their affection. This accounts for their outward appearance and the double message. Parental neurosis involves a two-mind split that corresponds to that of the ODD youth's. The rational agenda is to appear to side with the child's emotional brain, and the emotional agenda is to impose its own wants, to protect and educate, and exercise control. The parent talks about granting freedom but offers merely the illusion of choice. The child rebels, and the parent labels the protest as normal for the age. Thus: "All teenagers go through a period of rebellion. I remember how I was."

Neurotic parents give lip service to encouraging their children and to expressing faith in how they will eventually turn out, but doubt their children every step of the way. Neurotic parents learn to conceal their true intentions and use ulterior methods to control the child's choices and behaviors. They try to get others to tell the child the things they want to say themselves but don't. They ask peers and adults their children respect to intervene and help validate the protective agenda they are afraid to state. They embarrass their children in the process and invite seemingly unprovoked attacks.

RESOLVING PARENTAL NEUROSIS

Resolving parental neurosis is where the subtleties of a paradigm shift become acutely important. The discussion in Chapter 1 contrasted the paradigms of molding children versus fostering natural development. The molding paradigm mandates that adults teach their children how to adapt and force them to behave properly until proper behavior becomes habit. In this paradigm, a misbehaving child equals a child with a poor teacher. The developmental paradigm, on the other hand, mandates that adults remove dependencies to force their children to exercise vital mental abilities. This latter paradigm states that parents should allow their children to face reasonable challenges, make choices, and take the consequences. The intelligence is coded into the child's genetic blueprint. The suffering from the consequences triggers the development of new abilities. Trial-and-error learning through these experiences leads to growth.

The assumption that children need molding causes dependency and anxiety. Parents worry excessively because they can't see how the child will be able to respond wisely to failure without an external agent teaching them how to do so. Teenagers want to do things their own way. This is especially true of ODD teens seeking to grow in a unique way.

In support of the developmental paradigm one can use the observation that teenagers want to do things their own way. The natural urge to do things differently from the way their parents want may, in fact, invite the kinds of consequences and failures necessary to stimulate the natural growth process. Why else would adolescents seek to expose themselves to failure and pain? Why accept help and advice if they can survive without it?

Make-sure parents expect a discouraging response after each of their children's failures, with nothing new having been learned.

They fear that this will trigger a downward spiral, with each failure leading to discouragement, and each discouragement leading to a less secure response to the situation. Each insecure response will lead to another failure. The spiral can only be stopped with external teachings and forced success.

These parents need to understand that failure leads to growth because the intelligence to adapt lies dormant inside the individual's genetic blueprint. Suffering will activate the dormant program, and all the intelligence the parents have acquired over a lifetime will emerge from the youth when needed.

Parents must also realize that their children's negativity and selfishness are signs they have outgrown their usefulness as their children's protectors. Children need to develop their own motivations and determine their own reasons for wanting to succeed. They need to outgrow their oppositional phase and take responsibility for their own development. Parents need to let go, give up control, and trust that nature will assert itself. Parents who have come to live vicariously through their children's accomplishments will need to accept the reality of how the children actually turn out, and perhaps mourn the difference between that and what they had wished.

Once a parent has learned to let go, he can convey an attitude of confidence and support backed by calmness and wisdom even while his children are facing or experiencing failure. No more lectures, no more lessons, no more nagging, no more hidden urgencies. Now there is room for children to discover vital lessons, to share expert opinions, to include their parents (and therapist) in plotting new ways of conquering their worlds. Parents and their children can enjoy each other as never before once the parents abandon the make-sure parenting role and put their children in charge.

Parents will be surprised by the outcome of letting go. Their children will feel challenged by the opportunity to be in charge. They will try to prove to their parents that they can fulfill their obligations successfully, unaided. Unfortunately for the ODD teenagers, their initial attempts to prove their worth may be disappointing. They may fail to get up in the morning without help. They may not be productive during work time. However, they will soon rise to the challenges of life and begin to grow strong.

ODD youths will become more motivated and hungry for success once they are free of parental control. Their growth after each failure will provide all the evidence their parents need that they are on the right track, and their confidence and self-esteem as parents will grow. They will know that nature is backing them. When challenges come and their children begin to succeed, they will find the experience exhilarating. They will glow with pride over their children's accomplishments.

I have asked numerous mothers who had been deeply involved in daily control-poker battles what helped them master the process of letting go. Their AD/HD children were developmentally at a standstill, their families dysfunctional. By simply relinquishing their make-sure roles, most of these mothers witnessed tremendous growth in their children.

They reported the following factors as having been helpful in their efforts to let go: (1) realizing how their make-sure efforts had led to nothing but immaturity and problems; (2) realizing that their children needed help badly; (3) having confidence in a professional who exuded confidence, and gave them permission to let go and try something different; and (4) seeing my simple prediction—that their children would take pride in their abilities once they felt in charge and once their success mattered to them more than to their parents—come true. This prediction serves to create awareness of a destructive pattern in which parents hitherto have been blindly involved, and against which they have been rendered helpless. The resulting awareness helps to establish rational mind dominance over a recurring pattern that involved emotional hijacking (to use Goleman's term) and emotional mind dominance.

I also predicted that the children would set the highest standards for themselves under these conditions—a sign of their inner parenting ability kicking in and taking over. On the other side of the coin, I predicted that their children would turn off and become difficult once the parents wanted success for their children more than the children wanted it for themselves.

These predictions underscore the importance of parents' accepting whatever limitations their children settle for. No more living vicariously through children's accomplishments. Parents must endure living supportively with children who, for significant periods of time, are failing to realize their potential. In due time, this level of acceptance will foster the development of vital abilities in children.

Parents who suffer from severe neurosis will not be able to relinquish control over their children, no matter how hard they try. This is due to the trauma resulting from their having been in a position of extreme stress for a long period of time. They may allow others to exploit them because they had grown accustomed to giving way too much. They may be mistreated and taken for granted by those whom they have helped the most. Stress has a way of becoming traumatic, and trauma has a way of producing irrational worry.

The clinician can still make this failure-based intervention program work even if parents suffer from serious neurosis. But they will need regular counseling to process their worries about their children. As parents relinquish their make-sure roles, however, they will see their children's inherent strength and their ability to succeed take over. They will begin to enjoy them in a new way. This will ultimately bring their excessive worry to an end.

THERAPY WITH THE NEUROTIC PARENT

Parental neurosis can be diagnosed on the basis of the parents' response to treatment of the ODD child. All parents of ODD children develop a certain level of parental neurosis. In fact, they adopt an ODD stance toward the clinician. When it's time to intervene at home, they resist and undermine his work.

The inability to adopt a paradigm shift, disengage from control, and change the dysfunctional behavior is what differentiates a diagnosis of anxiety disorder from common neurotic behavior in parents of ODD children. Normal parents can fall into neurotic behavior patterns simply by operating with mistaken child-rearing assumptions. However, they will be able to adopt a paradigm of natural development and adjust their behavior in accordance with clinical prescription.

The clinician's treatment for parental neurosis parallels the one prescribed for ODD in the child. That is, he joins the parents' emotional agenda of needing to be a good parent, and puts them through the same four steps of treatment: (1) taking failure to the limit, (2) turning failure into growth, (3) addressing the resistance (mind split in the teen), and (4) providing opportunities.

THE FAILURE PHASE

The moment of truth for parental neurosis comes when the teenager takes failure to the limit while adopting a stance of contempt for authority that he feels is justified by the advice he received from his therapist. The neurotic parent will have formal anxiety symptoms and display varying forms of resistance. I recommend that the clinician see the parent alone to address his concerns, unless, at that time, it has been established that the teenager is well intentioned and relatively reasonable.

The parent presents a reasonable story at the start of the session. However, there are signs of the parent having lost it. He questions the clinician's work and fails to follow through on recommendations for handling the anticipated failure. The parent, composure regained, comes to the clinician with a reasonable report. However, the clinician senses the parent's concern that this level of failure indicates a poor treatment response.

There is a possibility that the parent will develop strong reservations about proceeding with this program and show some level of resistance. The clinician should look for it if it is not visible. Strong resistance and neurotic behavior from parents is most likely to occur in the turning-failure-into-growth phase, when it is time to deliver consequences. Managing the resistance of neurotic parents is discussed below.

The remedy for individuals who interfere with the treatment of ODD is always the same. The clinician invites those who resist his recommendations to wrestle with the ODD symptoms on their own ineffective terms until they are overcome by exhaustion, and are ready to change their approach. This is similar to taking failure to the limit for the teenager.

This treatment method demands that the therapist either gets the parents to allow the teenager to take failure to the limit or goes the opposite route and has the parent protect the teenager from all failure. The latter course becomes the parent's failure and the parental counterpart of taking failure to the limit. The neurotic parent will not allow extreme failures to take place easily. Therefore, parental neurosis will often require the clinician to facilitate the parent's taking make-sure tactics to the extreme—until the neurotic parent has had enough. The clinician simply waits until the parent has thoroughly failed and then provides the opportunity to follow with dedication the program described here.

The clinician prescribes taking it to the limit by clarifying that dedication to a new strategy cannot precede the conviction that one must give up on an earlier established and preferred method. He tells the parents that their emotional mind needs evidence that their present beliefs won't yield the kind of results desired. They must be fully convinced that there isn't a better control tactic to guide and teach the teenager mature behavior and help him succeed. They must be completely convinced that every method of protecting their children has been given every opportunity, and failed, before allowing the teenager to choose his own protection.

Parents must be fully committed to this intervention strategy before taking the attendant risks. Otherwise they will be betraying their emotional mind wants and losing trust in themselves. So the clinician asks them to go all the way with their old method so they can test its validity, once and for all. Only then will they succeed with the new intervention, as single-minded and dedicated parents with the full backing of the emotional and rational minds.

This challenge sets the stage for the prescription to take it to the limit. The clinician does not want to waste time. The teenager is growing older and the problem is not getting better. So the clinician must determine in which ways the parents have been holding back in their attempts to control, and ask them to go all the way: "Let's find out now, once and for all, whether the method you've been following can save your child." Now the clinician prescribes going all out with all the neurotic things they have refrained from doing. He challenges them for not having tried them, and asks them to try whatever they think is best and return to him in a few weeks.

TURNING FAILURE INTO GROWTH

Dealing with Moderate Parental Neurosis

Once the moderately neurotic parent is convinced that intensified attempts to implement the same old make-sure tactics only make matters worse, he will commit to the paradigm shift and allow failure. Moderately neurotic parents can maintain this shift with regular therapy support.

The stage of treatment in which the teenager has failed and needs to face consequences for infractions is very tough on the neurotic parent. It is one thing for these parents to sit back with clenched teeth and fists and endure watching their children as they think, "Oh my God! See, I knew it!" It is an entirely different matter when they remain calm and detached in relation to their teenagers' choices, are accepting and friendly, and dole out reasonable consequence for infractions, giving the offender an opportunity to demonstrate respect for the violated privilege.

The clinician will probably have to diagnose the parent with an anxiety disorder separate from that of the ODD child, and initiate a formal course of individual therapy with the parent. The clinician treating the ODD must act as the therapist for the neurotic parent, and the therapy needs to remain close to the concerns about the ODD teenager's choices and behaviors.

In each session with them, the clinician gets the parents' stories, exposes the creatures-of-habit assumptions that propel the anxiety, and facilitates the reconstruction of the stories, this time from the perspective of the natural development paradigm. The clinician can use the alliance with the emotional mind of the neurotic parent to challenge the rational mind that remains loyal to the old paradigm. The clinician challenges the unwillingness of the rational brain to experiment, asking, "How many years have you been doing the very same thing? Where has it gotten you? What kind of a rational brain doesn't try new things?" The clinician always supports the emotional mind. He says something like, "I can't believe you didn't panic even more given how you look at things."

Dealing with Severe Parental Neurosis

Some parents will be too far gone and require greater intervention. Processing episodes privately with the clinician will not suffice to remedy the condition of these parents. He needs, in dealing with severe parental neurosis, an intervention that parallels the one used with the ODD teen. The teen gets tickets with loss of privileges as a consequence of having violated them, and must perform a reparation that demonstrates respect for the privilege violated to get it back. The parent with severe neurosis must do the same.

To set the stage for work with the parent, the clinician meets with the teenager alone to start the session and explains his concern about the parent not being able to follow the program. The clinician explains that he is licensed by the state to enforce certain health and safety standards, just like a cop. However, he works to maximize health and freedom for the teenager, unlike the cop who may restrict freedom and mete out punishment. So sometimes the clinician needs to obtain the help of the teenager to enforce his agenda, just as he sometimes uses the parent to represent him in instances where the teenager is being abusive or engaging in unacceptable behavior.

Next, the clinician sees the teenager and parent together. He points out how the parents' anxiety, to the detriment of the entire family, hasn't allowed the teenager a fair try at implementing the program. The clinician puts the child in charge, representing him to help stop the parental violation of privileges. He gives the teenager a ticket pad, just like the one the parents used in Chapter 6.

Possible infractions include spoiling the family atmosphere, unfairness, personal attacks, public embarrassment, destroying property, and deception.

I have developed a ticket pad that I use to help parents and children document infractions and find the record of reparations rapidly and easily. The pad has carbon copies, which create a diary of the infractions. The clinician asks the teenager to give the parent a ticket (see Appendix B), and keep the carbon copy. The teenager will not remove privileges or demand that reparations be carried out now, but merely document the infractions and the resulting assignment of reparations. As a gesture of good faith, the parent can choose to be a good sport and perform the reparations indicated on the ticket.

In future weeks, when necessary, the teenager will remove parental privileges until reparations are performed. Once the ticket is delivered, the parents will be temporarily without control or influence over the child. The child is instructed to refuse to respond to parental authority until the parent performs a reparation. In extreme cases, I suggest that the teenager find a friend to stay with for as long as needed. This preempts the manipulative "running away" tactic that teenagers use so frequently as a desperate call for help or an aggressive manipulation. It allows the manipulative teenager to perform the same act, with, however, a different mind-set. Instead of rebellion, the teenager leaves home with the appearance of honor and the opportunity to be honorable. Inevitably, such episodes lead to the child's wearing out his welcome and needing to come home. Thus, the change in emphasis turns a pathological act of defiance into a sanctioned lesson for the teenager and the parent.

The clinician will probably have to see the severely neurotic parent on an emergency basis while the teenager is having a sleepover. He uses the session to plan the reparation the parent may perform or the consequence the parent will deliver if the child abuses the authority given him by the clinician. The child would be guilty of deception and would lose the privilege of having the ticket pad. Leaving home by prescription is very difficult for teenagers to accept. It feels very different from running away in the heat of anger. Leaving home under duress is a burden that will grow on them. In some cases leaving home to take up residence in a nice apartment for an extended period without the privilege of returning yields a very powerful lesson to a teenager who was dying for an apartment and defying the family to intolerable extremes.

This kind of consequence doled out by the ODD teenager to the severely neurotic parent could have the effect of forcing him to leave the house for a period so that the parent would temporarily lose the privilege of having a son. This will force the parent to separate and lose control, which is the reason for the neurosis in the first place. The severely neurotic parent is left with the choice of either detaching to deliver a consequence or detaching because his child has forced him to as a penalty for exercising excessive control.

ADDRESSING THE RESISTANCE

The method I recommend for managing resistance is to identify it, join it, and prescribe magnifying it. I do this in the same way I invite teens to take to the limit their quest to do things their own way. I tell them, "I just want you to come back to me saying that you're happy with your day." We've covered taking failure to the limit in the section on prescribing failure above. Here, I will limit the scope of discussion to exposing the resistance.

The clinician exposes the resistance by confronting its indirect expressions and by asking everything about it, without giving any opinion about it whatsoever. He simply asks general questions about reservations that parents experience about allowing failure. He asks: "What is the down side [and later the up side] of allowing your child to experience this?" He follows by asking for concise descriptions of the reservations: "What are you saying?" And then he can speculate: "Are you saying that the risk is too great?" Then he asks for more information: "Do you have other reservations?"

The obvious way to increase awareness of resistance is to interpret it. This means helping the parent become aware of it in a rational, straightforward manner. The clinician explains to the parent that he faces an inherent conflict of interest when it comes to failure and his ODD teenager.

The parent must allow the failure to loom larger and larger so the teenager experiences sufficient pressure to get past his denial, or any other resistance, to the point of dealing with it. Once more, the parent may manifest a parallel form of resistance. Instead of refusing to notice the problem, the parent resists exposure of the teenager's problems. The teen needs failure magnification and the parent seeks failure minimization.

The clinician mirrors the resistance by imitating the body language in cases where the parent doesn't respond to interpretation, probably due to lack of insight. Usually the parent's attitude expresses the resistance indirectly and nonverbally. He does this in the same way he deals with the resistance of the teenager when he is addressing the two-mind split (Chapter 7). He exaggerates the parent's irrational fears, imitates his body language and attitude, prescribes excessive control, and counts the number of times they avoid a subject, or perform a defensive operation.

PROVIDING OPPORTUNITIES

Parents suffering from neuroticism about their children have often neglected their personal lives. They have devoted all of their energies to controlling the uncontrollable (the ODD teenager). Their lives have been limited to incessant lectures, demands for correct living in their kids, and a constant need to check up on them. By concentrating their parental efforts on making sure their kids live correctly, they have ignored their own personal development every bit as much as their ODD teenagers.

These parents need to get back their own lives. They need to resume responsibility for the pursuit of their own dreams. They need to pick up where they left off. They may need to set new personal goals. They need to work on their primary relationships, their friendships, their career, their health, and their art. They need to remain present as parents and offer their teenagers the supports they request. However, once they have performed their two wake-up calls, or provided a ride or a tutor, they will assume their kids will manage their own affairs. They will then turn their primary attention to living their lives to the fullest.

These parents will help their children most effectively by setting an example of correct living. The teenager will follow in the footsteps of the parent whose primary investment is in self-improvement. The parent cannot mold and teach growth. People develop naturally through the trial-and-error learning process that accompanies the struggle for the coming true of dreams. When youths see their parents avoid life they fear ending up like them. When they see their parents blossom they gain confidence and are prepared to struggle to reach their goals. Parents will be shifting from a paradigm of molding and shaping to a paradigm of natural development once they become absorbed in their personal development.

These parents will have ample chances to teach and protect their children once the children turn to them for support and advice. The children will do so when they see their parents struggling to succeed in their own endeavors instead of overinvesting in efforts to run their children's lives. There will be ample time for bonding as the parents offer support to the teenager's efforts to live life his own way. There will be rides, help with homework, sleepover hosting, and doing chores together.

The therapy with neurotic parents should shift at this time from processing fears about the teenager's possible misbehavior to satisfying their own needs and realizing their own potential. The opportunity for this shift presents itself once the teenager begins to make better decisions. Once the parents have let go and the teenager has failed sufficiently, the clinician can address the two-mind split in the teenager, get past the resistance, and provide opportunities for the teenager to succeed on his own. This will give the parents hope and a chance to breathe more easily.

The clinician encourages parents to focus on their own lives once he has suppported them in completing the treatment steps outlined earlier in this book. They will have taken failure to the limit, arranged consequences to turn failure into growth, and seen how one can help integrate the mind split in the teenager. The teenager will become more honest. The parent will see the teenager's resistance (like externalizing blame) exposed and dissolved in the sessions. They will see the youth work harder and gain confidence. There will be future failures, but these will lead to growth as well.

A personal development agenda for the parents can be constructed in the period of time between failures during which the growth of the teenager becomes apparent. Each cycle of crisis resolution, success, and return to failure is a step in the direction of growth for the teenager. Each cycle can also become a step in the personal growth of the parent given focused therapy intervention. A solid foundation for growth in the entire family can be built this way.

10

Special Problem 3: Excessive Aggression

CHARACTERISTICS OF THE EXCESSIVELY AGGRESSIVE TEENAGER

I use the term *excessive aggression* to describe a series of behaviors that involve violations of the basic rights of others. The most common manifestations of excessive aggression involve physical and verbal attacks, tormenting others, and destruction of property. However, aggressive behaviors are not always direct and blatant. Individuals who possess these tendencies frequently employ a host of more subtle manipulations that represent as great a threat to the well-being of the family as do more visible forms of aggression. These maneuvers usually involve some form of dishonest behavior, including stealing, lying, and cheating.

Excessive aggression makes oppositional-defiance extremely troublesome, persistent, and toxic to families. Aggressive individuals tend to commit their violations when their personal interests are jeopardized. This can take place because of a conflict with the needs of another individual or of the group.

Oppositional children in general tend to recognize the disrespect for their true nature that traditional child-rearing methods cultivate. These youths in turn lose respect for the adults who promote these methods and respond to them with increased levels of disrespect and defiance. The excessively aggressive teenager will express his disrespect in unreasonable and destructive ways. The family becomes accustomed to these aggressive outbursts after years of exposure. These families learn to respond to the constant threat of abuse by walking on eggshells in the presence of the oppositional child.

The excessively aggressive teenager learns to turn every situation into an excuse to argue endlessly about the fairness of punishments or rewards. Perceived unfairness in turn justifies personal attacks. Thus, any attempt to set a limit feeds right into the coercive cycle that pits parents who attempt to remain calm against children who push all the buttons needed to start a fight. Family members will take a beating in this cycle, ultimately, though unwittingly, showing their children how to gain power through negative and aggressive behavior.

These youths elevate dawdling, coercion, retaliation, manipulation, disrespect, badgering, and self-destructive behavior to art forms, using these strategies to extort a hefty ransom—cash, a trip to the mall, the latest game or toy, or a sleepover at a friend's house. They achieve mastery over their parents, luring them in with irresponsible behavior, manipulating them with badgering and deception, and then hitting them hard with violent personal attacks: "Shut up or I'll rearrange your face! I hate you!" The aggressive teenager cannot lose here, because this strategy can lead to only two possible outcomes—a good fight or yet another indulgence, either of which satisfies the youth's deviant quest for stimulation. The root of the problem often seems to lie in the young person's inability to derive satisfaction from normal levels of stimulation. Individuals of this type need intense stimulation to experience reasonable levels of satisfaction. Normal stimulation simply doesn't register.

Excessively aggressive teenagers' feelings of entitlement increase, and they develop a seemingly insatiable appetite for excitement. These youths come to expect that they will get whatever they want. They believe that no one can stop them. Their heedless pursuit of excitement leads them to take unnecessary risks, leaving them vulnerable to school failure, problems with the law, sexually transmitted diseases, unwanted pregnancy, and drug involvement.

The aggressive teenagers' absorption with personal stimulation leaves them unable to feel the experience of others. They simply argue against the complaints of other persons about their conduct, dissociate themselves from their victims' expressions of pain, and feed off their targets' other emotions. They often transform the painful expressions of their victims into emotional states they can enjoy. For example, they may get angry at their victims' pain, become excited by their fear, or find humor and entertainment in their futile attempts to protect themselves or retaliate. They derive a sense of power and determination from the emotional discharges of their victims.

The constitutional inability to derive sufficient satisfaction from reasonable stimulation leads these individuals to view others as possessions. As a result, they attempt to exercise the rights of ownership over them. This means insisting on control of them, hurting them, frightening them, violating their right to privacy, taking from them, or simply exercising power over them for the sake of power.

Aggressive youths become parasites because they do not have the resources to create a stimulating life through their own honest efforts. They rationalize their tendency to take the fruits of the labor of others, and justify such acts by citing their own lack of opportunities: "I can't afford it, and you have it, so I have no choice but to take it from you."

Aggressive tendencies don't reside exclusively in the teenager who is identified as the patient. Many families are plagued with several members who have these characteristics and use similar tactics. The various aggressors in the family engage in coercive tactics intended to satisfy personal cravings for escalation of violence. Other family members adopt roles of victims, rescuers, peacemakers, and enablers in response to the risk of harm to others in the family.

REFRAMING RONNIE'S CONDITION

My first intervention with Ronnie's family was to reframe his problem as one of trust, not boredom. Ronnie continually complained of being bored and blamed all of his shortcomings on his hearing impairment. His parents, Helen and Mario, did, in fact, feel guilty about their son's deafness, and, to atone, catered to him. Mom worked herself to the bone. She was like an indentured servant to her entitled children. Dad bought them whatever they wanted.

Ronnie's expectations were completely unrealistic. He wanted a BMW, an apartment of his own in which he could live with his friends, a state-of-the art computer (he had one that was a few months old), lots of cash, and girls. He wanted a $100-a-week allowance for doing his schoolwork. All of this was justified by his need for stimulation. He was bored. He was defiant. It was his parents' fault, so they owed it to him to provide all of this. He, in turn, did nothing for the family, and actually tormented and traumatized other family members, particularly his youngest brother.

I made it clear to the parents that Ronnie needed to shift his focus away from the one sensory system that didn't work and seek satisfaction and stimulation from the four senses that remained. The reason he was bored was his lack of connection to other people. He was disconnected because he was violating the trust of others in a variety of ways.

I explained to the parents that trust depended on three basic factors: (1) respect for boundaries, meaning no attacks or violations of personal space, including cheating, lying, stealing, or hurting; (2) follow-through, meaning keeping promises made to members of the family; and (3) fairness, meaning a balance in give and take. I clarified that it was up to the family to establish a culture of trust by forcing the members to earn privileges through trust-enhancing behaviors.

I explained that trust is the lifeblood of the mind, and violations of trust represent the mental equivalent of cuts that caused bleeding. Sufficient bleeding kills the relationship by draining it of all trust. Violations of boundaries with behaviors such as cheating, lying, and physical or verbal attacks cause a profuse loss of trust. Not following through on a promise causes moderate loss of trust, and unfairness an ebbing away of trust.

Ronnie was bored because he lived in a home where there were constant violations of boundaries. The children did very little giving and a lot of taking, and no one followed through on promises. The children would demand things, promising to earn them somehow in the future, and then refuse to make good on their end of the deal.

These violations caused a loss of trust, and, in defense, all family members automatically shut down their sensory systems and felt disconnected, except for the stimulation provided by the fights. Ronnie also violated the trust of peers and other adults, but didn't know it. He didn't know how to make himself valued and accepted in social groups.

In short, Ronnie was cutting off all avenues for trust in his life because of the deficit in his thinking. He blamed the boredom that came from lack of belonging on his hearing problem. This fueled the very behavior that violated trust in others and condemned him to isolation.

In the weekend that had just passed, Ronnie had committed the following violations of trust against his family: He had run up a $100 Internet debt, but wouldn't acknowledge it. Also, he had used a household aerosol spray bottle and a lighter to create a torch to intimidate others and to destroy property. He had tormented his siblings, swearing them to secrecy about the torch device. If they told, he threatened, he would torch them and their mother. The threat traumatized the young ones.

Ronnie was convinced that other family members drove him to committing these violations. If they hadn't looked so nerdy and gotten in his way, he would not have had to go after them with a torch. If they had given him what he wanted, he would not have had to use his father's credit card on the Internet.

Helen made an important observation that validated the reframe of her son's problem as entailing boredom and hatred of his condition, and not the hearing impairment itself. She noticed that the deviant acts took place largely in the absence of social contacts. When he had friends or quality contact with Helen, Ronnie was very docile. This is a common pattern in cases that involve excessive aggression. The subjects seek positive stimulation, and if they don't get it, they'll take the negative.

I made it clear to Mario and Helen that Ronnie and his younger siblings couldn't learn the meaning of trust through a lecture or a book. Understanding of the trust concept has to come from the consequences of violations. My observation about positive stimulation called for a specific strategy around which we could organize our interventions. We had to (1) defeat Ronnie's attempts to derive negative stimulation by making sure they didn't lead to payoffs; (2) eliminate the power of Ronnie's expressions of hatred to induce feelings of guilt in his parents, leading them to indulge their son with whatever he wanted; and (3) provide opportunities for him to earn positive stimulation through trust-enhancing behaviors involving the family. That is, Ronnie needed to respect the boundaries of others, follow through on his commitments to the family, and contribute fairly to the household.

We needed a strategy that could help us achieve these treatment objectives. Ronnie wouldn't change his perspective on his problem easily. He wouldn't release his hatred, and certainly didn't want to relinquish his control over others or his avenues for negative stimulation.

THE INTERVENTION STRATEGY

Children who respond to loss of privileges with undue rebelliousness require a special intervention to facilitate a constructive response to treatment. Strategic therapy offers the best possible system of knowledge for this purpose. Strategic interventions rely on crafty induction of perceptual shifts and paradox to resolve symptoms. Since oppositional states are negative, they worsen with direct pressure, but rapidly resolve themselves with paradox. Strategic therapists use methods like paradox and counter-paradox to achieve sudden and dramatic changes in the most deeply entrenched irrational behaviors.

In *Ordeal Therapy* (1984), Jay Haley describes a kind of intervention that is ideally suited to dealing with excessively aggressive ODD teenagers. Ordeal therapy is designed to reverse the most extreme and entrenched symptoms possible, such as health- and life-threatening levels of insomnia, or compulsive behavior such as eating, smoking, gambling, and hand-washing.

The essence of ordeal therapy is to wait until the symptoms have become intolerable to the individual and then arrange it so that it becomes harder for him to indulge in the symptoms than it does to desist. The emotional mind is the driving force behind all symptoms and is always looking for the easiest way out of any situation. It is usually easier for the emotional brain to exhibit a symptom than to refrain from it and behave adaptively. Haley designed a sophisticated method for making it increasingly weighty to manifest the symptoms, until it became exhausting for the emotional mind to fall into the symptom pattern. Ultimately, the emotional mind developed an aversion to launching the symptom.

The severely oppositional child pushes much more intensely than is usual among young people, and hence is more easily thrown off balance. Strategic intervention can turn the formidable adolescent bully into a cooperative one in a short period of time. The problem posed by a proclivity for aggression is the danger that it will return, even though the strategy seems to have worked. The return of the problem means having to repeat most strategic interventions over and over. Ordeal therapy solves this problem by automatically searching for a level of consequence that makes the symptoms burdensome enough to encourage adaptive behavior.

Encouraging the Development of a Conscience

Strategic methods suffer from the same limitations as behavioral programs in their disregard of the internal workings of the organism they seek to modify. They use a trial-and-error process until they come upon the unique combination of cues and consequences that will increase or decrease a target behavior. They focus on eliminating specific symptoms but not much else. They can be used to change behaviors in any direction. They make no value judgments on whether behaviors other than the symptom should be encouraged or discouraged, or whether they might be healthy or unhealthy. We need to establish a direction for the changes we seek to make with our strategic intervention.

To make the therapeutic ordeal healthy, the clinician must arrange for more adaptive outlets for the ingrained tendencies of these oppositional individuals to aggress or seek excessive stimulation. The therapeutic ordeal interrupts the deviant expression of these tendencies. However, the clinician must subsequently provide alternative opportunities for their healthy expression. The central goals are to side with the emotional mind's agenda and to promote integration of the two minds. (For these purposes, I discuss below the provision of opportunities for healthy satisfaction of aggressive and sensation-seeking tendencies.)

The intervention presented here also supplements strategic intervention for oppositional-defiance with methods designed to foster the development of a healthy conscience. One way to do this is by prescribing reparative activities. Children who have made positive contributions to their families feel better about themselves, value their families more, and more easily grasp the difference between right and wrong.

It is hard for a person to feel empathy for someone he has treated immorally. If a person has shown disrespect for and hurt others, but has subsequently honored and supported them, he will feel more connected and welcomed in those people's lives than if he had simply been punished for his infractions.

For the clinician to foster the development of a conscience, he must understand how children outgrow their inherent self-centeredness and develop a genuine ability for concern. This requires an understanding of narcissism and the psychology of reparations, which provides the clinician with explanations of the self-centered tendencies that underlie oppositional defiance. The strategic intervention takes care of the rest.

The clinician often needs a special intervention at the start of a case to resolve narcissism. The cases described in this chapter present with excessive aggression, an urgent need for sensation-seeking, and a history of manipulating family members with aggression to satisfy unreasonable demands. The next section emphasizes the importance of this initial intervention. It presents a step-by-step process for deflating narcissism.

After the initial intervention, families can be taught to reverse the negative escalations that usually accompany the routine outbursts of the ODD teenager. The clinician can encourage reparations that will foster the development of a conscience.

UNDERSTANDING NARCISSISTIC RAGE

Narcissism in older children and adults implies an inflated ego, excessive self-importance, and disregard for the needs of others. The ability to make others feel important is all but lost, and often this obstructs the development of relationships.

Narcissism is a normal state of development but it must be corrected with narcissistic injury or it can become pathological. Delivering a narcissistic injury is bursting the bubble of an overly inflated ego. This process takes place naturally when parents let go of their servant roles. They begin to expect more. They invest their time and efforts in other matters. They want their children to wait patiently for their needs to be attended to. They expect their children to take more responsibility for managing their own affairs.

Narcissistic injury invariably leads to what self-theorists call narcissistic rage, a state that invariably passes quickly. For children at age 2, this takes the form of tantrums, the equivalent of murderous rage in older persons. Young children feel entitled to hurt adults but are too small to pose any threat. I instruct parents to put raging children in a time-out until the fit passes. After a few minutes, there is a complete change of mood.

Once narcissistic rage passes, the deflation of the excessive ego leads to a reduction of expectations. Thereafter, children are satisfied more easily and more frequently, and end up happier, prouder, and more appreciative. The process fosters moral development. It deflates narcissism in order to build self-esteem, interrupts negative cycles with loss, and introduces positive reparations to reverse the negative cycle.

There is a culture, however, that encourages narcissism and offers belonging and success to attention-deficit and oppositional-defiant teenagers who have been denied these advantages at home and in school. This is the culture of the street gangs and clubs, which cater to the needs of the morally immature, narcissistic youth. The philosophy of this culture is one of excessive indulgence. The clinician must understand this culture before he can counter its irrational logic.

The Problem of Excessive Indulgence

It is the task of the clinician to open the parents' eyes to the way their aggressive, entitled teenagers have been achieving deviant mastery by indulging in peer-related play activities that I call *hook items*, such as TV, sports, video games, graffiti, music, pranks, cigarettes, and drugs. These youths fight against adults in positions of authority to gain freedom and avoid responsibilities, which they equate with conformity. The youth culture's response to adult-mandated conformity is instinctive and elaborates on institutional mandates. The logic is simple. If one ice cream is good, three are better. If one hour of TV is good, six are better. If staying up until 10 P.M. is good, then staying up until 3 A.M. is better. If taking risks is fun, then taking more dangerous risks is better.

Enslaved by their own self-indulgence, these youths become slackers, thinking that if badgering Mom gets them what they want or gets them out of doing work, then why not badger all the time? If causing a fight at home is more fun than being bored, why not start wars? If getting Dad to do homework for them saves them the trouble, why not? If taking basic math is easier than advanced math, why struggle? This is how these youths seek to compensate for their constitutional need for greater stimulation, and escape from boredom.

This kind of lifestyle produces children who have lost all motivation, who have allowed their capacity for disciplined effort to atrophy, and who have become habituated to excessive indulgence, making them insatiable, easily bored, and vulnerable to depression. In helping parents to understand the consequences of their ODD adolescent's propensity for indulgence, the clinician empowers them to stop giving in to their children. For the only way to free a teenager from his misdirected quest for mastery is to cut off the avenues that lead to its fulfillment, that is, to starve it of attention, fights, hook items, and other family and relationship privileges.

The narcissistic logic of the youth culture is dead wrong because the more we indulge in something, the more our brains develop a tolerance for it, and the less pleasure we derive from each subsequent indulgence. Excessive gratification, in fact, quickly yields diminishing returns and leaves us in a trap. Once the newness wears off, we end up needing the item or activity constantly, just to feel the same happiness we felt before we ever had it. Once we lose it, we feel depressed. This is the basis of drug addiction. Taking this into account, we can see the wisdom of balance, moderation, and mastery. If we learn to appreciate music at lower volumes, drink alcohol in smaller amounts, or watch only an occasional TV show, our capacity for happiness is greater.

The key to a philosophy of moderation, balance, and mastery is to have a large pool of challenging and productive activities to choose from, and to balance these with the kinds of indulgences we have come to depend upon. That is, we need to strike a balance between the satisfaction that comes with suffering through and mastering difficult challenges and the pleasures resulting from indulging in TV, ice cream, candy, and electronics.

Resolving Narcissism through Hook Items

I have introduced the term hook items to describe the few specific privileges that have a spellbinding impact on narcissistically entitled children. Special terminology is called for to address the unique and addictive quality of these privileges. These are the only privileges that influence such children. They are all the children seem to care about when they are in their narcissistic and defiant states. Hook items quickly become obsessions, and easily become the basis for deviant behaviors. These youths seem ready to sell their souls to gain access to them.

Hook items involve specific privileges usually related to the peer world, either electronic, including TV, stereo, phone, and video games; or social, including having friends over, sleepover dates, and involvement in clubs and sports. Drugs and alcohol represent the ultimate in hook items.

V. R. Sherwood (1990) proposed a method for getting past the narcissistic resistance of rebellious ADD youths. He identified this resistance as the key obstacle to helping these children accept aid. He established the importance of overcoming resistance as the first stage of treatment for conduct disorders.

Sherwood recommended a three-step process to counter narcissistic resistances. First, join the child in his grandiose self-importance and anti-authority attitude, which translates into joining the child in his feelings toward activities. Second, deliver a reasonable but significant blow to his ego (a narcissistic injury) when he displays excessive entitlement. This deflates the child, but earns his respect and encourages him to take a more realistic view of the relationship. Third, praise the child for having risen to the challenge in a realistic, productive, and respectful manner.

The clinician wants the consequences of narcissistic injury to resemble closely what results in the natural peer world from misusing a relationship. The leader of a clique has the power to cut children off from their peers. The clinician wants to command this kind of respect, and wants the parents of the ODD teenager to have the same influence. He wants the parents to become like the once-familiar, take-charge TV character, "the Fonz." As it was in the case of the Fonz when he was dealing with his teenage friends, at the first sign of disrespect the parents snap their fingers and poof, the peer world is closed down, both electronic and flesh and blood. The enforcement of fair consequences does not harm the client. Once parents have established this position of respect, the ODD teenager will never see them with the same eyes again.

Consequences for Deflating Narcissism

A conduct-disordered teenager will be a formidable opponent for any adult who tries to enforce the discipline of conformity. As I noted earlier in this book, the conduct-disordered youth seeks to borrow the frontal lobes of others to do his work. At the same time, he becomes a consummate fighter against authority figures, and an expert player of peer-world games. He has developed a talent for fighting and for indulging in excessive play that makes him a mean adversary. The conduct-disordered teenager feels comfortable in a vicious battle with the school principal, or even a police officer, after having skipped school to spend the day at the local pool hall.

However, the child has one obvious weak spot, which becomes evident in the light of the new understanding of the addictive property of hook items. The narcissistically entitled youth is extremely vulnerable to having his hitherto constant supply of hook items cut off. As long as he can cut off access to hook items and to the peer world and as long as he can avoid fighting, the clinician will be able to counter narcissistic resistance. The effect is like kryptonite on Superman. The nervous system that has become dependent on a constant flow of hook items to provide satisfaction will quickly crash. The child will fall into a depressive state for the moment.

When hook items are cut off for the first time, the ensuing crash will lead to a major tantrum, and an attempt to start a fight. However, when the adult refuses to be drawn in, the tantrum will run its course and fade and the teenager will reach a healthy state of depression. This dysphoric state is healthy because it results from puncturing the teenager's massively overinflated ego. Once the child has had to endure this depressive position, the brain will reset and respond normally to indulgence.

There is no fair and reliable system that can contain the narcissistically entitled teenager because the youth uses the across-the-board character of rules as a way of spoiling things for other members of the family. The parents decide on what they think is an equitable division of obligations and responsibilities among the members of the family. For violations, access to the peer world is cut off. Lists of duties are handed out. Then, however, the ODD teenager figures it out that if he is deprived of watching TV, no one else will be able to watch either until he has completed his work assignments. He asks, "So if I don't finish all of my work, my sister doesn't get to watch TV? Is that right?" He then refuses to work and gladly does without hook items, meanwhile deriving his excitement from seeing his sister suffer and wondering exactly when the situation will cause his parents to lose their poise. In this way, the ODD teenager is able to make the loss-of-privileges program inconvenient for the family as a whole, and fights to have the family declare the clinician's intervention a failure.

The teenager is ever alert to the possibilities for disrupting the family. For example, he agrees to cooperate following the dispensing of consequences for routine violations of family privileges. He waits for an appropriate moment to strike, for example, when the parents must obtain cooperation to get to church on time. Sensing the family's need, the youth strikes without mercy. He refuses to cooperate, fights the consequences, and holds the parents hostage: "If I get dressed, will you take me to the mall afterward?"

The parents' answer to the ODD teenager's attempts to spoil the clinician's intervention is to be strategically inconsistent. The clinician informs the parents that they must be consistent in their dealings with the ODD teenager only to the extent of making sure his manipulations don't pay off. The family must, without qualms, change the rules so that the teenager's sister can still watch TV when he hasn't done his chores. The parents promise him the world, effective after church, and change their minds later. In short, parents must be trained to be whatever it takes—honest or dishonest, consistent or inconsistent—to avoid delivering the payoff the ODD teenager expects his manipulations will produce. This maintains the integrity of the intervention. The only exception to the rule comes when there is a threat of immediate physical violence. On such an occasion the parents give in to the child as much as is necessary to calm the situation at that moment. Privileges are removed later when the circumstances have improved.

Once more, the therapist will use the psychology of managing consequences and privileges introduced in Chapter 6. The teenager who has misused the privilege of being part of the family loses it. The infraction usually impacts directly on the family. Accordingly, the clinician arranges to have the parents remove all family privileges. He shows them how to remove themselves from any request for privileges until reparation has been completed. The major aspects that make this application unique include (1) a much trickier way of removing the privileges; (2) an emphasis on losing the hook item, with much less emphasis on other privileges, since they don't matter; and (3) a reparation that will be especially difficult, in keeping with Haley's (1984) ordeal therapy, as discussed above.

COUNTERING NARCISSISTIC RAGE

As stated earlier, the clever ODD teenager will soon figure out the rules and attempt to twist them to his advantage. The child may, for example, provoke a situation in which the TV is turned off for everyone, just when the program his sister has been waiting for all week comes on.

That's where the ticket comes into play. Like some traffic cops, the parents quietly let the driver break the rules, and then surprise him, pull him over, and write out a ticket. In this instance, the surprise is to delay the removal of TV privileges until the sister's favorite show has ended, or arrange ahead of time for her to view it at a neighbor's house.

The clinician must instruct the parents not to fight, but rather to write the ticket. They allow the teenager to think he's getting away with the deceptive tactics. While the ODD teenager is quietly indulging, the parent is writing up the ticket; a detailed description of the infraction (see Appendix B), giving the reasons the parent is upset and explaining the impact of the behavior on other family members. This fosters integration of the two minds by creating awareness in the rational mind of the deceptive tactics deployed by the emotional mind. A prescribed reparation process follows. To restore fairness in the family, the teenager who had become a taker must now become a giver.

During the first stage of this process, all hook items and access to friends are cut off and jobs are assigned to restore fairness. Once the child completes these jobs, he graduates to *humble status,* during which time he must put the needs of the family ahead of his own needs. As a humble family member, the child can indulge in activities like TV, but only with family members, and can watch only the programs that other family members choose. Having been in humble status for a day or two—depending on the severity of the infraction—the rebellious child is now ready for the exam, in which the original complaint is read aloud, and the child has to demonstrate an understanding of the problem, offer a different way to handle the same situation in the future, and answer all questions the family may have. Again, this step is designed to promote self-awareness, a crucial step in integrating the two minds. If the child does not want to discuss the episode, fine, he can remain humble until he is ready to try again.

THE INITIAL TICKET: FIVE STEPS TO NARCISSISTIC DEFLATION

The first time he prescribes an intervention for an excessively aggressive ODD youth, the clinician will have to prepare the parents for a true ordeal. The objective of this intervention is to challenge the assumption of the ODD teen that he owns his parents. It should be remembered that these youngsters are accustomed to terrorizing their families for their own gain. The first time parents challenge the ODD teenager's assumption of supremacy, the youths laugh and make things even more difficult for them.

The parents, therefore, must steel themselves for an ordeal lasting anywhere from a couple of days to a month. They ready the home for the worst. This includes removing valuables, being prepared to call police, and providing for the safety of younger siblings. They must anticipate that the child will punch holes in walls, physically threaten them, and retaliate in other ways. The clinician must prepare the parents for all this.

Following is the specific protocol for dispensing tickets to deflate excessive narcissism. I have tested the intervention and have found it effective with extremely aggressive teenagers. It is important that parents understand the details.

Step 1: Write the Ticket

The parents with whom the clinician deals should adopt the slogan: "Don't fight, write." It works. When the narcissistic teenager invites trouble, the parents walk away quietly rather than fight, and start writing a ticket (see Appendix B). The parent mentions briefly the necessity of having to write up a complaint. If the child continues to indulge and argue the parents should become, in effect, tricky. They should pretend they are giving up and allow the ODD teen to indulge. They want no confrontation because that's excitement. Instead, they want calm so they can think clearly when they write.

The parents should take their time as they write and even inject some playfulness into the process. They should seek an inspired consequence for the child's latest ploy. The consequence is always a loss of privileges. The reparation is something constructive that will reestablish respect for the parents and fairness for the family.

The reparation should always include (1) extra chores to compensate for wasted time; (2) a day of humble behavior, during which the ODD teenager's needs are made less important than those of the rest of the family; and (3) proof of having learned from the experience. I call the day of humble behavior *humble status*, meaning that the youth must consider people more important than objects and activities. The humble one wants to be with the family, no matter what the family does. Finally, the teenager is required to do some research that demonstrates learning from the experience, the opposite of blaming everyone else and being defensive. The ODD teen can present at the dinner table an explanation of what happened that shows he understood what he did wrong, and tell how he will handle matters differently next time. No rushing through it, because this would imply that the process is not important. In complex cases, the exam can take place in the consulting room of the clinician.

With the ticket written and copies made, the parents remove themselves and all family privileges, leaving no hook items behind.

Step 2: Administer the Ticket

To carry out the plan, the parents deliver the ticket at their convenience, not the child's. They concede that the child got away with things yesterday without immediate penalties, but they remove all privileges after he goes off to school today. The ticket awaits him after school. The element of surprise is on the parents' side.

Step 3: Watch with Detachment

When parents remove privileges there is normally a period of eruption that precedes the extinction of a behavior. The parents should expect an attack, recognizing, however, that the storm is relatively short, the calm that follows relatively long. The eruptions become shorter and the calms longer and longer until the maladaptive behaviors vanish. When attacked, parents say nothing. They remain poker-faced, businesslike, and distant. These tactics throw the teenager's disruptive side off balance because he expected the parents to become frantic, controlling, and intense. The parents witness maneuvers to charm, manipulate, deceive, explode, or quietly cause harm. Then will follow the longest campaign of revenge the child can manage. If the parents are not present as an audience, however, the child may decide to save face and get on with the fulfillment of the reparations.

Step 4: Eliminate Hook Items

The key from this point on is to pile up enough reparations to keep the child starved for excitement and hook items for days, or for weeks, if necessary. The three steps of the reparation—(1) work detail (while off privileges), (2) humble status (with conditional privileges), and (3) the exam (which restores full privileges)—require a graduation to move on to the next step. Failure at any step means going back to the previous one. For example, a humble one who has been destructive goes back to work duty. A failure in the exam means going back to humble status.

When the parent hands the child the ticket with its list of complaints and reparations, he discovers all hook items are cut off and extra chores need to be done. This is like being off privileges, and it lasts until all the work is done. A work detail often brings out the best in the child because his self-centered attitude has been deflated. The child's brain chemistry has had a chance to normalize.

Once the chores are completed, the child graduates to humble status. At this point, the child recognizes that there are others more important than himself. Now, he has access to hook items, but only where, when, and how other family members want them used. The child goes from no hook items and work duty to regaining partial privileges, as long as he can make others feel important. The clinician should instruct parents to be kind to the child in humble status and plan activities that are potentially enjoyable for everyone. The parents must be patient as they watch their child gradually become demanding, placing his needs before those of others. This is to be expected with an AD/HD child. The parents should remind him of his status by saying, "Didn't you want this to count as a humble day? Aren't you supposed to say, 'Whatever we do is fine with me as long as we're together?' You're not supposed to demand anything. Remember?"

After a day of work detail without privileges and a day or two on humble status, the child is ready for the final exam. If the child doesn't want to talk, or doesn't have good answers, that's fine. He can remain humble another day and try again tomorrow. Of course, the parents should keep their approach reasonable. They shouldn't expect to see a level of moral development that isn't there.

It's difficult to put a child through such an ordeal. The parents only want to operate at this level if all the exercises described above fail to alter the child's attitude. Parents can find consolation in knowing that eventually their child will emerge from the experience happy, trustworthy, well adjusted, and without a trace of resentment over what has happened. The process is the same thing as removing a parasite from the child's body. The result is a happier child and a healthier family.

Step 5: Empower the Humbled Teenager

Once the reparations have been fulfilled, it's time to empower the child, time to give him a sense of authority by encouraging his access to the peer world. Restore a state of full privileges. However, expect the child to continue to contribute to the family, and fulfill all responsibilities according to a list of priorities in order of importance, that is, family jobs first, personal household duties second, responsibilities outside the home third, and fun and friends last. It doesn't matter whether the teenager allocates the majority of his time and energies to responsibilities outside of home, fun, and friends. What matters is that he make good on his domestic commitments first.

Parents need to avoid the common mistake of going from one extreme to the other in their relationship with their children. Some parents avoid the extreme of grounding their children in favor of extending only minimal privileges until the misbehavior has reached intolerable proportions. Once the children return to their best behavior, however, the parents go overboard in providing hook items or they become lenient in their demands. They return to doing things for the children to make sure they are happy and successful. Initially, the good behavior continues with this pampering. However, the manipulative, narcissistic tactics gradually return, along with extreme misbehavior.

Each time a parent goes through the process of ticketing to remove hook items the child's tactics become less extreme. The reparations are completed more easily, and the ensuing happiness will last longer. The end result is a well-adjusted teenager who has mastered narcissism.

REVERSING THE NEGATIVE CYCLE

The parents will have passed the first test of authority once they have deflated excessive narcissism. The ODD teenager has tested the wisdom and strength of the parents. The parents have taken the worst blow that their child can deliver and come out empowered. Now the parents must show emotional intelligence in handling future outbursts.

These aggressive ODD youths present a natural proclivity to aggress, and the clinician must suggest an intervention that the teenager's emotional mind can respect. An effective intervention for individuals who suffer from a constitutional proclivity for aggressive behavior must emphasize reversal of the direction of the individual's disposition from negative to positive. Most intervention programs for children, however, seek to dole out a consequence that fits the crime. The more extreme the violation, the greater the punishment. The assumptions behind these interventions revolve around justice and deterrence. People don't want to reward aggressive behavior. They don't want to send the message that the infraction was taken lightly.

The problem with these deterrent-oriented consequences is their tendency to prolong the escalation of negative behavior. Each aggressive act by the teenager is a negative that invites a deterrent. The deterrent is another negative that invites retaliation from the aggressive teenager. This invites another deterrent, and so on.

Greene (1998) points out that most ODD youths already know the behaviors that adults want from them and are motivated not to spoil things for themselves or those around them. He emphasizes, however, that explosive youths cannot access this knowledge in the midst of a frustrating event, with the result that their emotional minds take over and their behavior contradicts their best intentions. Therefore, the goal is to counter narcissism and endure narcissistic rage only in select situations. It is wiser to create what Greene refers to as a user-friendly environment, which is goodness of fit in terms used by this book. It is necessary to identify the negative cycle of frustration and aggression before the youth reaches the point of no return, then take the steps necessary to replace the disturbing associations that have been imprinted in the emotional mind with pleasant ones.

The clinician wishing to design an intervention to reverse the direction of family interactions from negative to positive interrupts the negative cycle quickly and invites a positive behavior right away. The key to interrupting the negative cycle is loss. The key to initiating and maintaining a positive cycle is camaraderie.

> Steve, a good-looking 14-year-old, called me after hours, pleading for a moment to confer with me. His story illustrated the important role that loss and camaraderie play in reversing the flow of interactions from negative to positive.
>
> Steve had been to court for threatening his mother with a knife. He had visited a violence prevention youth program, but immediately told those in charge how stupid their program was. He also told them that he only listened to me because I was "the finest mind in child psychology." The basis for the remark was that I had joined his emotional mind and become his ally, and that was enough to gain his loyalty.
>
> Steve would cause disruptions in most settings. He was seething with anger. He loved and idealized his mother and older brother, but even they would report that when Steve wanted something they didn't want to give him, he became extremely demanding, and soon became almost diabolical in the ways he demonstrated his oppositional characteristics. The director of the special school where Steve was placed—a school psychologist by training—called me to ask if it was possible that the boy was psychotic. Steve's arrogance and expressions of contempt for authority were so pronounced that they seemed to reach pathological proportions.
>
> School made Steve feel sick to the stomach. He was recommended for a psychiatric school placement by the end of eighth grade. I recommended, instead, a home-schooling option so that I could continue to work with him without the pressure of another authority for awhile (see Chapter 8). Steve wouldn't attend the home-schooling center his mother was struggling to pay for. He wouldn't accept any feedback from

her on the schoolwork he produced, even though she was responsible for supervising his education. He had been abusive to a couple of conventional adult tutors who had offered to help him. Steve began to write a book based on the theme "I Did It My Way." The few pages I read were dynamic, but he went on for over a page without a comma or a period. Steve was impressive, but failure took its toll and he was ready to try something new. I could tell by his distraught tone when we met.

I invited Steve to take a walk with me. He was relieved. Apparently, his aggressive tendencies had finally upset his mother to the extent that he was convinced he was losing her affections for real. Steve's father had died a couple of years before, and the boy had symbolically adopted me as a substitute father. The possibility of also losing his mother was making him visibly ill.

Steve hated a woman who boarded with his family. He referred to her as the "fat lady." He insulted and upset her repeatedly. The woman complained to Steve's mother. Like many ODD teenagers with aggressive tendencies, Steve tended to externalize responsibility, and blame his victims for the problem. She was a crybaby, he would complain, after she protested his treatment of her. The boarder would approach Steve's mother looking traumatized. Steve's mother couldn't stand to see others hurt. She seemed to have had enough this time. And Steve was convinced she had given up on him.

The situation was ripe to confront his resistance, so I asked Steve to stop wasting my time telling me what was wrong with his mother, the "fat lady," and everyone else. "Deal with yourself," I said.

"What do you want me to do?" he asked. It took me a while to come up with a suggestion, but I found some inspiration. I set the intervention up with a paradox, just as Haley (1984) would recommend setting up an ordeal.

"As upset as you are, if I told you what it would take to get Mom back, you still wouldn't do it," I said. Steve pleaded for me to tell him. I hesitated, hemmed and hawed. I knew we were in good shape because Steve persisted. I said, "Be nice to the fat lady."

Steve responded with the resistance I had predicted. "It's too late for even that to work," he began. I interrupted: "You see what I mean! So don't do it. You wouldn't want to just try something. God knows. You might go through the humiliation and pain of being nice to the poor woman and have no guarantee of getting your mom back from it," I said.

Steve stopped me. "All right! I'll try it," he said. I feigned surprise, and said, "You will! That's awesome, dude. While you're at it, I'll tell you a couple of other things you could do. Let your mom teach you, and visit the home-schooling center like I asked you to."

Steve called me in a state of delight the day before our next scheduled session. He reported that he and his mom were on better terms than ever. They had been hugging the day after I gave him the advice. He then instructed me on the value of camaraderie in reversing the negative escalations that tend to occur with excessively aggressive teens.

Steve was playing with a mini-basketball in my office, sounding confident and content. "I'm still pissed at the fat lady," he said with a body language that showed that he was questioning himself. He stopped to think and continued, "It's hard to stay pissed at someone you've been nice to."

The clinician makes the ODD symptoms intolerable to the adolescent by taking failure to the limit. This invites loss. All that remains is to prescribe positive reparations that initiate a cycle of camaraderie in the family. The prescription can be, for example, repairing a damaged object, followed by playing well with others, or enjoying a movie.

Loss of the privilege of belonging to the family creates the therapeutic ordeal necessary to make indulging in the symptoms harder to accomplish than to curb. Bullying must be made more taxing to the ODD teenager than earning stimulation through honest and respectful means.

ESTABLISHING FAMILY FAIRNESS

A family must establish a fair balance of give and take to achieve a healthy enough position to counter the aggressive teenager's deviant quest for mastery. Typically, in dysfunctional families one member (in this case, the excessively aggressive ODD teenager) takes and takes and takes from other family members, who, for their part, give and give and give in an attempt to avoid the negative consequences of refusing to give. This makes it imperative for the clinician to implement a standard that individual needs, though important, must be subordinate to family needs. The ODD teenager who wants to receive family support needs to learn how to give to others as well as to take. Parents learn to enforce fairness by making their support (symbolized by hook items) contingent on the child's contributions to the household and fulfillment of school responsibilities. This concept of family fairness will alter family dynamics in a way that will promote development of genuine self-esteem and growth in every member of the family.

Once the clinician has reversed the flow of the interaction between himself and the child, he needs to achieve balance. Trust is everything when it comes to family health, and trust depends, among other things, on fairness. It would not suffice to stop a negative interaction and replace it with a positive one by eliciting a gesture of camaraderie. For the child would deplete the family with infractions, and then brush it off with a friendly gesture, then back to more selfishness. This would feed narcissism. The important thing is to demand fairness and a positive and cooperative family atmosphere.

CASE ILLUSTRATION: A CLINICIAN
TURNED POLICE OFFICER

It didn't take long for Ronnie, the hearing-impaired boy introduced earlier, to take failure to the limit once we put him in charge. His choice of actions quickly exposed his angry and manipulative intentions. Within a short time he had violated the rights of several family members. He disappeared for hours. It turned out he had gone into town, no note, no call, nothing to disclose his whereabouts. He refused to help his family. He broke promises that he had made to earn privileges. He destroyed family property. He verbally abused his little brother and mother. When his mother, Helen, stepped in to protect Ronnie's younger brother, Ronnie threatened her in a way that horrified the little one.

I received an emergency call late one night from Helen, who reported that she had just lost her cool and was ready to call the police to intervene. Ronnie, as mentioned previously, had taken out his anger on the washing machine and had poured laundry detergent all over Helen and all over the floor. He then dropped several buckets full of water on the soap-covered floor, creating a huge mess.

Ronnie had also tormented his little brother to the point where the younger child had developed a diagnosable case of separation anxiety. Ronnie had then purposely aggravated his brother's condition by threatening to murder his mother right in front of him. He had been warned to stop this kind of behavior and had promised to do so.

I instructed Helen to document all of these infractions. We would meet the next day to implement the first stage of the treatment—the therapeutic ordeal.

Turning Failure into Growth

At the session, we processed Ronnie's infractions and prepared the following letter, which served as an elaborate ticket:

"Ronnie, do not destroy this paper. It has instructions for getting your privileges back and getting your car loan," the paper read. Ronnie's birthday was coming up and he would soon be old enough to drive. He wanted a car. He felt so entitled but was unrealistic in that he fully expected his dad to get him a BMW, even though he had done nothing to earn it.

"Do not cause further damage when you read this because it will only add to the money you owe and slow the chances of getting privileges and a car," the paper continued. "Once you follow the instructions in this document, you will be in good standing. This letter is meant to help.

"The following are your infractions:

"Freedom to go out: Wednesday, going downtown without saying where you were. This is a violation of freedom to go out because it makes the family nervous when you disappear.

"Work group participation: This was the day you had promised to do your chores so you wouldn't lose privileges. Not doing the chores violates work group participation.

"Family property: When you did your laundry, you took family laundry and threw it all over the counter. This made a mess. When you were doing your laundry Thursday night, you were banging on the door of the dryer, abusing the machine, and saying, 'Piece of shit.'

"Family atmosphere: Bob was practicing the clarinet, you came down and said, 'Stop the fucking noise, you're giving me a fucking headache.' You wouldn't remove your ear piece to keep the sound from bothering you. You then used physical force to take the clarinet away from Bob. Bob needs to practice the clarinet. These insults and use of force spoil the mood of the family. They hurt and upset people who are smaller and weaker than you.

"Hurting family members: When Mom asked you to stop forcing Bob, you threatened her. You got in her face, waving your finger menacingly, and said, 'Don't mess with me!' Mom lost control and threw a pot at you. She will perform reparation to you for having done it. The pot landed near you and scared you, but didn't actually hit you. You retaliated by throwing detergent on Mom, which got all over her. You then created a mess by pouring water on the detergent. Also, when your brother Charlie was roller-blading, he became scared. When your mom reminded you of your responsibility to be gentle and stop scaring him, you said, 'Charlie, I'm going to kill Mom.' This is a direct violation of the reparation you were to do.

"Parental help: When Mom was cooking, or reminding you of your responsibilities, you were demanding and insulted her frequently.

"Refusing to honor reparation: When you were asked to help Charlie with his fears, you said to Charlie you didn't mean to carry out your threats. Then, a few days later, you threatened to kill your mother in a moment when your brother was visibly struggling with his fears. You did chores in ways that destroyed property, like the dryer door. You also did your chores angrily, or took shortcuts when doing the work. For example, you were doing the dishes and decided certain dishes weren't your problem because they weren't yours. You said, 'These aren't mine.' Yet, you expect to be paid for doing the dishes.

"Here are your reparations—the keys to your privileges and the car loan. It's your choice whether you complete them or not, and no one will force you.

"Arrange an outing where your parents know where you will be and get home on time. This can be a fun outing with friends. You can go on this outing after you have completed all your work around the house.

"Complete the following jobs with a friendly attitude: clean your room, finish all your laundry, vacuum upstairs, clean your bathroom, make a meal that everyone likes, and clean up afterward.

"When doing your laundry and other jobs, treat the equipment gently.

"Speak respectfully to everyone for the entire weekend, eliminate the words *fuck, bitch,* and *ho* from your vocabulary. No profanity in front of the family. Use old-fashioned polite terms like *Please* and *Thank you* and *Can I help?* all weekend. Be friendly to your brothers whenever you talk to them.

"Go out with the family and do what your parents ask. They will decide where you go. Stay home with the family and do what we ask. Watch what your parents want you to watch on TV, if anything. Parents will only buy things for themselves. Do not expect money. Do not ask for it.

"Cook a meal with Mom, have fun, and clean up afterward.

"Pass an inspection on the quality of all your jobs and do all of these reparations willingly. Once you complete these reparations, Mom will do her reparation for having thrown a pot at you. She will conduct a kid day, during which the parents do what the kids want, for fun. Mom will also walk away rather than scream when she is upset.

"There will be a family meeting at the end of these reparations to see that you understand all of these infractions. The bank will want to see that you can explain how these problems can be avoided before approving a car loan.

"Good luck."

Ronnie's first reaction was mean-spirited. He verbally attacked Helen and destroyed the ticket. He shouted in a menacing tone, "I'll kill you!" Helen asked him to read the letter. He questioned her about it with a hostile attitude. "I'm sick of Dr. B.," he finally said.

Helen responded. "This has nothing to do with Dr. B. It's you and me. Do you want to do it or not? I'm going to give you some time to think." Then she walked away. She had kept a copy of the ticket that he had torn.

Ronnie didn't know at this time that everything electronic had been cut off in the entire house, including his television, computer, video games, stereo, and phone. Helen expected a blowup within ten minutes.

Helen had administered tickets a few times before but had never enforced them fully. Ronnie had done some reparations but in a false and withholding way. This time the privilege loss and detachment from Helen were genuine.

Ronnie came back shortly demanding the power cord. She offered him a chance to make amends. "You know how this works. You know what you have to do." She exposed his attitude. He was inappropriately angry and she made him aware of it with a gesture, shrugging him off. She walked away.

Much to Helen's surprise, Ronnie broke down and talked about his pain: "I hate God for making me damaged. Fuck you, God! Fuck you, God! Fuck you, God!"

Helen played the role of friend who had been mistreated and was ready to give up on the relationship. She pretended this in a way that we had role-played in her sessions with me. She never took on the role of the authority figure. Her position was, "You've hurt me. You've taken things too far. Now it's your problem. You're on your own." The sense of loss left Ronnie desperate.

At this point, Ronnie seemed anxious to communicate. Helen talked to him about how she prefers to look at the healthy side of things. She told him to look at the four remaining senses he has. She talked about making peace, working with what he does have, killing boredom. "You'll like life if you do," she said, "but if you tell me to fuck off I won't give you the time of day."

Ronnie responded by shifting the focus to Dad and his anger. "Dad does it," he said. "Dad does the screaming." Helen responded that screaming doesn't get Dad what he wants either.

Hinting perhaps that he might be considering suicide, Ronnie talked about how life wasn't worth much to him. This summoned up Helen's worst fantasies and fears. She remained understanding, and then offered to restore her friendship with her son once he had completed his reparations. Ronnie worked to complete the chores on the list and to fulfill all the terms of the reparation letter.

The entire weekend was strikingly different from the customary chaos, dysfunction, and abuse. The kids got along with each other. They cooperated with their parents. The entire family played and worked together respectfully. The parents reported enjoying each other more once they were alone. This was a pleasant surprise for them. Typically, their disagreements surrounding the handling of the children's conflicts caused enough resentment between them to ruin the quality of their subsequent time together. It was better this time. However, Helen still harbored some resentment toward her husband for having caused the fight in the first place. Ronnie had convinced her of Mario's involvement.

Helen had humbled Ronnie, and, in the process, found a renewed sense of power. She would never revert to being intimidated by her son. Dad was in awe of his wife's fortitude. He discovered that she could take care of herself with the boys, even when Ronnie was at his worst. He didn't have to rush in to save the day every time Helen was in trouble. He didn't have to become aggressive and fight violence with violence. In fact, the couple agreed from this point on that if things got sufficiently heated, he would take the younger children out with him, and she would enforce the tickets.

Addressing the Resistance to Promote Integration

This case required addressing the resistance of Helen and Mario, as well as that of Ronnie. Helen placed the blame for Ronnie's excessive aggression on Mario's problem with anger and the way he dealt with his son. Helen believed that Mario was so disappointed in his son that he was cold toward him, and noticeably favored his other children. The only form of affection that Mario displayed was monetary support.

Helen used this belief to justify becoming involved in Ronnie's and his father's conflicts. As a result, any time that Ronnie experienced difficulty with his father, he turned to Helen, who then sided with him and attacked her husband. Ronnie would become arbitrarily disrespectful of his father and then convince Helen that Dad had provoked it.

I urged Helen to avoid getting into this position when disputes arose. We arranged for Helen to take the younger children for an overnight stay, with Ronnie and Mario remaining at home to work and play together. We also had Mario supervise Ronnie's school and family work. Helen was not to interfere. The two males worked things out. Ronnie's complaints about his father dwindled within a couple of months.

The new and relatively harmonious relationship between father and son was not to last, however. Mario eventually began to resist the program despite its initial successes. He absented himself from sessions with me and let Helen operate almost as a single parent for extended periods of time. Once Mario saw that Helen could handle Ronnie's outbursts by herself, he withdrew from all involvement in the conflict resolution process. He gradually reverted to screaming at his son rather than detaching and ticketing. Ronnie would become abusive in response, and Mario would transfer responsibility for the situation to his wife, as they had agreed to do once she managed to deflate Ronnie's narcissism.

To summarize, Mario would remain absent for extended periods, then enter the family system, provoke Ronnie's anger, and again disappear, leaving Helen to clean up the mess. However, he remained available to support Ronnie's schoolwork and to compensate him for completion of family chores.

I confronted Mario on the relapse in his attitude. He had canceled three appointments with me in a row, each time pleading involvement with business matters. I informed him that he could let his wife do all the work while he continued a conflict-laden relationship with his son. If he did, however, he would risk marital problems, and, in the long run, loss of his son.

I told Mario that he needed to set limits and use tickets in the same way that his wife had. He agreed and promised to resume the treatment. Mario was a man of his word and got back on track. He was legitimately busy, so he could not become as involved as previously. However, his attitude improved significantly and he took responsibility for helping with his son's schoolwork and supervising his chores and money. This was a significant help, and he managed to fulfill these responsibilities in a positive way.

Ronnie's own resistance manifested itself in two ways. He would refuse to see me for individual sessions, and ask that his parents stop consulting with me any time they attempted to set limits on his behavior. He protested, "I'm sick of Dr. B.," whenever he received a ticket. His second form of resistance was to have nothing to say in his individual sessions with me or to cancel an appointment at the last minute because he wanted to watch a TV show.

I dealt with the resistance that stemmed from ticket issuance by presenting myself as a police officer. I scheduled another house call to announce that I was an undercover cop, of sorts. The fact is that I am licensed as a psychologist by the state and mandated to report any abuse that involves a minor. Since Ronnie was abusing his younger siblings and his mother, I was technically mandated to report him to the Department of Social Services. My report would lead to an investigation that could lead to probation.

I informed the parents that I would tell Ronnie that I was a cop before presenting this at the family meeting. They were surprised by this tactic, but it made sense to them once I explained.

I have used this method with children who disregard the rights of others and refuse to honor the tickets that I have prescribed. Once I have joined the emotional mind's agenda, the idea of me as a policeman throws teenagers off balance, while at the same time it empowers the parents. The teenagers recuperate from the shock right away because I remain an ally and give them every chance possible to improve their behavior. I also provide them with a very reasonable explanation for why I can't allow them to abuse others.

At times, ODD teenagers accept me as their ally, but continue to disrespect their parents. Clinicians must establish that siblings and parents have emotional-mind agendas of their own, one as deserving of satisfaction as the other. It is my responsibility to represent the rights of all family members.

I fight for the right of the ODD teenager to live a life that makes him happy. I advocate for family support to generate opportunities for the teenager to find such a life. However, the ODD teenager needs to spread the happiness he derives from life to his family, and needs to earn these opportunities. He cannot be encouraged to love his clinician while at the same time he is showing disrespect to the parents who created his opportunities. He cannot enjoy his day and then abuse members of his family.

I informed Ronnie that I had two jobs. The first was helping him find a life that he liked. The second was securing the safety of the rest of his family. I informed him that he could fire me from the job of helping him find a happier, less boring life. However, he could not fire me from the job of stopping abuse in the family. I asked him whether he preferred to have me take the role of the cop or whether he preferred to have his parents report him to the courts in the traditional way.

Ronnie chose to keep me on both tasks. He wanted me to continue to advocate and he preferred my brand of tickets over having to go to court for his abuse of his family. I clarified that his parents acted as my agents when they handed out tickets. I informed him that if he ripped up one of my tickets I would have to dispense stronger consequences. Ronnie respected the tickets from that point on.

I addressed Ronnie's second form of resistance easily enough. He would act as though he didn't want to talk to me. I simply exposed his attitude and the different manifestations of his resistance. I told him that it was too bad he wouldn't let me help him, because his life seemed very boring.

It became very easy to address the reasons for Ronnie's resistance once I had exposed its manifestations. This led to arranging the opportunities he needed.

Providing Opportunities

Ronnie asserted that I had done nothing for him. He said, "I've been talking to you for two months, and I still don't have a car or a girl."

I responded by confronting him on his own lack of effort. I said, "You don't have a car because you haven't done what you have to do to get one. I can't give you things as though I'm Santa Claus, because if I did, you would never grow up. You would remain a baby forever."

Ronnie protested, "I am not a baby. I'm a man." He talked proudly about how big and strong he was.

I responded with an explanation of the difference between adult wants and baby wants. "You may be large, but the world is full of very large babies. Babies simply cry for what they want and grown-ups do everything that has to be done to give it to them. Every 'want to' has a 'have to' that accompanies it. Grown-up wants mean that you do what you have to to get it." From here on in we discussed what he has to do to earn a car.

Ronnie complained that he was too young to get a job or a bank loan. So how was he supposed to get a car? I explained that I had arranged for him to get a salary from his family for his work contributions, and for his help in improving the family atmosphere. He could use this salary from his parents to guarantee payment to a bank. However, he had to prove that he could earn that income. He could do this by completing all of his chores, schoolwork, and family play for twelve weeks in a row.

Ronnie's father and I put together a make-believe bank agreement that granted him a car loan with specific stipulations. Ronnie was to do his work, respect his family, and do well in school. This would earn him enough money to make payments for car and insurance. His father had connections and could get him a job that would provide money for gas and socializing. On any week that he didn't do the work he would lose his driving privileges, along with the other family privileges that he would normally lose. The bank would repossess his car until he made appropriate reparations.

We were able to put together a realistic-looking contract using desktop publishing technology. Mario invented a bank name and created a professional-looking letterhead. The contents of the documents were not very realistic. However, Ronnie's social-reality testing was relatively immature. Ronnie, in fact, suspected that there was something odd about the contract. However, he agreed to it, probably because it was worth his while to play along. Ronnie received a package via Federal Express with a cover letter and a contract. The cover letter read as follows.

Dear Mr. [Ronnie's last name]:

At the request of Dr. Eduardo Bustamante, we are enclosing this automobile loan agreement for your review. This document will also require the review and signature of your father, Mr. Mario [last name].

We are a bank that will offer loans to minors, given the recommendation of a professional and the guarantee of a parent with a good credit rating. The bank will base its loan on whatever conditions the professional and parents consider reasonable. As a service to your parents, the bank will enforce these terms in the same way that it does any of its contracts with adults.

If the enclosed condition and terms are acceptable, please sign and date the document. We will be in contact with Dr. Bustamante and your father weekly to confirm that you are adhering to terms 1 to 3 in your agreement.

Please note that if the enclosed conditions are not met every week, this agreement will become null and void. Thank you so much for giving us the opportunity to provide you with the financing you requested.

The letter was signed by a fictitious person, given the title Loan Officer. The accompanying contract read as follows.

Loan agreement made this _____ day of _____, _____ between the Regis Bank of Portland and Ronnie [last name].

Ronnie [last name]'s date of birth is _____, _____, and he will be eligible to receive a driver's license later this year. Although it is customary for an individual to be working for several years in order to establish a credit history, at the request of Dr. Eduardo Bustamante, this requirement is being waived. In order for Ronnie [last name] to be eligible for this loan of which Mr. Mario [last name] will co-sign, certain requirements must be met as per your agreement with Dr. Bustamante.

The requirements are: (1) Effective immediately, you must treat your family with respect. This means that you cannot use profane language, hit, punch, scream, or tease any member of the family. You must take responsibility for making your home a happy place. (2) You must do some homework and reading each night and review it daily with your mother or father. (3) You must assist your mother with cleaning the kitchen after dinner each and every night. These three items will require your attention on a daily basis. A successful week is doing all the work described above (items 1, 2, and 3) and reparations for any tickets.

Now, if you fail to adhere to all the items described above before purchasing the automobile, this loan will not occur and will be canceled. Upon receipt of your automobile, if the above requirements (1, 2, and 3) are not fulfilled, you will lose access to the car until you get caught up. Refusal to honor loss of access will lead to repossession of the car.

Whereas Ronnie [last name] is purchasing a car and the Regis Bank is going to provide the financing to purchase such car, the following financial details are part of this agreement. Each week, provided that items 1, 2, and 3 are completed, Mario [last name] will pay you $100.00. Now, $40.00 will be provided to you for weekly spending money and the balance ($60.00) will be set aside by Mr. [last name] to provide the down payment on the automobile.

Mario [last name] has informed us that you owe him $330.00 for destroying property (a hole in the kitchen wall) and the unauthorized purchase of a 56K modem for the computer. To satisfy that debt, $20.00 per week will be deducted from your spending money until the $330.00 is fully paid. That process should take about 16 weeks.

Monthly car payments will come to $240.00 per month for 48 months. This loan will provide you with $12,400.00. Depending on the down payment you amass, you could have as much as $14,400.00 for the purchase of a car. In addition, the Regis Bank and the State of Oregon require automobile insurance. For a first-time male driver, the premium will be $1,400.00/year or $116.00/month. Mario [last name] has agreed to pay the $356.00/month as long as items 1, 2, and 3 are adhered to AT ALL TIMES.

If you are in agreement with the above provisions, kindly sign in the space provided below and return one copy to our office for our files. If you have any questions, please don't hesitate to contact me. Thank you.

Many of the details of this agreement were necessary because of the scope of Ronnie's entitlement and aggressive behavior and the immature nature of his expectations. We had to spell out the details of what would constitute disrespectful behavior, and the chores that Ronnie needed to complete because he felt entitled to mistreat his family in a variety of ways. Mario felt that Ronnie would argue that such behaviors would not count as disrespectful. We included details about the cost of the car because we felt this was likely to become a source of conflict. I asked Ronnie to shop around for a car within his budget capabilities so auto dealers could give him a dose of reality.

Other opportunities we provided for Ronnie were a personal trainer and a nutritional counselor. Ronnie admitted that he needed to lose weight and get in shape if he were to have any chance of finding a girlfriend. He readily accepted the idea of a personal trainer. I referred him to one whom I use for AD/HD children. The training worked. It gave Ronnie confidence and improved his appearance. The nutritional counseling also helped him. He changed his poor eating habits.

I informed Ronnie that he needed to learn to be kind to smaller people to make himself worthy of a girlfriend, that females tend to like males who are strong but kind, and that he couldn't expect to be mean and bitter and charm ladies. He could practice better behavior on his own family, I said, and reparations would guide him in this process. He needed to view them in a positive light. Ronnie was not entirely convinced of the wisdom of this advice, but went along with it. He didn't have much choice. The positive flow that resulted in his family provided sufficient reward to teach Ronnie to value treating others respectfully.

Finally, Mario used his connections to get Ronnie a part-time job in the maintenance department of the company he worked for. Once again, Ronnie accepted this opportunity eagerly, as $20 to $40 per week was not enough money to cover the expenses he anticipated.

The combination of these opportunities amounted to a very different life than Ronnie was accustomed to. He had been a very lazy and demanding youngster who did little else but watch TV and play electronic games all day. Given his present opportunities, on the other hand, he would exercise, go to school, hold a job, help his family, do homework, and drive a car to social events. He would also become a positive influence in his home. He would have to pay for the damage he had done and save for a down payment on a car.

Once we had established sufficient authority and deflated Ronnie's narcissism, I trained the parents to use loss and acts of camaraderie to reverse the flow of interactions from negative to positive. Once things had become positive, Mom insisted that Ronnie make things fair. She learned to quickly induce loss by cutting privileges and moving out of range whenever he became aggressive. Ronnie learned to respect the tickets, which requested simple acts of camaraderie. These acts would quickly restore privileges. Mom would then establish fairness by requesting contributions that were consistent with Ronnie's contract.

Whenever Ronnie became unreasonably demanding, Mom would take time to think about his requests, and get back to him with a counteroffer. He would have to earn his request with contributions above and beyond those stated in the contract. If the requests were extreme, the conditions for gaining his objectives would be made so difficult that Ronnie would not want to pay the price. Mom would then offer the next best thing to Ronnie's original demand. He would usually acquiesce and earn a reasonable approximation of his initial request, or drop the request altogether. The best part of the process was that it was carried out in a friendly and respectful manner.

Ronnie learned to live with this sequence of consequences. His innate aggressive tendencies would surface regularly. However, for every aggressive moment, Mom would elicit a significant period of positive interactions. The dynamics of the family changed dramatically, and a few months after the initial house call we were able to stop family sessions. From this point on, I would provide individual counseling for Ronnie to help him establish mind–body integration and learn to take risks that would promote his development.

Ronnie subsequently did commit a fair share of infractions. However, he got tickets for them and completed appropriate reparations. I trained the parents to interrupt the negative cycle that triggered Ronnie's outbursts by removing themselves temporarily from his life. Next, they triggered a positive cycle by requesting token acts of camaraderie. They responded generously when these acts occurred. Then, once the cycle was positive, they established a reasonable level of fairness by demanding greater contributions from him to the family.

A memorable moment occurred in my office during a visit from Ronnie's little brother, who had endured a great deal of abuse from him. He was hesitant to come to a psychologist's office at first, but warmed up as soon as I offered him a hot chocolate and played a Nintendo game with him. He looked at me and said, "I gotta hand it to you. Whatever you did to my brother, it made a big difference. He's actually nice now a lot of the time. What was wrong with him, anyway?"

11

Special Problem 4: Negative Peer Influences

Carlos and I were approaching a breakthrough in understanding. We had made an important connection many months before, but were starting to click in a special way. The emotional-mind link was there. As a result, Carlos was being completely open. We were talking about experiences he said he had never before communicated to an adult, including the use of drugs.

"M'boy and I were talking," he said, referring to a friend who shared his problems. "We were saying how we'd love to go home right now and tell our parents everything. But not in the state we were in, not to hear, 'Look at your eyes. What have you been doing?' But oh! I have such stories to tell you. I've been through so much!"

Carlos had told me that he wanted to end the session ten minutes earlier than usual. However, he was entering a state of truth and openness that would keep him talking nonstop for the rest of the hour. He wanted to schedule a follow-up appointment as soon as possible to continue our conversation.

We had dispensed with our business for the session. Carlos's parents had been angry with him. They couldn't understand the way he was managing his affairs. The fact that he was still smoking marijuana caused them to misinterpret his actions. They seemed convinced that he was reverting to old ways. The fact was, he was maintaining very good grades. He was holding a job. He was dealing with peer situations in a much more mature way then he had in the reckless days of a year before.

Carlos was learning to resist peer pressure. He wasn't behaving like a follower. He stood up to bullies. He commanded the respect of peers from different groups, and he learned that most of the kids he had considered his friends were not trustworthy. He could identify violations against fair give and take, promises and commitments made, and the boundaries and rights of others. He had learned to trust and value only one friend out of the entire group with which he had been involved. He was taking important steps to become trustworthy.

Carlos was committing one important infraction against his family that he needed to do something about. He was negotiating a curfew time, but then violating it, and he wasn't calling to let his parents know where he was. This caused his parents, and particularly his mom, considerable anxiety. Carlos was not retaliating or showing disrespect to his parents. He was doing a fair share of work around the house. Violating curfew and disappearing without a word about where he was going were his major infractions. He was coming home late because he was getting into states that would warrant his parents' disapproval. This brought us to the point of his story. He wished he could tell his parents everything, the way he was telling me.

"I have so many stories to tell you, but I want to get to the one with the crazy night," Carlos said. "I came back to visit old friends after moving. This was before I used to get high. My boys were holding a beach party for me and they had a keg. But there were so many people there that the keg disappeared in no time. I didn't even get to taste one cup of beer.

"At first my buddy and I saw something like a light and yelled cops! We ran like hell. The other kids called us back. They said, 'There are no cops, relax.' Then there were these lights, and everyone ran one way. But the next thing we knew there was another light coming in the opposite direction." Carlos drew an outline of the setting and explained how the group scattered in every direction possible as it faced cop lights. The cops had them surrounded.

"Lucky for a group of us that we had parked our car a few blocks away. We had thought it looked chancy to have our car right by the beach in case the cops showed up. Everyone ran. We got to our car."

I was about to comment on his story, but Carlos clarified that this was only the beginning. My questions would be answered as the story unfolded. Carlos avoided an encounter with police, but had nowhere to go. He settled for having his friends take him to an ex-girlfriend's house.

Carlos was welcome there, but the situation quickly got complicated. The girl's mother was in her early thirties, and was, as Carlos put it, "hot." She had been divorced and remarried—to a millionaire this time. She lived in a beautiful house. Carlos had always joked about this with his friends. The mother really liked Carlos, who was 15 at the time they met, and inexperienced. Carlos had asked his ex-girlfriend if he could sleep over. She had assured him this would be okay, and called to her mom to announce their surprise visitor. "Mom! Guess who's here!" Obviously they were excited about having Carlos tell the story of his adventure on the beach.

"She [the mom] was drunk as hell," he told me. "She came over and started to hug and kiss me. It was kind of funny. We all laughed. I went back to the beach to find my friends. But no one was there. It was late, like two or three in the morning. I asked people at the beach and they told me that my good friend had gone off to buy more kegs. I got some weed, which wasn't very good, but it got me wrecked anyway. That's how new I was at smoking. So I went back to the girl's house.

"She asked me to go downstairs to stay in her mom's room. I felt funny, like it was a setup. When I get down there, this woman is sitting there in the dark. She's smoking bowls, cranking the music. She has an incredible stereo. She was wearing boxers and a tee shirt. She looked at me and purred."

I interrupted: "What? She did what?"

"She purred, like a cat." I laughed in disbelief. We both laughed.

"I swear!" Carlos said. "We started to hug, kiss. We were making out. We didn't take our clothes off or anything, but we were going at it. This was a mom that my family knew. Then the daughter comes into the room and catches us. She freaks out but she was cool. She was the normal one. But her older sister was a nut. She would have gone nuts if she had found out. The girl said to me, 'You need to get out of here so my sister doesn't find out.'"

Carlos was back out on the street and it was now about 4 A.M., and he was still looking for a place where he could spend what was left of the night.

"I found some kids around the beach that were drunk as hell. I don't know how I did it, but I ended up talking to them. We got friendly. I asked them if they had a car. They didn't, but they pointed to a kid who did. He was completely trashed, passed out on a bench. I went over to him, woke him up, and started talking to him. It was a coincidence, but we lived in the same town. So he gave me a ride to a few friends' houses and I finally ended up entering the bedroom of a friend through a screen door. The kid hadn't seen me for months and was shocked. 'Carlos, I can't believe it! What are you doing here? Where did you come from?'"

Carlos's friend allowed him to spend the night in a closet but he had to get up by 7:30 A.M. so he could play in a ballgame. He had a game at eight. Carlos explained that the closet was roomy. However, he overslept, and the next thing he knew it was time for him to sneak out of the closet. He woke up to the loud voice of his friend's father saying, "The problem is in this closet." A handyman doing some work in the house needed access to the closet. It wasn't long before Carlos was out on the street again.

Carlos took advantage of friends with job schedules that made them easy to find. They had cars and could be very helpful.

Carlos's story next had him driving along dark roads, about to try tripping on mushrooms for the first time. The mushroom effect was magical, and he felt he understood how the universe worked. He had touched ultimate truth. He knew that he would be fine. His life and his future would turn out fine. School would be fine. He had nothing to worry about.

Most of the ODD teens described in this book maintained some level of involvement with drugs. Typical scenarios involve alcohol and marijuana, with some dabbling in the most popular drugs, including LSD, mushrooms, downers, and speed, as opposed to cocaine or heroin.

Carlos's story illustrates a case where drug involvement was the core of the behavior problem. Managing the problem of drugs and the perils that come with the street drug culture is by far the hardest part of the work with these patients.

THE VALUE OF PEER ATTACHMENTS

Stories like the one Carlos shared with me reveal the strength of the bond teenagers form with each other. We all know intellectually that adolescents transfer their familial bonds to their peer group. However, this abstract concept comes to life in stories like the one above for those fortunate enough to be trusted with such stories.

The clinician faces a conflict between two extremes. On the one hand, there is the possibility of inviting drug use by encouraging teenagers to tell stories about their experiences with it. On the other, growth cannot be fostered in any realm of the teenager's being prior to the formation of the attachment often helped along by frank discussion. The clinician has to accept the areas that have been judged and rejected in the teenager's life before development can take place. The attachment is an indicator that the teenager wishes to please, to live better, to improve. Teenagers need this kind of attachment to develop healthy social skills and a strong sense of self. They get it from their peers. No matter how bad the influence of a peer group may seem, there is always wisdom in the choice. If the teenager had the wisdom to take what he needed from the relationship and leave the rest, these bonds would constitute essential steps in development. However, as it is, these peer influences turn out to be traps and produce more harm than good.

To summarily cut children off from undesirable peers will cause more problems sooner or later. Authority must demonstrate emotional intelligence when dealing with today's youth. It is a vital first step to demonstrate strength in the exercise of authority (see Countering Narcissistic Rage, and The Initial Ticket: Five Steps to Narcissistic Deflation in Chapter 10). However, young people know that these peers offer wonderful growth opportunities. Their emotional minds tell them so. They will not respect the authority of a parent who does not acknowledge this fact or give the child reasonable opportunities to earn the privilege of bonding with peers he finds attractive.

THE POSITIVE SIDE OF POOR
PEER SELECTION

The clinician must explain to parents the inherent wisdom in their children's peer selections, even when the child makes poor choices. This allows the parents to demonstrate wisdom in their authority, which lessens the need for the ODD. The teenager will trust the parent for understanding and accepting something he knows at the emotional-mind level but cannot explain cognitively, and trust the clinician for having facilitated the understanding.

The clinician must explain that we all start out incomplete beings, and the driving force in development is to unfold and become whole, and that we all have a way of developing parts of ourselves by forming attachments. Individuals identify with other persons and pick up traits from them, down to their mannerisms and idiosyncrasies. Our attraction to peers naturally directs us to the attachments we need so as to pick up essential pieces to the completed puzzle we seek to become.

Youths who attract negative influences need to learn to take what they need from the peers they select and leave the rest. This is an advanced skill even for adults. Hence, the best we can do with teenagers is to use their mistakes to train them to avoid the bad and take the good. The clinician can show them how to become a positive influence on some misguided youths. If he does his job well, he can help reverse the process so that instead of the negative peers bringing the positive down with them, the positive have an elevating effect on those who are negative.

The only way to accomplish a reversal of the usual negative influences cycle is by learning to bond with the emotional-mind agenda of the peers in a powerful way that competes with the corrupt path of the negative influences. The technique offers just as much acceptance and fun, but in a more adaptive and positive way. Successful results can be considered a community service.

THE CONSEQUENCES OF SUSTAINING A DEVIANT ATTACHMENT

The clinician can offer parents a sound understanding of attachment theory to prepare them for the task of reversing the problem of negative peer influences. Proper preparation enables the parents to operate intelligently while their children are trying to cope with the pressures that peers exert on each other to become negative influences. The parents can speak to their children in private about the pitfalls of peer pressures, and show them how they can use their own families to enjoy their friends even more, and help them grow.

Attachment theory can prepare families to face many of the irrational behaviors they will encounter. It can explain the driving force behind much of the narcissistically dominated adolescent's behavior. The clinician can explain attachment theory to the parents of the ODD teenage client in a simplified way as shown below.

Starting early in life, our emotional growth is determined by the nature of our attachments. A healthy attachment humanizes and promotes basic abilities that allow us to evolve in a healthy direction, possessed of qualities including trust, the ability to empathize, the ability to self-soothe, a sense of security, self-esteem, and a conscience. An anxious, neglectful, or traumatic attachment promotes distrust, callousness, insensitivity, insecurity, anxiety, depression, aggression, shame, and immorality. Youths who are traumatized early in life often fail to develop empathy or a conscience, and thus their socialization process is crippled, sometimes for life.

I use the term *corrective relationship* to describe an attachment that can withstand the deviant behaviors stemming from earlier traumatic experiences, that can reverse these deviant attachment patterns, and that can forge a new bond that will fundamentally change the course of that individual's development.

Attachment theory presents us with grave concerns but also gives us great hope. Youths emulate the behavior of those to whom they are attached. Hence, by forming a strong bond with a child's emotional mind, we can mold and largely determine his basic attitude toward the world. When a child attaches in a healthy way, he is capable of a complete transformation in a positive direction, all in a very short period of time. Similarly, when a child attaches in a deviant way, we see a fast and profound transformation in a destructive direction. Children remain malleable and open to such sweeping changes.

An unhealthy and traumatic attachment later in life can temporarily undermine key developmental breakthroughs that have been achieved through earlier attachments. This is the tragedy behind trauma. It is in the nature of the attachment system (the emotional brain, see Chapter 2) to repeat the trauma, and it does so with intensity. Hence, a parent can imbue a young child with deep love and devotion, and, later on in life, an abusive peer or authority figure can undo a significant portion of that parent's work by forming and maintaining an unhealthy attachment with the child. This later bond can cause deviant development.

Traumatic attachments to a destructive adult can dramatically alter a young person's view of authority, from seeing teachers as desirable role models, for example, to viewing them as oppressors. Should parents make the mistake of attempting to enforce the disciplinary edicts of such individuals, the traumatic attachment will spread from school to home. This will undermine the parents' earlier bond of trust with their child, and create in him an attitude of rebellion toward all authority, as well as a susceptibly to antisocial influences.

Escape is the most common route for teenagers to take once they have been traumatized and lured into antisocial behavior. This process easily leads to addiction.

ADDICTION: A MISGUIDED QUEST FOR FREEDOM

Teenagers often see drugs as an escape route. They want to escape boredom. Teenagers who don't care about what they do with their day stop caring about themselves. Once they don't care about themselves, they become self-destructive. Many ODD teenagers suffer from an anxious response to scholastic pressure that can reach traumatic proportions (see Chapter 8). They instinctively and involuntarily shut down and have little to look forward to. These ODD teenagers prefer to escape into drugs rather than face depression and self-destructive tendencies. They settle for the lesser of two evils. In the same way that a prisoner might see his escape from jail as a flight to freedom, teenagers see turning to drugs as freedom. The phenomenon of turning to drugs as an escape runs rampant both in such stultifying conditions as high-poverty areas and prisons and in such high-pressure areas as competitive academics, sports, and business.

ADDICTION TO PEERS

The problem with the escape into drugs is that addiction steals the addict's freedom in a subtle but certain way. It is one of nature's brilliant traps, and teenagers lack the wisdom to foresee the trap. Teenagers turn to each other for help and guidance on all these matters because they know that in their group there is mutual acceptance of emotional-mind agendas.

Peer pressure is thus the leading cause of the spread of drug abuse in the youth culture. No adult message, health education, scientific demonstration, or propaganda can compete with the influence of a peer group that feels like family and is firmly bonded with the emotional mind of the teenager who is considering whether to use drugs.

Youths resent the label of addict. In fact, exposure of drug use, followed by advice on getting help, leads to rage and deception. It is the instinctive response of most "good" parents and teachers to catch children who are using drugs and teach them a lesson. It is the instinctive response of youths who are caught to feel shame, then rage, and then to externalize blame, and lie.

> Tim's mother had caught him red-handed. She had been a very accepting ally to her son for the most part, but had always given in to him too easily. This time she had asked him to absent himself from the house while she was away and he had agreed. She came home unexpectedly because a neighbor had called her at work to report that a van-full of his friends had entered her house.
>
> Tim's mother felt violated by the broken promise and reacted angrily. She surprised the group of youths by breaking the door to Tim's room open. She caught the group smoking marijuana. Tim subsequently attacked her for violating his privacy by breaking into his room without knocking. Tim couldn't see the relationship between his promise to his mom that he wouldn't bring anyone home and her forced entry of his room.
>
> Tim and his mom calmed down, and were able to reach an understanding of each other's position once I pointed out that each of them had committed a boundary violation.

THE ADDICTIVE CYCLE

The addictive cycle explains how using pain as an excuse to escape responsibilities causes addiction. The cycle does not have to involve any particular substance or activity to make itself addictive. The key elements involve an experience of pain, use of the pain as an excuse to escape responsibility, and an activity that lessens pain, distracts, or provides pleasure.

The cycle goes like this. The person enters a state of pain. He escapes responsibility to relieve the discomfort. He indulges in some desired activity to reduce the pain. However, once the indulgence is over, the person faces circumstances that are more painful than before. Nothing was resolved. So in addition to whatever was causing pain before, the person now suffers the discomfort of a pile-up of unmet responsibilities, and dreads facing those he has let down by failing to fulfill commitments.

The pain that follows the indulgence after facing the unmet responsibilities invites further escape and indulgence and this completes the cycle (Figure 11–1).

The person's response to facing an even worse situation than that prompting the initial escape is to tell lies and offer further excuses to pacify the people he has disappointed. The deception causes a subtle restlessness that the teenager can easily shut off

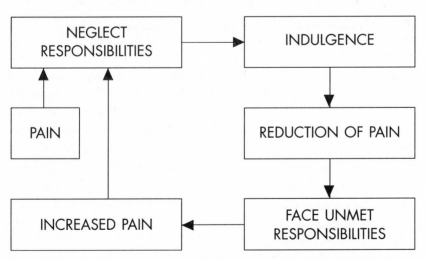

Figure 11–1. The pain that follows the indulgence after facing the unmet responsibilities invites further escape and indulgence, and this completes the cycle.

but that makes peace of mind unattainable by natural means. The teenager will be building a basement full of secret facts that are obstacles to openness. Relationships become less satisfying.

It is very useful to present the addictive cycle without attributing the problem to a particular substance. The clinician wants to remain an ally of the emotional mind and doesn't want to induce the shame, rage, and deception that results from exposure. So he explains the cycle to the teenager as an adaptively unintelligent way to utilize a simple tool—the activity, person, or illegal substance.

TALKING TO TEENAGERS ABOUT THEIR ADDICTIONS

Carlos seemed tense when I first confronted him on his drug use. It was early in his treatment, long before the conversation described at the start of this chapter. He had been caught at school with marijuana, and had been referred to a drug counselor. He had tried to connect with the counselor in the same open way he had with me and had felt he was being judged. He was turned off but was obligated to continue.

I used a couple of different techniques to reestablish my connection to his emotional mind, and prepared to criticize the rational mind's lack of adaptive intelligence. First, I explained the addictive cycle in a nonjudgmental way. Second, I criticized the way Carlos was counseled at school. I also told him how to eliminate the fear he had of being referred to a more extensive program. This fear was unfounded, it turned out, since the overworked drug counselor was able to offer only a few educational sessions.

I used the content of the counseling session at school to confront Carlos on his addiction. I then used the diagram in Figure 11–1 to counter his initial shame and impending resistance to my use of the word *addict*.

Carlos said, "I told her that I didn't have a problem, that I only smoke and drink on weekends."

I interrupted him. "Dude, you have an addiction," I said. Carlos was shocked, caught off guard. This was a calculated move to get past his denial. I continued, "I notice that you turned red when I said the word *addiction*. What's the big deal?"

Carlos smiled defensively and began to mumble under his breath, barely audibly. "I just don't like that word. Something about it bothers me."

I continued. "People talk like they don't have addictions, like the only addicts are the ones that smoke pot, drink, do heavy drugs, overeat, stuff like that. Like it has to involve a substance. I'll tell you, though, that's a narrow way of looking at things. People are addicted to power, money, other people, sex, gambling, games, and control. Control is a good one. Do you know how many parents are addicted to controlling their kids? Your parents were headed that way.

"The only thing you have to do to make something an addiction is to avoid dealing with your own responsibilities, or commit irresponsible acts to escape a bad feeling. Then you feel bad for having done something wrong, which kills the good feeling. This sets you up to indulge again. You can go make more money, give your kid one more lecture, beg for sex one more time, gamble on another number, pig out one more time, work longer hours to get more money and power—whatever! Let me show you how it looks, because once you understand what I call the addictive cycle, you can reverse it."

Here I showed Carlos the diagram on the addictive cycle (Figure 11–1) to make sure he understood. It is easy from this point on to show how to break the cycle, even if the patient, like Carlos, is indulging in an addictive substance. Some youths possess the will power to exercise reasonable mastery over their behavior. With them, the objective is to have them reverse the cycle. Some cannot change their behavior. With them, the first step is to have them realize their lack of freedom and how they cannot handle the substance they find themselves involved with.

I explained to Carlos that some substances are addictive in and of themselves, no matter how responsibly you try to use them. "They are traps of nature," I said. "Given everything I just said, some things are more addictive than others because of the way nature made them. These substances pull hard for addictions even if you don't enter into an addictive cycle with them. What they do is give you a pleasurable feeling, like love. Then they take you to a painful low called withdrawal.

"The really addictive substances continue to generate cravings for a very long time. Then comes the high, then the low. Then come more cravings. You see these substances occupy your life to the point of creating their own addictive cycle. You have the discomfort of the unfulfilled craving. You have the escape to pleasure and then the coming down from pleasure onto greater pain than when you first indulged," I said as I pointed out to Carlos the various steps on the diagram.

Finally, I sided with Carlos's emotional-mind devotion to smoking by calling marijuana a kind drug. I told him that compared to cocaine, and especially heroin, the addictive properties of marijuana were relatively kind. The high is good, the low not as bad as others. So if he had to be addicted to something, that choice is not too bad.

I gave Carlos one final example of addiction that did not involve substance use. I used the example of a pimp, knowing that he would find this politically incorrect topic pleasing. I didn't want him to associate me with a lecturing adult on the side of goodness.

I said, "The pimp creates a high by giving the lady jewelry, fine clothes, fine dining, and what seems to be love. They really make their new girls feel special. Then they force them to commit an irresponsible, deceptive act that deeply betrays the emotional mind they have just loved, fed, and entrusted. They get them to have sex with another person who offers no emotional bond, no attraction. If the girl resists, the pimp induces pain by beating her and insulting her. Either way, the initial high is followed by a low, much like a drunken stupor is followed by a hangover."

IDENTIFYING UNMET NEEDS

Besides reversing the addictive cycle, the addicted individual will have to identify and meet unrecognized needs that have been causing his need to escape. Chapter 2 cited the work of Joseph

(1992) in explaining the role of unmet needs in the formation of addictions. When an important need remains unmet for prolonged periods, the amygdala learns to launch substitute drives that can be more easily satisfied to divert its attention from the frustration of the unmet need. Hence, if an individual yearns for loyal friendship, romance, or some meaning in his life, but sees no hope of gratifying these needs, he may repeatedly drink, gamble, eat, or fight.

The substitute drives must be launched with abnormal frequency because they fail to provide a normal satiation period. This is because the refractory period is interrupted by awareness of the original unmet need. Increasingly frequent indulgence yields reduced gratification because of the natural tolerance properties of any drive that is abused. The more one drinks, smokes, or eats, the more one needs to engage in these activities to derive the same level of satisfaction.

This pattern eventually leads to painful addictions and massive denial as the organism strives to reduce awareness of a dissatisfying life. The individual ends up in a life of sharp fluctuations between states of acute need, fleeting satisfaction, and intense pain or boredom. It is difficult to develop self-awareness under these conditions.

The only solution to this problem is to identify and learn to gratify the unmet needs. The intervention I use for this problem is incorporated into the core of the protocol presented in this book—the commitment to developing a happy life. From the moment of the preassessment trial intervention we have put the ODD teenager in charge of his life and asked him to commit to making choices that will yield a day that he can look forward to.

Severe addictions need to implement this same protocol but take it to a new level. The clinician must help the youth to identify and learn to feel the unmet need, rather than fear it. The addicted individual will initially use the freedom to indulge more and more in the substitute drives that serve to conceal the unmet need.

The clinician must target this problem in individual sessions. He must side patiently with the emotional brain, and point out the futility of the addicted youth's lifestyle. This will become increasingly possible as the substitute gratification brings on life failures entailing consequences and suffering. He will have to challenge the individual to suppress the substitute gratification long enough to feel the unmet needs. He will then have to teach him how to use the rational mind to develop more adaptive strategies for gratifying the unmet needs. The youth who has faith in the clinician will develop hope that, with a new level of knowledge and coaching, satisfaction of these needs can be available as it has never been before.

ESCAPE VERSUS FREEDOM

It is important to explain to addicted teenagers that freedom comes from responsibility, and responsibility is the only thing that can break the addictive cycle. Escape leads to pleasure followed by pain and the need for more escape. Each time, the cycle gets worse. Each time, the person trusts less.

The absence of trust is the curse of the addict. The problem is that only trust offers the antidote to addiction. The only thing that can compete with drugs is love of life, love of others, mastery, pride, and the pursuit of meaning. This is living a life that makes a person happy to wake up and start a new day. For this kind of energy transfer to take place it is important to have trust. Only in trusting relationships can one open up one of the sensory systems of the emotional mind and truly feed it this kind of energy. Indulgence in drugs usually makes people untrustworthy, and thus makes the replacement of drugs by love unattainable.

The moral of the story is that escape leads to addiction. Responsible action leads to freedom, trust, and love. The trustworthy person who has love could indulge in a drink and still have love and trust. The addicted person who escapes responsibility cannot have trust and lasting love. That is a high price to pay. It is imperative that the clinician presents this perspective to the addicted ODD teenager.

I refer to the inability to have trust and lasting love while the victim is trapped in the addictive cycle as the curse of drug addiction. I use it to predict relationship problems in the future. It works wonders with older teenagers who fall in love. The more valuable and serious the relationship, the greater the likelihood of losing trust and love to the addictive cycle. These teenagers will most likely fail in their first serious relationships anyway. Why not attribute at least part of the failure to the drugs?

The clinician can apply a parallel strategy for youths who cannot relate to the problem of losing love. Teens who have no prospect of romantic involvement will stand to lose the affection of their best friends and valued peers. Those who have social problems and few friends stand to lose the trust of family. Such socially deficient youths tend to depend to extreme extents on a parent who has allowed himself to be taken for granted, knowing that the youth has no one else. The clinician will have to arrange for this parent to make his support conditional, so the youth can lose it, and make this intervention possible.

The next section discusses the only way to save ODD teenage clients from the consequences of a deviant attachment forged by unreasonable authority or by the deviance of the streets. I utilize the protocol described in this book to expose the negative influence of these peers and to reverse the process until we achieve two goals: (1) to teach these teenagers how to take the best that their peers have to offer and leave the undesirable traits behind, and (2) to achieve mind–body integration, honesty, and a happy, meaningful life for the ODD teenager.

REVERSING THE ADDICTIVE CYCLE

A step toward reversing the addictive cycle is to get the parents to measure baseline behaviors of their ODD teenager to demonstrate the impact of negative peer influences. They should document grades, school attendance, fulfillment of responsibilities at home, productive activities, and health-related habits.

The parents must have a reasonable understanding of the positives and negatives of peer influences, and a sound understanding of the addictive cycle. The teenager also understands these matters and is dying to prove that his friends won't be a bad influence.

Placing an Interesting Bet

The clinician can show the teenager a picture of his baseline functioning before exposure to peer influences and bet him, literally, that there will be a drop. The clinician can collect data on the child's functioning or can estimate it based on past experience. The ODD teenager can participate in the process.

Carlos believed that the problem of negative peer influences was a myth. At best, it applied to others. His friends haven't caused his problems—no way!

The bet puts the teenager in a positive frame of mind. The willful stubbornness that drives the ODD symptoms now gets turned into determination to maintain healthy functioning while he is participating freely in peer activities. Good luck to the teenager. Social psychology has demonstrated that Carlos was dead wrong. The labeling process causes all kinds of problems for hordes of teenagers. Attachment theory would bet against Carlos as well. The influence of these attachments runs deep.

The bet on the effect of peer influences thus pits two powerful forces against each other. The end result is a bout between the stubbornness of the teenager on the one hand and the forces of labeling and attachment theory on the other. The results are always interesting.

Inviting Failure

Failure should be taken to its limits once the bet has been made. This can be done by arranging for the peer-addicted ODD teenager to make choices. The clinician can remain an ally of the teenager throughout this process, as long as the teenager values his input.

Carlos made a valiant attempt to become responsible when he was first put in charge. He came to sessions with me willingly and reported all kinds of improvement. He described his intentions to do really well and showed me just how much he knew about real life on the streets, which was considerable.

It wasn't long, however, before Carlos got himself into trouble. He broke curfew repeatedly. It turned out that he was getting so "trashed" that he couldn't afford to go home, where his parents would be able to see him in this state. He invited friends to the house when his parents were out. He became belligerent whenever his parents mentioned that he was violating their trust. His grades dropped dramatically. He was caught with a girl in his room. She was supposed to get up early and leave before being noticed, but she overslept.

Carlos's worst problems were being caught with marijuana at school and having friends turn against him and beat him up. The very troubled girl who had overslept at his house had a big and aggressive boyfriend. She began to blackmail Carlos with threats about what the boyfriend might do to him. She would ask him to do things that she wanted. She thought Carlos was cute, so she wanted him available. She also wanted him to break up with his very nice girlfriend.

This girl pushed Carlos to the point where he had to say no. Her response was to tell her menacing boyfriend about the sleepover. She also spread rumors about the episode so that Carlos's girlfriend would find out and leave him.

I received phone calls from Carlos's mother every time a problem surfaced. She was an ally of Carlos and of the treatment. It was important to have Carlos face his problems, but I needed it done in a way that wouldn't shame him excessively.

I arranged two meetings every time I received an alarm call with some bad news about Carlos. I would first meet with the mother and get the facts. Then I would meet with Carlos to process what we had found. When I met with him, I made it a high priority to maintain an alliance with his emotional mind, yet challenge his rational mind.

I had him tell me stories of his transgressions like those at the start of this chapter. I always made it clear that I would function as his lawyer to protect him, no matter what mess he had created. I would listen to his stories in an accepting way, as would a friend, and keep them secret. I would challenge his rational mind for making a mistake once the story was complete. Then I would generate an adaptive plan to help him get a fresh start and avoid repetition of mistakes. This provided a corrective emotional experience.

I asked Mom to sit in and monitor, but to refrain from taking a punitive or overly controlling role as Carlos's problems came to the surface. I had her monitor without intruding. I helped her adopt an accepting stance, using the tenets of peer attachment described at the start of his chapter. Then I encouraged her to see the problem as Carlos's, not hers. These are steps I would take with any parent dealing with the problem of peers and addiction.

Monitoring without Intruding

Most parents instinctively become nosy and sneaky when dealing with drug use by their teenagers. They search their children's rooms for evidence of substance use. They interrogate, they check up on what their children are doing. If they find evidence of substance use, they will confront their children with it.

The teenagers will lie, protest, and manufacture excuses when they're caught. Once caught, they learn to be more clever in concealing drug use. Many act entitled and demand that they be allowed to smoke marijuana. They cite examples of parents who not only allow it but also join with their children in using it. These "cool" parents boast that they have a very close relationship with their children.

Regardless of the form of defense the teenager uses, it isn't long before a sophisticated cat-and-mouse game begins and goes on indefinitely as the substance use progresses. The parents cut off allowances and cash for lunches. The teenager makes drug deals to get the cash he needs. The parents threaten to involve the police. The teenager threatens to run away.

I have learned through trial-and-error that it is much more effective to have the parent play dumb, yet monitor closely, instead of inviting confrontations. I instruct the parents to gather evidence quietly. I tell them to pretend they didn't see or smell anything suspicious. The hope is that the teenager will become increasingly careless, making it easier for the parent to know what is really going on. Proof of substance use combined with documentation of a decline in functioning can serve as powerful evidence with which to confront the teenager when the time is right.

It is crucial to prepare parents to intervene without reservations should it become necessary. They should monitor quietly, and take action on the problem only if it seems essential to do so. They should use significant force when they decide it is essential to stop the teenager for his own good.

For parents to intervene, it may be possible to arrange a situation where the teenager is out of town, and beyond the reach of his peer group. This becomes necessary when the drug-involved peer group has ample money and resources and can support the clients' child, which they do gladly. They sustain him, party with him, and then make him useful by having him deal, steal, fight, or have sex for money.

Tony was out of control in his defiance. At age 15, he announced that he had a mind of his own, didn't belong to his mother or anyone else, and could do what he pleased. His "bros" were all cool and trustworthy, or so he thought. His mother found a substantial number of marijuana plants in Tony's room. This was enough proof for her to decide to put an end to the problem.

His mother and I knew that Tony would run away from home if she confronted him with her findings. His peer group would support Tony indefinitely, as he was popular and his friends had extensive resources. Therefore, we orchestrated an elaborate plan that was sure to surprise Tony. It took about a month to plan it but it circumvented the problem of running away.

The plan was to arrange an out-of-state visit to Tony's father. Tony didn't know when he boarded the bus to go visit Dad that he wouldn't be coming back. Mom called Tony at his father's house a day after he had arrived and informed him that she had found the marijuana plants. She told him they would have to do something about this. The next day Tony learned that he would be staying with his dad for the foreseeable future. The disclosure enraged him. He pleaded with Mom not to throw the plants away, as he needed to return them to his friends. She threw them out anyway. Tony threatened to run away, but Dad, who was cooperating, kept a close eye on him, and helped him weather the storm.

The Role of Private Investigators

The problems of teenagers have become so complex that I have found it necessary to maintain a working relationship with a private investigating agency to help ensure the safety of those who are out of control. This measure is to be used only in extremely difficult cases, when the parents can afford it, and then only when they feel the gravity of the situation outweighs ethical considerations involving the teenager's right to privacy. It is a difficult and expensive decision to make.

A runaway child warrants the hiring of a private investigator when it is feared he is living in dangerous circumstances. Other reasons are peer-related abuse threatening the teenager's emotional and physical health; abuse by authority figures, suspected by the parents but kept secret by the child out of fear of retaliation, and driving while intoxicated with its associated perils for life, limb, and public safety. Families themselves can sometimes take corrective steps and resolve these problems by careful monitoring of their child. In situations when police departments or other social agencies must be asked for help in removing a child from dangerous surroundings or preventing further abuse, however, the private investigator may be able to provide the evidence needed to justify such action.

Peers may be teaching a runaway drug use or encouraging him to traffic in drugs. A parent who has left the household because of a divorce, or a school or church figure, may be guilty of abuse but able to terrorize the victim into silence. A teenager with a license may be breaking a promise not to drive after drinking. These situations are grist for the private investigator if the parents cannot cope by themselves.

When I deal with investigators, I instruct them to consider the privacy needs of the teenager and to report only such information as relates to my patient's safety and well-being. It is important to avoid exposing problems that would embarrass the teenager but aren't a serious threat in regard to health and the law.

Sophie was driving drunk and speeding. At 16, she had just gotten her license and thought she knew all about life. She swore that she could drink eight or ten ounces of alcohol and drive perfectly well at high speeds. She was driving a family car. Hence, she was jeopardizing the well-being of everyone in the family, as well as her own health and that of other drivers and pedestrians.

I had warned Sophie repeatedly about the dangers of drinking and driving. I would also say that she could get caught very easily. I would warn her that her family could be sued for a lot of money. She would agree on the dangers but was confident that she wouldn't get caught. In fact, the police had stopped her numerous times without serious consequences to her, and she was still driving.

Sophie had the look of maturity needed in order to be served alcoholic drinks in public places even though she was not yet 21. She was attractive and wore sophisticated and alluring clothes. She was fearless about confronting authority figures, including police, when she didn't get her way.

Sophie's mother suspected her daughter was driving after drinking and asked for my opinion on how to handle the problem. I referred her to a private investigator who placed surveillance equipment in the family car to gather evidence. I advised the family to warn Sophie that she might be followed. We also discussed how the findings would be handled, and I emphasized Sophie's right to privacy in matters not related to her driving.

The investigator was to pass any information through me before taking it to the parents. I would then discuss it with

Sophie. I would tell her that the information had been gathered and the investigator was obligated to see that her parents got the material from him. However, if she wanted to admit her drinking problem and honor the consequences for violating her driving privilege, it would be unnecessary to pursue the matter further. I thought it would be good for her when she was sober to be confronted with the evidence of how out of control her driving looked after she had been drinking.

Issues of Confidentiality

Confidentiality becomes a sensitive area in the treatment of negative peer influences, drugs, and other illegal or harmful activities. Confidentiality becomes more of an issue in cases where these problems develop after treatment has been started.

Cases that present these problems from the start are no problem in respect to confidentiality, however. The clinician does not meet with the teenager until he has prepared the parents to manage their children's problem. This allows the clinician to do all the investigative and limit-setting work with the parents alone, before he meets the teenager. He can set limits and work with parents to curb teenager rebellion and the problem of excessive aggression, as well as the problems of peers and drugs.

I inform teenagers at the outset that I will maintain some communication with their parents throughout the case. I let them know that I will not reveal what they tell me but will use whatever I know to be in their best interests. Sometimes I use information to help them gain privileges. Sometimes I use it to help them become aware of ways they are hurting the family. However, I make it clear to the teenagers that I always use my influence to provide them optimal freedom, empowerment, and opportunities for the pursuit of their dreams. I make it clear to the parents that my ultimate goals are a healthy resolution of the addiction, the integration of the two minds, and maturation. Much of the work described next on turning failure into growth cannot take place without collaborating with the parents.

The clinician can treat anxiety, depression, and identity issues with teenagers while maintaining complete confidentiality. Teenagers need privacy, and the traditional frame of complete privacy can prove effective in cases where the teenager has connected and opened up to the clinician.

However, the problems of impulsive adolescents cannot be treated with that kind of frame. These youths require that family and other important figures in their lives contribute to the treatment effort in whatever way they can. This holds especially true for authority figures who are experiencing difficulties with the youth's ODD. A coordinated effort to help an impulsive child often requires the formation of a "team," to deal with his case, and it is essential that this team maintain open lines of communication. Likely members are educators, relatives, close friends, caseworkers, and court officials. It behooves the clinician to identify the authority figures who can contribute to the treatment effort, and establish the right to maintain open lines of communication with them from the start of treatment. He should clarify that this is what he needs to be successful and make this a condition for taking the case.

The clinician must negotiate the authority issues by adopting the perspectives of both sides on each issue. It has been my experience that teenagers easily come to accept my open communication with family and other authority figures. Most of the time they look forward to having the clinician advocate for them. It has also been my experience that parents appreciate and welcome the clinician contacting significant people in the youth's life. They want other authority figures to understand the plight of their children in the way they themselves have come to appreciate it, but find it difficult to convey to others. It is very important not to reveal what the teenager says in confidence. Conversely, the clinician should summarize for the teenager what others say about him.

The clinician can work with the parents on the constructions and assumptions they have about their children and can advise them. It helps that he has the patient's perspective. The information from both sides can put him in a unique position to dispense good advice. He can tell parents not to worry about an issue. He can ask them to support the child against school authority. He can urge them to support activities that will help the child be happy. In general, he can serve as an advocate for a teenager who knows the needs of his emotional mind but doesn't have the credibility with others that is necessary to make the case for behaving as he does.

I informed Sophie that the investigator had witnessed her and her friends breaking the law, and that he had the powers of a constable and could arrest and charge her. Sophie had experienced failure. It was time to turn the failure into growth.

Turning Failure into Growth

Once the problems have been exposed and the teenager has failed, it is time to dispense consequences for those infractions occurring in connection with peers and drugs. The clinician turns failure into growth by having the teen lose the privilege of access to the peers and situations of the kind that got him into trouble. He will have to put his life back in order before he can get the privilege back.

The clinician has now measured baseline behavior and allowed the teenager to make choices that expose his underlying intentions to escape responsibility and indulge himself, whatever the cost. The teenager's hidden intentions have directed choices that have caused him to fail. The clinician now confronts the teenager in a session or meets with the parents to prepare them to confront their teenager at home. The choice depends on whether the parents are likely to handle it well on their own and whether having the clinician participate in the confrontation is something he feels the teenager can handle without being overcome by shame.

The upshot of the confrontation is the loss of peer-related privileges. The clinician can serve as an ally to the ODD teenager's emotional-mind agenda and discuss earning the privilege back.

Sometimes the teenager cannot be forced to stop seeing the prohibited peers. However, support for peer access can be withheld. Peers can be prevented from coming to the house, and the teenager can be denied access to money, rides, telephone, or entertainment at home such as TV, video games, and computers (see Chapter 10). Life will become tough enough with this level of privilege loss to persuade the teenager to set things straight and respect the privilege he violated.

Once the teenager has put his affairs in proper order, he has earned the right to take a second step toward restoring peer-related privileges. He should arrange an activity that parallels the one where the violation took place. But his time he will handle matters in a trustworthy manner. The clinician can use individual counseling throughout these steps to accept the bond between the teenager and his friends, yet challenge its adaptive limitations. In this way, the process moves toward integration of the two minds.

It didn't take much persuasion for Carlos to accept the consequences of his failures and get his life back in order. He taunted and dared his mother when he first heard that he might lose privileges. However, his mother was prepared. She had spoken to the drug officer and was ready to proceed with a program that would put Carlos on probation and subject to random drug testing. I also spoke to Carlos about the privileges he would lose and talked to him about being a good sport.

Carlos had lost his bet but wanted to try again. He accepted the help of a tutor. He began to help out at home. He got a part-time job and respected the curfew. He spent more time with his girlfriend, a good student and a good influence on him.

Sophie was a different story. She fought when she lost the privilege of driving a car. How was she to get to work? This was nuts. She damaged property, ran away from home, and personally attacked her parents at every opportunity. She got drunk and caused a scene outside the house that the entire neighborhood witnessed.

Sophie's parents held strong. She eventually lost her job, got sick of her fighting, and settled down to appreciate her family. She accepted using the car only during the day, and gradually proved herself trustworthy. A history of sexual abuse at the hands of older teenagers in the neighborhood would eventually explain Sophie's ODD and drinking habits. This would become treatable once the limit had been set. We were moving into truth and the mending of the two-mind split.

Selecting a Type of Drug Treatment

Clinicians must offer a choice between traditional drug treatment and the protocol outlined in this chapter. The traditional approach involves locking the patient up in a hospital or rehab center. Some clinicians will not offer any outpatient counseling until after the teenager has been through rehab. The rationale for this position is simply that the patient would act out anything stirred up by the therapy rather than feel it, express it, and do something about it.

This rationale for this approach may sound good, but there are limitations. Young people must volunteer for help in conquering the drug habit. Success of twelve-step programs, as pioneered by Alcoholics Anonymous, requires exercise of free will, surrender of will, acceptance of help, and the desire to change things. Forcing ODD youths to undergo residential drug treatment often breeds resistance and requires unreasonably long stays. The treatments are expensive. The recidivism rate is high.

Involuntary residential drug treatment can yield better results when the youths face the choice of jail versus treatment. The conditions of probation can include routine drug screening to help the ODD teenager remain off drugs. However, the end result is often what twelve-steppers have come to call "dry drunks"—people who abstain from consumption but remain as dysfunctional as ever. The chances of long-term relapse are great. The problem is that peer influences will eventually return, and, following a relapse, the child won't go near treatment again. He will recall the forced program as a violation. Long-term hatreds and grudges are common in these cases.

> Barry had come a long way in his treatment. We sat with his family tying up loose ends. Barry's mom was expressing concern about the resentment that she felt he harbored. Barry, now 17, sat in front of a video game machine, playing 007. He had never done this before because there had always been important business to take care of. This time he began the session by saying, "Everything is cool so I want to play video games."

The father jokingly responded, "Great, now we get to sit here and talk while this guy plays James Bond."

"It's the nineties," I bantered. "Besides, the game is a classic." Barry agreed.

The parents set the agenda. Things were certainly going very well. The nightmare of theft, school failure, fights, and truancy had ended. Barry had failed, learned from failure, and changed his life to one that he genuinely liked. He had become truthful, very truthful. Now Mom wanted to address a bit of remaining sibling rivalry, but the big issue was resentment over decisions she had made as a mother. The biggest item of contention was forcing Barry to attend an inpatient drug treatment program, with an aftercare program to keep him straight.

"It's one of the dumbest things you've ever asked me to do," Barry said to his mother.

I clarified that I would help them look at the proposal from a different angle. Barry was open. I explained the pressure on parents to follow the established protocol and pointed out some of the positives that resulted from the residential stay. Based on history that I had gleaned over a year before, I stated my impression that Barry had come out of rehab straight, and glad he had stopped using drugs. One month later, upon re-entering school, Barry had relapsed and gotten worse than ever.

Barry interrupted me right away. "No way!" He protested. "I got blitzed the night I got out."

Mom agreed. A group of his friends had been waiting for him and induced him to become high on large amounts of marijuana. Mom explained that he had come home hours later still looking completely out of it, his eyes bright red. Barry had then accepted some help from a mentor and baseball coach who had taken the time to provide a positive influence. However, he never stopped smoking and staying out with his peer group. As soon as he returned to school he reached new levels of self-destructive behavior, resentment, and attacks on his family.

The intervention presented in this chapter takes the opposite tack and allows the clinician to offer the family a choice. Rather than force the child to stop indulging when he refuses to admit the problem, the clinician can take him through the critical components of the twelve-step program. There is no need to obtain parental approval.

The twelve-step program offers several elements to work with, even while the teenager continues to use drugs. These include acknowledging that one has a problem, accepting a higher power, accepting help, taking a moral inventory, and making amends to those the individual has hurt.

The clinician can approximate some of these critical steps of the twelve-step program by helping the drug-dependent teenager accept that he has a problem (though he may choose to continue to indulge in it). The teenager can learn to accept the influence and help of a caring and wise authority figure allied with his emotional-mind agenda. He can learn to accept his shortcomings and to complete reparations for infractions committed. The clinician can also help the teenager benefit from growth in other aspects of his life by encouraging him to plan his day to his satisfaction.

Having taken these steps, and decided to stop using drugs, he will be more than a "dry drunk." He will have a desirable life to fall back on. I have seen many cases, such as Carlos's, that have spontaneously reduced the intake of drugs and alcohol and fought hard to clean themselves up. I have seen them try to conquer their cigarette-smoking habit to achieve a healthier life. I have seen them try, relapse, and try again.

The clinician can recommend either the traditional forced abstinence approach or the approach outlined in this chapter for those situations in which drug dependency or abuse have been exposed as the core problem. This will become apparent in the treatment model, once the clinician places the teen in charge and takes failure to the limit. The drug dependency will drive the child's misuse of freedom, and all aspects of the child's life will suffer, including school, sports, and his life at home.

Carlos's family chose outpatient work, once the drug problem proved to be at the core of the difficulties. I knew about the problem, based on reports of peers.

This chapter makes the best of the situation by offering the child anything he can benefit from, rather than holding to the rigid policy that the drug problem must be resolved before counseling can be offered. Many components of this program can be offered while the drug problem persists. However, the drug problem must eventually be addressed. The objective of this approach is to maximize growth in other domains and make life so attractive that happiness is attainable without drugs. The clinician should emphasize the importance of openness and honesty and resolve other difficulties. Finally, he should help the teen accept and work on his problem. Rehab will succeed once the child is ready to accept help. Life after the drug rehab, if rehab is needed, will yield success.

Frequently, children attempt to quit drugs on their own. Eventually, their love of life and the exposure of the ugliness of the problem converge to furnish the motivation for accepting help.

What Parents Can Do to Counter the Problem of Drugs

An effective way for parents to counter the problem of drugs is to focus on increasing discipline and reducing laziness because these are areas they can control, and because drug problems become most severe in lazy children who are underachieving. Parents spend far too much time trying to catch their children in acts of deception, punishing them, and removing their privileges. However, unless the children become stronger, and develop more discipline, these punishments and humiliating violations of privacy will also provide a strong incentive for them to improve their ability to deceive.

Parents may, indeed, be able to keep their teenagers looking good during those formative years by uncovering and defeating their deceptions. With hard work, they may be able to get their uncooperative teens to conform and accept enough help from them to appear successful, with passing grades in school and a good reputation in the community. But until the parents deflate narcissism and strengthen their teens, they have achieved very little to improve the long-term picture.

I explained this to Carlos's parents as follows. "Think about it. If you were to send a narcissistically dominated child to Harvard or any other prestigious college or university, what do you think you would get for your money? You would get a lazy, manipulative child.

"You would be much better served by making sure your child is evolving, growing stronger, and investing in family, in work, and in self-development. You can invest the time you would otherwise have spent acting like a CIA agent on enforcing the exercise of will, which will promote honesty. Accomplishing this would allow you to give Carlos the freedom and privacy he needs without worrying about whether he's using drugs or is involved in other self-destructive behavior. A child who is strong and successful will do a lot less damage in hard-earned free time than a child who has been allowed to become lazy, demanding, self-centered, and bored, and who has lots of time to kill."

Breaking the Addictive Cycle

The key to breaking the addictive cycle is to replace escape with responsibility at the initial point of pain. The teenager can earn a pain-reducing indulgence after all responsibilities have been met. The challenge for the teenager is to remain trustworthy and responsible despite experiencing considerable pain, discomfort, boredom, or loneliness. In this event, the indulgence can become a reward for the sacrifice, rather than an escape from responsibility with the use of pain as an excuse.

The indulgence that the clinician recommends is the privilege of joining the peer world after the teenager has met responsibilities to family, school, sports, and other activities. Obviously, there will be times when the peer relationships will involve the use of illegal substances. That is the reality of today's peer culture. However, the message must not be conveyed that it's okay to use drugs as a reward. The reason for this is obvious. It can be argued that teenagers who choose to use drugs and alcohol are better off consuming these substances after all responsibilities have been met. However, they are minors, and the indulgence always involves breaking the law.

A clinician should always model the capacity to accept teenager rebellion and respect for the laws and rules of society. The message is that some of our social rules are obviously stupid. However, it is possible to lead a happy and honest life within our society. It just takes adaptive intelligence.

Figure 11–2 can be used to explain to the teenager the lifestyle necessary to break the addictive cycle.

The following guidelines can be helpful in the use of desirable peers as incentives for the teenager to learn trust and respect for others. The idea is to treat the peers the same way substances are treated to break the addictive cycle. Instead of using his pain as an excuse to escape into the peer world, the teenager works to create a life he likes, and meets his responsibilities. Then he can indulge in peer-world access.

The clinician does not talk to teenagers about controlling drug use at this stage of the game. He talks instead about controlling

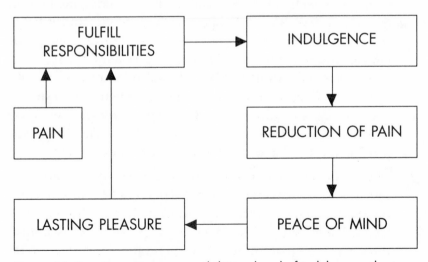

Figure 11–2. By putting responsibilities ahead of indulgence, the teenager can break the cycle.

access to the peer world. He assumes that drug use is very much linked to peer pressure, and he addresses using peers as motivators who will enhance life, not detractors who will breed distrust, dysfunction, and failure. With this in mind, he asks the teenager, who has just lost his first bet that he would be able to handle life successfully despite peer influences and drugs, to take the following steps to make things right. The goal is a life full of peer-related as well as family fun and success in other spheres of functioning.

Following are the basic principles the clinician introduces to the families with whom he works:

- *Put family first.* The obligations to family must come before peers whenever there is a conflict of interests. Family obligations may require an investment of less than one hour, and peer activity may last eight hours. The family obligation may seem petty and boring. Nonetheless, *family comes first.* For example, the teenager has a great party coming up. Yet, at home, the laundry needs to be done. The teenager must do the laundry before leaving for the party. This way, the family helps the teenager reverse the addictive cycle. It does this by having the teenager meet family responsibilities before indulging in peer life. This parallels what happens in outside life, and it helps the child develop the willpower necessary to overcome problems including addiction. ODD teenagers want the freedom that comes with adulthood. Yet, they also want the home life of a child. They want to handle their affairs in their own way and yet have everything done for them at home. Teenagers, however, should take responsibility for their home life in approximately the same way adults manage these affairs.

- *Make peers important.* The family should encourage the teenager to spend as much time with his peers as he wants. It's fine for the teenager to prefer spending time with friends over family. Parent support for peer activities can include money, rides, a private place in which to spend time, and sleepovers. Encouragement means giving the teenager and his peers opportunities to try new freedoms and prove they can handle them well. It also means allowing them second chances after they misuse their freedom. The limits to providing encouragement and freedom involve what is legal and supported in the community. Parents cannot condone anything that breaks the law, like drinking parties. The teenager cannot have friends over without supervision unless the other parents approve. The teenager does not want his parents making him look bad or otherwise embarrassing him in front of his friends, because this would hurt his standing within the peer group. In like manner, the parents do not want their kids engaging in activities that will hurt their standing in the community.

- *Involve peers in family life.* The family should encourage the teenager to invite friends to family events. However, the peer must work and contribute to the family work load, just like everyone else. It is also essential to have the peers improve the family atmosphere as much as possible. Often older siblings torment and exclude those younger when a friend visits. These youths attempt to gain status by putting others down and they make their siblings the target. Some teenagers will visit expecting to torment little ones because it's a cool thing to do. The family should prepare to remove peer privileges the moment this happens. The teenager can have one reminder of his responsibility to enhance the atmosphere of the family. After that, if the warning is unheeded, the friend goes, and the privilege of having peers over is gone.

- *Establish peer access as a privilege.* It is important to establish that having access to peers is a privilege requiring responsible management of the risks involved. The misuse of the privilege means the teenager must voluntarily surrender it until he is ready to earn it back. The guiding principle is illustrated in the movie *Groundhog Day*. The idea in the movie is for an individual to have multiple opportunities to act in a situation, with various options available to try until he gets it right. This means that the teenager puts himself in a situation that parallels the one that got him in trouble before, then makes another choice of action. Of course, the teenager must make amends for the harm done in the previous attempt before taking another chance. If something was broken, it must be repaired. If someone was lied to, the violation of trust must be addressed.

- *Break freedom into manageable chunks.* This principle is common sense. The teenager wants certain freedom. He may, for example, want to travel out of state overnight with friends to attend concerts. That desire can be broken down into chunks that the teenager must earn over the course of time to prove himself worthy of the ultimate freedom. The first step may involve meeting all obligations, going to a local concert, coming home by 1 A.M., and enjoying a family activity the next day. The next step may add an overnight, and the next, traveling further and staying at a hotel. The teenager must maintain a certain level of responsibility before and after each event. If the teenager promises to avoid drugs on these trips, the parents may reserve the right to take a surprise drug test after any of these events. Other items in this method of breaking freedom up into manageable chunks can include curfew extensions, access to vehicles like four-wheelers, dirt bikes, and cars, and the right to stay home alone. The teenager must agree to be a good sport and refrain from taking more freedom than was granted. If the teenager violates the freedom granted, the parents should remove the privilege and set conditions for the teenager to earn another chance.

- *Use specific experiments to increase freedom.* This condition entails making another bet, like that discussed at the start of this chapter. To start, the clinician takes a baseline reading of responsible behaviors, such as contributions to the family. He then looks at the responsible behaviors he would like to see continue after the new freedom is granted. He puts all of this in writing. Once he has established the necessary parameters for measuring the effect of increased freedom, the clinician invites everyone to bet on the outcome. The parents should bet on things going badly. The teen will bet on them going well. The clinician should bet as well. Have some fun. Put some real money on the line.

- *Learn from failures.* The clinician should schedule appointments with the parents and later with the teenager. He estimates how long it will take to evaluate the impact of the new freedom granted. He meets with the parents first to evaluate the relative success or failure of the trial. Then he meets with the teenager to side with the emotional mind, and help him feel good about having tried. He challenges the adaptive brain about anything that went wrong, comes up with a new plan for the next time it happens, and prepares the teenager for a second try.

- *Describe second-opportunities conditions.* The clinician establishes criteria for repairing the damage caused by a failed attempt, takes an inventory of all the people affected by the error, and makes a list of the activities the teenager can engage in to make up for the trouble he caused. For example, if the family lost sleep because of his behavior, the teenager must come home early a sufficient number of times to ensure that his worried parents get some rest. If a parent had to drive a long way and interrupt what he was doing to deal with a problem, the teenager must complete enough work time to make up for the time lost and work undone. The teenager is encouraged to come up with a plan for doing things differently once he has completed the list of reparations. The clinician oversees the preparation of this plan during an individual session with the ODD teenager. This gives him a chance to ally with the emotional-mind agenda and a chance to challenge the rational mind. Present the plan to the parents and set a target date for the *Groundhog Day* experience, with its range of options.

- *Manage the obvious dangers.* Before increasing the amount of freedom a teenager will have, the clinician discusses the possible dangers and problems that the parents can anticipate. He guides the family in arranging reasonable precautions to minimize risk. For example, a young teenage girl can take a cell phone with her to avoid being left alone late at night after a car breakdown. Parents can guarantee a ride back from anywhere at anytime without question. This assurance can prevent problems in situations where teenagers may be drinking and driving or have become involved in a violent or otherwise dangerous scene. (For a detailed presentation of how to set up these kinds of buffers, see Chapter 6.)

Addressing the Two-Mind Split

The conversation with Carlos at the start of this chapter illustrates the integration process. The key is to have the teenager reach a point where he describes all the good and bad things about his peer life and his experiences with drugs. It becomes possible, once this level of communication has been reached, to challenge the adaptive intelligence of misusing addictive substances.

The primary concern of the clinician is that he must fulfill the role of confidant in a way that parents cannot. He cannot advise most parents to speak in a tone of camaraderie with their children about their partying experiences. It is not an appropriate conversation for most families. The only people that teenagers truly can be open with are other peers, the exception being the clinician who has been successful in bonding with the teenager's emotional mind, understands its agenda, and has achieved a peer standing wth the parient.

The topic of drug-related adventures is of the utmost importance to teenagers who choose to surround themselves with questionable peer influences and drugs. The clinician enters a unique position of trust with his client if the teenager can speak to him in the way that Carlos spoke to me. We also spoke about the dumber use of drugs and the violations of trust that he committed and saw his friends commit.

The next section addresses the work the clinician must do, following this acceptance and truth phase, to promote adaptive intelligence in teenage clients who present with drug-related problems.

Preparing Teenagers to Accept Help

The clinician needs to side with the emotional-mind agenda for all the benefits and wonders of the teenager's desired lifestyle. Then he will work to challenge the adaptive problems. That is, he will work to point out the pitfalls in the lifestyle that have become evident as the teenager takes failure to the limit and can't correct matters. The clinician's intention is to help the teenager meet the needs of the emotional mind with more fun and greater trust.

Some of the adaptive pitfalls of drug addiction are obvious. There is tar in the lungs, constant breaking of the law, and drug friends (similar to fair-weather friends) who are there when the client has a supply of drugs but never when he doesn't. Distrust abounds among the teenager's cohorts. There are rip-offs, dry times, ratting, and other forms of betrayal.

Other adaptive pitfalls are subtler, and must be exposed. The biggest pitfall is the attendant loss of freedom. I explain it to teenagers this way:

> Imagine that you are invited to an incredible party. It has everything you could possibly want, including live music, food, drink, and drugs. It has pool, darts, video games, dancing. It has the best-looking kids of both sexes. It is completely private. Everything is free. However, there is one drawback. You can never leave. You can never stop partying and enjoy some serious moments. You can't clean up your act. You can't go home and clean your room. You can't resume your work or studies or decide on your own future. You can't settle down into a relationship or start a family. You can't even go home to spend quiet time with your family.

Once I lay out this metaphor, I explain how drug use gradually consumes the teenager's life. He lives for the next high and violates the rights of everyone around him in order to have just one more fix. Before he knows it, he has no trust, no hope. Before he knows it, he is supporting his partying by selling, or buying from a friend, and taking some for the sake of the risk. His other choice is to freeload. Finally, his problems are exposed. And he becomes an embarrassment to the family.

Here, I tell the teenager stories of young people who have lost sports careers, who have ended up in jail, who have lost the girlfriends or boyfriends they really loved. I tell them about teenagers who have rolled over in their cars and subsequently lost their licenses. I tell them about one kid who lost $5,000 and couldn't pay off his debts. I select a story that approximates the interests of the teenager I'm working with.

One of the most effective stories concerns a young man who squandered a $50,000 court settlement resulting from a car accident. This story often shocks the teenagers. They can't understand how someone could spend that much money. At first they assume that he was stupid, but I tell them that he isn't stupid, just addicted, and in a state of denial.

I explain that the young man didn't waste all $50,000 on drugs. There were other luxury items contributing to his lifestyle. He bought a car. He bought VCRs, TVs; he went to gambling casinos. He also spent money on cocaine, champagne, and expensive dinners with his beautiful girlfriend. Along the way he began to run short of money, and couldn't pay for $90-an-hour therapy, as he had promised himself he would—but not when he could buy a "bag" for that much, and it would last him almost two weeks. In the end, all the bags he smoked couldn't change his life, and he wound up working at a minimum-wage job. Luckily, he had enough foresight to enroll in a training program that eventually got him started on a good career. However, his life had become hell within a year of the accident settlement.

This intervention is most effective once the teenager has taken failure to the limit. Otherwise the talk won't get past the rational mind. The emotional mind will tune it out.

> Tim greeted me with a hug. I hadn't seen him for more than a fleeting moment in over two years. He looked great. He wore that tongue ring really well. That was Tim, always the extremes. He was now 21, and I had known him since he was 14. His parents offered to pay for a few therapy sessions because they felt that he had arrived at an important point in his life. They thought I would be a positive influence. Tim was excited to see me.
>
> Tim told a lengthy story about how his drug-addicted friends had let him down and violated his trust again and again.

I finally said, "Dude, I couldn't talk to you about this until you felt this kind of pain. I'm sorry you've been through all of this, but I'm glad, too."

I then discussed the meaning of trust with him, how he was responsible for being trustworthy, and how he could learn to identify people who also had those qualities. He needed a way to gauge the trustworthiness of others. He listened attentively. I concluded, "If you hadn't gone through all that pain, everything I have said here to you would sound like a huge lecture. You would have thought, 'These are my friends. They'll always look out for me.' And I would have wasted my breath."

Tim agreed. He said that in a way he was glad he had endured all of the extremes and hardships he had talked about. We then considered how he could get on with his life and how to test the trustworthiness of others. We talked about people needing to be fair, keeping their promises, and respecting boundaries. We went over tests for each of these qualities and saw which of his friends fit and which didn't.

Everything possible had been done to help Tim with his peer and drug problems. But there was no guarantee that he had overcome them. Voluntary involvement in a twelve-step program is the closest thing to a guarantee of beating the epidemic of difficult problems in today's youth culture. The methods outlined in this chapter count on the passage of time for help. Teenagers mature, improve their lives, and accomplish the goals of this treatment method while viewing their drug and peer problems in a more grown-up way. I have used the method to persuade many of them to stop using drugs and alcohol. I have seen many more teenagers reduce their drug use, as Carlos did. Many have formed a strong therapeutic alliance with me as a result of using this method. I have never seen a case of long-term drug use worsen as a result of this method.

This concludes the discussion of the basic structure of the method I recommend for dealing with ODD patients. The next chapter is a description of contraindications and problems the clinician is likely to face when using this treatment approach. The chapter describes ways to anticipate and avoid these possible pitfalls.

12

Other Special Problems and Contraindications

It distressed me to turn him away, but I had to tell Andrew that his mother's instructions that he no longer come to see me must be honored. The occasion for the rejection came on a day when a group of patients were gathered in my waiting room to drink coffee, play video games, relax, chat, and escape from the bitter cold outside. The waiting room was a favorite hangout for them and I knew Andrew wanted in the worst way to be able to join in.

I had seen Andrew for a few sessions and knew that he was desperate, unstable, and, in the long run, probably dangerous to himself. At age 13, he was experiencing an identity crisis. His speech and mannerisms were clearly effeminate, yet it was evident that he was ashamed of his presentation. He was depressed. He was indulging in shoplifting and other high-risk behaviors. The last thing Andrew needed was another rejection.

In the unfortunate aftermath of a vindictive divorce situation,

Andrew's mother prohibited him from entering my office and canceled sessions arranged by the father. She didn't realize that Andrew was desperate to fit in with older youths who considered my office a place of status. Keeping Andrew from visiting me had the effect of barring him from contact with the peers he admired. I worried about Andrew's potential for self-harm.

> His mother had become anxious when Andrew started to challenge her authority. This took place shortly after I began to see him. Increased rebellion is a very common initial response to treatment in adolescents. Andrew's mother was extremely controlling. Her son was failing school. He was talking back. I was still trying to help Andrew open up. Mom felt threatened by the increased rebellion in her son, and considered my influence a threat to her controlling ways.
>
> I asked my lawyer whether I could help Andrew on my own, in view of the fact that his mother was dealing with him in a way that would further traumatize him with rejection and undermine his development. My lawyer was clear about it. Andrew must not come anywhere near my office. His mother, as the custodial parent, had the right to do whatever she wanted with him.
>
> The next day I turned Andrew away. I knew what this would do to him. However, I could not prevent it. He was not imminently suicidal. I had nothing to report. Andrew continued to try to sneak his way into my building. I had to ask him to leave.

This chapter discusses how the clinician can benefit from mistakes such as those I made with Andrew, and prevent them from ever taking place. Andrew's case, which unfolded many years ago, illustrates some of the special problems and contraindications that can surface in this treatment approach to adolescent ODD. These include the absence of parental support, the possibility of increased rebellion and acting out, and challenges to authority by the teenager, who will misconstrue and misquote statements the clinician made in the process of joining the teenager's emotional mind. Youths who have been severely traumatized can also pose problems in a model that is based on joining their agenda.

LACK OF PARENTAL SUPPORT

The clinician should never enter into this treatment method unless at least one parent with custodial rights is well informed and strongly supports the approach. Otherwise, complications can become unmanageable and the risks unacceptable.

Parents must be warned that other adults they talk to about the prescribed methods will not understand. These outsiders will question the competence of the clinician working on the case. This happens because most people view child rearing from the perspective of the creatures-of-habit paradigm. They expect to tell their children what they must do. They expect parents to avoid failure at all costs. They emphasize sending youths the right message and instilling proper habits.

Outsiders will recommend greater structure and control even after these methods have caused ODD and a host of other problems. If the control tactics don't work, parents will tell themselves, implement them with greater intensity. If a time-out doesn't work, use grounding. If grounding doesn't work, use probation. If probation doesn't work, use jail or residential treatment. The idea is to keep enforcing proper behavior until the child surrenders the ODD and becomes easy to manage.

The parents must back the clinician fully before he can safely form an alliance with the emotional mind of the ODD teenager. Otherwise, it is the clinician and the ODD teenager against the rest of the world. Parents who don't grasp the method can fire the clinician when they object to what they see, based on the assumption that he is putting the wrong ideas into the teenager's head, rather than creating a breathing space in which the teenager can express primary wants, have these accepted as natural, and then have them challenged. The last thing needed is parents saying that the clinician is filling their child's mind with antisocial ideas, and that the child is helplessly under his spell.

Norma had been in counseling for depression and identity problems. Individual sessions were required to help her identify and process sources of loss and trauma in her life. Suddenly she made a breakthrough and began to open up. She began to take risks in response to my challenges. Reasonable risk-taking behavior in teenagers is essential to the development and strengthening of weak areas.

Norma suddenly decided to date a young man who had a problem with marijuana. He encouraged her to rebel against authority. Norma then developed ODD characteristics, and directed these toward her mother because her mother tried to stop her from seeing him.

I was suddenly caught up in a situation in which I had a strong bond with Norma's emotional mind and no support from Norma's mother. I tried to talk to the mother to improve matters but it was too late. Norma didn't want me talking to her mother, who was deeply enmeshed in the parental neurosis process (see Chapter 9) by the time we made contact.

This manifestation of rebellion without parent support cost Norma and me the therapy at a very critical time. In addition, Norma's mother complained to other parents about my influence on her daughter. Norma continued to misquote me to her mother, and rely on me for guidance. The mother repeated her daughter's biased statements about me to school personnel and other parents.

It turned out that I was starting treatment with the young man in whom Norma was interested. I normally could have used the coincidence of their relationship to influence them both to become increasingly trustworthy and positive influences on each other's lives. Instead, because of the gossip, I lost access to both cases, and several parents in the community were left with the impression that I was dispensing unsound advice to teenagers.

INCREASED ACTING OUT AT THE
START OF TREATMENT

The clinician must always warn parents that it is common to see increased acting out and defiance in the early part of the treatment, and provide them with an overview of the entire treatment philosophy and effort. Sophisticated parents can read parts of this book, such as Chapter 1, to clarify the paradigm in which we are working.

> David had refused to go to school for weeks. The more his parents tried to force him, the more devious he became. David's parents were good parents. They had four other children and had always been able to set limits and teach them the right lessons. But David was different. He never complained, acted out, or rebelled. He was always very quiet. However, he was determined. He would listen quietly to instructions from his parents, then do whatever he wanted. Mom realized that she was not equipped to deal with David and brought him to me.
>
> At the outset, I took the parents aside and warned them of what to expect. I said, "In the early part of this treatment, all kinds of ugly things come out. It's an evaluation phase [see Chapters 3 and 4], and it's like draining an infection. Everything that's buried and secret will surface. This is desirable, though it will make you nervous. The process helps me to know what to treat. Believe me, we will turn today's problems into tomorrow's growth. And, once children begin to grow naturally, they turn out beautifully no matter how ugly things look at times."
>
> Within weeks of my delivering this explanation, David was caught for shoplifting, marijuana possession, and setting a fire in the house. Every couple of weeks we had a new emergency to deal with involving some shocking behavior by this otherwise cute and quiet child.
>
> "This kid seems so quiet, but there's more than meets the

eye here," I would say, trying to inject a trace of humor into the situation as the stories of his transgressions unfolded. I would shake my head, perplexed, and exclaim, "David did that! Are you kidding? This kid is too much!" We were able to form an alliance around getting at the truth of his activities.

David's parents struggled, and had their moments of doubt, but we got through it all. Once we had uncovered everything and allowed David to make choices, he became extremely lazy and entered a period of inactivity. When I got to the individual therapy (two-mind integration) work, David explained that he wasn't doing anything because peers had unjustly excluded him from their company. The parents of one of them had found some marijuana paraphernalia that her son blamed on David. The parents had spread the word that David was a bad influence and all the families had ostracized him.

David gave me permission to solicit his parents' help on this matter, and we arranged for him to have supports for finding new peers. He was eventually caught smoking marijuana with several peers, one of whom was the teenager who had lied to his mother about David to conceal his own drug use. This time he had been caught red-handed, and couldn't shift the entire responsibility for his involvement to David.

David was placed on probation. We used this event and other consequences to help him change peer groups and select a program of studies that he liked. David ended up planning a schedule for himself, and this provided the motivation that he needed to drop his do-nothing attitude. The consequences at home for his infraction combined to convert failure into growth, and David's case turned out fine after a few months.

I am certain that if I hadn't warned the parents at the start about the difficult part of the program, I would not have received their support, and I would not have been able to establish the connection with David that I needed for success in this case.

Increased rebellion against authority is a common side effect of different forms of child therapy. Children of all ages can become more challenging to parents and teachers, and this can represent a desirable by-product of the growth induced by the therapy. The child develops confidence, feels worthwhile, and is comfortable demanding more independence. Increased rebellion in response to therapeutic intervention is most common in teen-agers, and even more so when starting this treatment method.

It is easy for uninformed parents and well-intentioned friends to conclude mistakenly that the clinician is putting strange ideas into children's heads. The clinician can count on this happening unless he prepares the parents for what is to take place.

I have described numerous case studies where the parents called me in a state of alarm because of a teenager who had come home completely defiant as a result of his talks with me. However, in each case where this actually took place, I had predicted to the parents that the initial response to my forming an emotional-mind alliance with their ODD teenager would be increased acting out.

The clearer the warning about what will happen, the less likely it is that parents will panic and revert to the old ways in their child-rearing methods. Nonetheless, whatever the degree of their un-derstanding, the clinician should remain available for urgent calls to schedule a meeting soon after the precipitating event takes place.

MISQUOTING SESSION MATERIAL TO CHALLENGE AUTHORITY

ODD teenager patients can be expected to misrepresent what the clinician tells them when he initially joins their emotional-mind agenda. They are apt to take quotes out of context and use them to challenge authority figures at home and at school. They may misrepresent what is said to them to gain their own ends, though in some cases their failure to report the clinician's words accurately may be the result of genuine misunderstandings and involve no ulterior motives.

As the teenager sees it, the world is divided into cool peers and dumb old adults. When he argues with his parents he has no credibility because he's just a kid. Now comes this person who has more status than parents or teachers and who speaks the language of the emotional mind. The teenager skews whatever the clinician says to him in the direction of his selfish agenda. The clinician knows the teenager is going to misquote him and use his words as a weapon to strike at authority.

The misuse of his words to defy authority is, to some extent, the unavoidable by-product of the clinician's having become the first adult to side with the youth's emotional-mind agenda. Such misrepresentation may make the clinician look bad in the short run. However, adults exposed to this treatment will be impressed by the clinician's influence over the difficult teenager, and often will understand that what he is doing is in the interests of forming an alliance.

Once more, the best way to deal with this problem is to predict it. The clinician cannot control what people do with his words. He can be clear and precise in what he says and he can try to determine if his words have been understood, but he cannot keep the ODD teenager from taking advantage of them. Nonetheless, he will gain tremendous influence over the teenager with his work to join the emotional-mind agenda and will eventually use this influence to accomplish what no one else can, namely growth, trustworthiness, and mind–body integration. However, all of that will come later. Meanwhile, the clinician must maintain credibility or forfeit forever his chance of providing his patient with the benefits of therapy.

The clinician must alert the parents to everything he will be doing to form a bond with the child's emotional mind. They should understand that the clinician will be playing games, swearing, and criticizing the authority that the child distrusts at the emotional-mind level. The clinician should explain that he will later challenge the teenager to bring out the best side of the authority figures he is complaining about. For example, it is easy to judge a teacher. But few can learn to turn the situation into a positive and get the best from the teacher that he has to offer. I challenge teenagers to develop their own imagination to transform dull information into something interesting. This is the kind of skill that can make the teenager successful as he proceeds to higher education and to the challenges of later life. The clinician should explain to the parents that he cannot arrive at such a response from the teenager until he has joined him in negativity toward others.

The clinician can also try to prevent this problem by asking the teenager not to misquote him to other adults. He explains that others won't understand the clinician's perspective, and he could lose credibility if the teenager quotes him in order to get away with bratty and selfish behavior. Sometimes the teenager will value the connection with the clinician enough to protect his reputation.

> Alan was starting to act out in school again. He was a 14-year-old with the playfulness of a young child, and a history of school struggles caused by AD/HD and severe dyslexia. He had been responsible and well behaved for several months, but was starting to be verbally abusive to his resource-room teacher.
>
> The school had been good to Alan. His teachers had given him everything I had recommended to help him enjoy his school day and be honest with them. Alan came from a socio-economically disadvantaged home. His school had determined that he needed counseling for his emotional problems, and offered to pay for private therapy. This would avoid having to place him in an expensive residential school. Alan's mother had requested that the school hire me as the outside expert to treat Alan and consult with the school. The school first tried other counselors who were unable to manage Alan's behavior. They eventually granted the mother's wishes and hired me. They had paid for Alan to come see me for two years.
>
> Alan loved the visits. In fact, the only punishment his mother could threaten that had any meaning for him was losing the right to see me. His mom would say, "Do your chores or you aren't going to Dr. B.'s tonight." Usually I tell parents not to use therapy as a negotiating tactic because the ODD teenager may begin to resist or become indifferent in his attitude. Alan was different. He would do anything to see me.
>
> Alan's family would travel from out of state every other week for an extended two-hour session. Our bond at the emo-

tional-mind level was solid and it allowed me to challenge his rational mind readily. Alan had been extremely manipulative in sessions during the first year that I saw him, but I had reached a point at which I could confront these forms of resistance and he would open up readily.

I told Alan that he needed to find different outlets for his frustration or it would make our work look bad. I said, "You wouldn't want the school to think that everything they've done for us and their payment for you to come see me was a waste. They might think that you had been good for a few months as a honeymoon period, but were now heading back to your old ways."

Alan agreed with me. We decided to look at what the need of the emotional mind to act out was telling us. Perhaps we needed to make a life change. However, the adaptive intelligence of that outlet (abusing the resource-room teacher) was not smart.

Alan stopped the acting out. He felt that he needed a vacation from being so good, and he was tired of the resource-room help. He wanted it three times weekly instead of five. He wanted more peer access time on the other two days of the week. We met with his teachers and made adjustments.

INCOMPETENT CUSTODIAL PARENTS

Sometimes the clinician receives information that a custodial parent is neglecting or abusing the child, or otherwise behaving incompetently. This gives rise to numerous complications, considering the power a custodial parent holds over a minor. In the rivalry existing between parents, it is difficult to know whose story to believe and to identify the incompetent parent. The clinician, in fact, may not have an ally who supports the treatment in the immediate family. He may need to report the problem to the Department of Social Services for a resolution.

I handle these cases by exposing the problem and finding a reliable ally in the family system who can offer the youth a reasonably satisfying living situation. I have the ally monitor the problem. I allow the ODD to grow naturally to the point that it brings the incompetent parent to surrender. The parent then becomes open to receiving help.

In the segment "Issues of Confidentiality" in Chapter 11, I introduce the necessary parameters to establish an effective frame around confidentiality. I suggest that the clinician gain permission from the start of treatment to maintain an open flow of communication with significant others in the ODD youth's life. He should encourage the formation of a "treatment team," and strive to keep all members informed and involved. The clinician should act as an advocate for the youth, able to make suggestions that will gain his client valuable opportunities, and should gather information that he can use to give his client feedback. He can use the feedback that he gathers to help foster self-awareness in his client, and thereby two-mind integration.

I believe that the same principles of confidentiality apply to impulsive or otherwise incompetent parents. Relatives and well-intentioned supporters of the family system will usually contact the clinician to inform him of the nature of the problems they witness as these arise. If the child is experiencing neglect or abuse, the clinician will be informed.

Complications involving confidentiality occur once the clinician starts to gather information about the case without the permission of the custodial, but perhaps incompetent, parent. Much depends on who brings the child in for treatment, and who pays the fee.

I inform the family that in working with teenagers I handle the issue of privacy differently. I inform the teenager and his parents that I will listen to people who have something to say about him. I speak with the parents about whatever they feel they can do to help. I ask to be informed of any relative I should not listen to and ask for the rationale. I inform the teenager that I will not reveal anything he tells me, and, if information comes to me another way, I will tell him someone called, and give him a summary of what I was told.

I find this relatively open policy on confidentiality useful in gathering material for challenging the adaptive brain of the teenager. I was trained in this method in my internship by my adolescence supervisor and have seen it work well. Many times teens think they are doing wonderfully well while others see major problems. I tell teenagers that I will use my best judgment in making recommendations to their parents and other adults. I clarify that I am their ally and will arrange to get them multiple chances to secure the life they want. I clarify that I cannot accept responsibility for the case without the freedom to operate this way.

Teenagers need privacy. However, they don't have the resources to secure the things they need to make their lives better. They don't have the credibility they need to advocate effectively for their emotional-mind agenda. Therefore, I need to be in a position to represent them, in much the same way that a lawyer represents a client. They can choose to trust me or seek a different kind of help. Most parents welcome my speaking to school personnel or relatives. The teenagers find my advocacy on their behalf very useful. I will not speak to anyone a teenager asks me to avoid.

If the clinician operates this way in a case that involves parental incompetence, he will soon have evidence of what's going on. He can then decide what course of action to take. He may need to report the problem to a social agency, recommend a lawyer, or offer the struggling parent reasonable help.

He must, of course, keep an open mind when he is seeking to judge the competence of any adult and wait until the evidence is in. He doesn't live with the family. He is not there to witness neglect, abuse, or incompetence, so he must proceed with caution. People have all kinds of hidden motives when it comes to the custody of children.

> Tammy, the concerned mother of two boys, decided to come see me even though I had told her prior to the appointment that I wasn't certain I could do much for her. She was worried because her ex-husband suffered from a drinking problem, and she could tell that his habits were being transmitted to the children. For example, they showed signs of enabling and parentification (adopting a parental role toward the alcoholic).

The boys would be resistant to seeing a clinician because they had already been through a bad experience with a counselor who had pressured them into betraying their father. They remained loyal to him, but complained continually of the father's incompetence.

Jason and Bob, 15 and 11, seemed increasingly out of patience with their dad's authoritative and restrictive parenting style, and were tired of him being extremely friendly, albeit in an insincere way, early in the day, and extremely aggressive at night. They were tired of the mess, the lack of food, and the responsibility for doing the housework. The boys often contacted their mother, cousin, or grandmother, asking to be fed or driven to an activity that their father had neglected to take them to. They were tired of worrying constantly about adult matters, like how the family would pay rent and make ends meet.

Jason and Bob were good boys. They were closely bonded to each other, dutiful, polite, charming, and successful in school. These characteristics might have seemed like evidence of good child rearing, but they presented other aspects that, to the trained eye, matched the syndrome of parentification that occurs in alcoholic families. It demonstrated a need to agree on most matters, as though having an independent thought violated some unspoken rule. They were clingy and showed hints of neediness and defensiveness.

On the surface, Tammy lacked credibility because she had given up on herself for a couple of years. This was largely a response to having voluntarily surrendered custody of her kids. She had fallen into a depression in response to some tragic losses in her family and, in a moment of weakness, agreed to hand over the children to her former husband. Once he had gained custody he developed various excuses for depriving her of access to the boys. She was devastated and, to a large extent, felt she had lost her reason for living. She let her travel business go, neglected to file income tax returns, and failed to collect money she was owed by customers.

I learned, though, that Tammy was basically a reliable

woman who kept her word. I learned this after testing her for competence. I didn't use psychological tests on Tammy, though I might have. Instead, I told her that if she wanted to help her sons she would have to demonstrate competence. She would have to earn their trust. I asked her to straighten out her business and find herself a place to live that was suitable for herself and her boys. Tammy told me that she had a devoted extended family that would do anything to help. I asked her to bring them in to meet with me if she was willing to bare her troubles.

Tammy's ex-husband, Ted, was in many ways her opposite. On the surface, he looked extremely competent. He was a pillar of the community, involved in the Boy Scouts, church activities, and school events. He was friendly with numerous teachers in his sons' schools. He talked about his devotion to the children and saw his overly obedient sons as validating his parenting style.

However, Ted showed all the signs of alcoholism. His denial was extreme and he manipulated and lied to cover things up. He would blame all his troubles on Tammy, who was a hopeless enabler. She had been programmed over a ten-year period to do anything needed to satisfy Ted. She couldn't stop doing things for him. She set herself up to take the blame for her ex-husband's incompetence.

I was surprised by how quickly Tammy accomplished everything I asked of her. She got her life together, and saw to it that her extended family would visit my office. Family members independently told stories of trying to help Ted with the boys but felt taken advantage of. Tammy's elderly mother seemed traumatized in her dealings with Ted. She was near tears as she recalled being put in the position of having to promise the boys money she didn't have, only to disappoint them later. All the data fit.

My position in cases like this is to do whatever is in the best interests of the children within the context of the family. There does not have to be a conflict between what's good for the parent and what's good for the children. Conflict takes place only when a parent harbors an ulterior motive that becomes more important than the children's well-being. Such motives include getting even with a spouse, getting more than a fair share of time with the children, and raising them in a way that disagrees with the ideas of the other spouse. In general, two parents are better than one. The more allies the children have, the better, as long as the alliances are healthy.

My objectives were to gather direct evidence of incompetence on the father's side and to find suitable living quarters for the boys. I did not want the courts to have to rely on the boys as primary witnesses in action to take custody away from their father, even on a short-term basis. As to where they would stay in the event the father was relieved of custody, I was confident that the mother's side of the family would provide for the boys very well. The relatives would arrange a living situation that met the boys' needs, but would not exclude their father once he had dealt with his drinking problem.

My next step was to have Tammy gather evidence of the drinking and neglect at home. I also referred Tammy to an attorney with whom I work closely, and to a private investigator to gather evidence. I asked Tammy to find out what kind of evidence was admissible in court that would help make the case for the change in custody.

The boys came to see me much sooner than I expected. Reducing the enabling had increased the pressure. When the boys reached a state of crisis, the extended family unanimously recommended their coming to see me. I met with them alone and then with the extended family. Both meetings went well. The boys quickly connected. They responded well to my siding with their emotional-mind agenda and my challenge to them to plan a better life.

I met with Ted and got a firsthand demonstration of the extent of his denial. He assured me that he and the boys had enjoyed the happiest life imaginable until all of this legal challenge had come into play, and this was, of course, Tammy's fault. I asked whether he was referring to the legal challenge that Tammy had just initiated. He said that he was referring to the events that had taken place in the last two weeks and this confirmed his incompetence.

I had referred Tammy to an attorney and offered her a choice between hiring a private investigator or acting as her own (see Chapter 11, under "Monitoring without Intruding," "The Role of the Private Investigators," and "Issues of Confidentiality"). She chose the latter.

Tammy needed evidence to back up her claims that Ted was incompetent as a parent. She claimed that Ted's house was messy enough to present a health hazard, that the boys went without food, and that he drank in front of them. Her report was fine for the purposes of counseling but it would not hold up in court were she to seek custody of the boys. This was especially true because Ted had discredited her before the community on numerous occasions, claiming that she did drugs, was unfaithful, and that the marital problems were her fault.

When Ted claimed that everything had been perfect until two weeks ago, he didn't realize that Tammy had showed me disturbing pictures of his home from several weeks back. There were dozens of empty liquor bottles, and some left open with plenty of alcohol left in them, sitting in plain view in common living areas. Other pictures showed huge messes, including an area of the house that constituted a fire hazard. Of course there was a picture of an empty refrigerator. We had sealed these pictures in a letter and mailed them to my office to confirm the date on which they were gathered.

Ted didn't realize that I had photographs of the trashed house and alcohol bottles. I had guilt-trip letters and reports of neglect on the chart. I had numerous independent reports of the problem from the boys themselves. Most of this evidence was gathered long before the events of the last two weeks. I said nothing about my findings, but the evidence of denial was obvious.

It was important to explain to the boys and to Tammy's extended family that it was imperative for us to stop the enabling process if Ted were to have a chance of winning his struggle against alcoholism.

I explained the problem with enabling: "The disease of alcoholism feeds off people who surround the person dependent on the bottle. It's like a tug of war. On one side is the bottle pulling at the spirit of the drinker; on the other side are all the well-intentioned people who are striving to save the one who drinks. The enablers help him in various ways, rescue him from precarious situations, give him money, and make excuses for him. They put their own lives on hold, and remain loyal to the one with the problem.

"The people who immediately surround the one that drinks need help, just as the drinker does. So they turn to other friends and relatives, who in turn reach out to them and offer the same kind of support. It's a long chain of events that begins with the bottle and works itself through an entire network to friends and family.

"The best thing you can do is let go. Take care of yourselves and let the others decide if they want to invest their entire lives keeping the drinking going. Every time one person lets go, it puts more pressure on everyone else, making the situation more intolerable. This makes it more likely that others will let go. However, in the end, the person drinking has to make a choice to get help. Everyone must make the choice of life over death on their own."

I looked at the extended family, and said, "Every time you give Ted money to rescue him from a problem you prolong the disease."

I looked at the boys and said, "Every time you clean the house because your father is drunk you prolong the disease. If there is anyone that your dad will quit drinking for it's you boys."

I explained that inflicting hardships on him might make them feel bad in the short term. However, the side of his nature that is in pain is the one addicted to the drinking. Once the person stops drinking and receives the right kind of help, he will appreciate life as never before. I then explained the classic intervention strategy reserved for individuals with serious addictions, as at the Betty Ford Foundation.

"The way people in families help alcoholics in serious trouble is with what they call an intervention," I said. "An intervention takes place when the family gets together and tells the member who is drinking about the effect the addiction has on them, including the sacrifices they make in trying to furnish help for the drinker. The family may also make treatment a condition of remaining in the home. This kind of intervention can prompt an addicted individual to get the necessary help."

I assured the boys that once their father got treatment, they could welcome him back into the family. Most likely, Dad would be happier and thank them for it once he has entered a twelve-step program and feels the peace of mind that comes from living well.

I treated the boys successfully and they responded with a healthy increase in rebellion. I taught them how to counter guilt trips and refuse to give in to irrational control tactics. The healthy rebellion (ODD in response to unreasonable expectations) tried the father's patience. His authoritative and rigid parenting style didn't fit well with his teenage sons' needs for autonomy. The boys became increasingly difficult and Ted soon lost control. He hit one of the boys. The school reported this to the Department of Social Services and the case went to court.

Tammy and the extended family were given temporary custody of the boys. Dad was mandated to treatment and his therapist began preparations for him to enter a twelve-step program.

MEDICAL COMPLICATIONS

Many cases present with a medical component that accompanies ODD. These comorbid conditions present their own unique set of problems. Examples of these conditions are diabetes, epilepsy, and eating disorders. The complications are obvious. If the therapist works on the medical condition, he is bound to encounter the ODD. The ODD will make the treatment frustrating for the adults involved and difficult for the entire family. If the clinician treats the ODD, he may jeopardize the effectiveness of the medical treatment. Failure taken to the limit risks medical complications, which can reach a crisis point before the ODD reverses itself.

When he is facing medical complications, the clinician must work closely with the physician, update him regularly, and ask him to monitor the patient's condition frequently until the patient has passed through the failure phase of treatment. The clinician must inform the family of the risk of a worsened medical condition and let the family know he may want to treat the ODD for a trial period to determine whether the teenager can turn matters around quickly enough to avoid medical complications. The teenager should be placed in charge of his own health so that he takes pride in his actions and doesn't live under the mistaken impression that others are handling the problem for him. Life for the teenager should be made as positive as possible to minimize self-destructive tendencies. The teenager who loves his life learns to care about himself and doesn't entertain the idea of hurting himself.

Conditions like eating disorders thrive on control, much as drug addictions do. Hence, forcing the eating will only increase the ODD and make the teenager more determined in using illness to manipulate and spoil matters for the family. On the other hand, if he treats the ODD in the manner described in this book, the clinician may face medical complications as the ODD process reaches a stagnation point (see Chapter 1), and the teenager bottoms out and enters the mastery phase.

The clinician can expect a worsening of the teenager's self-destructive tendencies when he puts the teenager in charge of his own health and prescribes taking failure to the limit. Common sense dictates that he coordinate the treatment for ODD with the health care professional treating the medical condition. The health care professional should monitor the health factors and call a halt to the ODD treatment at any time if this becomes necessary.

Treatment for ODD should begin at a point where the medical condition is at its most stable. In the following case, a 15-year-old with a severe eating disorder had just been released from an intensive hospital-based program designed to restore her weight. At home, the teenager did fine for a while. Shortly thereafter, however, the struggle with her mother and the ODD pattern that had been ingrained for many years began to resurface. That's when I entered the case.

The Case of an Eating-Disordered Teenager

Anne presented a formidable array of problems. Not only was she the victim of a severe eating disorder, but, complicating treatment, she manifested symptoms of ODD. Well aware that something serious was wrong, Anne's mother, a creative educator and dedicated parent, blamed herself for her inability to communicate with her daughter. She felt vindicated, however, when a second daughter was born and she was able to connect with her.

Anne had been in individual therapy for about three years, but was only going through the motions when I first met her. She had also been under careful medical supervision in connection with her dietary problems. She was prone to tantrums and wouldn't open up to her mom. The therapist was highly qualified in the field of eating disorders, but not ODD. She informed me that Anne suffered from the most severe eating disorder that she had ever witnessed. Anne would produce buckets of vomit and could cheat on her weigh-ins with amazing cunning. She would lure her mother into pathological battles and resisted therapy with relentless determination. She could turn her mother against her therapist and vice versa. The therapist was well aware of what Anne was doing but could do little to stop it. It took all the effort that she could muster simply to minimize further deterioration.

The family had worked with this clinician to stop the struggles revolving around Anne's eating problem. However, these interventions had failed because they didn't go far enough. The control battles in the family went beyond food-related issues. Also, Mom would detach from the daughter's eating with a very judgmental attitude. She would detach on the outside but would be troubled on the inside. The girl sensed this and worked the attachment to spoil things for the family whenever she didn't get her way.

My intervention with the parents for the ODD was decisive, yet playful. The parents were ready to try anything. They knew of my work and had traveled a long way to see me. It wasn't practical for me to see them regularly. However, they were willing to consult with me to find out if I could resolve the ODD and enhance the benefits of other treatments Anne was receiving for her eating disorder.

The consultation consisted of what I referred to in the preassessment chapter (Chapter 3) as the trial intervention. I had the mother accept the blame for everything that had gone wrong and playfully invited the girl to prove that without Mom's expert opinion she could do just fine. Mom took my intervention of making everything her fault with good humor. Dad, who was Anne's ally, and tried to stop his wife from being overinvested, was delighted with the humor of this intervention.

Anne's initial response was positive. However, her eating disorder symptoms increased by about 50 percent. She stopped taking antidepressants. While it took her a few days, she soon managed to squeeze the playfulness out of this initial intervention and reestablished her ODD struggle with Mom. However, the ODD never returned to the levels reached prior to the initial trial intervention. The parents had made a significant breakthrough. They had implemented a new level of noncontrol, something they had never dared to try before this point. They had gotten a taste of the possible.

At our second visit, I adjusted the intervention to make them even more extreme and playful. Mom was to support and even prescribe certain kinds of bingeing. She was to ask, "Aren't you going to get rid of that meal? Do you want me to stay out of the house for a few hours more so you can have privacy?" This was to be done at times when Anne might be planning some eating disorder behavior.

The objectives were the same as those described in the early-intervention chapters of this book (Chapters 5 and 6). Anne was to run her life the way she wanted. Her school, her social life, her sleep, her medication, her eating, and her hygiene were her business. The parents would offer opportunities and buffers from harsh consequences, and Anne would decide the level of parental support she desired. Her parents were to be extra generous because we wanted her to enjoy her life and eliminate self-destructive urges.

The parents were to offer Anne extra money to purchase whatever she needed, even if she used it to feed her symptoms. We were hoping that she would herself experience anxiety about the progression of her illness and this actually transpired to some extent. It was, of course, a risky course of action to take, akin to giving an alcoholic a generous budget to spend at a liquor store. We designed this as limited trial because of the risk involved.

The parents were also to monitor everything closely from the perspective of emotional-mind allies. This meant they were on the side of her indulging in any way she wanted until she was ready to ask for help. She might also resolve her problems on her own, without interference from people who didn't know any better—such as her parents.

Anne had to earn this level of support by respecting her family. She would lose privileges and access to all family support if she became abusive, destructive, or unhelpful. She could binge and purge, but she had to clean up after herself, in both the kitchen and bathroom. There was no judgment involved.

The parents were in a positive and playful frame of mind regarding this intervention. We role-played the different ways that Anne had attempted to spoil things in the weeks following our first trial intervention. We came up with countertactics. Dad had a signal to use should Mom become too serious and controlling. The signal was purposely blaming problems on Mom to take the edge off Anne's usual tactic of doing the same thing. Dad was to use a loving tone and say to his wife, "Dear, you're screwing everything up again. Remember, she'll figure this all out. If she wants your help, she'll ask."

Mom was to respond in a loving and understanding tone while, at the same time, accepting the blame. The arrangement was designed to throw Anne off balance. Mom would say, "Oh yes, you're right, dear. I forgot again. Never mind. Do what you think is right, Anne." We role-played until Mom's body language was pleasant and nonjudgmental.

I prescribed a six-week trial period of these measures, with the stipulation that the family would consult with the therapist and the attending physician to obtain their approval. I figured that the eating had worsened enough already. Hence, these interventions might be inadvisable. I also felt, however, that if the parents tested this intervention briefly, it would provide data for use in the future, once the eating disorder was stabilized. We could attempt another intervention for the ODD at that time and benefit from what had learned from this go-round.

We tried the second level of intervention for a short time and the tension appeared to relax. However, the eating problem didn't improve. In fact, it worsened rapidly. Anne lost enough weight to warrant hospitalizing her again. Meanwhile, the parents had developed a much more accepting and emotional-mind–supporting stance. Anne had become increasingly defiant, but her parents had remained allies who did the right thing consistently, rather than react to Anne's escalating defiance.

Right after taking failure to the limit, Anne made a remarkable breakthrough. Anne had engaged in a tantrum that lasted long into the night. Her parents dispensed a consequence that she deserved for violating their rights. She was abusing them but they weathered the storm. The next morning Anne seemed calmer. However, she continued to display vestiges of her oppositional attitude.

Anne softened the moment she learned that she was headed for the hospital and that the attending physician would not budge from this decision. Anne dreaded the return to the hospital. She had experienced enough hardship. She allowed herself to become vulnerable and pleaded with her parents to let her stay at home. She swore she would follow their guidelines for nutrition and behavior. This was the first time that Anne's mother had seen her genuinely contrite.

The parents offered Anne their support. They informed the physician of their willingness to run the nutritional program the same way as the hospital did. They maintained that they had the training to do so after years of working on the same problem. The physician agreed, on the condition that the parents would call him if they encountered the slightest resistance. Emergency hospitalization would follow automatically.

It was essential for the parents to have this kind of power over Anne. The arrangement with the physician gave them leverage to dispense strong consequences should Anne go back on her word and revert to her oppositional behavior. However, Anne became a different child. The home stay was wonderful and physically productive.

We returned to the ODD protocol as before, but the parents remained in charge of structuring the food and the intake of medication. We put Anne in charge of her life and her decisions, her parents avoided struggles, and we framed her failures as positives. We also made her accountable for violations of privileges and set up consequences likely to turn her failures into growth, yet shelter her from trauma. The professionals involved didn't think it was prudent to increase Anne's budget for food and allocation of private time in which to indulge in her symptomatic behavior. We modified the treatment for ODD accordingly. In the meantime, the parents had been empowered to use all of the contingencies that didn't have to do with food. They found these very helpful, even though they would have to monitor and structure her eating, her medication, and other health-related behaviors. They were left having to manage an eating disorder but had made a breakthrough with the severe ODD of this teenage girl.

The parents asked that I see Anne shortly after this breakthrough. They wanted me to have a chance to bond with her emotional-mind agenda and attempt two-mind integration work with her. We agreed to a few sessions with Anne and her family and the established therapist and medical staff.

I began the session by joining Anne's emotional-mind agenda. I interested her in creating a wish list for a happy and meaningful life. She listed a private room, with phone, TV, and VCR. She wanted literature on nutrition. She wanted a different curfew, a different wardrobe, and money for social events and food. I suggested that she request immunity from consequences after she made mistakes, once she had taken charge of herself. She agreed. I made it clear that she would get only an approximation of her wish list.

I provided Anne with the rationale behind this intervention in the same way I had presented it to her parents. I explained that youths who don't care about their life end up not caring about themselves. They become self-destructive. Their parents become more controlling, and this makes their life worse, thus launching a cycle of increased conflict and self-destruction impulses.

I explained to Anne that individuals who care about what they do with their life end up caring about themselves. They wish to be well and help others. Their parents recognize their good intentions and grant them more freedom. The reason for the wish list was to interrupt the old cycle of control and trigger one of mutual respect, freedom, and growth.

I warned Anne that she would fail at times, once put in charge of her own life, but reassured her that failure would help her to learn and grow. I explained that nothing is as effective in building self-confidence as overcoming failure.

Anne became a willing patient, and this allowed me to do cognitive behavioral work with the parents in the room. I was able to maintain a playful tone at the sessions and plan games between Anne and her mom that avoided the ODD-related dynamic that invited the eating disorder.

A detailed description of the cognitive work is beyond the scope of this book. It is sufficient to say that I joined the emotional mind and criticized the weak attempts of the rational mind to meet its needs.

Anne fell into two different coping states. One was her "phony" side, which "lived in a pizza," meaning that she lived to count calories, fat, carbohydrates, and protein. She craved junk food, ate it, and purged it. That side of her simply sought approval and was pathetically dependent. The other coping style was the "free" side. This side of Anne lived a life surrounded by many activities. She loved school and her classes. She made friends. She had a job. She exercised. She loved nature. She loved this state of being, eating without giving it much thought, and enjoying life.

Anne's communication style served as an obvious way to detect which mind state dominated her. She was very open and communicative when in her free state. She was very closed and oppositional when in her phony state.

We soon learned that Mom could be lured into playing a role in the eating disorder problem once Anne had achieved her free state. Anne would become positive and communicative. Mom would grant her freedom and the family would become energized. They admired Anne. Her phony side secretly thrived on the positive attention, however, and would soon add to Mom's difficulties. She would ask her mom for advice on what to eat.

Mom would fall for the trap every time and treat Anne like a helpless child whenever she asked for advice. Mom gave advice that was good for the moment but she wouldn't stop there. Gradually, the interaction became pathological.

The key to the case was to have Mom refuse to give advice when Anne came asking. Her response needed to be playful, yet challenging, on the order of, "You expect me to believe that you, at age 15, cannot tell whether you should have a tuna sandwich? Am I supposed to pretend you have the intelligence of a preschooler?" We also came up with the idea we hoped was humorous of having Anne wear a T-shirt that said, "Phony loser." That way she didn't have to try to earn approval. Mom should say, "Not bad for a phony loser," whenever Anne did something right.

The eating disorder symptoms decreased dramatically after only a few sessions. Anne agreed to take nutritional supplements and participate in sports that challenged her to eat healthy foods. There were setbacks, and we needed biweekly sessions in addition to her regular therapy to maintain the gains. However, prior to becoming involved in the new approach, Anne had been in intensive treatment for almost three years with little remission of her extreme symptoms. Resolving the ODD and engaging in some two-mind integration work made a dramatic difference in this high-risk case.

The eating disorder was not resolved by my involvement in the case, but I was able to play an role in enhancing the treatment provided by the other specialists involved. Working closely with

Anne's established therapist, I was able to use my influence as an ally of her emotional mind to orchestrate some fundamental changes. The battles with Mom became so severe that we set up an apartment for Anne and her father to live in. We presented this to Anne in a positive light and she welcomed the change. This immediately stopped the ODD struggle, and from this position we had Anne earn time back at home. Meanwhile, Anne's mother entered her own individual therapy. I also used my influence to encourage Anne to check herself into an intensive inpatient treatment center for eating disorders, with a positive outlook and a willingness to cooperate. In this setting she received the kind of help she needed for her medical condition.

SERIOUS TRAUMA

Serious trauma in the ODD teenager usually contraindicates treatment with this model, except with significant modifications. The clinician can activate reenactment of trauma when he bonds with the emotional mind of a traumatized person. This stimulates pathological attachment patterns that can distort everything that takes place in the treatment. The attempt to bond can become overly personal and anxiety provoking. The distortion can prove dangerous to everyone involved.

Trauma runs in families. Therefore, the clinician may find evidence of it in a parent, and that parent may distort the treatment process as well. The risk is greatest in cases involving a history of sexual abuse.

Modifications for treating cases that involve serious trauma include (1) less ambitious goals; (2) minimal individual work; (3) reduced challenging of the resistance; (3) working with the parent in the room, if possible; (4) an initial agreement to work only for a trial period, and reevaluate the progress at a later date; and (5) prior approval by the parents of the treatment modifications.

The results of reality testing should determine whether the case is treatable with this paradigm. The paradigm involves changing the person's life and is practical and change-oriented. The clinician should screen out individuals who grossly distort reality. In fact, he should avoid these cases altogether, for the patients will not be able to follow through on life changes and will find the clinician's prescriptions frustrating. He can prescribe failure as a way to grow, only to find such patients distorting the process and failing to understand the benefit of failing.

Should the clinician decide to go ahead, he should understand that the goals of treatment change in cases that involve serious trauma. The objectives include (1) forming a safe alliance with the emotional mind by limiting contact to predictable, playful, and nonintrusive activities, (2) recommending for life changes that will help the traumatized teenager be happier, and (3) working with parents to administer consequences for acting out, using principles similar to those described in Chapter 10. In recommending life changes, the clinician should explain that emotional factors create special needs.

The manifestations of trauma will most likely surface in acting-out behavior outside the treatment setting. The consequences should involve a loss of privileges (without struggle), followed by acts of camaraderie that reverse the negative cycle, and reparative gestures that provide the opposite outcome from that of the original trauma. That is, if the youth reenacts past trauma in the family setting by provoking others into abandoning or hitting him, make the reparation a constructive conversation and quality time with the parties involved.

The clinician may eventually have an opportunity to process the trauma in more intensive therapy. However, that would come with time. The family would need the financial resources to keep treatment going for a long time and the teenager would have to come to trust the clinician enough to challenge him with resistance and other manifestations of trauma.

The Case of a Traumatized Teenager

George, a cute and young-looking 13-year-old, had been sexually abused at age 3 by another teenager who had held him down against his will for hours. The imprint of this experience was trig-

gered anytime he faced physical restraint. Yet, his aggressive behavior provoked restraints repeatedly at home and in social settings. This is the tragedy of trauma. The organism seeks the repetition of the traumatic event and ends up trapped in constantly
reliving the trauma.

George had been to more than ten specialists in AD/HD and
conduct disorder. None had helped much. Some caused more
harm than good, according to George's mother.

George's mother began her journey to find help with practitioners covered by her health plan. They all told her that her son
was fine. She knew better. Then she decided it was worth paying
the money herself if she could find someone who would help. She
tried and invested in numerous attempts, but still nothing helped.
The clinicians she enlisted for the case had tried traditional behavioral methods on George.

George had been extremely aggressive from a very early age.
The fires of hatred grew in him and he would tear into anyone
nearby. He had no mercy on his little brother.

One clinician prescribed holding him down until the tantrum
passed. This tactic didn't work because George wouldn't calm
down. In fact, his bad behavior escalated. The next prescription
was to lock him in a room. George found the experience traumatic.
He looked horribly lifeless and hurt after each restraint. The frequency of his aggressive behavior toward his younger sibling increased with these restraints. This was a clear instance of a mainstream behavioral intervention exacerbating the child's condition
each time it was implemented. George's condition worsened
steadily. Mom worried.

The other therapies failed because George experienced them
as violations. I analyzed all of the therapies by obtaining a history
of each from his mother. The common theme was an initial bonding when the therapists engaged George in play during the sessions, and then a sudden turnoff and an ODD response as soon as
the therapists attempted to engage in serious psychological work.
They would explore, question, and interpret, and George would
immediately turn off to treatment. It was impossible to reengage
him once this had occurred.

The ODD response to the probing was probably protective in nature (see Chapter 1). The violent urges that seemed to come out of nowhere were most likely a manifestation of posttraumatic stress disorder (PTSD). The trauma was the violent initial rape, which was kept alive by behavioral interventions that involved physical restraint. The clinicians missed the parallel in the child's experience between the rape and the restraint.

Meanwhile, Mom described a loving child who would suddenly seem possessed by a hateful, evil force. When he was in this condition, he would take obvious delight in violating the rights of others and causing them pain. He thought nothing of threatening murder. He had become a teenager, and to some key authority figures had become a waste of time. They saw him as unwilling to change and as a trouble maker and they treated him accordingly.

One clinician, after working with him for a few months, concluded that George was fine and didn't need treatment. This was because the clinician never triggered the destructive side of George by trying to get him to do some processing of psychological material. This clinician offered nothing but play, yet was the closest to doing George any good. He had set up the kind of relationship in which George eventually could have opened up. The bond would have flourished, and, with time, George would have instinctively challenged the therapist to experience some of the destructive impulses. These would have presented in the play material, in some form of resistance, or in acting out in a way that would have led others to report problems to the therapist.

This clinician, however, offered no system of consequences to address behavioral problems outside of the treatment room. Meanwhile, George was traumatizing other children. Mom considered this purely playful relationship a waste of time. She wanted the therapist to dig out the buried trauma and when he made no attempt to do so, she stopped the therapy.

Mom had heard me speak at a conference and liked what I had to say. So when her son began to get in trouble with the law, she came to see me.

I explained to the mother that George needed treatment that

was a calculated waste of time. There would be no mention of exploratory material. I would play video games, buy him treats, and advocate for his needs in case any problems surfaced. Mom would be present as George played video games. She would report on what had happened at home and I would advise her on the removal and restoration of privileges.

Mom agreed to a six-month trial of my method. If my approach made no difference, we could stop. Mom was glad to go along once she understood the importance of maintaining a nonintrusive frame. The improvement in George was notable. He responded to detachment in a nonpunitive way when he was aggressive and performed reparations to regain lost privileges. He agreed to these conditions from early on. I could already see a bond developing and a bit of softening in George.

As I stated earlier, my objective was to increase the positives in George's life so that they would outweigh the negatives and George could enjoy his life. Then he would experience minimal self-destructive urges. I would arrange for changes in school schedule, new toys, and privileges. I would protect him from legal consequences. I would earn his trust.

The incidents of aggression and other forms of ODD at home and school would become the manifestations of failure. The privilege removal and subsequent reparations would become the tools for turning failure into growth. I would not conduct individual therapy to address the two-mind split with George. I would play music and speak like he spoke, including cursing. I would not teach him moral lessons until later on. I would not confront resistance, and most important, I would not allow him to talk about his problems or interpret any material. He could come for sessions or not.

I would say at the start of the sessions, "So, George, what's it going to cost me to have you here today?" The price would usually be a hot chocolate and a cookie, plus access to video games or darts.

I would not have tried any other approach with George if it didn't make a difference. The dangers because of the trauma made the risk too great. As of this writing, George's treatment continues.

Epilogue

I would like to leave readers with the thought that behind the dramatically different and potentially destructive behavior of the oppositional child there is a lonely someone longing to be recognized for what he really is—a person with his own special needs, talents, and desires, with his own special feelings, and with an accumulation of frustrations because nobody seems to understand.

Such an understanding of the root cause of ODD and the child's real state of mind is necessary before those attempting to treat the condition can make a productive start on the road to lasting success, and is the foundation of the method I have described in this book.

Because of its nontraditional approach, the method is not without its hazards. It is sure to try the patience and test the understanding of the parents, if not the clinician himself. It flies in the face of public opinion and the preponderance of professional views. Indeed, traditional counseling may lead to improvement in the troubled teenager's conduct and may seem to provide a prompt and early answer to the problem. But the results, satisfactory to everyone except the patient, are short term at best, and the oppositionalism, though papered over at the start, reasserts itself in terms of resistance and deception.

By contrast, the method I recommend produces early complications while the clinician is seeking to establish the groundwork for an alliance with the teenager's emotional mind at the expense of the standard of conduct parents and teachers would much prefer to see. It replaces coercion with friendship and persuasion, and allows failure to become the precursor of achievement. The reward comes later when, with the teenager's trust and confidence gained, the clinician at last produces in his patient the two-mind integration required for mature, positive, and healthy action, and a productive and satisfying life.

To have participated in such a transformation is more than satisfying. It is sometimes awesome. The successful outcome of what inevitably has been a long and countercurrent struggle more than justifies the efforts of all those whose understanding and dedication have combined to make the process work.

Appendix A: The Prevalence and Prognosis of Disruptive Behavior Disorders in Children

(written in collaboration with Andrew M. Bustamante)

D isruptive behavior disorders (DBDs) of childhood make up the greatest single source of referrals to mental health clinics. Estimates of prevalence among school-age children range from 3 to 5 percent for AD/HD (Barkley 1990), with an estimated 200,000 new cases referred to mental health clinics each year. For conduct disorder (CD) and oppositional defiant disorder (ODD), estimates have been reported as high as 16 percent, depending on the sample and methodology used. In clinical populations, estimates of hyperactivity have been reported between 23 and 50 percent, depending on the operational definition of hyperactivity (Campbell 1985).

Comorbidity of these disorders is quite common. AD/HD has been found to be associated with learning disabilities (LD), ODD, CD, academic underachievement, and social-skill deficits (Barkley 1989, Hinshaw 1992). Over 80 percent of children diagnosed with hyperactivity qualify for a diagnosis of AD/HD during adolescence, and 60 percent meet criteria for an additional diagnosis of either ODD or CD (Barkley et al. 1990). Among children referred for CD, the rate of comorbidity for AD/HD has been as high as 90 percent (Abikoff et al. 1987). The overlap between externalizing disorders and academic underachievement occurs with estimates between less than 10 percent and more than 50 percent, depending on how underachievement is defined (Hinshaw 1992).

DISTINGUISHING FEATURES

AD/HD, previously referred to as hyperkinesis, or minimal brain dysfunction (Sattler 1974), consists of developmentally inappropriate and persistent levels of inattention, impulsivity, and hyperactivity (Barkley 1990, Hinshaw 1992, Pennington and Ozonoff 1991). In a broader sense, it may be considered a deficit of executive functioning, which refers to organizing, planning, self-regulation, selective attention, inhibition, and future-oriented behaviors (Pennington and Ozonoff 1991), all of which are regulated by the prefrontal regions of the brain. Others view AD/HD as a biologically rooted deficiency in the sensitivity to environmental reinforcement that usually motivates children to inhibit their behaviors, sustain their responses on assigned tasks, and perform work (Haenlein and Caul 1987). The behavioral difficulties often arise during the preschool years and appear to be chronic over time (Weiss and Hechtman 1986). As many as 50 to 70 percent may continue to manifest these symptoms into adulthood (Barkley 1990).

ODD is a recurring pattern of negativistic, hostile, noncompliant, and defiant behaviors toward authority figures that persists for at least six months. These children often argue, deliberately annoy people, blame others for their misbehaviors, and become angry, resentful, and vindictive (Barkley 1990, Hinshaw 1992).

CD is a repetitive and persistent pattern of behaviors characterized by violating the basic rights of others or age-appropriate societal norms and rules. These behaviors include aggression against people and animals (e.g., bullying, threats, fighting, use of weapons), destruction of property, deceitfulness or theft, and serious violations of rules (e.g., truancy, running away from home, breaking curfews before age 13). Most symptoms of ODD will be present. Barkley (1990) estimates that over 95 percent of CD children have ODD; hence, CD preempts ODD, diagnostically.

ASSOCIATED FEATURES AND OUTCOMES

Various studies have established peer, academic, familial, and outcome correlates of DBDs. The relative contributions of each DBD and related LDs have also been ascertained to further the understanding of the many interactive variables that together shape this relentless condition.

PEER AND SCHOOL DIFFICULTY

AD/HD children have been known to have significant peer problems (Landau and Moore 1991). Flicek (1992) investigated the relative contributions of low achievement (LA), LD, and AD/HD toward social status and peer problems. In their study, AD/HD was shown to have contributed to peer disruption and oppositional behavior. These children were also deficient in cooperation and self-control. The LD group contributed problems with peer popularity, cooperation, and leadership. Taken together, however, the AD/HD/LD subgroup contributed to significantly more rejection and less popularity than controls, though neither subgroup alone differed from controls in this regard.

Moffitt (1990) analyzed the trajectories of a birth cohort of 435 boys, ages 3 to 13, to delineate developmental precursors and correlates of delinquency. At the age-13 stage for the boys, the subgroups were classified by self-reports and professional diagnosis as ADD and delinquent, ADD only, delinquent only, or nondisordered. Measures of antisocial behavior, verbal intelligence, reading difficulties, and family adversity were taken throughout childhood. Results showed that the ADD and delinquent group (4 percent of cohorts and 50 percent ADD cases) had significantly greater family adversity and reading difficulties, and less verbal intelligence than the other groups.

At the school entry level, these boys experienced reading failure and fell further and further behind their peers as they approached high school. An exacerbation of antisocial behavior coincided with school entry and reading failure and remained remarkably consistent throughout the study. In contrast, the ADD nondelinquents (4 percent of cohorts and 46 percent of ADD cases) had no deficits, according to the various measures. Their antisocial behavior was mild, transient, and occurred only during middle childhood. The non-ADD delinquents (12 percent of cohorts and 73 percent of all delinquents), like the ADD nondelinquent group, had no deficits. Their antisocial behavior began after age 11.

MOTHER–CHILD DYSFUNCTIONAL RELATING

Researchers have attempted to discern the dynamics of families with DBDs. In two separate studies (Barkley et al. 1991, Barkley, Anastopoulos et al. 1992) investigators assessed family interactions, conflicts, and maternal psychopathology. In addition, they had teased out the differential effects of DBDs on family dynamics by analyzing the contributions of appropriate subgroups: AD/HD, AD/HD/ODD, and controls. Relative to controls, families of adolescent hyperactives (both subgroups) were less positive and facilitative, and more negative, angry, and controlling, based upon mother and teen reports, and objective family interaction measures (Barkley et al. 1991, 1992). Hyperactive mothers reported more conflict (Barkley, et al. 1991, 1992), more stressful life events, and more hostility in their relations with others than mothers of controls (Barkley, et al. 1991).

Mothers and teens of AD/HD/ODD subgroups attributed exaggerated and distorted beliefs (e.g., malicious intent, somatization ruination) toward each other's behaviors, and had greater levels of negative interactions (e.g., defends, complains) than the other two subgroups (Barkley et al. 1992). Mothers of AD/HD/ODD adolescents reported greater levels of psychiatric morbidity (e.g., obsessive-compulsive symptomatology, depression) (Barkley et al. 1991, 1992) and interpersonal hostility than mothers of pure AD/HD and control subgroups (Barkley et al. 1992).

Mothers of both pure AD/HD and mixed AD/HD/ODD subgroups reported less satisfying marriages. This suggests that AD/HD alone is associated with marital dissatisfaction. ODD accounts for most of the differences between hyperactive and controls in family interactions and conflicts. This suggests that ODD brings about greater levels of family dysfunction and pathology (Barkley et al. 1991, 1992).

A regression analysis revealed that maternal hostility contributed toward parent–adolescent conflict variance above and beyond that contributed by ODD. Hence both factors (ODD and maternal hostility) contribute greatly toward parent–teen conflict (Barkley et al. 1992). This finding is similar to that of Anastopoulos and colleagues (1992), who found that a substantial amount of parenting stress variance was accounted for by the child's ODD behavior and maternal psychopathology.

Various studies have attempted to determine the effects of methylphenidate hydrochloride on dysfunctional interactions in families of AD/HD children. Findings suggest that AD/HD children become more compliant and mothers respond by becoming less negative and directive than when the children are without medication or are on placebo (Barkley 1988, Pollard et al. 1983). Though it seems that child behaviors are weighted in these reciprocal interactions, it is interesting to note that mothers' controlling behaviors have been found to be highly predictive of conduct problems, whereas children's negative behaviors were not related to such problems in a six-year follow-up study (Campbell and Ewing 1990).

Vostanis and colleagues (1994) investigated the relationship between maternal criticism, warmth, emotional overinvolvement, and positive comments, and externalizing (CD) and emotional disorders (ED), that is, internalizing symptoms. They found that children with CDs received less maternal warmth and more criticism than emotional disordered or control children. Emotional over-involvement was not found to differ across groups, however.

THE COERCIVE CYCLE

Heslin and Patterson (1982) described a pattern of family interaction that serves to progress and stabilize childhood conduct disorders, referred to as the coercive family process or family coercion model. In this process, a negatively reinforcing and escalating cycle ensues between parent and child as they vie for control. For example, a parental command that is aversive to the child may be met with an aversive response, such as noncompliance. The noncompliance fuels an escalation of parental commands and subsequent threats that, in turn, evoke escalating noncompliance, until either parent or child acquiesces or aggresses. Each learns that an escalation of aversive responses can lead to quick conflict resolution.

The coercive cycle is said to be reinforced by ignoring children's positive behaviors, selectively tracking and overreacting to their negative behaviors, and applying inconsistent discipline, or by withdrawing from the interaction leading to systematic reinforcement of childhood aggression. Barkley (1987) has shown that the escalation forms a communication loop between parent commands and child noncompliance that repeats three to seven times upon initial parent request. Acquiescence or aggression follows a subsequent and elevated communication loop between parental threats and child noncompliance that repeats one to three times.

Baden and Howe (1992) have contributed to understanding the coercive cycle by assessing mothers' attributions and expect-ancies of CD children. They found that mothers of CD children were more likely to perceive their children's misbehaviors as intentional (blaming) than controls, attributed their children's misbehaviors to stable and global causes beyond their control (helplessness), and perceived their own parenting as less effective (helplessness). Baden and Howe hypothesized that attributing intentionality to their CD children's misbehaviors may fuel participation in the coercive cycle. The attribution of their parenting as ineffective may manifest in inconsistent parenting and withdrawal from the escalating CD child's aggressions. Hence, blaming and helplessness as a cognitive set would seemingly explain the incompatible behaviors of coercion and withdrawal that describes the coercive cycle.

Speltz and colleagues (1990) proposed a developmental-organizational model that conceptualizes disruptive behavior as children's attempt to regulate the proximity and attention of caregivers who have been unresponsive and unpredictable. The conception supports Heslin and Patterson's (1982) coercion/control model. Speltz and colleagues (1990) assessed the attachment style of preschoolers referred to a psychiatry clinic in an effort to establish attachment relations as only one of many contributing factors toward the etiology of DBDs. They found a significant difference in the insecure attachment status of clinic-referred children in comparison to nonproblem peers (84 percent vs. 28 percent). Interestingly, the clinic-referred children were mostly categorized as insecure-controlling.

SUBSTANCE ABUSE AND PARENTING STYLE

Stice and colleagues (1993) investigated the relation between parental support and control of adolescents' externalizing behaviors and illicit substance use, and found a negative quadratic relation. Specifically, either extreme of parental control or support was associated with externalizing symptoms and the use of illicit substances. Results suggested that teens who are exposed to extremes of either parental support or control are at risk for disruptive behaviors and illicit substance use. These findings parallel those of family systems theorists and investigators (e.g., Minuchin 1974, Olson et al. 1989), who suggest that moderate levels of cohesiveness are ideal for family functioning, whereas extremes of disengagement or enmeshment lead to problematic outcomes.

HYPERACTIVITY AND ADOLESCENT OUTCOME

Barkley and colleagues (1990) reported on the adolescent outcome of their eight-year longitudinal study of hyperactive children diagnosed with rigorous research criteria. Their clinical sample ($N = 189$) and rigorous research criteria (based on normed rating instruments) are the most representative of hyperactives to date, yielding clinically valid adolescent outcome data.

Adolescents had the most difficulty with attention and following instructions. Pronounced ODD symptoms in this sample were arguing, irritability, and touching behaviors. The mean age of onset of hyperactivity was 3.7 years (preschool), and of ODD and CD, approximately 6 years. This confirms previous studies that CD manifests after the onset of school, and hence may be a reaction to academic demands (Moffitt 1990).

The social outcome revealed antisocial and illicit substance use. Relative to controls, the hyperactive mothers reported significantly greater theft. The hyperactive teens reported greater drug use, theft, assaults, and possession or use of a weapon. In looking at subgroup differences, pure hyperactives did not differ significantly from controls with respect to cigarette or marijuana smoking. However, the AD/HD/CD subgroup reported two to five times more use of these substances than either the pure AD/HD group or controls.

The academic outcome showed that the hyperactives were inferior to controls. The hyperactives had at least three times as much grade retention (29.3 percent vs. 10.6 percent), suspensions (46.3 percent vs. 15.2 percent), and school expulsions (10.6 percent vs. 1.5 percent), 9.8 percent of the hyperactives had dropped out of school compared to none of the controls. In teasing out the differential effects of CD, it was found that, in comparison to pure hyperactives, the risk for school suspension more than doubled (67.4 percent vs. 30.6 percent) and the risk of dropping out almost tripled (13 percent vs. 4.8 percent). The pure hyperactive group did not differ from normal hyperactives in the rates of expulsion (1.6 percent vs. 1.5 percent), while the rate of expulsion for the AD/HD/CD subgroup was 21.7 percent. In contrast, the AD/HD subgroup did not differ from the AD/HD/CD subgroup with respect to grade retention.

Barkley and colleagues (1990) also found that the fathers of hyperactives had higher rates of antisocial behavior than did normal adolescents' fathers. By the *Diagnostic and Statistical Manual of Mental Disorders* (*DSM III-R*) criteria, the fathers of hyperactives had significantly higher rates of antisocial personality than normal adolescents (11.2 percent vs. 1.6 percent). Another interesting observation derived from this study was that the hyperactive group received significantly more psychological, pharmacological, and academic services than the normal teens. Yet, the extra support did not seem to curb the negative psychosocial outcomes reported.

RESEARCH SUMMARY

DBDs are chronic and persistent over time and interact with environmental (peer, school, and family) and neurobiological (e.g., learning disabilities) variables to result in family dysfunction, academic failure, peer rejection, illicit substance use, and other antisocial/criminal behaviors. Specifically, AD/HD is associated with an increased risk of grade retention, parental psychopathology, negative and angry family interactions, conflicts, marital dissatisfaction, peer disruption, and rejection.

Children with CD have an increased risk for illicit substance use, school expulsions, suspensions, and dropping out. They are associated with less maternal warmth and more criticism and controlling behaviors, and are exposed to more coercive family dynamics with underlying maternal blaming and helplessness. Comorbidity is associated with greater family conflict and negative interactions than pure AD/HD. It is also associated with heightened maternal hostility and psychopathology, coercive family dynamics, distorted family beliefs, increased risk for chronic and persistent criminal behavior beyond adolescence, and greater peer rejection than pure AD/HD.

These findings add support for the contention that AD/HD is a disorder of cognitive and neuromaturational development that involves impulsivity, inattention, and hyperactivity, but, when combined with a disorganized and psychiatrically disturbed family life, increases the risk for later ODD and CD (Barkley 1990). Strong verbal skills and good family circumstances combine to combat CD. This very important finding underscores the need for early educational and psychological intervention (Moffitt 1990).

EXISTING TREATMENTS

The most widely evaluated treatments for DBDs are psychopharmacological, behavior modification of home and classroom settings, and cognitive behavioral therapy (Abikoff and Klein 1992, Barkley 1989, Hinshaw 1992). The most widely used intervention for children with DBDs in clinical settings is thought to be individual play therapy. However, this modality has not shown to be effective in the symptom reduction of externalizing behaviors (Gard and Berry 1986, Kazdin 1987).

Psychopharmacology

Methylphenidate hydrochloride (MPH) (Ritalin), is the most widely used and studied psychostimulant for AD/HD (Abikoff and Klein 1992, Barkley 1991). Other psychostimulants that are used less often but are known to be effective are dextroamphetamine sulfate (Dexedrine) and pemoline (Cylert). These psychostimulants act to enhance certain catecholamine neurotransmitters that are presumed to control attention, arousal, and inhibitory processes (Evans et al. 1986). There is much research that attests to the effects of MPH in reducing the primary symptoms of AD/HD (Klein and Last 1989). Improvements in associated features—academic performance, task motivation, and interactions with others—have also been documented (e.g., Pelham 1986).

For example, Douglas and colleagues (1988) tested the effects of three dosages of MPH (0.15, 0.30, and 0.60 mg/kg) on AD/HD children on a multitude of cognitive academic and behavioral measures, in both the laboratory and in the classroom. Results showed a linear pattern of improvement on all measures across and within domains as a function of increasing dosages of medication. Other studies have documented improvements in peer status with increasing dosages of psychostimulants (Whalen et al. 1989). MPH has been shown to reduce aggression during naturalistic observation, but showed only minimal effects in a response to provocation laboratory tasks (Murphy et al. 1992).

Though the short-term effects of psychostimulant medication are impressive, several investigators have concluded that in AD/HD children, there is little evidence of improved long-term outcome or adjustment (e.g., Weiss and Hechtman 1986). Further, medication alone does not bring all social behaviors and academic achievement into the normal range (Pelham and Hinshaw 1992, Weiss and Hechtman 1996). Some studies show that not all children respond to stimulants (Loney et al. 1981) and others suffer a rebound effect, characterized by a worsening of behavioral control beyond what is usually observed when the child is off MPH. The rebound occurs when the effect of medication wears off by the day's end (Barkley 1989). During this time, family management problems and parent–child conflicts increase (Abikoff and Klein 1992).

Cognitive-Behavioral Treatment

Cognitive-behavioral therapy (CBT) is based on the postulate that AD/HD children lack self-talk and other mediation skills that facilitate introspection and self-regulation. CBT includes techniques such as anger control training, self-reinforcement, and self-monitoring (Braswell et al. 1985). It is believed that children internalize the mediation skills they are taught upon successfully implementing the strategies and attributing the subsequent behavioral changes to themselves, rather than to the external actions of others (Meichenbaum 1977). Though there has been some demonstrated short-term effectiveness with self-monitoring and self-reinforcement in improving classroom and playground behaviors, the expectation of internalizing self-regulation skills has not been reached. CBT has not demonstrated generalization and maintenance of gains in AD/HD children, either as a single modality, or as an adjunct treatment (Abikoff 1987, 1991, Horn and Ialongo 1988).

CBT has been used to target social skill deficits of non-AD/HD, aggressive children who are thought to misperceive neutral social skills as hostile (Lochman et al. 1993). Studies have reported immediate posttreatment gains that were maintained at one-year follow-up with both inpatient and outpatient children (Kazdin 1987, Kazdin et al. 1989). Kendall and colleagues (1990) reported significant results in CD youngsters at a psychiatric day hospital. However, only prosocial behaviors increased, while disruptive behaviors changed minimally. Therapeutic gains were not maintained. Other studies have shown either mixed results or a lack of generalization (e.g., Lochman et al. 1984). Evidence that CBT decreases aggressive behaviors by targeting social-cognitive deficits has been inconsistent (Abikoff and Klein 1992).

Behavior Modification

Behavioral treatment in home settings is based upon implementing behavior modification principles, such as token economies, point programs, response costs, and time-outs. These techniques are used to increase positive, prosocial behaviors while decreasing negative, noncompliant behaviors by appropriate contingency management. Typically, these programs utilize parents to act as agents of change for their children in the home and are typically referred to as parent training programs. The findings of behavioral parent training studies in reducing disruptive behaviors for clinically meaningful periods in children and on maintaining these gains are inconsistent.

For example, one study reported the maintenance of post-treatment gains for 34 mother–child pairs from 1 to 4.5 years, based on parent perceptions of child adjustment with corroborating independent home observations (Baum and Forehand 1981). Webster-Stratton and colleagues (1989) reported clinically significant improvements in approximately two-thirds of the entire sample based on parent reports, teacher reports, and home observations.

In a subsequent three-year follow-up, the rate of clinically improved children dropped to between less than one-quarter to less than one-half (22 to 46 percent) based on parent and teacher perceptions alone. Other investigators have reported that gains were not maintained at follow-up (Bernal et al. 1980, Christensen et al. 1980, Ferber et al. 1974, Wahler 1980).

Efforts have been made to discern the predictor variables of parent training outcomes. Dumas and Wahler (1983) reported on a discriminant analysis model of mother insularity (measure of community contacts) and socioeconomic disadvantage (income, maternal education, family size) for two studies that accounted for 49 percent of the variance in treatment outcome. The model predicted a linear effect of treatment failure as a function of both variables. The fact that 51 percent of the variance remained unaccounted for suggests that many factors other than socioeconomic disadvantage and insularity may impede parent training outcome as well.

In Webster-Stratton's (1990) three-year follow-up study, the children who remained maladjusted were associated with single-parent status, maternal depression, social class status, and family history of alcoholism and drug abuse. Frankel and Simmons (1992) found that treatment dropouts were associated with greater negativity and helplessness than treatment remainders. Other variables were parental psychopathology, socioeconomic status, and distance from the clinic.

Parent training has shown effectiveness in reducing specific defiant behaviors within the context of the treatment environment for clinically meaningful periods, though inconsistently. Family adversity and sociodemographics have accounted for a substantial portion of the variance in treatment outcome. However, as reported by Forehand and colleagues (1983) in a seven-year systematic follow-up study, treated subjects are still perceived by teachers as having more adjustment problems and academic difficulties than their nonproblem peers. It should also be noted that although there have been decrements in overt behaviors, the effect of these programs on covert behaviors is unknown (McMahon and Wells 1989). Also, the efficacy of behavioral parent training programs is limited to young oppositional children who are in preschool and elementary schools (Patterson and Narrett 1990).

Multi-Modal Treatments

Research has not established the efficacy of behavioral parent training for AD/HD children (Barkley 1990). In well-controlled studies of diagnosed cases, therapeutic gains have not been maintained at post-treatment (Murphy et al. 1992, Pelham 1986, Rapport et al. 1985). Because of the limitations of behavioral treatments and psychostimulants, investigators have moved toward combining treatment modalities expecting to facilitate child management at home (Abikoff and Klein 1992, Barkley 1991).

Abikoff and Klein (1992) cite the few controlled studies combining behavioral treatments and medication (e.g., Gittelman et al. 1983, Murphy et al. 1992) and concluded that behavioral treatment is not as effective as medication. Also, the treatment does not have the advantage of being able to withdraw the use of medication. However, a study investigating the effects of medication and behaviorism in the classroom suggests that medication alone requires higher dosages than the combined effects of the two modalities (Carlson et al. 1992). Specifically, a combination of behavior therapy and 0.3 mg/kg MPH resulted in behavioral improvements comparable to using 0.6 mg/kg MPH alone.

Other studies have assessed the combined effects of behavioral parent training and self-control therapy in comparison to each alone and to a normal control group (Horn et al. 1991). The AD/

HD subjects remained deviant in multiple measures at post-treatment and follow-up with the exception of one measure—self-concept. However, a greater proportion of subjects in the multimodal group experienced a reduction in externalizing behaviors by parent reports. Therapeutic gains did not generalize to the school setting. Results did not support the additive effect hypothesis.

CONCLUSIONS AND RECOMMENDATIONS

Based on the treatment outcome findings and documented associated features of DBDs, investigators have concluded that DBDs are chronic, persistent, and debilitating conditions that are resistant to existent treatment modalities. The emphasis is on delivery to children and parents of integrated, long-term, multimodal, multidisciplinary interventions for these disorders. These include social, academic, self-esteem, organizational skills, parenting skills, and family counseling (Abikoff and Klein 1992, Barkley 1991, Griest and Wells 1983, Hinshaw 1992, Horn et al. 1991, Kazdin 1987, Kazdin et al. 1989, Nathan 1992, Wetchler 1986, Whalen and Henker 1991).

Abikoff and Klein (1992) and others (e.g., Nathan 1992) emphasize that medication alone is insufficient to address the multiple problems of these disorders, although its use should be given serious consideration. Medication ameliorates severe symptoms and may facilitate other treatment modalities. Nathan emphasizes that though medication may, in the short term, reduce the cardinal symptoms of AD/HD, there remains much work in processing years of guilt, rage, and distorted perceptions of self and others.

Hinshaw (1992) recommends early intervention of specific problem areas due to the strong association between AD/HD and achievement problems in childhood, and between delinquency and school failure in adolescence. The overlap between learning difficulty and problem behaviors usually has its onset in the preschool years with causal factors (e.g., family distress, developmental delays) eventually shaping comorbidity (Moffitt 1990).

There has been little documented success for the treatment of these highly prevalent and debilitating conditions. The cost is devastating to the families involved and to society at large. The integrated, long-term, multimodal, multidisciplinary interventions for children and parents of these disorders entail a prohibitive cost for all but the most affluent families. Yet, there is little evidence that it would make any difference in the long-term prognosis of these children, even if society were to make this unrealistic level of treatment available to all DBDs.

Science has established the diagnosis of AD/HD and accurately described related DBDs. However, the process of finding effective treatments for these conditions is in its infancy. Extensive research is needed, beginning with small-scale trials of different intervention programs that could be studied further as they demonstrated their effectiveness. The most successful protocols could eventually be made systematic, replicable, cost-effective, and widely available.

In the meantime, it would be wise to adjust our expectations of these teenagers and to offer them different avenues for becoming productive, well-adjusted citizens, as well as multiple opportunities to correct their errors when they stray from the socially sanctioned path. This will minimize unnecessary casualties in these youths until science can find a more effective answer to their problems. Here are some adjustments that we can make to keep these youths from falling into the antisocial path: (1) offer opportunities to pursue special interests, including art, music, dance, and sports; (2) provide work and social opportunities for teenagers who are failing school; (3) monitor more closely and offer more constructive consequences for violating social rules; and (4) create chances to reenter the educational system and/or work force in the early adult years.

These interim interventions would certainly not remedy the problem of DBDs. However, these social adjustments could be tested on a small scale to determine their long-term effectiveness. Society at large can generate policies based on the adjustments that prove effective in reintegrating youths who have alienated themselves from society. This may be the best we can offer as we await significant breakthroughs in the treatment of DBDs.

Appendix B: Family Ticket

VIOLATED PRIVILEGE(S)

1. Family atmosphere
2. Work give and take
3. Parent help
4. Hurting sibling
5. Family outings
6. Family property
7. Freedom to go out
8. Deception

REPARATION

Note that reparations correspond to violated privileges in numerical order. The first violation warrants the first reparation, the second the second, and so on.

1. Make family fun for a day
2. Complete work list
3. Play with sibling as best friend for one day
4. Arrange parental help, work well as partners
5. Arrange socially successful outing with family
6. Repair, pay for, and/or use property well
7. Arrange a trustworthy outing with peers
8. Demonstrate understanding of trust

PRIVILEGE LOSS

1. Loss of all privileges
2. Parent support
3. Specific property
4. Peer access

References

Abikoff, H. (1987). An evaluation of cognitive behavior therapy for hyperactive children. In *Advances in Clinical Child Psychology*, ed. B. B. Lahey and A. Kazdin, vol. 10, pp. 171–216. New York: Plenum.

——— (1991). Cognitive training in ADHD children: less to it than meets the eye. *Journal of Learning Disabilities* 24: 205–209.

Abikoff, H., and Klein, R. G. (1992). Attention-deficit hyperactivity and conduct disorder: co-occurrence and implication for treatment. *Journal of Consulting and Clinical Psychology* 60: 881–892.

Abikoff, H., Klein, R., Klass, E., and Ganeles, D. (1987). Methylphenidate in the treatment of conduct disordered children. *Diagnosis and Treatment Issues in Children with Disruptive Disorders.* Symposium conducted at the Annual Meeting of the American Academy of Child and Adolescent Psychiatry, Washington, DC.

Anastopoulos, A. D., Guevremont, D. C., Shelton, T. L., and DuPaul, G. J. (1992). Parenting stress among families of children with attention deficit hyperactivity disorder. *Journal of Abnormal Child Psychology* 20(5): 503–520.

Baden, A. D., and Howe, G. W. (1992). Mothers' attributions and expect-ancies regarding their conduct-disordered children. *Journal of Abnormal Child Psychology* 20(5): 467–485.

Barkley, R. A. (1987). *Defiant Children. A Clinician's Manual For Parent Training.* New York: Guilford.

——— (1988). Attention deficit disorder with hyperactivity. In *Behavioral Assessment of Childhood Disorders*, ed. E. J. Mash and L. G. Terdal, 2nd ed. pp. 552–585. New York: Guilford.

——— (1989). Hyperactive girls and boys: stimulant drug effects on mother-child interactions. *Journal of Child Psychology and Psychiatry and Allied Disciplines* 30(3): 379–390.

——— (1990). *Attention-Deficit Hyperactivity Disorder: A Handbook For Diagnosis and Treatment.* New York: Guilford.

Barkley, R. A., Anastopoulos, A. D., Guevremont, D. C., and Fletcher, K. E. (1992). Adolescents with attention deficit hyperactivity disorder: mother-adolescent interactions, family beliefs and conflicts, and maternal psychopathology. *Journal of Abnormal Child Psychology* 20(3): 263–288.

Barkley, R. A., Fischer, M., Edelbrock, C. S., and Smallish, L. (1990). The adolescent outcome of hyperactive children diagnosed by research criteria: an 8-year prospective follow-up study. *Journal of the American Academy of Child and Adolescent Psychiatry* 29(4): 546–557.

——— (1991). The adolescent outcome of hyperactive children diagnosed by research criteria: III. Mother-child interactions, family conflicts and maternal psychopathology. *Journal of Child Psychology and Psychiatry and Allied Disciplines* 32(2): 233–255.

Baum, C. G., and Forehand, R. (1981). Long term follow-up assessment of parent training by use of multiple outcome measures. *Behavior Therapy* 12: 643–652.

Beck, A. T., Wright, F. D., Newman, C. F., and Liese, B.S. (1993). *Cognitive Therapy of Substance Abuse.* New York: Guilford.

Bernal, M., Klinnert, M., and Schultz, L. (1980). Outcome evaluation of behavioral parent training and client-centered parent counseling for children with conduct problems. *Journal of Applied Behavioral Analysis* 13(4): 677–691.

Bierman, S. E., (1998). Mind matters. *Advances* 12(3): 51–60.

Bion, W. R. (1962). Learning from experience. In *Seven Servants*, pp. 1–105. New York: Jason Aronson, 1997.

Bogen, J. E. (1985). The dual brain: Some historical and methodological aspects. *UCLA Forum in Medical Sciences* 26: 27–43.

Braswell, L., Koehler, C., and Kendall, P. (1985). Attributions and outcomes in psychotherapy. Special issue: the emergence of research at the interface of social, clinical, and developmental psychology. *Journal of School and Clinical Psychology* 3(4): 458–465.

Bustamante, A. M. (in press). *Outcome of a Standardized Strategic Family Intervention for Disruptive Disorders: A Multi-Site, Randomized Trial.* Ann Arbor, MI: University Microfilms International.

Bustamante, E. (1997). *Parenting the AD/HD child: A New Approach.* Springfield, MA: Whitcomb.

Campbell, S. (1985). Hyperactivity in preschoolers: correlates and prognostic implications. *Clinical Psychology Review* 5(5): 405–428.

Campbell, S., and Ewing, L. (1990). Follow-up of hard-to-manage preschoolers: adjustment at age 9 and predictors of continuing symptoms. *Journal of Child Psychology and Psychiatry and Allied Sciences* 31(6): 871–889.

Carlson, C., Pelham, W., and Milich, R. (1992). Single and combined effects of methylphenidate and behavior therapy on the classroom performance of children with attention deficit hyperactivity disorder. *Journal of Abnormal Child Psychology* 20(2): 213–232.

Chess, S., and Thomas, A. (1984). *The Origins and Evolution of Behavior Disorders.* New York: Brunner/Mazel.

Christensen, A., Johnson, S., Phillips, S., and Glasgow, R. (1980). Cost effectiveness in behavioral family therapy. *Behavior Therapy* 11(2): 208–226.

Douglas, V. I., Barr, R. G., Amin, K., et al. (1988). Dosage effects and individual responsivity to methylphenidate in attention deficit disorder. *Journal of Child Psychology and Psychiatry* 29: 453–475.

Dumas, J. E., and Wahler, R. G. (1983). Predictors of treatment outcome in parent training: mother insularity and socioeconomic disadvantage. *Behavioral Assessment* 5: 301–313.

Ekman, P. (1992). An argument for basic emotions. *Cognition and Emotion* 6: 169–200.

Evans, R., Gaultieri, C., and Amara, I. (1986). Methylphenidate and memory: dissociated effects in hyperactive children. *Psychopharmacology* 90(2): 211–216.

Ferber, H., Keeley, S., and Shemberg, K. (1974). Training parents in behavior modification: outcome of and problems encountered in a program after Patterson's work. *Behavior Therapy* 5(3): 415–419.

Flicek, M. (1992). Social status of boys with both academic problems and attention-deficit hyperactivity disorder. *Journal of Abnormal Child Psychology* 20(4): 353–366.

Forehand, R., Middlebrook, J., Rogers, T., and Steefe, M. (1983). Dropping out of parent training. *Behavior Research Therapy* 21 (6): 663–688.

Frankel, F., and Simmons, J. Q. (1992). Parent behavioral training: why and when some parents drop out. *Journal of Clinical Child Psychology* 21 (4): 322–330.

Freeman, A., Simon, K. M., Beutler, L. E., and Arkowitz, H. (1989). *Comprehensive Handbook of Cognitive Therapy*. New York: Plenum.

Gard, G., and Berry, K. (1986). Oppositional children: taming tyrants. *Journal of Clinical Child Psychology* 15 (2): 148–158.

Gittelman, R., Klein, D. F., and Feingold, I. (1983). Children with reading disorders: ii. Effects of methylphenidate in combination with reading remediation. *Journal of Child Psychology and Psychiatry* 24: 193–212.

Goleman, D. (1996). *Emotional Intelligence: Why It Matters More Than I.Q.* New York: Bantam.

Greene, R. W. (1998). *The Explosive Child: A New Approach for Understanding and Parenting Easily Frustrated, "Chronically Inflexible" Children*. New York: Harper Collins.

Griest, D. L., and Wells, K. C. (1983). Behavioral family therapy with conduct disorders in children. *Behavior Therapy* 14: 37–53.

Griffith, J. L. (1998). The importance of nondichotomized thinking. In *Integrated Primary Care: The Future of Medical and Mental Health Collaboration*, ed. A. Blount, et al., pp. 44–62. New York: Norton.

Grotstein, J. (1997). "Mens sane in corpore sano": the mind and the body as an "odd couple" and as an oddly coupled unity. *Psychoanalytic Inquiry* 17 (2): 204–222.

Haenlein, M., and Caul, W. (1987). Attention deficit with hyperactivity: a specific hypothesis of reward dysfunction. *Journal of the American Academy of Child and Adolescent Psychiatry* 26 (3): 356–362.

Haley, J. (1984). *Ordeal Therapy*. San Francisco, CA: Jossey-Bass.

Hepburn, J. M. (1997). The mind–body split and body memory. *Free Associations* (40 pt 4): 539–606.

Heslin, R., and Patterson, M. (1982). *Nonverbal Behavior and Social Psychology*. New York: Plenum.

Hinshaw, S. P. (1992). Academic underachievement, attention deficits, and aggressions: co-occurrence and implications for intervention. *Journal of Consulting and Clinical Psychology* 60: 893–903.

Hoffman, M. L. (1984). Empathy, its limitations and its role in a comprehensive moral theory. In *Morality, Moral Behavior, and Moral Devel-*

opment, ed. W. M. Kurtines and J. L. Gewirtz, pp. 284–302. New York: Wiley.

Horn, W., and Ialongo, N. (1988). Multimodal treatment of attention-deficit hyperactivity disorder in children. In *Theory and Research in Behavioral Pediatrics,* ed. H. E. Fitzgerald, A. H. Lester, and M. W. Yogman, vol. 4, pp. 175–219. New York: Plenum.

Horn, W., Ialongo, N., Pascoe, J., et al. (1991). Additive effects of psychostimulants, parent training, and self-control therapy with ADHD children. *Journal of the American Academy of Child and Adolescent Psychiatry* 30(2): 233–240.

Johnson, K. R., and Layng, T. V. J. (1992). Breaking the structuralist barrier: literacy and numeracy with fluency. *American Psychologist* 47: 1475–1490.

Joseph, R. (1992). *The Right Brain and the Unconscious: Discovering the Stranger Within.* New York: Plenum.

Kazdin, A. E. (1987). *Treatment of Antisocial Behavior in Children and Adolescents.* Homewood: Dorsey.

Kazdin, A., Bass, D., Siegel, T., and Christopher, T. (1989). Cognitive-behavioral therapy and relationship therapy in the treatment of children referred for antisocial behavior. *Journal of Consulting and Clinical Psychology* 57(4): 522–535.

Kendall, P., Reber, M., McLeer, S., et al. (1990). Cognitive-behavioral treatment of conduct-disordered children. *Cognitive Therapy and Research* 14(3): 279–297.

Klein, R., and Last, C. (1989). *Anxiety Disorders in Children.* Newbury Park, CA: Sage.

Landau, S., and Moore, L. (1991). Social skills deficits in children with attention deficit hyperactivity disorder. *School Psychology Review* 20(2): 235–251.

LeDoux, J. E. (1992). Emotional memories in the brain. In *Neuropsychology of Memory,* ed. L. R. Squire, N. Butters, et al., 2nd ed., pp. 463–469. New York: Guilford.

———— (1993). Brain systems and emotional memory. In *International Review of Studies on Emotion,* ed. K. T. Strongman et al., vol 2, pp. 23–29. Chichester, England: Wiley.

Lochman, J., Burch, P., and Curry, J. (1984). Treatment and generalization effects of cognitive-behavioral and goal-setting interventions with aggressive boys. *Journal of Consulting and Clinical Psychology* 52(5): 915–916.

Lochman, J., Wayland, K., and White, K. (1993). Social goals: relationship to adolescent adjustment and to social problem solving. *Journal of Abnormal Child Psychology* 21(2): 135–151.

Locke, S. E., and Colligan, D. (1986). *The Healer Within: The New Medicine of Mind and Body*. New York: E. P. Dutton.

Loney, J., Kramer, J., and Milich, R. (1981). The hyperkinetic child grows up: predictors of symptoms, delinquency and achievement at follow-up. In *Psychosocial Aspects of Drug Treatment for Hyperactivity*, ed. K. D. Gadow and J. Loney, pp. 381–415. Boulder, CO: Westview.

McMahon, R., and Wells, K. (1989). Conduct disorders. In *Treatment of Childhood Disorders*, ed. E. Mash and R. Barkley, pp. 73–132. New York: Guilford.

Meichenbaum, D. (1977). Cognitive behavior modification: an integrative approach. New York: Plenum.

———— (1985). *Stress Inoculation Training: A Clinical Guidebook*. New York: Plenum.

———— (1990). Paying homage: providing challenges. *Psychological Inquiry* 1(1): 96–100.

Meichenbaum, D., and Biemiller, A. (1998). *Nurturing Independent Learners. Helping Students Take Charge of their Learning*. Cambridge, MA: Brookline Books.

Meichenbaum, D., and Jaremko, M., eds. (1983). *Stress Reduction and Prevention*. New York: Plenum.

Meichenbaum, D., Price R., Phares, E. J., et al. (1989). *Exploring Choices: The Psychology of Adjustment*. Genview, IL: Scott, Foresman.

Meichenbaum, D., and Turk, D. (1987). *Facilitating Treatment Adherence: A Practitioner's Guidebook*. New York: Plenum.

Minuchin, S. (1974). *Families and Family Therapy*. Cambridge, MA: Harvard University Press.

Moffitt, T. E. (1990). Juvenile delinquency and attention deficit disorder: boys' developmental trajectories from age 3 to age 15. *Child Development* 61: 893–910.

Murphy, D., Pelham, W., and Lang, A. (1992). Aggression in boys with attention deficit hyperactivity disorder: methylphenidate effects on naturalistically observed aggression, response to provocation, and social information processing. *Journal of Abnormal Child Psychology* 20(5): 451–466.

Nagy, I. B., and Krasner, B. R. (1986). *Between Give and Take: A Clinical Guide to Contextual Therapy*. New York: Brunner/Mazel.

Nathan, W. A. (1992). Integrated multimodal therapy of children with attention-deficit hyperactivity disorder. *Bulletin of the Menninger Clinic* 56(3): 283–312.

National Center for Education in Maternal and Child Health (1991). *A Data Book of Child and Adolescent Injury.* Washington, DC: U.S. Department of Health and Human Services and Children's Safety Network.

Office of Educational Research and Improvement (1997). *Digest of Educational Statistics,* pp. 109–112. Washington, DC: U.S. Department of Education.

Olson, D. H., McCubbin, H. I., Barnes, H., et al. (1989). *Families: What Makes Them Work,* 2nd ed. Los Angeles: Sage.

Pally, R. (1998). Emotional processing: the mind–body connection. *International Journal of Psycho-Analysis* 79(2): 349–362.

Patterson, G., and Narrett, C. (1990). The development of a reliable and valid treatment program for aggressive young children. Special issue: unvalidated, fringe, and fraudulent treatment of mental disorders. *International Journal of Mental Health* 19(3): 19–26.

Pelham, W. E. (1986). The effects of psychostimulant drugs on learning and academic achievement in children with attention-deficit disorders and learning disabilities. In *Psychological and Educational Perspectives on Learning Disabilities,* ed. J. K. Torgeson and B. Y. L. Wong, pp. 259–296. San Diego, CA: Academic Press.

Pelham, W. E., and Hinshaw, S. P. (1992). Behavioral intervention for attention-deficit hyperactivity disorder. In *Handbook of Clinical Behavior Therapy,* ed. S. M. Turner, K. S. Calhoun, and H. E. Adams, 2nd ed., pp. 259–283. New York: Wiley.

Pelletier, K. R., and Herzing, D. L. (1996). Psychoneuroimmunology: toward a mind–body model. In *Healing East and West: Ancient Wisdom and Modern Psychology,* ed. A. A. Sheikh, K. S. Sheikh et al., pp. 344–394. New York: Wiley.

Pennington, B., and Ozonoff, S. (1991). A neuroscientific perspective on continuity and discontinuity in developmental psychopathology. In *Rochester Symposium on Developmental Psychopathology,* ed. D. Cicchetti and S. Toth, vol. 3, pp. 117–159. Rochester, NY: University of Rochester Press.

Pollard, S., Ward, E., and Barkley, R. (1983). The effects of parent training and Ritalin on the parent–child interactions of hyperactive boys. *Child and Family Behavior Therapy* 5(4): 51–69.

Royer, J. M., and Carlo, M. S. (1991). Assessing the language acquisition progress of limited English proficient students: Problems and a new alternative. *Applied Measurement in Education* 4: 85–114.

Royer, J. M., and Sinatra, G. M. (1994). A cognitive theoretical approach to reading diagnostics. *Educational Psychology Review* 6(2): 81–113.

Sattler, J. (1974). *Assessment of Children's Intelligence*. Philadelphia: Saunders.

Schachter, J. (1997). The body of thought: psychoanalytic considerations on the mind–body relationship. *Psychoanalytic Psychotherapy* 11(3): 211–219.

Shadmehr, R., and Holcomb, H. (1997). Neural correlates of motor memory consolidation. *Science* 277: 821–825.

Sherwood, V. R. (1990). The first stage of treatment with the conduct disordered adolescent: overcoming narcissistic resistance. *Psychotherapy* 27(3): 380–387.

Speltz, M., Greenberg, M., and Deklyen, M. (1990). Attachment in preschoolers with disruptive behavior: a comparison of clinic-referred and nonproblem children. *Development and Psychopathology* 2(1): 31–46.

Stice, E., Barerra, M., and Chasen, L. (1993). Relation of parental control to adolescents externalizing symptomatology and substance abuse: a longitudinal evaluation of curvilinear effects. *Journal of Abnormal Child Psychology* 21(6): 609–629.

Talbot, F., Pepin, M., and Loranger, M. (1992). Computerized cognitive training with learning disabled students: a pilot study. *Psychological Reports* 71(3, pt. 2): 1347–1356.

Vostanis, P., Nicholls, J., and Harrington, R. (1994). Maternal expressed emotion in conduct and emotional disorders of childhood. *Journal of Child Psychology and Psychiatry and Allied Disciplines* 35(2): 365–376.

Wahler, R. (1980). The insular mother: her problems in parent-child treatment. *Journal of Applied Behavior Analysis* 13(2): 207–219.

Webster-Stratton, C. (1990). Long-term follow-up with young conduct problem children: from preschool to grade school. *Journal of Clinical Child Psychology* 19(2): 144–149.

Webster-Stratton, C., Hollinsworth, T., and Kolpacoff, M. (1989). The long-term effectiveness and clinical significance of three cost-effective training programs for families with conduct-problem children. *Journal of Consulting and Clinical Psychology* (4): 550–553.

Weiss, G., and Hechtman, L. T. (1986). *Hyperactive Children Grow Up: Empirical Findings and Theoretical Considerations*. New York: Guilford.

Wetchler, J. L. (1986). Family therapy of school-focused problems: a macrosystematic perspective. *Contemporary Family Therapy: An International Journal* 8(3): 224–240.

Whalen, C., and Henker, B. (1991). Therapies for hyperactive children: comparisons, combinations, and compromises. *Journal of Consulting and Clinical Psychology* 59(1): 126–137.

White, M. (1995). *Re-authoring Lives: Interviews and Essays.* Adelaide, South Australia: Dulwich Centre Publications.

Winnicott, D. W. (1979). *The Maturational Processes and the Facilitating Environment: Studies in the Theory of Emotional Development.* New York: International Universities Press.

Zaslow, M. J., and Takanishi, R. (1993). Priorities for research on adolescent development. *American Psychologist* February, 48(2): 185–193.

SUPPLEMENTARY READINGS

Abikoff, H., and Klein, R. (1987). Cognitive training in treatment of hyperactivity in children. *Archives of General Psychiatry* 43(3): 296–297.

Allen, J. P., Hauser, S. T., Bell, K. L., and O'Connor, T. G. (1994). Longitudinal assessment of autonomy and relatedness in adolescent–family interactions as predictors of adolescent ego development and self-esteem. *Child Development* 65(1): 179–194.

Baker, A. K., Barthelemy, K. J., and Kurdek, L. A. (1993). The relation between fifth and sixth graders' peer-classroom social status and their perceptions of family and neighborhood factors. *Journal of Applied Developmental Psychology* 14(4): 547–556.

Bank, L., Patterson, G. R., and Reid, J. B. (1987). Delinquency prevention through training parents in family management. *Behavior Analyst* 10(1): 75–82.

Barkley, R. A., Guevremont, D. C., Anastopoulos, A. D., and Fletcher, K. E. (1992). A comparison of three family therapy progrms for treating family conflicts in adolescents. *Journal of Consulting and Clinical Psychology* 60: 450–462.

Biederman, J., Munir, K., and Knee, D. (1987). Conduct and oppositional disorder in clinically referred children with attention deficit disorder: a controlled family study. *Journal of the American Academy of Child and Adolescent Psychiatry* 26: 777–784.

Bowlby, J. (1969). *Attachment and Loss.* New York: Basic Books.

Burland, J. R. (1986). One of the family—a behavioral approach. *Maladjustment and Therapeutic Education* 4(2): 74–79.

Dangel, R. F., Deschner, J. P., and Rasp, R. R. (1989). Anger control training for adolescents in residential treatment. Special Issue: empirical research in behavioral social work. *Behavior Modification* 13(4): 447–458.

Eisenberg, L., Lachman, R., Molling, P. A., et al. (1963). A psychopharmacological experiment in a training school of delinquent boys. *American Journal of Orthopsychiatry* 33: 431–447.

Fischer, M. (1990). Parenting stress and the child with attention deficit hyperactivity disorder. *Journal of Clinical Child Psychology* 19(4): 337–346.

Gottfried, A, E., Fleming, J. S., and Gottfried, A. W. (1994). Role of parental motivational practices in children's academic intrinsic motivation and achievement. *Journal of Educational Psychology* 86(1): 104–113.

Greene, B. A., Royer, J. M., and Anzalone, S. (1990). A new technique for measuring listening and reading literacy in developing countries. *International Review of Education* 36: 57–68.

Haley, J. (1973). Strategic therapy when the child is presented as the problem. *Journal of the American Academy of Child Psychiatry* 12(4): 641–659.

Harter, S. (1978). Effectance motivation reconsidered: toward a developmental model. *Human Development* 21(1): 34–64.

Henderson, L. J. (1913). *The Fitness of the Environment.* New York: Macmillan.

Jacob, T., Krahn, G., and Leonard, K. (1991). Parent–child interactions in families with alcoholic fathers. *Journal of Consulting and Clinical Psychology* 59(1): 176–181.

Lewis, M., Feiring, C., McGuffog, C., and Jaskir, J. (1984). Predicting psychopathology in six-year-olds from early social relations. *Child Development* 55(1): 123–136.

Main, M., Kaplan, N., and Cassidy, J. (1985). Security in infancy, childhood, and adulthood: a move to the level of representation. *Monographs of the Society for Research in Child Development* 50(1–2): 66–104.

Mueller-Braunschweig, H. (1997). The current state of body-oriented psychotherapy. *Psychotherapeut.* 43(3): 132–144.

Reeves, J. C., Werry, J. S., Elkind, G. S., and Sametkin, A. (1987). Attention deficit, conduct, oppositional and anxiety disorders in children. II. Clinical characteristics. *Journal of the American Academy of Child and Adolescent Psychiatry* 26: 144–155.

Rey, J. M., Bashir, M. R., Schwartz, M., et al. (1988). Oppositional disorder: Fact or fiction? *Journal of the American Academy of Child and Adolescent Psychiatry* 27: 157–162.

Saggino, A. (1996). Integrating verbal and body therapies: a proposal. *Psychiatria e Psicoterapia Analitica* 15(2): 131–136.

Schachar, R., and Wachsmuth, R. (1990). Hyperactivity and parental psychopathology. *Journal of Child Psychology and Psychiatry* 31: 381–392.

Schreier, H. A. (1990). A multimodality approach to the treatment of children and families. *New Directions for Mental Health Services* 46: 75–80.

Stein, D. B., and Smith, E. D. (1990). The "rest program": a new treatment system for the oppositional defiant adolescent. *Adolescence* 25(100): 891–904.

Walker, L., and Taylor, J. (1991). Family interactions and the development of moral reasoning. *Child Development* 62(2): 264–283.

Werry, J. S., Reeves, J. C., and Elkind, G. S. (1987). Attention deficit, conduct, oppositional and anxiety disorders in children: I. A review of research on differentiating characteristics. *Journal of the American Academy of Child and Adolescent Psychiatry* 26: 133–143.

Winnicott, D. W. (1965). From dependence toward independence in the development of the individual. In *The Maturational Processes and the Facilitating Environment*, pp. 83-93. New York: International Universities Press.

———— (1971). *Playing and Reality.* New York: Penguin.

Index

About the Author

Eduardo M. Bustamante was born in Havana in 1951 but spent his teen years in Miami after his family left Cuba. He is a clinical and child psychologist and has been practicing in Amherst, Massachusetts, for the past 15 years, specializing in the diagnosis and treatment of older children and adolescents with AD/HD, ODD and other learning and behavior problems, and is generally called "Dr. B" by his patients. He received his doctorate in clinical/school psychology in 1983 from Adelphi University's Derner Institute, School of Advanced Psychological Studies. He has been an instructor in clinical psychology at Antioch/New England Graduate School in Keene, New Hampshire, and for several years coordinated children's services at University of Massachusetts Health Services, Amherst. In addition to seeing patients and families at his clinic in Amherst, he lectures widely and conducts workshops for parents, school systems, and fellow professionals on his method of treating and managing disruptive young people and how to use its principles successfully in home, classroom, and office settings. He is the author of *Parenting the AD/HD Child: A New Approach*. Dr. Bustamante lives in Amherst with his wife and three children.